PHILOSOPHY OF RELIGION

SOURCES IN CONTEMPORARY PHILOSOPHY

FRANK A. TILLMAN, CONSULTING EDITOR

HARPER & ROW, PUBLISHERS

NEW YORK
EVANSTON
LONDON

PHILOSOPHY
OF RELIGION

Edited

by

STEVEN M. CAHN

New York University

CONTENTS

EDITOR'S INTRODUCTION

No volume by a single scholar can recreate the incessant dialectic of contemporary phliosophic inquiry; hence we are offering a series that is a collaboration of many hands. The present series is intended to provide students, teachers, and interested nonprofessionals with collections of essays in every major problem area of contemporary philosophy. Each volume is devoted to a single set of interconnected issues; each issue is currently the subject of intense philosophic discussion. The editors have been uncompromising in their attempt to bring together essays of great clarity and high technical excellence. Most of the essays were written during the last ten years, some newly written for this series; a number have already become contemporary classics. Each collection is large enough to display a cumulative diversity of viewpoint and detail.

In making relatively inaccessible essays available, this series will enable teachers of philosophy to find strategic or supplementary materials for a wide range of courses. To the student it offers the luxury of possessing essays formerly buried in bound journals or closeted in library reserves. To readers other than teachers and students, the series offers an opportunity to explore contemporary philosophy at first hand. To all readers, it offers original formulations of new ideas and fresh insight into topics of ancient ancestry.

FRANK A. TILLMAN

PHILOSOPHY OF RELIGION

INTRODUCTION

STEVEN M. CAHN

In the past two decades, work in philosophy of religion has exhibited enormous vitality, particularly in the direction of uncovering and clarifying crucial theological problems inherent in supernaturalist religious beliefs. This volume of contemporary essays charts the course of these recent developments and presents the central arguments which have been utilized by proponents on opposing sides of major issues.

There is a clear pattern to the philosophical attacks which have been launched on supernaturalist religious commitments. The first wave of these attacks consists in calling attention to possible inconsistencies in commonly accepted theological tenets. The classic example of such a possible inconsistency is the problem of evil: how can God be all-good and all-powerful if the world which He created contains evil? The first two selections in this volume, those by J. L. Mackie and H. J. McCloskey, pose this problem, consider various proposed solutions, and claim to dispose of them all. The authors' conclusion is that if God is understood to be a Being who is all-good and all-powerful, then the existence of evil precludes God's existence. Their conclusion is disputed by Alvin Plantinga, who argues that it is possible for an all-good, all-powerful Being to have created a world which contains evil. He defends his view by claiming that the evil in the world is a result of the free actions of God's creatures. In the next selection, Nelson Pike argues that there is an inconsistency between the claim that God is omniscient and the claim that man has free will. According to Pike, one of these claims must be relinquished in order to avoid a contradiction. In the succeeding article, Norman Kretzmann argues that there is an inconsistency between the claim that God is omniscient and the claim that He is immutable. Again, according to Kretzmann, one of these claims must be relinquished to avoid a contradiction.

Though attacks of this sort may disturb those who wish to maintain the traditional attributes of God, such believers are always in a position to meet these attacks by suitable modifications of what they understand God's attributes to be. There is no similar defense against the second wave of attack, for this wave, relying upon linguistic considerations, raises doubts regarding not the attributes of God but the very meaningfulness of talk about God. Those philosophers who adopt this approach argue not that God does not exist, but that it does not even make sense to say that God exists. Antony Flew's article is a classic presentation of this view. The selections by R. M. Hare, Basil Mitchell, I. M. Crombie, R. B. Braithwaite, and John Hick present various responses to Flew's challenge. These responses are answered in Flew's reply and in Kai Nielsen's article. The selection by Paul Ziff analyzes the word 'God' itself, and Ziff concludes by denying the existence of God as traditionally conceived while admitting that new conceptions of the Divine are possible. The essay by Paul Edwards strongly criticizes one such new conception, that of the noted theologian Paul Tillich.

It is customary for some defenders of religious orthodoxy to seek refuge from linguistic attacks by appealing to the occurrence of special religious experiences which are relied upon to prove beliefs which cannot be validated otherwise. The rationale behind this defense is explained in my own article, which begins part 3. C. B. Martin's article strongly opposes the view that there is any special religious way of acquiring knowledge. The selection by Paul Henle expresses some sympathy for the claim of religious mystics that language is inadequate to express their insights. The alleged ineffability of mystical experience is critically examined in the articles by William Alston and Richard Gale.

For those defenders of religious orthodoxy who acknowledge that neither their use of reason nor their appeal to experience can withstand philosophical attacks, what defense is there but an appeal to pure faith, unhampered by logical or empirical considerations? This position is presented and discussed in Arthur Danto's article, a dialogue between representatives of faith and reason. The position of faith is further developed and defended in the article by Richard Taylor, who maintains that the choice between faith and reason is an arbitrary one. This position is attacked in the essay by Sidney Hook, who argues that the appeal to faith is intellectual capitulation and that those who cannot support their positions through the use of reason have lost the battle. Alasdair MacIntyre then claims that Christianity is outmoded and that understanding Christian doctrines is incompatible with believing in them.

In the selection that concludes the book, Jack Cohen argues that mankind has gone beyond the need for supernatural religion and that the time has come for those who believe in the utility of religion to take up a new position, not opposed to reason but alongside it, treating reason not as an enemy but as an ally. Cohen calls upon religious spokesmen "to abandon outmoded positions and strike out in new directions." Whether this can be done is one of the central questions which must be considered by philosophers of religion.

One final note: this book contains neither selections opposing or defending traditional proofs for the existence of God, nor discussions of the practices of religious institutions. Many other collections of articles are devoted to these subjects. This book is intended to emphasize some other important and equally fascinating issues in philosophy of religion.

1

THE ATTRIBUTES OF GOD

EVIL AND OMNIPOTENCE

J. L. MACKIE

The traditional arguments for the existence of God have been fairly thoroughly criticised by philosophers. But the theologian can, if he wishes, accept this criticism. He can admit that no rational proof of God's existence is possible. And he can still retain all that is essential to his position, by holding that God's existence is known in some other, non-rational way. I think, however, that a more telling criticism can be made by way of traditional problem of evil. Here it can be shown, not that religious beliefs lack rational support, but that they are positively irrational, that the several parts of the essential theological doctrine are inconsistent with one another, so that the theologian can maintain his position as a whole only by a much more extreme rejection of reason than in the former case. He must now be prepared to believe, not merely what cannot be proved, but what can be *disproved* from other beliefs that he also holds.

The problem of evil, in the sense in which I shall be using the phrase, is a problem only for someone who believes that there is a God who is both omnipotent and wholly good. And it is a logical problem, the problem of clarifying and reconciling a number of beliefs: it is not a scientific problem that might be solved by further observations, or a practical problem that might be solved by a decision or an action. These points are obvious; I mention them only because they are sometimes ignored by theologians, who sometimes parry a statement of the problem with such remarks as "Well, can you solve the problem yourself?" or "This is a mystery which may be revealed to us later" or "Evil is something to be faced and overcome, not to be merely discussed".

Reprinted from *Mind, 64* (1955), by permission of *Mind* and the author.

In its simplest form the problem is this: God is omnipotent; God is wholly good; and yet evil exists. There seems to be some contradiction between these three propositions, so that if any two of them were true the third would be false. But at the same time all three are essential parts of most theological positions: the theologian, it seems, at once *must* adhere and *cannot consistently* adhere to all three. (The problem does not arise only for theists, but I shall discuss it in the form in which it presents itself for ordinary theism.)

However, the contradiction does not arise immediately; to show it we need some additional premises, or perhaps some quasi-logical rules connecting the terms 'good', 'evil', and 'omnipotent'. These additional principles are that good is opposed to evil, in such a way that a good thing always eliminates evil as far as it can, and that there are no limits to what an omnipotent thing can do. From these it follows that a good omnipotent thing eliminates evil completely, and then the propositions that a good omnipotent thing exists, and the evil exists, are incompatible.

A. Adequate Solutions

Now once the problem is fully stated it is clear that it can be solved, in the sense that the problem will not arise if one gives up at least one of the propositions that constitute it. If you are prepared to say that God is not wholly good, or not quite omnipotent, or that evil does not exist, or that good is not opposed to the kind of evil that exists, or that there are limits to what an omnipotent thing can do, then the problem of evil will not arise for you.

There are, then, quite a number of adequate solutions of the problem of evil, and some of these have been adopted, or almost adopted, by various thinkers. For example, a few have been prepared to deny God's omnipotence, and rather more have been prepared to keep the term 'omnipotence' but severely to restrict its meaning, recording quite a number of things that an omnipotent being cannot do. Some have said that evil is an illusion, perhaps because they held that the whole world of temporal, changing things is an illusion, and that what we call evil belongs only to this world, or perhaps because they held that although temporal things *are* much as we see them, those that we call evil are not really evil. Some have said that what we call evil is merely the privation of good, that evil in a positive sense, evil that would really be opposed to good, does not exist. Many have agreed with Pope that disorder is harmony not understood, and that partial evil is universal good. Whether any of these views is *true* is, of course, another question. But each of them gives an adequate solution of the problem of evil in the sense that if you accept it this problem does not arise for you, though you may, of course, have *other* problems to face.

But often enough these adequate solutions are only *almost* adopted. The thinkers who restrict God's power, but keep the term 'omnipotence', may reasonably be suspected of thinking, in other contexts, that his power is really unlimited. Those who say that evil is an illusion may also be thinking, inconsistently, that this illusion is itself an evil. Those who say that "evil" is merely privation of good may also be thinking, inconsistently, that privation of good is an evil. (The fallacy here is akin to some forms of the "naturalistic fallacy" in ethics, where some think, for example, that "good" is just what contributes to evolutionary progress, and that evolutionary progress is itself good.) If Pope meant what he said in the first line of his couplet, that "disorder" is only harmony not understood, the "partial evil" of the second line must, for consistency, mean "that which, taken in isolation, falsely appears to be evil", but it would more naturally mean "that which, in isolation, really is evil". The second line, in fact, hesitates between two views, that "partial evil" isn't really evil, since only the universal quality is real, and that "partial evil" is really an evil, but only a little one.

In addition, therefore, to adequate solutions, we must recognise unsatisfactory inconsistent solutions, in which there is only a half-hearted or temporary rejection of one of the propositions which together constitute the problem. In these, one of the constituent propositions is explicitly rejected, but it is covertly re-asserted or assumed elsewhere in the system.

B. Fallacious Solutions

Besides these half-hearted solutions, which explicitly reject but implicitly assert one of the constituent propositions, there are definitely fallacious solutions which explicitly maintain all the constituent propositions, but implicitly reject at least one of them in the course of the argument that explains away the problem of evil.

There are, in fact, many so-called solutions which purport to remove the contradiction without abandoning any of its constituent propositions. These must be fallacious, as we can see from the very statement of the problem, but it is not so easy to see in each case precisely where the fallacy lies. I suggest that in all cases the fallacy has the general form suggested above: in order to solve the problem one (or perhaps more) of its constituent propositions is given up, but in such a way that it appears to have been retained, and can therefore be asserted without qualification in other contexts. Sometimes there is a further complication: the supposed solution moves to and fro between, say, two of the constituent propositions, at one point asserting the first of these but covertly abandoning the second, at another point asserting the second but covertly abandoning the first. These fallacious solutions often turn upon some equivocation with the words 'good' and 'evil', or upon some vagueness about the way in which good and evil are opposed to one another, or about how much is meant by 'omnipotence'. I propose to examine some of these so-called solutions, and to exhibit their fallacies in detail. Incidentally, I shall also be considering whether an adequate solution could be reached by a minor modification of one or more of the constituent propositions, which would, however, still satisfy all the essential requirements of ordinary theism.

1. "Good cannot exist without evil" or "Evil is necessary as a counterpart to good."

It is sometimes suggested that evil is necessary as a counterpart to good, that if there were no evil there could be no good either, and that this solves the problem of evil. It is true that it points to an answer to the question "Why should there be evil?" But it does so only by qualifying some of the propositions that constitute the problem.

First, it sets a limit to what God can do, saying that God *cannot* create good without simultaneously creating evil, and this means either that God is not omnipotent or that there are *some* limits to what an omnipotent thing can do. It may be replied that these limits are always presupposed, that omnipotence has never meant the power to do what is logically impossible, and on the present view the existence of good without evil would be a logical impossibility. This interpretation of omnipotence may, indeed, be accepted as a modification of our original account which does not reject anything that is essential to theism, and I shall in general assume it in the subsequent discussion. It is, perhaps, the most common theistic view, but I think that some theists at least have maintained that God can do what is logically impossible. Many theists, at any rate, have held that logic itself is created or laid down by God, that logic is the way in which God arbitrarily chooses to think. (This is, of course, parallel to the ethical view that morally right actions are those which God arbitrarily chooses to command, and the two views encounter similar difficulties). And *this* account of logic is clearly inconsistent with the view that God is bound by logical necessities—unless it is possible for an omnipotent being to bind himself, an issue which we shall consider later, when we come to the Paradox of Omnipotence. This solution of the problem of evil cannot, therefore, be consistently adopted along with the view that logic is itself created by God.

But, secondly, this solution denies that evil is opposed to good in our original sense. If good and evil are counterparts, a good thing will not "eliminate evil as far as it can". Indeed, this view suggests that good and evil are not strictly qualities of things at all. Perhaps the suggestion is that good and evil are related in much the same way as great and small. Certainly, when the term 'great' is used relatively as a condensation of 'greater than so-and-so', and 'small' is used correspondingly, greatness and smallness are counterparts and cannot exist without each other. But in this sense greatness is not a quality, not an intrinsic feature of anything; and it would be absurd to think of a movement in favour of greatness and against smallness in this sense. Such a movement would be self-defeating, since relative greatness can be promoted only by a simultaneous promotion of relative smallness. I feel sure that no theists would be content to regard God's goodness as analogous to this—as if what he supports were not the *good* but the *better,* and as if he had the paradoxical aim that all things should be better than other things.

This point is obscured by the fact that 'great' and 'small' seem to have an absolute as well as a relative sense. I cannot discuss here whether there is absolute magnitude or not, but if there is, there could be an absolute sense for 'great', it could mean of at least a certain size, and it would make sense to speak of all things getting bigger, of a universe that was expanding all over, and therefore it would make sense to speak of promoting greatness. But in *this* sense great and small are not logically necessary counterparts: either quality could exist without the other. There would be no logical impossibility in everything's being small or in everything's being great.

Neither in the absolute nor in the relative sense, then, of 'great' and 'small' do these terms provide an analogy of the sort that would be needed to support this solution of the problem of evil. In neither case are greatness and smallness *both* necessary counterparts *and* mutually opposed forces or possible objects for support and attack.

It may be replied that good and evil are necessary counterparts in the same way as any quality and its logical opposite: redness can occur, it is suggested, only if non-redness also occurs. But unless evil is merely the privation of good, they are not logical opposites, and some further argument would be needed to show that they are counterparts in the same way as genuine logical opposites. Let us assume that this could be given. There is still doubt of the correctness of the metaphysical principle that a quality must have a real opposite: I suggest that it is not really impossible that everything should be, say, red, that the truth is merely that if everything were red we should not notice redness, and so we should have no word 'red'; we observe and give names to qualities only if they have real opposites. If so, the principle that a term must have an opposite would belong only to our language or to our thought, and would not be an ontological principle, and, correspondingly, the rule that good cannot exist without evil would not state a logical necessity of a sort that God would just have to put up with. God might have made everything good, though *we* should not have noticed it if he had.

But, finally, even if we concede that this *is* an ontological principle, it will provide a solution for the problem of evil only if one is prepared to say, "Evil exists, but only just enough evil to serve as the counterpart of good". I doubt whether any theist will accept this. After all, the *ontological* requirement that non-redness should occur would be satisfied even if all the universe, except for a minute speck, were red, and, if there were a corresponding requirement for evil as a counterpart to good, a minute dose of evil would presumably do. But theists are not usually willing to say, in all contexts, that all the evil that occurs is a minute and necessary dose.

2. "Evil is necessary as a means to good."

It is sometimes suggested that evil is necessary for good not as a counterpart but as a means. In its simple form this has little plausibility as a solution of the problem of evil, since it obviously implies a severe restriction of God's power. It would be a *causal* law that you cannot have a certain end without a certain means, so that if God has to introduce evil as a means to good, he must be subject to at least some causal laws. This certainly conflicts with what a theist normally means by omnipotence. This view of God as limited by causal laws also conflicts with the view that causal laws are themselves made by God, which is more widely held than the corresponding view about the laws of logic. This conflict, would, indeed, be resolved if it were possible for an omnipotent being to bind himself, and this possibility has still to be considered. Unless a favourable answer can be given to this question, the suggestion that evil is neces-

sary as a means to good solves the problem of evil only by denying one of its constituent propositions, either that God is omnipotent or that 'omnipotent' means what it says.

>   3. "The universe is better with some evil in it than it
> could be if there were no evil."

Much more important is a solution which at first seems to
be a mere variant of the previous one, that evil may contribute
to the goodness of a whole in which it is found, so that the
universe as a whole is better as it is, with some evil in it, than
it would be if there were no evil. This solution may be developed
in either of two ways. It may be supported by an aesthetic
analogy, by the fact that contrasts heighten beauty, that in a
musical work, for example, there may occur discords which
somehow add to the beauty of the work as a whole. Alternatively,
it may be worked out in connexion with the notion of progress,
that the best possible organisation of the universe will not be
statis, but progressive, that the gradual overcoming of evil by
good is really a finer thing than would be the eternal unchal-
lenged supremacy of good.

In either case, this solution usually starts from the assumption that the evil whose existence gives rise to the problem of
evil is primarily what is called physical evil, that is to say, pain.
In Hume's rather half-hearted presentation of the problem of
evil, the evils that he stresses are pain and disease, and those who
reply to him argue that the existence of pain and disease makes
possible the existence of sympathy, benevolence, heroism, and
the gradually successful struggle of doctors and reformers to
overcome these evils. In fact, theists often seize the opportunity
to accuse those who stress the problem of evil of taking a low,
materialistic view of good and evil, equating these with pleasure
and pain, and of ignoring the more spiritual goods which can
arise in the struggle against evils.

But let us see exactly what is being done here. Let us call
pain and misery 'first order evil' or 'evil (1)'. What contrasts
with this, namely, pleasure and happiness, will be called 'first

order good' or 'good (1)'. Distinct from this is 'second order
good' or 'good (2)' which somehow emerges in a complex situation in which evil (1) is a necessary component—logically, not
merely causally, necessary. (Exactly *how* it emerges does not
matter: in the crudest version of this solution good (2) is simply
the heightening of happiness by the contrast with misery, in
other versions it includes sympathy with suffering, heroism in
facing danger, and the gradual decrease of first order evil and
increase of first order good.) It is also being assumed that
second order good is more important than first order good or
evil, in particular that it more than outweighs the first order evil
it involves.

Now this is a particularly subtle attempt to solve the problem of evil. It defends God's goodness and omnipotence on the
ground that (on a sufficiently long view) this is the best of all
logically possible worlds, because it includes the important
second order goods, and yet it admits that real evils, namely
first order evils, exist. But does it still hold that good and evil
are opposed? Not, clearly, in the sense that we set out originally: good does not tend to eliminate evil in general. Instead,
we have a modified, a more complex pattern. First order good
(*e.g.* happiness) *contrasts with* first order evil (*e.g.* misery):
these two are opposed in a fairly mechanical way; some second
order goods (*e.g.* benevolence) try to maximize first order
good and minimise first order evil; but God's goodness is not
this, it is rather the will to maximise *second* order good. We
might, therefore, call God's goodness an example of a third
order goodness, or good (3). While this account is different
from our original one, it might well be held to be an improvement on it, to give a more accurate description of the way in
which good is oposed to evil, and to be consistent with the
essential theist position.

There might, however, be several objections to this solution.

First, some might argue that such qualities as benevolence
—and *a fortiori* the third order goodness which promotes benevolence—have a merely derivative value, that they are not higher

sorts of good, but merely means to good (1), that is, to happiness, so that it would be absurd for God to keep misery in existence in order to make possible the virtues of benevolence, heroism, etc. The theist who adopts the present solution must, of course, deny this, but he can do so with some plausibility, so I should not press this objection.

Secondly, it follows from this solution that God is not in our sense benevolent or sympathetic: he is not concerned to minimise evil (1), but only to promote good (2); and this might be a disturbing conclusion for some theists.

But, thirdly, the fatal objection is this. Our analysis shows clearly the possibility of the existence of a *second* order evil, an evil (2) contrasting with good (2) as evil (1) contrasts with good (1). This would include malevolence, cruelty, callousness, cowardice, and states in which good (1) is decreasing and evil (1) increasing. And just as good (2) is held to be the important kind of good, the kind that God is concerned to promote, so evil (2) will, by analogy, be the important kind of evil, the kind which God, if he were wholly good and omnipotent, would eliminate. And yet evil (2) plainly exists, and indeed most theists (in other contexts) stress its existence more than that of evil (1). We should, therefore, state the problem of evil in terms of second order evil, and against this form of the problem the present solution is useless.

An attempt might be made to use this solution again, at a higher level, to explain the occurrence of evil (2): indeed the next main solution that we shall examine does just this, with the help of some new notions. Without any fresh notions, such a solution would have little plausibility: for example, we could hardly say that the really important good was a good (3), such as the increase of benevolence in proportion to cruelty, which logically required for its occurrence the occurrence of some second order evil. But even if evil (2) could be explained in this way, it is fairly clear that there would be third order evils contrasting with this third order good: and we should be well on the way to an infinite regress, where the solution of a problem of evil, stated in terms of evil (n), indicated the existence of an evil $(n + 1)$, and a further problem to be solved.

4. "Evil is due to human freewill."

Perhaps the most important proposed solution of the problem of evil is that evil is not to be ascribed to God at all, but to the independent actions of human beings, supposed to have been endowed by God with freedom of the will. This solution may be combined with the preceding one: first order evil (*e.g.* pain) may be justified as a logically necessary component in second order good (*e.g.* sympathy) while second order evil (*e.g.* cruelty) is not *justified*, but is so ascribed to human beings that God cannot be held responsible for it. This combination evades my third criticism of the preceding solution.

The freewill solution also involves the preceding solution at a higher level. To explain why a wholly good God gave men freewill although it would lead to some important evils, it must be argued that it is better on the whole that men should act freely, and sometimes err, than that they should be innocent automata, acting rightly in a wholly determined way. Freedom, that is to say, is now treated as a third order good, and as being more valuable than second order goods (such as sympathy and heroism) would be if they were deterministically produced, and it is being assumed that second order evils, such as cruelty, are logically necessary accompaniments of freedom, just as pain is a logically necessary pre-condition of sympathy.

I think that this solution is unsatisfactory primarily because of the incoherence of the notion of freedom of the will: but I cannot discuss this topic adequately here, although some of my criticisms will touch upon it.

First I should query the assumption that second order evils are logically necessary accompaniments of freedom. I should ask this: if God has made men such that in their free choices they sometimes prefer what is good and sometimes what is evil, why could he not have made men such that they always freely choose the good? If there is no logical impossibility in a man's freely choosing the good on one, or on several, occasions, there cannot be a logical impossibility in his freely choosing the good on every occasion. God was not, then, faced with a choice between making innocent automata and making beings who, in acting freely, would sometimes go wrong: there was open to him the obviously better possibility of making beings who would act freely but always go right. Clearly, his failure to avail himself of this possibility is inconsistent with his being both omnipotent and wholly good.

If it is replied that this objection is absurd, that the making of some wrong choices is logically necessary for freedom, it would seem that 'freedom' must here mean complete randomness or indeterminacy, including randomness with regard to the alternatives good and evil, in other words that men's choices and consequent actions can be "free" only if they are not determined by their characters. Only on this assumption can God escape the responsibility for men's actions; for if he made them as they are, but did not determine their wrong choices, this can only be because the wrong choices are not determined by men as they are. But then if freedom is randomness, how can it be a characteristic of *will*? And, still more, how can it be the most important good? What value or merit would there be in free choices if these were random actions which were not determined by the nature of the agent?

I conclude that to make this solution plausible two different senses of 'freedom' must be confused, one sense which will justify the view that freedom is a third order good, more valuable than other goods would be without it, and another sense, sheer randomness, to prevent us from ascribing to God a decision to make men such that they sometimes go wrong when he might have made them such that they would always freely go right.

This criticism is sufficient to dispose of this solution. But besides this there is a fundamental difficulty in the notion of an omnipotent God creating men with free will, for if men's wills are really free this must mean that even God cannot control them, that is, that God is no longer omnipotent. It may be objected that God's gift of freedom to men does not mean that he *cannot* control their wills, but that he always *refrains* from controlling their wills. But why, we may ask, should God refrain from controlling evil wills? Why should he not leave men free to will rightly, but intervene when he sees them beginning to will wrongly? If God could do this, but does not, and if he is wholly good, the only explanation could be that even a wrong free act of will is not really evil, that its freedom is a value which outweighs its wrongness, so that there would be a loss of value if God took away the wrongness and the freedom together. But this is utterly opposed to what theists say about sin in other contexts. The present solution of the problem of evil, then, can be maintained only in the form that God has made men so free that he *cannot* control their wills.

This leads us to what I call the Paradox of Omnipotence: can an omnipotent being make things which he cannot subsequently control? Or, what is practically equivalent to this, can an omnipotent being make rules which then bind himself? (These are practically equivalent because any such rules could be regarded as setting certain things beyond his control, and *vice versa*.) The second of these formulations is relevant to the sugestions that we have already met, that an omnipotent God creates the rules of logic or causal laws, and is then bound by them.

It is clear that this is a paradox: the questions cannot be answered satisfactorily either in the affirmative or in the negative. If we answer "Yes", it follows that if God actually makes things which he cannot control, or makes rules which bind himself, he is not omnipotent once he has made them: there are *then* things which he cannot do. But if we answer "No", we are immediately asserting that there are things which he cannot do, that is to say that he is already not omnipotent.

It cannot be replied that the question which sets this paradox is not a proper question. It would make perfectly good sense to say that a human mechanic has made a machine which he cannot control: if there is any difficulty about the question it lies in the notion of omnipotence itself.

This, incidentally, shows that although we have approached this paradox from the free will theory, it is equally a problem for a theological determinist. No one thinks that machines have free will, yet they may well be beyond the control of their makers. The determinist might reply that anyone who makes anything determines its ways of acting, and so determines its sub-

sequent behaviour: even the human mechanic does this by his
choice of materials and structure for his machine, though he
does not know all about either of these: the mechanic thus determines, though he may not foresee, his machine's actions. And
since God is omniscient, and since his creation of things is total,
he both determines and foresees the ways in which his creatures
will act. We may grant this, but it is beside the point. The question is not whether God *originally* determined the future actions
of his creatures, but whether he can *subsequently* control their
actions, or whether he was able in his original creation to put
things beyond his subsequent control. Even on determinist principles the answers "Yes" and "No" are equally irreconcilable
with God's omnipotence.

Before suggesting a solution of this paradox, I would point
out that there is a parallel Paradox of Sovereignty. Can a legal
sovereign make a law restricting its own future legistlative
power? For example, could the British parliament make a law
forbidding any future parliament to socialise banking, and also
forbidding the future repeal of this law itself? Or could the
British parliament, which was legally sovereign in Australia in,
say, 1899, pass a valid law, or series of laws, which made it no
longer sovereign in 1933? Again, neither the affirmative nor
the negative answer is really satisfactory. If we were to answer
"Yes", we should be admitting the validity of a law which, if
it were actually made, would mean that parliament was no
longer sovereign. If we were to answer "No", we should be
admitting that there is a law, not logically absurd, which parliament cannot validly make, that is, that parliament is not now
a legal sovereign. This paradox can be solved in the following
way. We should distinguish between first order laws, that is
laws governing the actions of individuals and bodies other than
the legislature, and second order laws, that is laws about laws,
laws governing the actions of the legislature itself. Correspondingly, we should distinguish two orders of sovereignty, first
order sovereignty (sovereignty (1)) which is unlimited authority to make first order laws, and second order sovereignty
(sovereignty (2)) which is unlimited authority to make second
order laws. If we say that parliament is sovereign we might

mean that any parliament at any time has sovereignty (1), or we might mean that parliament has both sovereignty (1) and sovereignty (2) at present, but we cannot without contradiction mean both that the present parliament has sovereignty (2) and that every parliament at every time has sovereignty (1), for if the present parliament has sovereignty (2) it may use it to take away the sovereignty (1) of later parliaments. What the paradox shows is that we cannot ascribe to any continuing institution legal sovereignty in an inclusive sense.

The analogy between omnipotence and sovereignty shows that the paradox of omnipotence can be solved in a similar way. We must distinguish between first order omnipotence (omnipotence (1)), that is unlimited power to act, and second order omnipotence (omnipotence (2)), that is unlimited power to determine what powers to act things shall have. Then we could consistently say that God all the time has omnipotence (1), but if so no beings at any time have powers to act independently of God. Or we could say that God at one time had omnipotence (2), and used it to assign independent powers to act to certain things, so that God thereafter did not have omnipotence (1). But what the paradox shows is that we cannot consistently ascribe to any continuing being omnipotence is an inclusive sense.

An alternative solution of this paradox would be simply to deny that God is a continuing being, that any times can be assigned to his actions at all. But on this assumption (which also has difficulties of its own) no meaning can be given to the assertion that God made men with wills so free that he could not control them. The paradox of omnipotence can be avoided by putting God outside time, but the freewill solution of the problem of evil cannot be saved in this way, and equally it remains impossible to hold that an omnipotent God *binds himself* by causal or logical laws.

Conclusion

Of the proposed solutions of the problem of evil which we have examined, none has stood up to criticisim. There may be other solutions which require examination, but this study strongly suggests that there is no valid solution of the problem which does not modify at least one of the constituent propositions in a way which would seriously affect the essential core of the theistic position.

Quite apart from the problem of evil, the paradox of omnipotence has shown that God's omnipotence must in any case be restricted in one way or another, that unqualified omnipotence cannot be ascribed to any being that continues through time. And if God and his actions are not in time, can omnipotence, or power of any sort, be meaningfuly ascribed to him?

GOD AND EVIL

H. J. MCCLOSKEY

A. The Problem Stated

Evil is a problem for the theist in that a contradiction is involved in the fact of evil on the one hand, and the belief in the omnipotence and perfection of God on the other. God cannot be both all-powerful and perfectly good if evil is real. This contradiction is well set out in its detail by Mackie in his discussion of the problem.[1] In his discussion Mackie seeks to show that this contradiction cannot be resolved in terms of man's free will. In arguing in this way Mackie neglects a large number of important points, and concedes far too much to the theist. He implicity allows that whilst physical evil creates a problem, this problem is reducible to the problem of moral evil and that therefore the satisfactoriness of solutions of the problem of evil turns on the compatibility of free will and absolute goodness. In fact physical evils create a number of distinct problems which are not reducible to the problem of moral evil. Further, the proposed solution of the problem of moral evil in terms of free will renders the attempt to account for physical evil in terms of moral good, and the attempt thereby to reduce the problem of evil to the problem of moral evil, completely untenable. Moreover, the account of moral evil in terms of free will breaks down on more obvious and less disputable grounds than those indicated by Mackie. Moral evil can be shown to remain a problem whether or not free will is compatible with absolute goodness. I therefore propose in this paper to reopen the discussion of "the problem of evil", by apporaching it from a more general standpoint, examining a wider variety of solutions than those considered by Mackie and his critics.

Reprinted from *The Philosophical Quarterly*, *10* (1960), by permission of *The Philosophical Quarterly* and the author.

[1] Evil and Omnipotence," *Mind*, 1955. [The article may be found on p. 7 in this book.]

The fact of evil creates a problem for the theist; but there are a number of simple solutions available to a theist who is content seriously to modify his theism. He can either admit a limit to God's power, or he can deny God's moral perfection. He can assert either (1) that God is not powerful enough to make a world that does not contain evil, or (2) that God created only the good in the universe and that some other power created the evil, or (3) that God is all-powerful but morally imperfect, and chose to create an imperfect universe. Few Christians accept these solutions, and this is no doubt partly because such 'solutions' ignore the real inspiration of religious beliefs, and partly because they introduce embarrassing complications for the theist in his attempts to deal with other serious problems. However, if any one of these 'solutions' is accepted, then the problem of evil is avoided, and a weakened version of theism is made secure from attacks based upon the fact of the occurrence of evil.

For more orthodox theism, according to which God is both omnipotent and perfectly good, evil creates a real problem; and this problem is well-stated by the Jesuit, Father G. H. Joyce. Joyce writes:

> The existence of evil in the world must at all times be the greatest of all problems which the mind encounters when it reflects on God and His relation to the world. If He is, indeed, all-good and all-powerful, how has evil any place in the world which He has made? Whence came it? Why is it here? If He is all-good why did He allow it to arise? If all-powerful why does He not deliver us from the burden? Alike in the physical and moral order creation seems so grievously marred that we find it hard to understand how it can derive in its entirety from God.[2]

The facts which give rise to the problem are of two general kinds, and give rise to two distinct types of problem. These two general kinds of evil are usually referred to as 'physical' and as 'moral' evil. These terms are by no means apt—suffering for instance is not strictly physical evil—and they conceal sig-

[2] Joyce: *Principles of Natural Theology*, ch. XVII. All subsequent quotations from Joyce in this paper are from this chapter of this work.

nificant differences. However, this terminology is too widely-accepted, and too convenient to be dispensed with here, the more especially as the various kinds of evil, whilst important as distinct kinds, need not for our purposes be designated by separate names.

Physical evil and moral evil then are the two general forms of evil which independently and jointly constitute conclusive grounds for denying the existence of God in the sense defined, namely as an all-powerful, perfect Being. The acuteness of these two general problems is evident when we consider the nature and extent of the evils of which account must be given. To take physical evils, looking first at the less important of these.

(a) *Physical evils:* Physical evils are involved in the very constitution of the earth and animal kingdom. There are deserts and icebound areas; there are dangerous animals of prey, as well as creatures such as scorpions and snakes. There are also pests such as flies and fleas and the hosts of other insect pests, as well as the mutitude of lower parasites such as tapeworms, hookworms and the like. Secondly, there are the various natural calamities and the immense human suffering that follows in their wake—fires, floods, tempests, tidal-waves, volcanoes, earthquakes, droughts and famines. Thirdly, there are the vast numbers of diseases that torment and ravage man. Diseases such as leprosy, cancer, poliomyelitis, appear *prima facie* not to be creations which are to be expected of a benevolent Creator. Fourthly, there are the evils with which so many are born—the various physical deformities and defects such as misshapen limbs, blindness, deafness, dumbness, mental deficiency and insanity. Most of these evils contribute towards icnreasing human pain and suffering: but not all physical evils are reducible simply to pain. Many of these evils are evils whether or not they result in pain. This is important, for it means that, unless there is one solution to such diverse evils, it is both inaccurate and positively misleading to speak of *the* problem of physical evil. Shortly I shall be arguing that no one 'solution' covers all these evils, so we shall have to conclude that physical evils create not one problem but a number of distinct problems for the theist.

The nature of the various difficulties referred to by the

theist as the problem of physical evil is indicated by Joyce in a
way not untypical among the more honest, philosophical theists,
as follows:

> The actual amount of suffering which the human race
> endures is immense. Disease has store and to spare of torments
> for the body: and disease and death are the lot to which we
> must all look forward. At all times, too, great numbers of the
> race are pinched by want. Nor is the world ever free for very
> long from the terrible sufferings which follow in the track of
> war. If we concentrate our attention on human woes, to the
> exclusion of the joys of life, we gain an appalling picture of
> the ills to which the flesh is heir. So too if we fasten our
> attention on the sterner side of nature, on the pains which
> men endure from natural forces—on the storms which wreck
> their ships, the cold which freezes them to death, the fire
> which consumes them—if we contemplate this aspect of
> nature alone we may be led to wonder how God came to deal
> so harshly with His Creatures as to provide them with such
> a home.

Many such statements of the problem proceed by suggesting,
if not by stating, that the problem arises at least in part by concentrating one's attention too exclusively on one aspect of the
world. This is quite contrary to the facts. The problem is not one
that results from looking at only one aspect of the universe. It
may be the case that over-all pleasure predominates over pain,
and that physical goods in general predominate over physical
evils, but the opposite may equally well be the case. It is both
practically impossible and logically impossible for this question
to be resolved. However, it is not an unreasonable presumption,
with the large bulk of mankind inadequately fed and housed and
without adequate medical and health services, to suppose that
physical evils at present predominate over physical goods. In
the light of the facts at our disposal, this would seem to be a
much more reasonable conclusion than the conclusion hinted at
by Joyce and openly advanced by less cautious theists, namely,
that physical goods in fact outweigh physical evils in the world.
However, the question is not, Which predominates, physical

good or physical evil? The problem of physical evil remains a problem whether the balance in the universe is on the side of physical good or not, because the problem is that of accounting for the fact that physical evil occurs at all.

(*b*) *Moral evil:* Physical evils create one of the groups of problems referred to by the theist as 'the problem of evil'. Moral evil creates quite a distinct problem. Moral evil is simply immorality—evils such as selfishness, envy, greed, deceit, cruelty, callousness, cowardice and the larger scale evils such as wars and the atrocities they involve.

Moral evil is commonly regarded as constituting an even more serious problem than physical evil. Joyce so regards it, observing:

> The man who sins thereby offends God. . . . We are called on to explain how God came to create an order of things in which rebellion and even final rejection have such a place. Since a choice from among an infinite number of possible worlds lay open to God, how came He to choose one in which these occur? Is not such a choice in flagrant opposition to the Divine Goodness?

Some theists seek a solution by denying the reality of evil or by describing it as a 'privation' or absence of good. They hope thereby to explain it away as not needing a solution. This, in the case of most of the evils which require explanation, seems to amount to little more than an attempt to sidestep the problem simply by changing the name of that which has to be explained. It can be exposed for what it is simply by describing some of the evils which have to be explained. That is why a survey of the data to be accounted for is a most important part of the discussion of the problem of evil.

In *The Brothers Karamazov*, Dostoievsky introduces a discussion of the problem of evil by reference to some then recently committed atrocities. Ivan states the problem:

> "By the way, a Bulgarian I met lately in Moscow," Ivan went on . . . "told me about the crimes committed by Turks in all parts of Bulgaria through fear of a general rising of the

Slavs. They burn villages, murder, outrage women and children, and nail their prisoners by the ears to the fences, leave them till morning, and in the morning hang them—all sorts of things you can't imagine. People talk sometimes of bestial cruelty, but that's a great injustice and insult to the beasts; a beast can never be so cruel as a man, so artistically cruel. The tiger only tears and gnaws and that's all he can do. He would never think of nailing people by the ears, even if he were able to do it. These Turks took a pleasure in torturing children too; cutting the unborn child from the mother's womb, and tossing babies up in the air and catching them on the points of their bayonets before their mothers' eyes. Doing it before the mother's eyes was what gave zest to the amusement. Here is another scene that I thought very interesting. Imagine a trembling mother with her baby in her arms, a circle of invading Turks around her. They've planned a diversion: they pet the baby to make it laugh. They succeed; the baby laughs. At that moment, a Turk points a pistol four inches from the baby's face. The baby laughs with glee, holds out its little hands to the pistol, and he pulls the trigger in the baby's face and blows out its brains. Artistic, wasn't it?"[3]

Ivan's statement of the problem was based on historical events. Such happenings did not cease in the nineteenth century. *The Scourge of the Swastika* by Lord Russell of Liverpool contains little else than descriptions of such atrocities; and it is simply one of a host of writings giving documented lists of instances of evils, both physical and moral.

Thus the problem of evil is both real and acute. There is a clear *prima facie* case that evil and God are incompatible—both cannot exist. Most theists admit this, and that the onus is on them to show that the conflict is not fatal to theism; but a consequence is that a host of proposed solutions are advanced.

The mere fact of such a multiplicity of proposed solutions, and the widespread repudiation of each other's solutions by theists, in itself suggests that the fact of evil is an insuperable obstacle to theism as defined here. It also makes it impossible to treat of all proposed solutions, and all that can be attempted

[3] P. 244, Garnett translation, Heinemann.

here is an examination of those proposed solutions which are most commonly invoked and most generally thought to be important by theists.

Some theists admit the reality of the problem of evil, and then seek to sidestep it, declaring it to be a great mystery which we poor humans cannot hope to comprehend. Other theists adopt a rational approach and advance rational arguments to show that evil, properly understood, is compatible with, and even a consequence of God's goodness. The arguments to be advanced in this paper are directed against the arguments of the latter theists; but in so far as these arguments are successful against the rational theists, to that extent they are also effective in showing that the non-rational approach in terms of great mysteries is positively irrational.

B. Proposed Solutions to the Problem of Physical Evil

Of the large variety of arguments advanced by theists as solutions to the problem of physical evil, five popularly used and philosophically significant solutions will be examined. They are, in brief: (i) Physical good (pleasure) requires physical evil (pain) to exist at all; (ii) Physical evil is God's punishment of sinners; (iii) Physical evil is God's warning and reminder to man; (iv) Physical evil is the result of the natural laws, the operations of which are on the whole good; (v) Physical evil increases the total good.

(i) *Physical Good is Impossible without Physical Evil:* Pleasure is possible only by way of contrast with pain. Here the analogy of colour is used. If everything were blue we should, it is argued, understand neither what colour is nor what blue is. So with pleasure and pain.

The most obvious defect of such an argument is that it does not cover all physical goods and evils. It is an argument commonly invoked by those who think of physical evil as creating only one problem, namely the problem of human pain. However, the problems of physical evils are not reducible to the one problem, the problem of pain; hence the argument is simply irrelevant to much physical evil. Disease and insanity are evils, but health and sanity are possible in the total absence of disease and insanity. Further, if the argument were in any way valid even in respect of pain, it would imply the existence of only a speck of pain, and not the immense amount of pain in the universe. A speck of yellow is all that is needed for an appreciation of blueness and of colour generally. The argument is therefore seen to be seriously defective on two counts even if its underlying principle is left unquestioned. If its underlying principle is questioned, the argument is seen to be essentially invalid. Can it seriously be maintained that if an individual were born crippled and deformed and never in his life experienced pleasure, that he could not experience pain, not even if he were severely injured? It is clear that pain is possible in the absence of pleasure. It is true that it might not be distinguished by a special name and called 'pain', but the state we now describe as a painful state would nonetheless be possible in the total absence of pleasure. So too the converse would seem to apply. Plato brings this out very clearly in Book 9 of the *Republic* in respect of the pleasures of taste and smell. These pleasures seem not to depend for their existence on any prior experience of pain. Thus the argument is unsound in respect of its main contention; and in being unsound in this respect, it is at the same time ascribing a serious limitation to God's power. It maintains that God cannot create pleasure without creating pain, although as we have seen, pleasure and pain are not correlatives.

(ii) *Physical Evil is God's Punishment for Sin:* This kind of explanation was advanced to explain the terrible Lisbon earthquake in the 18th century, in which 40,000 people were killed. There are many replies to this argument, for instance Voltaire's. Voltaire asked: "Did God in this earthquake select the 40,000 least virtuous of the Portuguese citizens?" The distribution of disease and pain is in no obvious way related to the virtue of the persons afflicted, and popular saying has it that the distribution is slanted in the opposite direction. The only way of meeting the fact that evils are not distributed proportionately to the evil of the sufferer is by suggesting that all human beings, including children, are such miserable sinners, that our offences are of such enormity, that God would be justified in punishing all of us as severely as it is possible for humans to be punished; but even then, God's apparent caprice in the selection of His victims requires explanation. In any case it is by no means clear that young children who very often suffer severely are guilty of sin of such an enormity as would be necessary to justify their sufferings as punishment.

Further, many physical evils are simultaneous with birth— insanity, mental defectiveness, blindness, deformities, as well as much disease. No crime or sin of *the child* can explain and justify these physical evils as punishment; and, for a parent's sin to be punished in the child is injustice or evil of another kind.

Similarly, the sufferings of animals cannot be accounted for as punishment. For these various reasons, therefore, this argument must be rejected. In fact it has dropped out of favour in philosophical and theological circles, but it continues to be invoked at the popular level.

(iii) *Physical Evil is God's Warning to Men:* It is argued, for instance of physical calamities, that "they serve a moral end which compensates the physical evil which they cause. The awful nature of these phenomena, the overwhelming power of the forces at work, and man's utter helplessness before them, rouse him from the religious indifference to which he is so prone. They inspire a reverential awe of the Creator who made them, and controls them, and a salutary fear of violating the laws which He has imposed". (Joyce). This is where immortality is often alluded to as justifying evil.

This argument proceeds from a proposition that is plainly false; and that the proposition from which it proceeds is false is conceded implicitly by most theologians. Natural calamities do not necessarily turn people to God, but rather present the problem of evil in an acute form; and the problem of evil is said to account for more defections from religion than any other cause. Thus if God's object in bringing about natural calamities is to inspire reverence and awe, He is a bungler. There are many more reliable methods of achieving this end. Equally important, the use of physical evil to achieve this object is hardly the course one would expect a benevolent God to adopt when other, more effective, less evil methods are available to Him, for example, miracles, special revelation, etc.

(iv) *Evils are the Results of the Operation of Laws of Nature:* This fourth argument relates to most physical evil, but it is more usually used to account for animal suffering and physical calamities. These evils are said to result from the operation of the natural laws which govern these objects, the relevant natural laws being the various causal laws, the law of pleasure-pain as a law governing sentient beings, etc. The theist argues that the non-occurrence of these evils would involve either the constant intervention by God in a miraculous way, and contrary to his own natural laws, or else the construction of a universe with different components subject to different laws of nature; for God, in creating a certain kind of being, must create it subject to its appropriate laws; He cannot create it and subject it to any law of His own choosing. Hence He creates a world which has components and laws good in their total effect, although calamitous in some particular effects.

Against this argument three objections are to be urged. First, it does not cover all physical evil. Clearly not all disease can be accounted for along these lines. Secondly, it is not to give a reason against God's miraculous intervention simply to assert that it would be unreasonable for Him constantly to intervene in the operation of His own laws. Yet this is the only reason that theists seem to offer here. If, by intervening in respect to the operation of His laws, God could thereby eliminate an evil, it would seem to be unreasonable and evil of Him not to do so. Some theists seek a way out of this difficulty by denying that God has the power miraculously to intervene; but this is to ascribe a severe limitation to His power. It amounts to asserting that when His Creation has been effected, God can do nothing else except contemplate it. The third objection is related to this, and is to the effect that it is already to ascribe a serious limitation to God's omnipotence to suggest that He could not make sentient beings which did not experience pain, nor sentient beings without deformities and deficiencies, nor natural phenomena with different laws of nature governing them. There is no reason why better laws of nature governing the existing objects are not possible on the divine hypothesis. Surely, if God is all-powerful, He could have made a better universe in the first place, or one with better laws of nature governing it, so that the operation of its laws did not produce calamities and pain. To maintain this is not to suggest that an omnipotent God should be capable of achieving what is logically impossible. All that has been indicated here is logically possible, and therefore not beyond the powers of a being Who is really omnipotent.

This fourth argument seeks to exonerate God by explaining that He created a universe sound on the whole, but such that He had no direct control over the laws governing His creations, and had control only in His selection of His creations. The previous two arguments attribute the detailed results of the operations of these laws directly to God's will. Theists commonly use all three arguments. It is not without significance that they betray such uncertainty as to whether God is to be *commended* or *exonerated*.

(v) *The Universe is Better with Evil in it:* This is the important argument. One version of it runs:

> Just as the human artist has in view the beauty of his composition as a whole, not making it his aim to give to each several part the highest degree of brillancy, but that measure of adornment which most contributes to the combined effect, so it is with God. (Joyce)

Another version of this general type of argument explains evil not so much as *a component* of a good whole, seen out of its context as a mere component, but rather as *a means* to a greater good. Different as these versions are, they may be treated here as one general type of argument, for the same criticisms are fatal to both versions.

This kind of argument if valid simply shows that some evil may enrich the Universe; it tells us nothing about *how much* evil will enrich this particular universe, and how much will be too much. So, even if valid in principle—and shortly I shall argue that it is not valid—such an argument does not in itself provide a justification for the evil in the universe. It shows simply that the evil which occurs might have a justification. In view of the immense amount of evil the probabilities are against it.

This is the main point made by Wisdom in his discussion of this argument. Wisdom sums up his criticism as follows:

> It remains to add that, unless there are independent arguments in favour of this world's being the best logically possible world, it is probable that some of the evils in it are not logically necessary to a compensating good; it is probable because there are so many evils.[4]

Wisdom's reply brings out that the person who relies upon this argument as a conclusive and complete argument is seriously mistaken. The argument, if valid, justifies only some evil. A belief that it justifies all the evil that occurs in the world is mistaken, for a second argument, by way of a supplement to it, is needed. This supplementary argument would take the form of a proof that all the evil that occurs is *in fact* valuable and necessary as a means to greater good. Such a supplementary proof is in principle impossible; so, at best, this fifth argument can be taken to show only that some evil *may be* necessary for the production of good, and that the evil in the world may perhaps have a justification on this account. This is not to justify a physical evil, but simply to suggest that physical evil might nonetheless have a justification, although we may never come to know this justification.

Thus the argument even if it is valid as a general form of reasoning is unsatisfactory because inconclusive. It is, however, also unsatisfactory in that it follows on the principle of the argument that, just as it is possible that evil in the total context contributes to increasing the total ultimate good, so equally, it will hold that good in the total context may increase the ultimate evil. Thus if the principle of the argument were sound, we could never know whether evil is really evil, or good really good. (Aesthetic analogies may be used to illustrate this point.) By implication it follows that it would be dangerous to eliminate evil because we may thereby introduce a discordant element into the divine symphony of the universe; and, conversely, it may be wrong to condemn the elimination of what is good, because the latter may result in the production of more, higher goods.

So it follows that, even if the general principle of the argument is not questioned, it is still seen to be a defective argument. On the one hand, it proves too little—it justifies only some evil and not necessarily all the evil in the universe; on the other hand it proves too much because it creates doubts about the goodness of apparent goods. These criticisms in themselves are fatal to the argument as a solution to the problem of physical evil. However, because this is one of the most popular and plausible accounts of physical evil, it is worthwhile considering whether it can properly be claimed to establish even the very weak conclusion indicated above.

Why, and in what way, is it supposed that physical evils such as pain and misery, disease and deformity, will heighten the total effect and add to the value of the moral whole? The answer given is that physical evil enriches the whole by giving rise to moral goodness. Disease, insanity, physical suffering and the like are said to bring into being the noble moral virtues—courage, endurance, benevolence, sympathy and the like. This is what the talk about the enriched whole comes to. W. D. Niven makes this explicit in his version of the argument:

> Physical evil has been the goad which has impelled men to most of those achievements which made the history of man so wonderful. Hardship is a stern but fecund parent of invention. Where life is easy because physical ills are at a minimum we find man degenerating in body, mind, and character.

And Niven concludes by asking:

> Which is preferable—a grim fight with the possibility of splendid triumph; or no battle at all? [5]

[5] W. D. NIVEN, *Encyclopedia of Religion and Ethics.*
Joyce's corresponding argument runs:

> Pain is the great stimulant to action. Man no less than animals is impelled to work by the sense of hunger. Experience shows

The argument is: Physical evil brings moral good into being, and in fact is an essential precondition for the existence of some moral goods. Further, it is sometimes argued in this context that those moral goods which are possible in the total absence of physical evils are more valuable in themselves if they are achieved as a result of a struggle. Hence physical evil is said to be justified on the grounds that moral good plus physical evil is better than the absence of physical evil.

A common reply, and an obvious one, is that urged by Mackie.[6] Mackie argues that whilst it is true that moral good plus physical evil together are better than physical good alone, the issue is not as simple as that, for physical evil also gives rise to and makes possible many moral evils that would not or could not occur in the absence of physical evil. It is then urged

---

that, were it not for this motive the majority of men would be content to live in indolent ease. Man must earn his bread.

One reason plainly why God permits suffering is that man may rise to a height of heroism which would otherwise have been beyond his scope. Nor are these the only benefits which it confers. That sympathy for others which is one of the most precious parts of our experience, and one of the most fruitful sources of well-doing, has its origin in the fellow-feeling engendered by endurance of similar trials. Furthermore, were it not for these trials, man would think little enough of a future existence, and of the need of striving after his last end. He would be perfectly content with his existence, and would reck little of any higher good. These considerations here briefly advanced suffice at least to show how important is the office filled by pain in human life, and with what little reason it is asserted that the existence of so much suffering is irreconcilable with the wisdom of the Creator.

And:

It may be asked whether the Creator could not have brought man to perfection without the use of suffering. Most certainly He could have conferred upon him a similar degree of virtue without requiring any effort on his part. Yet it is easy to see that there is a special value attaching to a conquest of difficulties such as man's actual demands, and that in God's eyes this may well be an adequate reason for assigning this life to us in preference to another. . . . Pain has value in respect to the next life, but also in respect to this. The advance of scientific discovery, the gradual improvement of the organization of the community, the growth of material civilization are due in no small degree to the stimulus afforded by pain.

[6] Mackie, "Evil and Omnipotence," *Mind*, 1955.

that it is not clear that physical evils (for example, disease and pain) plus some moral goods (for example courage) plus some moral evil (for example, brutality) are better than physical good and those moral goods which are possible and which would occur in the absence of physical evil.

This sort of reply, however, is not completely satisfactory. The objection it raises is a sound one, but it proceeds by conceding too much to the theist, and by overlooking two more basic defects of the argument. It allows implicitly that the problem of physical evil may be reduced to the problem of moral evil; and it neglects the two objections which show that the problem of physical evil cannot be so reduced.

The theist therefore happily accepts this kind of reply, and argues that, if he can give a satisfactory account of moral evil he will then have accounted for both physical and moral evil. He then goes on to account for moral evil in terms of the value of free will and/or its goods. This general argument is deceptively plausible. It breaks down for the two reasons indicated here, but it breaks down at another point as well. If free will alone is used to justify moral evil, then even if no moral good occurred, moral evil would still be said to be justified; but physical evil would have no justification. Physical evil is not essential to free will; it is only justified if moral good actually occurs, and if the moral good which results from physical evils outweighs the moral evils. This means that the argument from free will cannot alone justify physical evil along these lines; and it means that the argument from free will and its goods does not justify physical evil, because such an argument is incomplete, and necessarily incomplete. It needs to be supplemented by factual evidence that it is logically and practically impossible to obtain.

The correct reply, therefore, is first that the argument is irrelevant to many instances of physical evil, and secondly that it is not true that physical evil plus the moral good it produces is better than physical good and its moral goods. Much pain and suffering, in fact much physical evil generally, for example in children who dies in infancy, animals and the insane passes unnoticed; it therefore has no morally uplifting effects upon

others, and cannot by virtue of the examples chosen have such
effects on the sufferers. Further, there are physical evils such as
insanity and much disease to which the argument is inapplicable.
So there is a large group of significant cases not covered by the
argument. And where the argument is relevant, its premiss is
plainly false. It can be shown to be false by exposing its implications in the following way.

We either have obligations to lessen physical evil or we
have not. If we have obligations to lessen physical evil then we
are thereby reducing the total good in the universe. If, on the
other hand, our obligation is to increase the total good in the
universe it is our duty to prevent the reduction of physical evil
and possibly even to increase the total amount of physical evil.
Theists usually hold that we are obliged to reduce the physical
evil in the universe; but in maintaining this, the theist is, in
terms of this account of physical evil, maintaining that it is his
duty to reduce the total amount of real good in the universe, and
thereby to make the universe worse. Conversely, if by eliminating
the physical evil he is not making the universe worse, then that
amount of evil which he eliminates was unnecessary and in
need of justification. It is relevant to notice here that evil is not
always eliminated for morally praiseworthy reasons. Some discoveries have been due to postively unworthy motives, and many
other discoveries which have resulted in a lessening of the
sufferings of mankind have been due to no higher a motive than
a scientist's desire to earn a reasonable living wage.

This reply to the theist's argument brings out its un-
tenability. The theist's argument is seen to imply that war plus
courage plus the many other moral virtues war brings into play
are better than peace and its virtues; that famine and its moral
virtues are better than plenty; that disease and its moral virtues
are better than health. Some Christians in the past, in consistency with this mode of reasoning, opposed the use of
anaesthetics to leave scope for the virtues of endurance and
courage, and they opposed state aid to the sick and needy to
leave scope for the virtues of charity and sympathy. Some have
even contended that war is a good in disguise, again in consistency with this argument. Similarly the theist should, in terms

of this fifth argument, in his heart if not aloud regret the discovery of the Salk polio vaccine because Dr. Salk has in one blow destroyed infinite possibilities of moral good.

There are three important points that need to be made concerning this kind of account of physical evil. (*a*) We are told, as by Niven, Joyce and others, that pain is a goad to action and that part of its justification lies in this fact. This claim is empirically false as a generalization about all people and all pain. Much pain frustrates action and wrecks people and personalities. On the other hand many men work and work well without being goaded by pain or discomfort. Further, to assert that men need goading is to ascribe another evil to God, for it is to claim that God made men naturally lazy. There is no reason why God should not have made men naturally industrious; the one is no more incompatible with free will than the other. Thus the argument from physical evil being a goad to man breaks down on three distinct counts. Pain often frustrates human endeavour, pain is not essential as a goad with many men, and where pain is a goad to higher endeavours, it is clear that less evil means to this same end are available to an omnipotent God. (*b*) The real fallacy in the argument is in the assumption that all or the highest moral excellence results from physical evil. As we have already seen, this assumption is completely false. Neither all moral goodness nor the highest moral goodness is triumph in the face of adversity or benevolence towards others in suffering. Christ Himself stressed this when He observed that the two great commandments were commandments to love. Love does not depend for its possibility on the existence and conquest of evil. (*c*) The 'negative' moral virtues which are brought into play by the various evils—courage, endurance, charity, sympathy and the like—besides not representing the highest forms of moral virtue, are in fact commonly supposed by the theist and atheist alike not to have the value this fifth argument ascribes to them. We—theists and atheists alike—reveal our comparative valuations of these virtues and of physical evil when we insist on state aid for the needy; when we strive for peace, for plenty, and for harmony within the state.

In brief, the good man, the morally admirable man, is he

who loves what is good knowing that it is good and preferring it because it is good. He does not ned to be torn by suffering or by the spectacle of another's sufferings to be morally admirable. Fortitude in his own sufferings, and sympathetic kindness in others' may reveal to us his goodness; but his goodness is not necessarily increased by such things.

Five arguments concerning physical evil have now been examined. We have seen that the problem of physical evil is a problem in its own right, and one that cannot be reduced to the problem of moral evil; and further, we have seen that physical evil creates not one but a number of problems to which no one nor any combination of the arguments examined offers a solution.

C. Proposed Solutions to the Problem of Moral Evil

The problem of moral evil is commonly regarded as being the greater of the problems concerning evil. As we shall see, it does create what appears to be insuperable difficulties for the theist; but so too, apparently, do physical evils.

For the theist moral evil must be interpreted as a breach of God's law and as a rejection of God himself. It may involve the eternal damnation of the sinner, and in many of its forms it involves the infliction of suffering on other persons. Thus it aggravates the problem of physical evil, but its own peculiar character consists in the fact of sin. How could a morally perfect, all-powerful God create a universe in which occur such moral evils as cruelty, cowardice and hatred, the more especially as these evils constitute a rejection of God Himself by His creations, and as such involve them in eternal damnation?

The two main solutions advanced relate to free will and to the fact that moral evil is a consequence of free will. There is a third kind of solution more often invoked implicitly than as an explicit and serious argument, which need not be examined here as its weaknesses are plainly evident. This third solution is to the effect that moral evils and even the most brutal atrocities have their justification in the moral goodness they make possible or bring into being.

(i) *Free will alone provides a justification for moral evil:* This is perhaps the more popular of the serious attempts to explain moral evil. The argument in brief runs: men have free will; moral evil is a consequence of free will; a universe in which men exercise free will even with lapses into moral evil is better than a universe in which men become *automata* doing good aways because predestined to do so. Thus on this argument it is the mere fact of the supreme value of free will itself that is taken to provide a justification for its corollary moral evil.

(ii) *The goods made possible by free will provide a basis for accounting for moral evil:* According to this second argument, it is not the mere fact of free will that is claimed to be of such value as to provide a justification of moral evil, but the fact that free will makes certain goods possible. Some indicate the various moral virtues as the goods that free will makes possible, whilst others point to beatitude, and others again to beatitude achieved by man's own efforts or the virtues achieved as a result of one's own efforts. What all these have in common is the claim that the good consequences of free will provide a justification of the bad consequences of free will, namely moral evil.

Each of these two proposed solutions encounters two specific criticisms, which are fatal to their claims to be real solutions.

(i) To consider first the difficulties to which the former proposed solution is exposed. (a) A difficulty for the first argument—that it is free will alone that provides a justification for moral evil—lies in the fact that the theist who argues in this way has to allow that it is logically possible on the free will hypothesis that all men should always will what is evil, and that even so, a universe of completely evil men possessing free will is better than one in which men are predestined to virtuous living. It has to be contended that the value of free will itself is so immense that it more than outweighs the total moral evil, the eternal punishment of the wicked, and the sufferings inflicted on others by the sinners in their evilness. It is this paradox that leads to the formulation of the second argument; and it is to be noted that the explanation of moral evil switches to the second argu-

ment or to a combination of the first and second argument,
immediately the theist refuses to face the logical possibility of
complete wickedness, and insists instead that in fact men do not
always choose what is evil.

(*b*) The second difficulty encountered by the first argument relates to the possibility that free will is compatible with
less evil, and even with no evil, that is, with absolute goodness.
If it could be shown that free will is compatible with absolute
goodness, or even with less moral evil than actually occurs, then
all or at least some evil will be left unexplained by free will
alone.

Mackie, in his recent paper, and Joyce, in his discussion of
this argument, both contend that free will is compatible with
absolute goodness. Mackie argues that if it is not possible for
God to confer free-will on men and at the same time ensure that
no moral evil is committed. He cannot really be omnipotent.
Joyce directs his argument rather to fellow-theists, and it is more
of an *ad hominem* argument addressed to them. He writes:

> Free will need not (as is often assumed) involve the
> power to choose wrong. Our ability to misuse the gift is due
> to the conditions under which it is exercised here. In our
> present state we are able to reject what is truly good, and
> exercise our power of preference in favour of some baser
> attraction. Yet it is not necessary that it should be so. And all
> who accept Christian revelation admit that those who attain
> their final beatitude exercise freedom of will, and yet cannot
> choose aught but what is truly good. They possess the kuowl-
> edge of Essential Goodness; and to it, not simply to good in
> general, they refer every choice. Moreover, even in our present
> condition it is open to omnipotence so to order our circum-
> stances and to confer on the will such instinctive impulses
> that we should in every election adopt the right course and
> not the wrong one.

To this objection, that free will is compatible with absolute
goodness and that therefore a benevolent, omnipotent God
would have given man free will and ensured his absolute virtue,
it is replied that God is being required to perform what is

logically impossible. It is logically impossible, so it is argued, for free will and absolute goodness to be combined, and hence, if God lacks omnipotence only in this respect, He cannot be claimed to lack omnipotence in any sense in which serious theists have ascribed it to Him.

Quite clearly, if free will and absolute goodness are logically incompatible, then God, in not being able to confer both on man does not lack omnipotence in any important sense of the term. However, it is not clear that free will and absolute goodness are logically opposed; and Joyce does point to considerations which suggest that they are not logical incompatibles. For my own part I am uncertain on this point; but my uncertainty is not a factual one but one concerning a point of usage. It is clear that an omnipotent God could create rational agents predestined always to make virtuous 'decisions'; what is not clear is whether we should describe such agents as having free will. The considerations to which Joyce points have something of the status of test cases, and they would suggest that we should describe such agents as having free will. However, no matter how we resolve the linguistic point, the question remains—Which is more desirable, free will and moral evil and the physical evil to which free will gives rise, or this special free will or pseudo-free will which goes with absolute goodness? I suggest that the latter is clearly preferable. Later I shall endeavour to defend this conclusion; for the moment I am content to indicate the nature of the value judgement on which the question turns at this point.

The second objection to the proposed solution of the problem of moral evil in terms of free will alone, related to the contention that free will is compatible with less moral evil than occurs, and possiby with no moral evil. We have seen what is involved in the latter contention. We may now consider what is involved in the former. It may be argued that free will is compatible with less moral evil than in fact occurs on various grounds. 1. God, if He were all-powerful, could miraculously intervene to prevent some or perhaps all moral evil; and He is said to do so on occasion in answer to prayers, (for example, to prevent wars) or of His own initiative (for instance, by producing calamities which serve as warnings, or by working miracles, etc.).

2. God has made man with a certain nature. This nature is often interpreted by theologians as having a bias to evil. Clearly God could have created man with a strong bias to good, whilst still leaving scope for a decision to act evilly. Such a bias to good would be compatible with freedom of the will. 3. An omnipotent God could so have ordered the world that it was less conducive to the practice of evil.

These are all considerations advanced by Joyce, and separately and jointly, they establish that God could have conferred free will upon us, and at least very considerably *reduced* the amount of moral evil that would have resulted from the exercise of free will. This is sufficient to show that *not all* the moral evil that exists can be justified by reference to free will alone. This conclusion is fatal to the account of moral evil in terms of free will alone. The more extreme conclusion that Mackie seeks to establish—that absolute goodness is compatible with free will—is not essential as a basis for refuting the free will argument. The difficulty is as fatal to the claims of theism whether all moral evil or only some moral evil is unaccountable. However, whether Mackie's contentions are sound is still a matter of logical interest, although not of any real moment in the context of the case against theism, once the fact that less moral evil is compatible with free will has been established.

(ii) The second free will argument arises out of an attempt to circumvent these objections. It is not free will, but the value of the goods achieved through free will that is said to be so great as to provide a justification for moral evil.

(a) This second argument meets a difficulty in that it is now necessary for it to be supplemented by a proof that the number of people who practice moral virtue or who attain beatitude and/or virtue after a struggle is sufficient to outweigh the evilness of moral evil, the evilness of their eternal damnation and the physical evil they cause to others. This is a serious defect in the argument, because it means that the argument can at best show that moral evil *may have* a justification, and not that it has a justification. It is both logically and practically impossible to supplement and complete the argument. It is necessarily incomplete and inconclusive even if its general principle is sound.

(*b*) This second argument is designed also to avoid the other difficulty of the first argument—that free will may be compatible with no evil and certainly with less evil. It is argued that even if free will is compatible with absolute goodness it is still better that virtue and beatitude be attained after a genuine personal struggle; and this, it is said, would not occur if God is conferring free will nonetheless prevented moral evil or reduced the risk of it. Joyce argues in this way:

> To receive our final beatitude as the fruit of our labours, and as the recompense of a hard-worn victory, is an incomparably higher destiny than to receive it without any effort on our part. And since God in His wisdom has seen fit to give us such a lot as this, it was inevitable that man should have the power to choose wrong. We could not be called to merit the reward due to victory without being exposed to the possibility of defeat.

There are various objections which may be urged here. First, this argument implies that the more intense the struggle, the gerater is the triumph and resultant good, and the better the world; hence we should apparently, on this argument, court temptation and moral struggles to attain greater virtue and to be more worthy of our reward. Secondly, it may be urged that God is being said to be demanding too high a price for the goods produced. He is omniscient. He knows that many will sin and not attain the goods or the Good free will is said to make possible. He creates men with free will, with the natures men have, in the world as it is constituted, knowing that in His doing so He is committing many to moral evil and eternal damnation. He could avoid all this evil by creating men with rational wills predestined to virtue, or He could eliminate much of it by making men's natures and the conditions in the world more conducive to the practice of virtue. He is said not to choose to do this. Instead, at the cost of the sacrifice of the many, He is said to have ordered things so as to allow fewer

men to attain this higher virtue and higher beatitude that result
from the more intense struggle.

In attributing such behaviour to God, and in attempting to
account for moral evil along these lines, thesist are, I suggest,
attributing to God immoral behaviour of a serious kind—of a
kind we should all unhesitatingly condemn in a fellow human
being.

We do not commend people for putting temptation in the
way of others. On the contrary, anyone who today advocated, or
even allowed where he could prevent it, the occurrence of evil
and the sacrifice of the many—even as a result of their own
freely chosen actions—for the sake of the higher virtue of the
few, would be condemned as an immoralist. To put severe
temptation in the way of the many, knowing that many and
perhaps even most will succumb to the temptation, for the sake
of the higher virtue of the few, would be blatant immorality;
and it would be immoral whether or not those who yielded to
the temptation possesed free will. This point can be brought out
by considering how a conscientious moral agent would answer
the question: Which should I choose for other pepole, a world
in which there are intense moral struggles and the possibility of
magnificent triumphs and the certainty of many defeats, or a
world in which there are less intense struggles, less magnificent
triumphs and fewer defeats, or a world in which there are
no struggles, no triumphs and no defeats? We are constantly
answering less easy questions than this in a way that conflicts
with the theist's contentions. If by modifying our own behaviour we can save someone else from an intense moral
struggle and almost certain moral evil for example if by refraining from gambling or excessive drinking ourselves we can help
a weaker person not to become a confirmed gambler or an
alcoholic, or if by locking our car and not leaving it unlocked
and with the key in it we can prevent people yielding to the
temptation to become car thieves, we feel obliged to act
accordingly, even though the persons concerned would freely
choose the evil course of conduct. How much clearer is
the decision with which God is said to be faced—the choice

between the higher virtue of some and the evil of others, or the higher but less high virtue of many more, and the evil of many fewer. Neither alternative denies free will to men.

These various difficulties dispose of each of the main arguments relating to moral evil. There are in addition to these difficulties two other objections that might be urged.

If it could be shown that man has not free will both arguments collapse; and even if it could be shown that God's omniscience is incompatible with free will they would still break down. The issues raised here are too great to be pursued in this paper; and they can simply be noted as possible additional grounds for which criticisms of the main proposed solutions of the problem of moral evil may be advanced.

The other general objection is by way of a follow-up to points made in objections (*b*) to both arguments (i) and (ii). It concerns the relative value of free will and its goods and evils and the value of the best of the alternatives to free will and its goods. Are free will and its goods so much more valuable than the next best alternatives that their superior value can really justify the immense amount of evil that is introduced into the world by free will?

Theologians who discuss this issue ask, Which is better— men with free will striving to work out their own destinies, or automata-machine-like creatures, who never make mistakes because they never make decisions? When put in this form we naturally doubt whether free will plus moral evil plus the possibility of the eternal damnation of the many and the physical evil of untold billions are quite so unjustified after all; but the fact of the matter is that the question has not been fairly put. The real alternative is, on the one hand, rational agents with free wills making many bad and some good decisions on rational and non-rational grounds, and 'rational' agents predestined always 'to choose' the right things for the right reasons—that is, if the language of automata must be used, rational automata. Predestination does not imply the absence of rationality in all senses of that term. God, were He omnipotent, could preordain the decisions and the reasons upon which they were based; and such a mode of existence would seem to be in itself a worthy mode of existence, and one prfeerable to an existence with free will, irrationality and evil.

D. Conclusion

In this paper it has been maintained that God, were He all-powerful and perfectly good, would have created a world in which there was no unnecessary evil. It has not been argued that God ought to have created a perfect world, nor that He should have made one that is in any way logically impossible. It has simply been argued that a benevolent God could, and would, have created a world devoid of superfluous evil. It has been contended that there is evil in this world—unnecessary evil— and that the more popular and philosophically more significant of the many attempts to explain this evil are completely unsatisfactory. Hence we must conclude from the existence of evil that there cannot be an omnipotent, benevolent God.

THE FREE WILL DEFENCE

ALVIN PLANTINGA

Since the days of Epicurus many philosophers have suggested that the existence of evil constitutes a problem for those who accept theistic belief.[1] Those contemporaries who follow Epicurus here claim, for the most part, to detect logical inconsistency in such belief. So McCloskey:

> Evil is a problem for the theist in that a *contradiction* is involved in the fact of evil, on the one hand, and the belief in the omnipotence and perfection of God on the other.[2]

and Mackie:

> I think, however, that a more telling criticism can be made by way of the traditional problem of evil. Here it can be shown, not that religious beliefs lack rational support, but that they are positively irrational, that the several parts of the essential theological doctrine are *inconsistent* with one another . . .[3]

and essentially the same charge is made by Professor Aiken in an article entitled 'God and Evil'.[4]

These philosophers, then, and many others besides, hold that traditional theistic belief is self-contradictory and that the problem of evil, for the theist, is that of deciding which of

[1] David Hume and some of the French encyclopedists, for example, as well as F. H. Bradley, J. McTaggart, and J. S. Mill.

[2] H. J. McCloskey, 'God and Evil'. *The Philosophical Quarterly*, Vol. 10 (April 1960), p. 97. [The article may be found on p. 23 in this book.]

[3] 'Evil and Omnipotence.' J. L. Mackie, *Mind*, Vol. 64, No. 254 (April 1955), p. 200. [The article may be found on p. 7 in this book.]

[4] *Ethics*, Vol. 48 (1957–58), p. 79.

the relevant propositions he is to abandon. But just which propositions are involved? What is the set of theistic beliefs whose conjunction yields a contradiction? The authors referred to above take the following five propositions to be essential to traditional theism: (*a*) that God exists, (*b*) that God is omnipotent, (*c*) that God is omniscient, (*d*) that God is wholly good, and (*e*) that evil exists. Here they are certainly right: each of these propositions is indeed an essential feature of orthodox theism. And it is just these five propositions whose conjunction is said, by our atheologians,[5] to be self-contradictory.

Apologists for theism, of course, have been quick to repel the charge. A line of resistance they have often employed is called *The Free Will Defence;* in this paper I shall discuss and develop that idea.

First of all, a distinction must be made between *moral evil* and *physical evil.* The former, roughly, is the evil which results from human choice or volition; the latter is that which does not. Suffering due to an earthquake, for example, would be a case of physical evil; suffering resulting from human cruelty would be a case of moral evil. This distinction, of course, is not very clear and many questions could be raised about it; but perhaps it is not necessary to deal with these questions here. Given this distinction, the Free Will Defence is usually stated in something like the following way. A world containing creatures who freely perform both good and evil actions—and do more good than evil—is more valuable than a world containing quasi-automata who always do what is right because they are unable to do otherwise. Now God can create free creatures, but He cannot causally or otherwise determine them to do only what is right; for if he does so then they do not do what is right *freely.* To create creatures capable of moral good, therefore, he must create creatures capable of moral evil; but he cannot create the posssibility of moral evil and at the same time

---

[5] *Natural* theology is the attempt to infer central religious beliefs from premises that are either obvious to common sense (e.g., *that some things are in motion*) or logically necessary. *Natural atheology* is the attempt to infer the falsity of such religious beliefs from premises of the same sort.

prohibit its actuality. And as it turned out, some of the free creatures God created exercised their freedom to do what is wrong: hence moral evil. The fact that free creatures sometimes err, however, in no way tells against God's omnipotence or against his goodness; for he could forestall the occurrence of moral evil only by removing the possibility of moral good.

In this way some traditional theists have tried to explain or justify part of the evil that occurs by ascribing it to the will of man rather than to the will of God. At least three kinds of objections to this idea are to be found both in the tradition and in the current literature. I shall try to develop and clarify the Free Will Defence by restating it in the face of these objections.

I

The first objection challenges the assumption, implicit in the above statement of the Free Will Defence, that free will and causal determinism are logically incompatible. So Flew:

> . . . to say that a person could have helped doing something is not to say that what he did was in principle unpredictable nor that there were no causes anywhere which determined that he would as a matter of fact act in this way. It is to say that if he had chosen to do otherwise he would have been able to do so; that there were alternatives, within the capacities of one of his physical strength, of his I.Q., of his knowledge, open to a person in his situation.
>
> . . . There is no contradiction involved in saying that a particular action or choice was: *both* free, and could have been helped, and so on; *and* predictable, or even foreknown, and explicable in terms of caused causes.
>
> . . . if it is really logically possible for an action to be both freely chosen and yet fully determined by caused causes, then the keystone argument of the Free Will Defense, that there is contradiction in speaking of God so arranging the laws of nature that all men always as a matter of fact freely choose to do the right, cannot hold.[6]

6 'Divine Omnipotence and Human Freedom', in *New Essays in Philosophical Theology*, ed. A. Flew and A. MacIntyre, London 1955, pp. 150, 151, 153.

Flew's objection, I think, can be dealt with in a fairly summary
fashion. He does not, in the paper in question, explain what he
means by 'casual determination' (and of course in that paper
this omission is quite proper and justifiable). But presumably
he means to use the locution in question in such a way that to
say of Jones' action *A* that it is *causally determined* is to say
that the action in question has causes and that given these
causes, Jones could not have refrained from doing *A*. That is
to say, Flew's use of 'causally determined', presumably, is such
that one or both of the following sentences, or some sentences
very much like them, express necessarily true propositions:

(*a*) If Jones' action *A* is causally determined, then a set
S of events has occurred prior to Jones' doing *A* such that,
given *S*, it is causally impossible for Jones to refrain from doing
A.

(*b*) If Jones' action *A* is causally determined, then there is
a set *S* of propositions describing events occurring before *A*
and a set *L* of propositions expressing natural laws such that

(1) the conjunction of *S*'s members does not entail that
Jones does *A*, and
(2) the conjunction of the members of *S* with the members
of *L* does entail that Jones does *A*.

And Flew's thesis, then, is that there is no contradiction in saying of a man, both that all of his actions are causally determined
(in the sense just explained) and that some of them are free.

Now it seems to me altogether paradoxical to say of anyone all of whose actions are causally determined, that on some
occasions he acts freely. When we say that Jones acts freely
on a given occasion, what we say entails, I should think, that
either his action on that occasion is not causally determined,
or else he has previously performed an undetermined action
which is causal ancestor of the one in question. But this is a
difficult and debatable issue; fortunately we need not settle
it in order to assess the force of Flew's objection to the Free
Will Defence. The Free Will Defender claims that the sentence

'Not all free actions are causally determined' expresses a necessary truth; Flew denies this claim. This strongly suggests that Flew and the Free Will Defender are not using the words 'free' and 'freedom' in the same way. The Free Will Defender, apparently, uses the words in question in such a way that sentences 'Some of Jones' actions are free' and 'Jones did action *A* freely' express propositions which are inconsistent with the proposition that all of Jones' actions are causally determined, Flew, on the other hand, claims that with respect to the ordinary use of these words, there is no such inconsistency. It is my opinion that Flew is mistaken here; I think it is he who is using these words in a non-standard, unordinary way. But we need not try to resolve that issue; for the Free Will Defender can simply make Flew a present of the word 'freedom' and state his case using other locutions. He might now hold, for example, not that God made men free and that a world in which men freely do both good and evil is more valuable than a world in which they unfreely do only what is good; but rather that God made men such that some of their actions are *unfettered* (both free in Flew's sense and also causally undetermined) and that a world in which men perform both good and evil unfettered actions is superior to one in which they perform only good, but fettered, actions. By substituting 'unfettered' for 'free' throughout this account, the Free Will Defender can elude Flew's objection altogether.[7] So whether Flew is right or wrong about the ordinary sense of 'freedom' is of no consequence; his objection is in an important sense merely verbal and thus altogether fails to damage the Free Will Defence.

II

Flew's objection, in essence, is the claim that an omnipotent being could have created men in such a way that although free they would be *causally determined* to perform only right actions. According to a closely allied objection, an omnipotent being could have made men in such a way that although

[7] And since this is so in what follows I shall continue to use the words 'free' and 'freedom' in the way the Free Will Defender uses them.

free, and free from any such causal determination, they would nonetheless *freely refrain* from performing any evil actions. Here the contemporary spokesman is Mackie:

> . . . if God has made men such that in their free choices they sometimes prefer what is good and sometimes what is evil, why could he not have made men such that they always freely choose the good? If there is no logical impossibility in a man's freely choosing the good on one, or on several occasions, there cannot be a logical impossibility in his freely choosing the good on every occasion. God was not, then, faced with a choice between making innocent automata and making beings who, in acting freely, would sometimes go wrong; there was open to him the obviously better possibility of making beings who would act freely but always go right. Clearly, his failure to avail himself of this possibility is inconsistent with his being both omnipotent and wholly good.[8]

The objection is more serious than Flew's and must be dealt with more fully. Now the Free Will Defence is an argument for the conclusion that (*a*) is not contradictory or necessarily false:[9]

(*a*) God is onmipotent, omniscient, and all-good and God creates free men who sometimes perform morally evil actions.

What Mackie says, I think, may best me construed as an argument for the conclusion that (*a*) *is* necessarily false; in other words, that *God is omnipotent, omniscient and all good* entails *no free men He creates ever perform morally evil actions.* Mackie's argument seems to have the following structure:

(1) God is omnipotent and omniscient and all-good.
(2) If God is omnipotent. He can create any logically possible state of affairs.
∴ (3) God can create any logically possible state of affairs. (1, 2)

---

[8] *Op. cit.*, p. 17.
[9] And of course if (*a*) is consistent, so is the set (*a*)–(e) mentioned on page 50, for (*a*) entails each member of that set.

(4) That all free men do what is right on every occasion is a logically possible state of affairs.

∴(5) God can create free men such that they always do what is right. (4, 3)

(6) If God can create free men such that they always do what is right and God is all-good, then any free men created by God always do what his right.

∴(7) Any free men created by God always do what is right. (1, 5, 6)

∴(8) No free men created by God ever perform morally evil actions. (7)

Doubtless the Free Will Defender will concede the truth of (4); there is a difficulty with (2), however; for

(a) that there are men who are not created by God is a logically possible state of affairs

is clearly true. But (2) and (a) entail

(b) If God is onipotent, God can create men who are not created by God.

And (b), of course, is false; (2) must be revised. The obvious way to repair it seems to be something like the following:

(2′) If God is omnipotent, then God can create any state of affairs S such that *God creates S* is consistent.

Similarly, (3) must be revised:

(3′) God can create any state of affairs S such that *God creates S* is consistent.

(1′) and (3′) do not seem to suffer from the faults besetting (1) and (3); but now it is not at all evident that (3′) and (4) entail

(5) God can create free men such that they always do what is right

as the original argument claims. To see this, we must note that (5) is true only if

(5a) God creates free men such that they always do what is right

is consistent. But (5a), one might think, is equivalent to:

(5*b*) God creates free men and brings it about that they always freely do what is right.

And (5*b*), of course, is *not* consistent; for if God *brings it about* that the men He creates always do what is right, then they do not do what is right *freely*. So if (5*a*) is taken to express (5*b*), then (5) is clearly false and clearly not entailed by (3′) and (4).

On the other hand, (5*a*) could conceivably be used to express:

(5*c*) God creates free men and these free men always do what is right.

(5*c*) is surely consistent; it is indeed logically possible that God creates free men and that the free men created by Him always do what is right. And conceivably the objector is using (5) to express this possibility—i.e., it may be that (5) is meant to express:

(5*d*) the proposition *God creates free men and the free men created by God always do what is right* is consistent.

If (5) is equivalent to (5*d*), then (5) is true—in fact necessarily true (and hence trivially entailed by (3′) and (4)). But now the difficulty crops up with respect to (6) which, given the equivalence of (5) and (5*d*) is equivalent to

(6′) If God is all-good and the proposition *God creates free men and the free men He creates always do what is right* is consistent, then any free men created by God always do what is right.

Now Mackie's aim is to show that the proposition *God is omnipotent, omniscient and all-good* entails the proposition *no free men created by God ever perform morally evil actions*. His attempt, as I outlined it, is to show this by constructing a valid argument whose premise is the former and whose conclusion is the latter. But then any additional premise appealed to in the deduction must be necessarily true if Mackie's argument is to succeed. (6′) is one such additional premise; but there seems to be no reason for supposing that (6′) is true at all, let alone necessarily true. Whether the free men created by God would always do what is right would presumably be up

to them; for all we know they might sometimes exercise their
freedom to do what is wrong. Put in a nutshell the difficulty
with the argument is the following. (5*a*) (God creates free men
such that they always do what is right) is susceptible of two
interpretations ((5*b* and (5*c*)). Under one of these interpretations (5) turns out to be false and the argument therefore fails.
Under the other interpretation (6) turns out to be utterly
groundless and question begging, and again the argument fails.

So far, then, the Free Will Defence has emerged unscathed
from Mackie's objection. One has the feeling, however, that
more can be said here; that there is something to Mackie's
argument. What more? Well, perhaps something along the
following lines. It is agreed that it is logically possible that
all men always do only what is right. Now God is said to be
omniscient and hence knows, with respect to any person he
proposes to create, whether that person would or would not
commit morally evil acts. For every person *P* who in fact
performs morally evil actions, there is, evidently, a possible
person *P'* who is exactly like *P* in every respect except that *P'*
never performs any evil actions. If God is omnipotent, He could
have created these possible persons instead of the persons He
in fact did create. And if He is also all-good, He *would*, presumably, have created them, since they differ from the persons He
did create only in being morally better than they are.

Can we make coherent sense out of this revised version of
Mackie's objection? What, in particular, could the objector
mean by 'possible person'? and what are we to make of the suggestion that God could have created possible persons? I think
these questions can be answered. Let us consider first the set of
all those properties it is logically possible for human beings to
have. Examples of properties *not* in this set are the properties of
*being over a mile long; being a hippotamous; being a prime
number; being divisible by four;* and the like. Included in the
set are such properties as *having red hair; being present at the
Battle of Waterloo; being the President of the United States;
being born in 1889;* and *being a pipe-smoker.* Also included
are such moral properties as *being kind to one's maiden aunt,
being a scoundrel, performing at least one morally wrong action,*

and so on. Let us call the properties in this set *H* properties. The complement $\bar{P}$ of an *H* property *P* is the property a thing has just in case it does not have *P*. And a *consistent set of H properties* is a set of *H* properties such that it is logically possible that there be a human being having every property in the set. Now we can define 'possible person' in the following way:

> *x* is a possible person = *x* is a consistent set of *H* properties such that for every *H* property *P*, either *P* or $\bar{P}$ is a member of *x*.

To *instantiate* a possible person *P* is to create a human being having every property in *P*. And a set *S* of possible persons is a *co-possible set of possible persons* just in case it is logically possible that every member of *S* is instantiated.[10]

Given this technical terminology, Mackie's objection can be summarily restated. It is granted by everyone that there is no absurdity in the claim that some man who is free to do what is wrong never, in fact, performs any wrong action. It follows that there are many possible persons containing the property *is free to do wrong but always does right*. And since it is logically possible that all men always freely do what is right, there are presumably several co-possible sets of possible persons such that each member of each set contains the property in question. Now God, if he is omnipotent, can instantiate any possible person and any co-possible set of possible persons he chooses. Hence, if He were all-good, He would have instantiated one of the sets of co-possible persons all of whose members freely do only what is right.

In spite of its imposing paraphernalia the argument, thus restated, suffers from substantially the same defect that afflicts Mackie's original version. There are *some* possible persons God obviously cannot instantiate—those, for example, containing the property *is not created by God*. Accordingly it is *false* that God can instantiate just any possible person He chooses. But of course the interesting question is whether

> (1) God can instantiate possible persons containing the property of always freely doing what is right

---

[10] The definiens must not be confused with: For every member *M* of *S*, it is logically possible that *M* is instantiated.

is true; for perhaps Mackie could substitute (1) for the premise just shown to be false.

Is (1) true? Perhaps we can approach this question in the following way. Let P be any possible person containing the property *always freely does what is right*. Then there must be some action A such that P contains the property of being free with respect to A (i.e., the property of being free to perform A and free to refrain from performing A). The *instantiation* of a possible person, S, I shall say, is a person having every property in S; and let us suppose that if P were instantiated, its instantiation would be doing something morally wrong in performing A. And finally, let us suppose that God wishes to instantiate P. Now P contains many properties in addition to the ones already mentioned. Among them, for example, we might find the following: *is born in 1910, has red hair, is born in Stuttgart, has feeble-minded ancestors, is six feet tall at the age of fourteen*, and the like. And there is no difficulty in God's creating a person with these properties. Further, there is no difficulty in God's bringing it about that this person (let's call him Smith) is free with respect to A. But if God *also* brings it about that Smith refrains from performing A (as he must to be the instantiation of P) then Smith is no longer free with respect to A and is hence not the instantiation of P after all. God cannot cause Smith to refrain from performing A, while allowing him to be free with respect to A; and therefore whether or not Smith does A will be entirely up to Smith; it will be a matter of free choice for him. Accordingly, whether God can instantiate P depends upon what Smith would freely decide to do.

This point may be put more accurately as follows: First, we shall say that an H property Q is *indeterminate* if *God creates a person and causes him to have Q* is necessarily false; an H property is *determinate* if it is not indeterminate. Of the properties we ascribed to P, all are determinate except *freely refrains from doing A* and *always freely does what is right*. Now consider P_1, the subset of P containing just the determinate members of P. In order to instantiate P God must instantiate P_1. It is evident that there is at most one instantiation of P_1, for among the members of P_1 will be some such individuating properties as for example, *is the third son of Richard and Lena Dykstra.* P_1 also contains the property of being free with respect to A; and if P_1 is instantiated, its instantiation will either perform A or refrain from performing A. It is, of course, possible that P_1 is such that if it is instantiated its instantiation I will perform A. If so, then if God allows I to remain free with respect to A, I will do A; and if God prevents I from doing A, then I is not free with respect to A and hence not the instantiation of P after all. Hence in neither case does God succeed in instantiating P. And accordingly God can instantiate P only if P_1 is *not* such that if it is instantiated, its instantiation will perform A. Hence it is possible that God cannot instantiate P. And evidently it is also possible, further, that *every* possible person containing the property *always freely does what is right* is such that neither God nor anyone else can instantiate it.

Now we merely supposed that P_1 is such that if it is instantiated, its instantiation will perform A. And this supposition, if true at all, is merely contingently true. It might be suggested, therefore, that God could instantiate P by instantiating P_1 and bringing it about that P_1 is *not* such that if it is instantiated, its instantiation will perform A. But to do this God must instantiate P_1 and bring it about that P_1 is such that if it is instantiated, its instantiation I will *refrain* from performing A. And if God does this then God brings it about that I will not perform A. But then I is not free to perform A and hence once more is not the instantiation of P.

It is possible, then, that God cannot instantiate any possible person containing the property *always freely does what is right.* It is also possible, of course, that He *can* instantiate some such possible persons. But *that* He can, if indeed He can, is a contingent truth. And since Mackie's project is to prove an entailment, he cannot employ any contingent propositions as added premises. Hence the reconstructed argument fails.

Now the difficulty with the reconstructed argument is the fact that God cannot instantiate just any possible person he chooses, and the possibility that God cannot instantiate any possible persons conaining the property of always freely doing what is right. But perhaps the objector can circumvent this difficulty.

The *H* properties that make trouble for the objector are the indeterminate properties—those which God cannot cause anyone to have. It is because possible persons contain indeterminate properties that God cannot instantiate just any possible person He wishes. And so perhaps the objector can reformulate his definition of 'possible person' in such a way that a possible person is a consistent set *S* of *determinate* properties such that for any determinate *H* property *P*, either *P* or $\bar{P}$ is a member of *S*. Unfortunately the following difficulty arises. Where *I* is any indeterminate *H* property and *D* a determinate *H* property, *D* or *I* (the property a person has if he has either *D* or *I*) is determinate. And so, of course, is $\bar{D}$. The same difficulty, accordingly, arises all over again—there will be some possible persons God can't instantiate (those containing the properties *is not created by God or has red hair* and *does not have red hair*, for example). We must add, therefore, that no possible person *entails* an indeterminate property.[11]

Even so our difficulties are not at an end. For the definition as no stated entails that there are no *possible free persons*, i.e., possible persons containing the property *on some occasions free to do what is right and free to do what is wrong*.[12] We may see this as follows: Let *P* be any possible free person. *P* then contains the property of refraining from performing *A*. Hence in Furthermore, *P* would contain either the property of performing *A* (since that is a determinate property) or the property of refraining from performing *A*. But if *P* contains the property of performing A and the property of being free with respect to *A*, then *P* entails the property of freely performing *A*—which is an indeterminate property. And the same holds in case *P* contains the property of refraining from performing *A*. Hence in either case *P* entails an indeterminate property and accordingly is not a possible person.

---

[11] Where a set *S* of properties entails a property *P* if and only it is necessarily true that anything having every property in *S* also has *P*.

[12] This was pointed out to me by Mr. Lewis Creary.

Clearly the objector must revise the definition of 'possible person' in such a way that for any action with respect to which a given possible person P is free, P contains neither the property of performing that action nor the property of refraining from performing it. This may be accomplished in the following way. Let us say that a person S is *free with respect to a property P* just in case there is some action A with respect to which S is free and which is such that S has P if and only if he performs A. So, for example, if a person is free to leave town and free to stay, then he is free with respect to the property *leaves town.* And let us say that a set of properties is free with respect to a given property P just in case it contains the property is *free with respect to P*. Now we can restate the definition of 'possible person' as follows:

x is a possible person $= x$ is a consistent set of determinate H properties such that (1) for every determinate H property P with respect to which x is not free, either P or $\bar{P}$ is a member of x, and (2) x does not entail any indeterminate property.

Now let us add the following new definition:

Possibly person P has indeterminate property $I =$ if P were instantiated, P's instantiation would have I.

Under the revised definition of 'possible person' it seems apparent that God, if he is omnipotent, can instantiate any possible person, and any co-possible set of possible persons, he chooses. But, the objector continues, if God is also all-good, He will, presumably, instantiate only those possible persons who have some such indeterminate H property as that of *always freely doing what is right.* And here the Free Will Defender can no longer make the objection which held against the previous versions of Mackie's argument. For if God can instantiate any possible person he chooses, he can instantiate any possible free person he chooses.

The Free Will Defender can, however raise what is essentially the same difficulty in a new guise: what reason is there for supposing that there are *any* possible persons, in the present sense of 'possible person', having the indeterminate property in question? For it is clear that, given any indeterminate *H* property *I*, the proposition *no possible person has I* is a contingent proposition. Further, the proposition *every possible free person freely performs at least one morally wrong action* is possibly true. But if every *possible* free person performs at least one wrong action, then every *actual* free person also freely performs at least one wrong action; hence if every possible free person performs at least one wrong action, God could create a universe without moral evil only by refusing to create any free persons at all. And, the Free Will Defender adds, a world containing free persons and moral evil (provided that it contained more moral good than moral evil) would be superior to one lacking both free persons and moral good and evil. Once again, then, the objection seems to fail.

The definitions offered during the discussion of Mackie's objection afford the opportunity of stating the Free Will Defence more formally. I said above [p. 54] that the Free Will Defence is in essence an argument for the conclusion that (*a*) is consistent:

 (*a*) God is omnipotent, omniscient, and all-good and God creates persons who sometimes perform morally evil actions.

One way of showing (*a*) to be consistent is to show that its first conjunct does not entail the negation of its second conjunct, i.e., that
 (*b*) God is omnipotent, omniscient and all-good
does not entail
 (*c*) God does not create persons who perform morally evil actions.

Now one can show that a given proposition *p* does not entail another proposition *q* by producing a third proposition *r* which is such that (1) the conjunction of *p* and *r* is consistent and

(2) the conjunction of *p* and *r* entails the negation of *q*. What we need here, then, is a proposition whose conjunction with (*b*) is both logically consistent and a logically sufficient condition of the denial of (*c*).

Consider the following argument:

(*b*)   God is omnipotent, omniscient and all-good.
(*r*1)   God creates some free persons.
(*r*2)   Every possible free person performs at least one wrong action.
∴ (*d*)   Every actual free person performs at least one wrong action. (*r*2)
∴ (*e*)   God creates persons who perform morally evil actions. ((*r*1), (*d*))

This argument is valid (and can easily be expanded so that it is *formally* valid). Furthermore, the conjunction of (*b*), (*r*1) and (*r*2) is evidently consistent. And as the argument shows, (*b*), (*r*1) and (*r*2) *jointly entail* (*e*). But (*e*) is the denial of (*c*); hence (*b*) and (*r*) jointly entail the denial of (*c*). Accordingly (*b*) does not entail (*c*), and (*a*) (God is omnipotent, omniscient and all-good and God creates persons who perform morally evil acts) is shown to be consistent. So stated, therefore, the Free Will Defence appears to be successful.

At this juncture it might be objected that even if the Free Will Defence, as explained above, shows that there is no contradiction in the supposition that God, who is all-good, omnipotent and omniscient, creates persons who engage in moral evil, it does nothing to show that an all-good, omnipotent and omniscient Being could create a universe containing as *much* moral evil as this one seems to contain. The objection has a point, although the fact that there seems to be no way of measuring or specifying amounts of moral evil makes it exceedingly hard to state the objection in any way which does not leave it vague and merely suggestive. But let us suppose, for purposes of argument, that there is a way of measuring moral evil (and moral good) and that the moral evil present in the universe amounts to ø. The problem then is to show that

(b) God is omnipresent, omniscient and all-good

is consistent with

(f) God creates a set of free persons who produce ø moral evil.

Here the Free Will Defender can produce an argument to show that (b) is consistent with (f) which exactly parallels the argument for the consistency of (b) with (c):

(b) God is omnipotent, omniscient and all-good.

(r3) God creates a set S of free persons such that there is a balance of moral good over moral evil with respect to the members of S.

(r4) There is exactly one co-possible set S' of free possible persons such that there is a balance of moral good over moral evil with respect to its members; and the members of S' produce ø moral evil.

Set S is evidently the instantiation of S' (i.e. every member of S is an instantation of some member of S' and every member of S' is instantiated by some member of S); hence the members of S produce ø moral evil. Accordingly, (b), (r3) and (r4) jointly entail (f); but the conjunction of (b), (r3) and (r4) is consistent; hence (b) is consistent with (f).

III

The preceding discussion enables us to conclude, I believe, that the Free Will Defence succeeds in showing that there is no inconsistency in the assertion that God creates a universe containing as much moral evil as the universe in fact contains. There remains but one objection to be considered. McCloskey, Flew and others charge that the Free Will Defence, even if it is successful, accounts for only *part* of the evil we find; it accounts only for moral evil, leaving physical evil as as intractable as before. The atheologian can therefore restate his position, maintaining that the existence of *physical evil*, evil which cannot be ascribed to the free actions of human beings, is inconsistent with the existence of an omniscient, omnipotent and all-good Deity.

To make this claim, however, is to overlook an important part of traditional theistic belief; it is part of much traditional belief to atrribute a good deal of the evil we find to Satan, or to Satan and his cohorts. Satan, so the traditional doctrine goes, is a mighty non-human spirit, who, along with many other angels, was created long before God created men. Unlike most of his (c) colleagues, Satan rebelled against God and has since been creating whatever havoc he could; the result, of course, is physical evil. But now we see that the moves available to the Free Will Defender in the case of moral evil are equally available to him in the case of physical evil. First he provides definitions of 'possible non-human spirit,' 'free non-human spirit', etc., which exactly parallel their counterparts where it was moral evil that was at stake. Then he points out that it is logically possible that

(r5) God creates a set S of free non-human spirits such that the members of S do more good than evil,
and

(r6) there is exactly one co-possible set S' of possible free non-human spirits such that the members of S' do more good than evil, and

(r7) all of the physical evil in the world is due to the actions of the members of S.

He points out further that (r5), (r6), and (r7) are jointly consistent and that their conjunction is consistent with the proposition that God is omnipotent, omniscient and all-good. But (r5) through (r7) jointly entail that God creates a universe containing as much physical evil as the universe in fact contains; it follows then, that the existence of physical evil is not inconsistent with the existence of an omniscient, omnipotent, all-good Deity.

Now it must be conceded that views involving devils and other non-human spirits do not at present enjoy either the extensive popularity or the high esteem of (say) the Theory of Relativity. Flew, for example, has this to say about the view in question:

> To make this more than just another desperate *ad hoc*
> expedient of apologetic it is necessary to produce independent
> evidence for launching such an hypothesis (if 'hypothesis' is
> not too flattering a term for it).[13]

But in the present context this claim is surely incorrect; to rebut
the charge of contradiction the theist need not hold that the
hypohesis in question is probable or even true. He need hold
only that it is not inconsistent with the proposition that God
exists. Flew suspects that 'hypothesis' may be too flattering a
term for the sort of view in question. Perhaps this suspicion
reflects his doubts as to the meaningfulness of the proposed view.
But it is hard to see how one could plausibly argue that the
views in question are nonsensical (in the requisite sense) without invoking some version of the Verifiability Criterion, a doctrine whose harrowing vicissitudes are well known. Furthermore,
it is likely that any premises worth considering which yield the
conclusion that hypotheses about devils are nonsensical will
yield the same conclusion about the hypothesis that God exists.
And if *God exists* is nonsensical, then presumably theism is not
self-contradictory after all.

We may therefore conclude that the Free Will Defence
successfully rebuts the charge of contradiction brought against
the theist. The Problem of Evil (if indeed evil constitutes a
problem for the theist) does not lie in any inconsistency in the
belief that God, who is omniscient, omnipotent and all-good,
has created a world containing moral and physical evil.

[13] *Op. cit.*, p. 17.

DIVINE OMNISCIENCE AND VOLUNTARY ACTION

NELSON PIKE

In Part V, Section III of his *Consolatio Philosophiae*, Boethius entertained (though he later rejected) the claim that if God is omniscient, no human action is voluntary. This claim seems intuitively false. Surely, given only a doctrine describing God's *knowledge*, nothing about the voluntary status of human actions will follow. Perhaps such a conclusion would follow from a doctrine of divine omnipotence or divine providence, but what connection could there be between the claim that God is *omniscient* and the claim that human actions are determind? Yet Boethius thought he saw a problem here. He thought that if one collected together just the right assumptions and principles regarding God's knowledge, one could derive the conclusion that if God exists, no human action is voluntary. Of course, Boethius did not think that all the assumptions and principles required to reach this conclusion are true (quite the contrary), but he thought it important to draw attention to them nonetheless. If a theologian is to construct a doctrine of God's knowledge which does not commit him to determinism, he must first understand that there is a way of thinking about God's knowledge which would so commit him.

In this paper, I shall argue that although his claim has a sharp counterintuitive ring, Boethius was right in thinking that there is a selection from among the various doctrines and principles clustering about the notions of knowledge, omniscience, and God which, when brought together, demand the conclusion that if God exists, no human action is voluntary. Boethius, I think, did not succeed in making explicit all of the ingredients in the problem. His suspicions were sound, but his discussion was incomplete. His argument needs to be developed. This is the task I shall undertake in the pages to follow. I should

Reprinted from *The Philosophical Review*, 74 (1965), by permission of *The Philosophical Review* and the author.

like to make clear at the outset that my purpose in rearguing this thesis is not to show that determinism is true, nor to show that God does not exist, nor to show that either determinism is true or God does not exist. Following Boethius, I shall not claim that the items needed to generate the problem are either philosophically or theologically adequate. I want to concentrate attention on the implications of a certain set of assumptions. Whether the assumptions are themselves acceptable is a question I shall not consider.

I

A. Many philosophers have held that if a statement of the form "*A* knows *X*" is true, then "*A* believes *X*" is true and "*X*" is true. As a first assumption, I shall take this partial analysis of "*A* knows *X*" to be correct. And I shall suppose that since this analysis holds for all knowledge claims, it will held when speaking of God's knowledge. "God knows *X*" entails "God believes *X*" and "*X*' is true."

Secondly, Boethius said that with respect to the matter of knowledeg, God "cannot in anything be mistaken."[1] I shall understand this doctrine as follows. Omniscient beings hold no false beliefs. Part of what is meant when we say that a person is omniscient is that the person in question believes nothing that is false. But, further, it is part of the "essence" of God to be omniscient. This is to say that any person who is not omniscient could not be the person we usually mean to be referring to when using the name "God." To put this last point a little differently: if the person we usually mean to be referring to when using the name "God" were suddenly to lose the quality of omniscience (suppose, for example, He came to believe something false), the resulting person would no longer be God. Although we might call this second person "God" (I might call my cat "God"), the absence of the quality of omniscience would be sufficient to guarantee that the person referred to was not the same as the person formerly called by that name. From

---

[1] *Consolatio Philosophiae*, Bk. V, sec. 3, par. 6.

this last doctrine it follows that the statement "If a given person is God, that person is omniscient" is an a priori truth. From this we may conclude that the statement "If a given person is God, that person holds no false beliefs" is also an a priori truth. It would be conceptually impossible for God to hold a false belief. " '*X*' is true" follows from "God believes *X*." These are all ways of expressing the same principle—the principle expressed by Boethius in the formula "God cannot in anything be mistaken."

A second principle usually associated with the notion of divine omniscience has to do with the scope or range of God's intellectual gaze. To say that a being is omniscient is to say that he knows everything. "Everything" in this statement is usually taken to cover future, as well as present and past, events and circumstances. In fact, God is usually said to have had foreknowledge of everything that has ever happened. With respect to anything that was, is, or will be the case, God knew, *from eternity*, that it would be the case.

The doctrine of God's knowing everything from eternity is very obscure. One particularly difficult question concerning this doctrine is whether it entails that with respect to everything that was, is, or will be the case, God knew *in advance* that it would be the case. In some traditional theological texts, we are told that God is *eternal* in the sense that He exists "outside of time," that is, in the sense that He bears no temporal relations to the events or circumstances of the natural world.[2] In a theology of this sort, God could not be said to have known that a given natural event was going to happen before it happened. If God knew that a given natural event was going to occur *before* it occurred, at least one of God's cognitions would then have occurred before some natural event. This, surely, would violate the idea that God bears no temporal relations to natural events.[3] On the other hand, in a considerable number of theological

---

[2] This position is particularly well formulated in St. Anselm's *Proslogium*, ch. xix and *Monologium*, chs. xxi-xxii; and in Frederich Schleiermacher's *The Christian Faith*, Pt. I, sec 2, par. 51. It is also explicit in Boethius, *op. cit.*, secs. 4-6, and in St. Thomas' *Summa Theologica*, Pt. I, Q. 10.

[3] This point is explicit in Boethius, *op. cit.*, secs. 4-6.

sources, we are told that God *has always* existed—that He
existed long *before* the occurrence of any natural event. In a
theology of this sort, to say that God is eternal is not to say
that God exists "outside of time" (bears no temporal relations
to natural events), it is to say, instead, God has existed (and
will continue to exist) at each moment.[4] The doctrine of omniscience which goes with this second understanding of the notion of eternity is one in which it is affirmed that God *has
always* known what was going to happen in the natural world.
John Calvin wrote as follows:

> When we attribute foreknowledge to God, we mean that
> all things have ever been and perpetually remain before, his
> eyes, so that to his knowledge nothing is further or past, but
> all things are present; and present in such manner, that he
> does not merely conceive of them from ideas formed in his
> mind, as things remembered by us appear to our minds, but
> really he holds and sees them as if (*tanquam*) actually placed
> before him.[5]

All things are "present" to God in the sense that He "sees" them
as if (*tanquam*) they were actually before Him. Further, with
respect to any given natural event, not only is that event "present" to God in the sense indicated, it has *ever been and has
perpetually remained* "present" to Him in that sense. This latter
is the point of special interest. Whatever one thinks of the idea
that God "sees" things as if "actually placed before him,"
Calvin would appear to be committed to the idea that God
has *always known* what was going to happen in the natural
world. Choose an event (E) and time (T_2) at which E occurred. For any time (T_1) prior to T_2 (say, five thousand, six
hundred, or eighty years prior to T_2), God knew at T_1 that

---

[4] This position is particularly well expressed in William Paley's
Natural Theology, ch. xxiv. It is also involved in John Calvin's discussion
of predestination, *Institutes of the Christian Religion*, Bk. III, ch. xxi;
and in some formulations of the first cause argument for the existence
of God, e.g., John Locke's *Essay Concerning Human Understanding*, Bk.
IV, ch. x.

[5] *Institutes of the Christian Religion*, Bk. III, ch. xxi; this passage
trans. by John Allen (Philadelphia, 1813), II, 145.

E would occur at T_2. It will follow from this doctrine, of course, that with respect to any human action, God knew well in advance of its performance that the action would be performed. Calvin says, "when God created man, He foresaw what would happen concerning him." He adds, "little more than five thousand years have elapsed since the creation of the world."[6] Calvin seems to have thought that God foresaw the outcome of every human action well over five thousand years ago.

In the discussion to follow, I shall work only with this second interpretation of God's knowing everything *from eternity*. I shall assume that if a person is omniscient, that person has always known what was going to happen in the natural world— and, in patricular, has always known what human actions were going to be performed. Thus, as above, assuming that the attribute of omniscience is part of the "essence" of God, the statement "For any natural event (including human actions), if a given person is God, that person would always have known that that event was going to occur at the time it occurred" must be treated as an a priori truth. This is just another way of stating a point admirably put by St. Augustine when he said: "For to confess that God exists and at the same time to deny that He has foreknowledge of future things is the most manifest folly. . . . One who is not prescient of all future things is not God."[7]

B. Last Saturday afternoon, Jones mowed his lawn. Assuming that God exists and is (essentially) omniscient in the sense outlined above, it follows that (let us say) eighty years prior to last Saturday afternoon, God knew, and thus believed) that Jones would mow his lawn at that time. But from this it follows, I think, that at the time of action (last Saturday afternoon) Jones was not *able*—that is, it was not *within Jones's power*—to refrain from mowing his lawn.[8] If at the time of

---

6 *Ibid.*, p. 144.

7 *City of God*, Bk. V, sec. 9.

8 The notion of someone being *able* to do something and the notion of something being *within one's power* are essentially the same. Tradi-

action, Jones had been able to refrain from mowing his lawn,
then (the most obvious conclusion would seem to be) at the
time of action, Jones was able to do something which would
have brought it about that God held a false belief eighty years
earlier. But God cannot in anything be mistaken. It is not possible that some belief of His was false. Thus, last Saturday afternoon, Jones was not able to do something which would have
brought it about that God held a false belief eighty years ago.
To suppose that it was would be to suppose that, at the time of
action, Jones was able to do something having a conceptually
incoherent description, namely something that would have
brought it about that one of God's beliefs was false. Hence, given
that God believed eighty years ago that Jones would mow his
lawn on Saturday, if we are to assign Jones the power on Saturday to refrain from mowing his lawn, this power must not be described as the power to do something that would have rendered
one of God's beliefs false. How then should we describe it
vis-à-vis God and His belief? So far as I can see, there are only
two other alternatives. First, we might try describing it as the
power to do something that would have brought it about that
God believed otherwise than He did eighty years ago; or,
secondly, we might try describing it as the power to do something that would have brought it about that God (Who, by
hypothesis, existed eighty years earlier) did not exist eighty
years earlier—that is, as the power to do something that would
have brought it about that any person who believed eighty
years ago that Jones would mow his lawn on Saturday (one of

---

tional formulations of the problem of divine foreknowledge (e.g., those
of Boethius and Augustine) made use of the notion of what is (and
what is not) *within one's power*. But the problem is the same when
framed in terms of what one is (and one is not) *able* to do. Thus, I shall
treat the statements "Jones was able to do X," "Jones had the ability to
do X," and "It was within Jone's power to do X" as equivalent. Richard
Taylor, in "I Can," *Philosophical Review*, LXIX (1960), 78-89, has
argued that the notion of ability or power involved in these last three
statements is incapable of philosophical analysis. Be this as it may, I
shall not here attempt such an analysis. In what follows I shall, however,
be careful to affirm only those statements about what is (or is not) within
one's power that would have to be preserved on any analysis of this
notion having even the most distant claim to adequacy.

whom was, by hypothesis, God) held a false belief, and thus was
not God. But again, neither of these latter can be accepted. Last
Saturday afternoon, Jones was not able to do something that
would have brought it about that God believed otherwise than
He did eighty years ago. Even if we suppose (as was suggested
by Calvin) that eighty years ago God knew Jones would mow
his lawn on Saturday in the sense that He "saw" Jones mowing
his lawn as if this action were occurring before Him, the fact
remains that God knew (and thus believed) eighty years prior
to Saturday that Jones would mow his lawn. And if God held
such a belief eighty years prior to Saturday, Jones did not have
the power on Saturday to do something that would have made it
the case that God did not hold this belief eighty years earlier.
No action performed at a given time can alter the fact that a
given person held a certain belief at a time prior to the time in
question. This last seems to be an apriori truth. For similar
reasons, the last of the above alternatives must also be rejected.
On the assumption that God existed eighty years prior to Saturday, Jones on Saturday was not able to do something that would
have brought it about that God did not exist eighty years prior to
that time. No action performed at a given time can alter the fact
that a certain person existed at a time prior to the time in
question. This, too, seems to me to be an a priori truth. But if
these observations are correct, then, given that Jones mowed his
lawn on Saturday, and given that God exists and is (essentially)
omniscient, it seems to follow that at the time of action, Jones
did not have the power to refrain from mowing his lawn. The
upshot of these reflections would appear to be that Jones's
mowing his lawn last Saturday cannot be counted as a voluntary
action. Although I do not have an analysis of what it is for an
action to be *voluntary*, it seems to me that a situation in which
it would be wrong to assign Jones the *ability* or *power* to do
other than he did would be a situation in which it would also
be wrong to speak of his action as voluntary. As a general remark, if God exists and is (essentially) omniscient in the sense
specified above, no human action is voluntary.[9]

    [9] In Bk. II, ch xxi, secs. 8-11 of the *Essay*, John Locke says that an
agent is not *free* with respect to a given action (i.e., that an action is

As the argument just presented is somewhat complex, perhaps the following schematic representation of it will be of some use.

1. "God existed at T_1" entails "If Jones did X at T_2, God believed at T_1 that Jones would do X at T_2.

2. "God believes X" entails "'X' is true."

3. It is not within one's power at a given time to do something having a description that is logically contradictory.

4. It is not within one's power at a given time to do something that would bring it about that someone who held a certain belief at a time prior to the time in question did not hold that belief at the time prior to the time in question.

5. It is not within one's power at a given time to do something that would bring it about that a person who existed at an earlier time did not exist at that earlier time.

6. If God existed at T_1 and if God believed at T_1 that Jones would do X at T_2, then if it was within Jones's power at T_2 to refrain from doing X, then (1) it was within Jones's power at T_2 to do something that would have brought it about that God held a false belief at T_1, or (2) it was within Jones's power at T_2 to do something which would have brought it about that God did not hold the belief He held at T_1, or (3) it was within Jones's power at T_2 to do something that would have brought it about that any person who believed at T_1 that Jones would do X at T_2 (one of whom

---

done "under necessity") when it is not within the agent's power to do otherwise. Locke allows a special kind of case, however, in which an action may be *voluntary* though done under necessity. If a man chooses to do something without knowing that it is not within his power to do otherwise (e.g., if a man chooses to stay in a room without knowing that the room is locked), his action may be voluntary though he is not free to forbear it. If Locke is right in this (and I shall not argue the point one way or the other), replace "voluntary" with (let us say) "free" in the above paragraph and throughout the remainder of this paper.

was, by hypothesis, God) held a false belief and thus was not God—that is, that God (who by hypothesis existed at T_1) did not exist at T_1.

7. Alternative 1 in the consequent of item 6 is false (from 2 and 3).

8. Alternative 2 in the consequent of item 6 is false (from 4).

9. Alternative 3 in the consequent of item 6 is false (from 5).

10. Therefore, if God existed at T_1 and if God believed at T_1 that Jones would do X at T_2, then it was not within Jones's power at T_2 to refrain from doing X (from 6 through 9).

11. Therefore, if God existed at T_1, and if Jones did X at T_2, it was not within Jones's power at T_2 to refrain from doing X (from 1 and 10).

In this argument, items 1 and 2 make explicit the doctrine of God's (essential) omniscience with which I am working. Items 3, 4, and 5 express what I take to be part of the logic of the concept of ability or power as it applies to human beings. Item 6 is offered as an analytic truth. If one assigns Jones the power to refrain from doing X at T_2 (given that God believed at T_1 that he would do X at T_2), so far as I can see, one would have to describe this power in one of the three ways listed in the consequent of item 6. I do not know how to argue that these are the only alternatives, but I have been unable to find another. Item 11, when generalized for all agents and actions, and when taken together with what seems to me to be a minimal condition for the application of "voluntary action," yields the conclusion taht if God exists (and is essentially omniscient in the way I have described) no human action is voluntary.

C. It is important to notice that the argument given in the preceding paragraphs avoids use of two concepts that are often prominent in discussions of determinism.

In the first place, the argument makes no mention of the

causes of Jones's action. Say (for example, with St. Thomas)[10] that God's foreknowledge of Jones's action was, itself, the cause of the action (though I am really not sure what this means). Say, instead, that natural events or circumstances caused Jones to act. Even say that Jones's action had no cause at all. The argument outlined above remains unaffected. If eighty years prior to Saturday, God believed that Jones would mow his lawn at that time, it was not within Jones's power at the time of action to refrain from mowing his lawn. The reasoning that justifies this assertion makes no mention of a causal series preceding Jones's action.

Secondly, consider the following line of thinking. Suppose Jones mowed his lawn last Saturday. It was then *true* eighty years ago that Jones would mow his lawn at that time. Hence, on Saturday, Jones was not able to refrain from mowing his lawn. To suppose that he was would be to suppose that he was able on Saturday to do something that would have made false a proposition that was *already true* eighty years earlier. This general kind of argument for determinism is usually associated with Leibniz, although it was anticipated in Chapter IX of Aristotle's *De Interpretatione*. It has been used since, with some modification, in Richard Taylor's article, "Fatalism."[11] This argument, like the one I have offered above, makes no use of the notion of causation. It turns, instead, on the notion of its being *true eighty years ago* that Jones would mow his lawn on Saturday.

I must confess that I share the misgivings of those contemporary philosophers who have wondered what (if any) sense can be attached to a statement of the form "It was true at T_1

[10] *Summa Theologica*, Pt. I, Q. 14, a. 8.
[11] *Philosophical Review*, LXXI (1962), 56-66. Taylor argues that if an even E fails *to* occur at T_2, then at T_1 it was true that E would fail to occur at T_2. Thus, at T_1, a necessary condition of anyone's performing an action sufficient for the occurence of E at T_2 is missing. Thus at T_1, no one could have the power to perform an action that would be sufficient for the occurrence of E at T_2. Hence, no one has the power at T_1 to do something sufficient for the occurrence of an event at T_2 that is not going to happen. The parallel between this argument and the one recited above can be seen very clearly if one reformulates Taylor's argument, pushing back the time at which it was true that E would not occur at T_2.

that E would occur at T_2."[12] Does this statement mean that had someone believed, guessed, or asserted at T_1 that E would occur at T_2, he would have been right?[13] (I shall have something to say about this form of determinism later in this paper.) Perhaps it means that at T_1 there was sufficient evidence upon which to predict that E would occur at T_2.[14] Maybe it means neither of these. Maybe it means nothing at all.[15] The argument presented above presupposes that it makes straightforward sense to suppose that God (or just anyone) held a true belief eighty years prior to Saturday. But this is not to suppose that *what* God believed *was true eighty years prior to Saturday*. Whether (or in what sense) it was true eighty years ago that Jones would mow his lawn on Saturday is a question I shall not discuss. As far as I can see, the argument in which I am interested requires nothing in the way of a decision on this issue.

I I

I now want to consider three comments on the problem of divine foreknowledge which seem to be instructively incorrect.

A. Leibniz analyzed the problem as follows:

> They say that what is foreseen cannot fail to exist and they say so truly; but it follows not that what is foreseen is necessary. For necessary truth is that whereof the contrary is impossible or implies a contradiction. Now the truth which states that I shall write tomorrow is not of that nature, it is not necessary. Yet, supposing that God foresees it, it is necessary that it come to pass, that is, the consequence is necessary,

---

[12] For a help discussion of difficulties involved here, see Rogers Albritton's "Present Truth and Future Contingency," a reply to Richard Taylor's "The Problem of Future Contingency," both in the *Philosophical Review*, LXVI (1957), 1-28.

[13] Gilbert Ryle interprets it this way. See "It Was To Be," *Dilemmas* (Cambridge, 1954).

[14] Richard Gale suggests this interpretation in "Endorsing Predictions," *Philosophical Review*, LXX (1961), 378-385.

[15] This view is held by John Turk Saunders in "Sea Fight Tomorrow?," *Philosophical Review*, LXVII (1958), 367-378.

namely that it exist, since it has been foreseen; for God is infallible. This is what is termed a *hypothetical necessity*. But our concern is not this necessity; it is an *absolute* necessity that is required, to be able to say that an action is necessary, that it is not contingent, that it is not the effect of free choice.[16]

The statement "God believed at T_1 that Jones would do X at T_2" (where the interval between T_1 and T_2 is, for example, eighty years) does not entail " 'Jones did X at T_2' is necessary." Leibniz is surely right about this. All that will follow from the first of these statements concerning "Jones did X at T_2" is that the latter is *true,* not that it is *necessarily true.* But this observation has no real bearing on the issue at hand. The following passage from St. Augustine's formulation of the problem may help to make this point clear.

> Your trouble is this. You wonder how it can be that these two propositions are not contradictory and incompatible, namely that God has foreknowledge of all future events, and that we sin voluntarily and not by necessity. For if, you say, God foreknows that a man will sin, he must necessarily sin. But if there is necessity there is no voluntary choice of sinning, but rather fixed and unavoidable necessity.[17]

In this passage, the term "necessity" (or the phrase "by necessity") is not used to express a modal-logical concept. The term "necessity" is here used in contrast with the term "voluntary," not (as in Leibniz) in contrast with the term "contingent." If one's action is necessary (or by necessity), this is to say that one's action is not voluntary. Augustine says that if God has foreknowledge of human actions, the actions are necessary. But the form of this conditional is "P implies Q," not "P implies N (Q)." "Q" in the consequent of this conditional is the claim that human actions are not voluntary—that is, that one is not able, or does not have the power, to do other than he does.

16 *Théodicée*, Pt. I, sec. 37. This passage trans. by E. M. Huggard (New Haven, 1952), p. 144.
17 *De Libero Arbitrio*, Bk. III. This passage trans. by J. H. S. Burleigh, *Augustine's Earlier Writings* (Philadelphia, 1955).

Perhaps I can make this point clearer by reformulating the original problem in such a way as to make explicit the modal operators working within it. Let it be *contingently* true that Jones did X at T_2. Since God holds a belief about the outcome of each human action well in advance of its performance, it is then *contingently* true that God believed at T_1 that Jones would do X at T_2. But it follows from this that it is *contingently* true that at T_2 Jones was not able to refrain from doing X. Had he been (contingently) able to refrain from doing X at T_2, then either he was (contingently) able to do something at T_2 that would have brought it about that God held a false belief at T_1, or he was (contingently) able to do something at T_2 that would have brought it about that God believed otherwise than He did at T_1, or he was (contingently) able to do something at T_2 that would have brought it about that God did not exist at T_1. None of these latter is an acceptable alternative.

B. In *Concordia Liberi Arbitrii,* Luis de Molina wrote as follows:

It was not that since He foreknew what would happen from those things which depend on the created will that it would happen; but, on the contrary, it was because such things would happen through the freedom of the will, that He foreknew it; and that He would foreknow the opposite if the opposite was to happen.[18]

Remarks similar to this one can be found in a great many traditional and contemporary theological texts. In fact, Molina assures us that the view expressed in this passage has always been "above controversy"—a matter of "common opinion" and "unanimous consent"—not only among the Church fathers, but also, as he says, "among all catholic men."

One claim made in the above passage seems to me to be truly "above controversy." With respect to any given action foreknown by God, God would have foreknown the opposite if

[18] This passage trans. by John Mourant, *Readings in the Philosophy of Religion* (New York, 1954), p. 426.

the opposite was to happen. If we assume the notion of omniscience outlined in the first section of this paper, and if we
agree that omniscience is part of the "essence" of God, this
statement is a conceptual truth. I doubt if anyone would be inclined to dispute it. Also involved in this passage, however, is at
least the suggestion of a doctrine that cannot be taken as an item
of "common opinion" among *all* catholic men. Molina says it is
not because God foreknows what He foreknows that men act as
they do: it is because men act as they do that God foreknows
what He foreknows. Some theologians have rejected this claim.
It seems to entail that men's actions determine God's cognitions.
And this latter, I think, has been taken by some theologians to
be a violation of the notion of God as self-sufficient and incapable of being affected by events of the natural world.[19] But
I shall not develop this point further. Where the view put forward in the above passage seems to me to go wrong in an interesting and important way is in Molina's claim that God can
have foreknowledge of things that will happen "through the
freedom of the will." It is this claim that I here want to examine
with care.

What exactly are we saying when we say that God can
know in advance what will happen *through the freedom of the
will?* I think that what Molina has in mind is this. God can
know in advance that a given man is going to *choose* to perform
a certain action sometime in the future. With respect to the case
of Jones mowing his lawn, God know at T_1 that Jones would
freely decide to mow his lawn at T_2. Not only did God know at
T^1 that Jones would mow his lawn at T_2, He also knew at T_1
that this action would be performed *freely*. In the words of
Emil Brunner, "God knows that which will take place in freedom
in the future as something which happens in freedom."[20] What
God knew at T_1 is that Jones would *freely* mow his lawn at T_2.

I think that this doctrine is incoherent. If God knew (and
thus believed) at T^1 that Jones would *do X* at T_2,[21] I think it

---

[19] Cf. Boethius' *Consolatio*, Bk. V, sec. 3, par. 2.
[20] *The Christian Doctrine of God*, trans. by Olive Wyon (Philadelphia, 1964), p. 262.
[21] Note: no comment here about *freely* doing *X*.

follows that Jones was not able to do other than X at T_2 (for reasons already given). Thus, if God knew (and thus believed) at T_1 that Jones would *do* X at T_2, it would follow that Jones did X at T_2, but *not freely*. It does not seem to be possible that God could have believed at T_1 that Jones would freely do X at T_2. If God believed at T_1 that Jones would do X at T_2 Jones's action at T_2 was not free; and if God *also* believed at T_1 that Jones would freely act at T_2, it follows that God held a false belief at T_1—which is absurd.

C. Frederich Schleiermacher commented on the problem of divine foreknowledge as follows:

> In the same way, we estimate the intimacy between two persons by the foreknowledge one has of the actions of the other, without supposing that in either case, the one or the other's freedom is thereby endangered. So even the divine foreknowledge cannot endanger freedom.[22]

St. Augustine made this same point in *De Libero Arbitrio*. He said:

> Unless I am mistaken, you would not directly compel the man to sin, though you knew beforehand that he was going to sin. Nor does your prescience in itself compel him to sin even though he was certainly going to sin, as we must assume if you have real prescience. So there is no contradiction here. Simply you know beforehand what another is going to do with his own will. Similarly God compels no man to sin, though he sees beforehand those who are going to sin by their own will.[23]

If we suppose (with Schleiermacher and Augustine) that the case of an intimate friend having foreknowledge of another's action has the same implications for determinism as the case of God's foreknowledge of human actions, I can imagine two positions which might then be taken. First, one might hold (with

[22] *The Christian Faith*, Pt. I, sec. 2, par. 55. This passage trans. by W. R. Matthew (Edinburgh, 1928), p. 228.
[23] *Loc. cit.*

Schleiermacher and Augustine) that God's foreknowledge of human actions cannot entail determinism—since it is clear that an intimate friend can have foreknowledge of another's voluntary actions. Or, secondly, one might hold that an intimate friend cannot have foreknowledge of another's voluntary actions —since it is clear that God cannot have foreknowledge of such actions. This second position could take either of two forms. One might hold that since an intimate friend *can* have foreknowledge of another's actions, the actions in question cannot be voluntary. Or, alternatively, one might hold that since the other's actions *are* voluntary, the intimate friend cannot have foreknowledge of them.[24] But what I propose to argue in the remaining pages of this paper is that Schleiermacher and Augustine were mistaken in supposing that the case of an intimate friend having foreknowledge of other's actions has the same implications for determinism as the case of God's foreknowledge of human actions. What I want to suggest is that the argument I used above to show that God cannot have foreknowledge of voluntary actions cannot be used to show that an intimate friend cannot have foreknowledge of another's actions. Even if one holds that an intimate friend *can* have foreknowledge of another's voluntary actions, one ought not to think that the case is the same when dealing with the problem of divine foreknowledge.

Let Smith be an ordinary man and an intimate friend of Jones. Now, let us start by supposing that Smith believed at T_1 that Jones would do X at T_2. Te make no assumption concerning the truth or falsity of Smith's belief, but assume only that Smith held it. Given only this much, there appears to be no difficulty in supposing that at T_2 Jones was able to do X and that at T_2 Jones was able to do not-X. So far as the above description of the case is concerned, it might well have been within Jones's power at T_2 to do something (namely, X) which would have brought it about that Smith held a true belief at T_1, and it might well have been within Jones's power at T_2 to do something

---

[24] This last seems to be the position defended by Richard Taylor in "Deliberation and Foreknowledge," *American Philosophical Quarterly*, I (1964).

(namely, not-X) which would have brought it about that Smith held a false belief at T_1. So much seems apparent.

Now let us suppose that Smith *knew* at T_1 that Jones would do X at T_2. This is to suppose that Smith correctly believed (with evidence) at T_1 that Jones would do X at T_2. It follows, to be sure, that Jones *did* X at T_2. But now let us inquire about what Jones was *able* to do at T_2. I submit that there is nothing in the description of this case that requires the conclusion that it was not within Jones's power at T_2 to refrain from doing X. By hypothesis, the belief held by Smith at T_1 was true. Thus, by hypothesis, Jones did X at T_2. But even if we assume that the belief held by Smith at T_1 was *in fact* true, we can add that the belief held by Smith at T_1 *might have* turned out to be false.[25] Thus, even if we say that Jones *in fact* did X at T_2, we can add that Jones *might not* have done X at T_2—meaning by this that it was within Jones's power at T_2 to refrain from doing X. Smith held a true belief which might have turned out to be false, and, correspondingly, Jones performed an action which he was able to refrain from performing. Given that Smith correctly believed at T_1 that Jones would do X at T_2, we can still assign Jones the *power* at T_2 to refrain from doing X. All we need add is that the power in question is one which Jones *did not exercise.*

These last reflections have no application, however, when dealing with God's foreknowledge. Assume that God (being essentially omniscient) existed at T_1, and assume that He believed at T_1 that Jones would do X at T_2. It follows, again, that Jones did X at T_2. God's beliefs are true. But now, as above, let us inquire into what Jones was *able* to do at T_2. We cannot claim now, as in the Smith case, that the belief held by God at T_1 was *in fact* true but *might have* turned out to be false. No sense of "might have" has application here. It is a conceptual truth that God's beliefs are true. Thus, we cannot claim, as in the

---

[25] The phrase "might have" as it occurs in this sentence does not express mere *logical* possibility. I am not sure how to analyze the notion of possibility involved here, but I think it is roughly the same notion as is involved when we say, "Jones might have been killed in the accident (had it not been for the fact that at the last minute he decided not to go)."

Smith case, that Jones *in fact* acted in accordance with God's beliefs but had the *ability* to refrain from so doing. The ability to refrain from acting in accordance with one of God's beliefs would be the ability to do something that would bring it about that one of God's beliefs was false. And no one could have an ability of this description. Thus, in the case of God's foreknowledge of Jones's action at T_2, if we are to assign Jones the ability at T_2 to refrain from doing X, we must understand this ability in some way other than the way we understood it when dealing with Smith's foreknowledge. In this case, either we must say that it was the ability at T_2 to bring it about that God believed otherwise than He did at T_1; or we must say that it was the ability at T_2 to bring it about that any person who believed at T_1 that Jones would do X at T_2 (one of whom was, by hypothesis, God) held a false belief and thus was not God. But, as pointed out earlier, neither of these last alternatives can be accepted.

The important thing to be learned from the study of Smith's foreknowledge of Jones's action is that the problem of divine foreknowledge has as one of its pillars the claim that truth is *analytically* connected with God's *beliefs*. No problem of determinism arises when dealing with human knowledge of future actions. This is because truth is not analytically connected with human belief even when (as in the case of human knowledge) truth is contingently conjoined to belief. If we suppose that Smith knows at T_1 that Jones will do X at T_2, what we are supposing is that Smith believes at T_1 that Jones will do X at T_2 and (as an additional, contingent, fact) that the belief in question is true. Thus having supposed that Smith knows at T_1 that Jones will do X at T_2, when we turn to a consideration of the situation of T_2 we can infer (1) that Jones *will* do X at T_2 (since Smith's belief is true), and (2) that Jones does not have the power at T_2 to do something that would bring it about that Jones did not *believe* as he did at T_1. But paradoxical though it may seem (and it seems paradoxical only at first sight), Jones can have the power at T_2 to do something that would bring it about that Smith did not have *knowledge* at T_1. This is simply to say that Jones can have the *power* at T_2 to do something that

would bring it about that the belief held by Smith at T_1 (which
was, in fact, true) was (instead) false. We are required only to
add that since Smith's belief was in fact true (that is, was knowledge) Jones *did not* (in fact) *exercise* that power. But when
we turn to a consideration of God's foreknowledge of Jones's
action at T_2 the elbowroom between belief and truth disappears
and, with it, the possibility of assigning Jones even the *power*
of doing other than he does at T_2. We begin by supposing that
God *knows* at T_1 that Jones will do X at T_2. As above, this is to
suppose that God believes at T_1 that Jones will do X at T_2, and
it is to suppose that this belief is true. But it is *not* an additional,
contingent fact that the belief held by God is true. "Good believes X" entails "X is true." Thus, having supposed that God
knows (and thus believes) at T_1 that Jones will do X at T_2, we
can infer (1) that Jones *will do* X at T_2 (since God's belief is
true) ; (2) that Jones does not have the power at T_2 to do something that would bring it about that God did not hold the belief
He held at T_1, and (3) that Jones does not have the power at
T_2 to do something that would bring it about that the belief held
by God at T_1, was false. This last is what we could *not* infer
when truth and belief were only factually connected—as in the
case of Smith's knowledge. To be sure, "Smith knows at T_1 that
Jones will do X at T_2" and "God knows at T_1 that Jones will do
X at T_2" both entail "Jones will do X at T_2" ("*A* knows X"
entails " 'X' is true"). But this similarity between "Smith knows
X" and "God knows X" is not a point of any special interest in
the present discussion. As Schleiermacher and Augustine rightly
insisted (and as we discovered in our study of Smith's foreknowledge) the mere fact that someone knows in advance how
another will act in the future is not enough to yield a problem
of the sort we have been discussing. We begin to get a glimmer
of the knot involved in the problem of divine foreknowledge
when we shift attention away from the *similarities* between
"Smith knows X" and "God knows X" (in particular, that they
both e...ail " 'X' is true") and concentrate instead on the logical
differences which obtain between Smith's knowledge and God's
knowledge. We get to the difference which makes the difference
when, after analyzing the notion of knowledge as true belief

(supported by evidence) we discover the radically dissimilar relations between truth and belief in the two cases. When truth is only factually connected with belief (as in Smith's knowledge) one can have the power (though, by hypothesis, one will not exercise it) to do something that would make the belief false. But when truth is analytically connected with belief (as in God's belief) no one can have the power to do something which would render the belief false.

To conclude: I have assumed that any statement of the form "*A* knows *X*" entails a statement of the form "*A* believes *X*" as well as a statement of the form " '*X*' is true." I have then supposed (as an analytic truth) that if a given person is omniscient, that person (1) holds no false beliefs, and (2) holds beliefs about the outcome of human actions in advance of their performance. In addition, I have assumed that the statement "If a given person is God that person is omniscient" is an a priori statement. (This last I have labeled the doctrine of God's essential omniscience.) Given these items (plus some premises concerning what is and what is not without one's power), I have argued that if God exists, it is not within one's power to do other than he does. I have inferred from this that if God exists, no human action is voluntary.

As emphasized earlier, I do not want to claim that the assumptions underpinning the argument are acceptable. In fact, it seems to me that a theologian interested in claiming both that God is omniscient and that men have free will could deny any one (or more) of them. For example, a theologian might deny that a statement of the form "*A* knows *X*" entails a statement of the form "*A* believes *X*" (some contemporary philosophers have denied this) or, alternatively, he might claim that this entailment holds in the case of human knowledge but fails in the case of God's knowledge. This latter would be to claim that when knowledge is attributed to God, the term "knowledge" bears a sense other than the one it has when knowledge is attributed to human beings. Then again, a theologian might object to the analysis of "omniscience" with which I have been working. Although I doubt if any Christian theologian would allow that an omniscient being could believe something false, he might claim that a given person could be omniscient although he did not hold beliefs about the outcome of human actions *in advance* of their performance. (This latter is the way Boethius escaped the problem.) Still again, a theologian might deny the doctrine of God's essential omniscience. He might admit that if a given person is God that person is omniscient, but he might deny that this statement formulates an a priori truth. This would be to say that although God is omniscient, He is not *essentially* omniscient. So far as I can see, within the conceptual framework of theology employing any one of these adjustments, the problem of divine foreknowledge outlined in this paper could not be formulated. There thus appears to be a rather wide range of alternatives open to the theologian at this point. It would be a mistake to think that commitment to determinism is an unavoidable implication of the Christian concept of divine omniscience.

But having arrived at this understanding, the importance of the preceding deliberations ought not to be overlooked. There is a pitfall in the doctrine of divine omniscience. That knowing involves believing (truly) is surely a tempting philosophical view (witness the many contemporary philosophers who have affirmed it). And the idea that God's attributes (including omniscience) are essentially connected to His nature, together with the idea that an omniscient being would hold no false beliefs and would hold beliefs about the outcome of human actions in advance of their performance, might be taken by some theologians as obvious candidates for inclusion in a finished Christian theology. Yet the theologian must approach these items critically. If they embraced together, then if one affirms the existence of God, one is committed to the view that no human action is voluntary.

OMNISCIENCE AND IMMUTABILITY

It is generally recognized that omniscience and immutability are necessary characteristics of an absolutely perfect being. The fact that they are also incompatible characteristics seems to have gone unnoticed.

In the main body of this paper I will present first an argument that turns on the incompatibility of omniscience and immutability and, secondly, several objections to that argument with my replies to the objections.

(1) A perfect being is not subject to change.[1]
(2) A perfect being knows everything.[2]
(3) A being that knows everything always knows what time it is.[3]

Reprinted from *The Journal of Philosophy*, *63* (1966), by permission of *The Journal of Philosophy* and the author.

[1] This principle of immutability is regularly supported by one of two arguments. (I) *From Supreme Excellence:* A perfect being is a supremely excellent being; thus any change in such a being would constitute corruption, deterioration, loss of perfection. (See Plato, *Republic*, II, 381B.) (II) *From Complete Actualization:* A perfect being is a being whose capacities for development are all fully realized. A being subject to change, however, is in that respect and to that extent a being with an unrealized capacity for development, a being merely potential and not fully actualized, a being in a state of process and not complete; hence not perfect. (See Aristotle, *Metaphysics*, XII, 9 1074b26.) The principle of immutability is a thesis of orthodox Christian theology, drawn from Greek philosophy and having among its credentials such biblical passages as Malachi 3.6 and James 1.17. (See Aquinas, *Summa theologica*, I, Q. 9, art. 1.)

[2] Being incapable of knowing all there is to know or being capable of knowing all there is to know and knowing less than that are conditions evidently incompatible with absolute perfection. Hence (2), which seems even more familiar and less problematic than (1).

[3] Part of what is meant by premise (3) is, of course, that a being that knows everything always knows what time it is in every time zone on every planet in every galaxy; but it is not quite in that horological sense that its knowledge of what time it is is most plainly relevant to con-

(4) A being that always knows what time it is is subject to change.[4]

∴ (5) A perfect being is subject to change.

∴ (6) A perfect being is not a perfect being.

Finally, therefore,

(7) There is no perfect being.[5]

In discussing this argument with others[6] I have come across various objections against one or another of its premises. Considering such objections here helps to clarify the line taken

---

siderations of omniscience and immutability. The relevant sense can be brought out more easily in the consideration of objections against the argument.

[4] Adopting 'it is now t_n' as a convenient standard form for propositions as to what time it is, we may say of a being that always knows what time it is that the state of its knowledge changes incessantly with respect to propositions of the form 'it is now t_n'. First such a being knows that it is now t_1 (and that it is not now t_2), and then it knows that it is now t_2 (and that it is not now t_1). To say of any being that it knows something different from what it used to know is to say that it has changed; hence (4).

[5] [1f] $(x)(Px \supset \sim Cx)$; [2f] $(x)(Px \supset (p)(p \equiv Kxp))$ [K: . . . knows that . . .]; [3f] $(x)((p)(p \equiv Kxp) \supset (p)(Tp \supset (p \equiv Kxp)))$ [T: . . . is of the form 'it is now t_n'] [4f] $(x)((p)(Tp \supset (p \equiv Kxp)) \supset Cx)$; [5f] $(x)(Px \supset Cx)$ [entailed by 2f, 3f, 4f]; [6f] $(x)(Px \supset \sim Px)$ [entailed by 1f, 5f]; [7f] $(x) \sim Px$ [equivalent to 6f]. The formalization [3f] is an instance of a logical truth; nevertheless, premise (3) is not one of the established principles in philosophical or theological discussions of the nature of a perfect being. Not only is it not explicitly affirmed, but it seems often to be implicitly denied. This circumstance may arouse a suspicion that the formalization [3f] is inaccurate or question-begging. Any such suspicion will, I think, be dissipated in the course of considering the objections to the argument, but it may be helpful in the meantime to point out that the validity of the argument does not depend on this formalization. It is of course possible to adopt less detailed formalizations that would not disclose the special logical status of premise (3) and would nevertheless exhibit the validity of the argument. For example, [2f'] $(x)(Px \supset Ox)$; [3f'] $(x)(Ox \supset Nx)$ together with a similarly imprecise formalization of premise (4) would serve that purpose.

[6] I am indebted especially to Miss Marilyn McCord and to Professors H. N. Castañeda, H. G. Frankfurt, C. Ginet, G. B. Matthews, G. Nakhnikian, W. L. Rowe, S. Shoemaker, and W. Wainwright.

in the argument and provides an opportunity to anticipate and turn aside several natural criticisms of that line.

Because premises (1) and (2) present the widely accepted principles of immutability and omniscience, objections against them are not so much criticisms of the line taken in the argument as they are attempts to modify the concept of a perfect being in the light of the argument. And since premise (3) gives every impression of being an instance of a logical truth, premise (4) is apparently the one most vulnerable to attacks that are genuinely attacks on the argument. The first four of the following seven objections are all directed against premise (4), although Objection D raises a question relevant to premise (3) as well.

Objection A: It must be granted that a being that always knows what time it is knows something that is changing—say, the state of the universe. But change in the object of knowledge does not entail change in the knower.

The denial that a change in the object necessitates a change in the knower depends on imprecise characterizations of the object. For example, I know that the Chrysler Building in Manhattan is 1,046 feet tall. If it is said that the Chrysler Building is the object of my knowledge, then of course many changes in it—in its tenants or in its heating system, for example—do not necessitate changes in the state of my knowledge. If, however, it is more precisely said that the object of my knowledge is the *height* of the Chrysler Building, then of course a change in the object of my knowledge does necessitate a change in me. If a 40-foot television antenna is extended from the present tip of the tower, either I will cease to know the height of the Chrysler Building or I will give up believing that its height is 1,046 feet and begin believing that its height is 1,086 feet. In the case of always knowing what time it is, if we are to speak of an object of knowledge at all it must be characterized not as the state of the universe (which might also be said to be the object of, for example, a cosmologist's knowledge), but as the *changing* of that state. To know the changing of anything is to know first that p and then that not-p (for some particular instance of p), and a

knower that knows first one proposition and then another is a
knower that changes.

Objection B: The beliefs of a being that always knows
what time it is are subject to change, but a change in a being's
beliefs need not constitute a change in the being itself. If last
year Jones believed the Platonic epistles to be genuine and this
year he believes them to be spurious, then Jones has changed his
mind; and that sort of change in beliefs may be considered a
change in Jones. But if last year Jones believed that it was 1965
and this year he believes that it is 1966, he has not changed
his mind, he has merely taken account of a calendar change;
and that sort of change in beliefs should not be considered a
change in Jones. The change in beliefs entailed by always knowing what time it is is that taking-account sort of change rather
than a change of mind, the sort of change in beliefs that might
reasonably be said to have been at least in part initiated by the
believer and that might therefore be reasonably attributed to
him.

It seems clear, first of all, that the sort of change in beliefs
entailed by knowing the changing of anything is the taking-
account sort of change rather than a change of mind. But once
that much has been allowed, Objection B seems to consist in no
more than an expression of disappointment in the *magnitude*
of the change necessitated by always knowing what time it is.
The entailed change in beliefs is not, it is true, sufficiently radical to qualify as a change of character or of attitude, but it is
no less incompatible with immutability for all that. If Jones had
been immutable from December 1965 through January 1966 he
could no more have taken account of the calendar change than
he could have changed his mind.

It may be worth noting that just such small-scale, taking-
account changes in beliefs have sometimes been recognized by
adherents of the principle of immutability as incompatible with
immutability. Ockham, for example, argues at length against the
possibility of a change in the state of God's foreknowledge just
because God's changelessness could not be preserved through
such a change. In Question Five of his *Tractatus de praedesti-*

natione et de praescientia Dei et de futuris contingentibus Ockham maintains that "if 'God knows that *A*' (where *A* is a future contingent proposition) and 'God does not know that *A*' *could* be true successively, it *would* follow that God was changeable," and the principle on which Ockham bases that claim is in no way restricted to future contingents. (As an adherent of the principle of immutability Ockham of course proceeds to deny that God could first know that *A* and then not know that *A*, but his reasons for doing so involve considerations peculiar to future contingent propositions and need not concern us here.)[7]

Objection C: For an omniscient being always to know what time it is to know the state of the universe at every instant, but it is possible for an omniscient being to know the state of the universe at every instant all at once rather than successively. Consequently it is possible for an omniscient being always to know what time it is without being subject to change.

The superficial flaw in this objection is the ambiguity of the phrase 'to know the state of the universe at every instant', but the ambiguity is likely to be overlooked because the phrase is evidently an allusion to a familiar, widely accepted account of omniscience, according to which omniscience regarding contingent events is nothing more nor less than knowledge of the entire scheme of contingent events from beginning to end at once. I see no reason for quarreling here with the ascription of such knowledge to an omniscient being; but the underlying flaw in Objection C is the drastic *incompleteness* of this account of omniscience regarding contingent events.

[7] The most interesting historical example of this sort that I have seen was called to my attention by Professor Hugh Chandler after I had submitted this paper for publication. It is Problem XIII in the *Tahdfut al-Faldsifah* of al-Ghazali (d. ea. 1111): "REFUTATION OF THEIR [i.e., the philosophers', but principally Avicenna's] DOCTRINE THAT GOD (MAY HE BE EXALTED ABOVE WHAT THEY SAY) DOES NOT KNOW THE PARTICULARS WHICH ARE DIVISIBLE IN ACCORDANCE WITH THE DIVISION OF TIME INTO 'WILL BE', 'WAS', AND 'IS' " (tr. S. A. Kamali; Lahore, Pakistan Philosophical Congress, 1963; pp. 153–162). This work was not known to medieval Christian philosophers. [See Etienne Gilson, *History of Christian Philosophy in the Middle Ages* (New York: Random House, 1955), p. 216.]

The kind of knowledge ascribed to an omniscient being in this account is sometimes characterized as "seeing all time at a glance," which suggests that if one sees the entire scheme of contingent events from beginning to end at once one sees all there is to see of time. The totality of contingent events, we are to suppose, may be known either simultaneously or successively, and an omniscient being will of course know it not successively but simultaneously. In his *Summa contra gentiles* (Book I, Ch. 55, sects. [6]-[9]) Aquinas presents a concise version of what seems to be the standard exposition of this claim.

> . . . the intellect of one considering *successively* many things cannot have only one operation. For since operations differ according to their objects, the operation by which the first is considered must be different from the operation by which the second is considered. But the divine intellect has only one operation, namely, the divine essence, as we have proved. Therefore God considers all that he knows not successively, but *together*. Moreover, succession cannot be understood without time nor time without motion . . . But there can be no motion in God, as may be inferred from what we have said. There is, therefore, no succession in the divine consideration. . . . Every intellect, furthermore, that understands one thing after another is at one time *potentially* understanding and at another time *actually* understanding. For while it understands the first thing actually it understands the second thing potentially. But the divine intellect is never potentially but always actually understanding. Therefore it does not understand things successively but rather understands them together.

On this view an omniscient being's knowledge of contingent events is the knowledge that event *e* occurs at time *t* (for every true instance of that form). Thus an omniscient being knows that my birth occurs at t_n, that my writing these words occurs at t_{n+x}, that my death occurs at t_{n+x+y}. This omniscient being also knows what events occur simultaneously with each of those events—knows, for example, that while I am writing these words my desk calendar lies open at the page bearing the date "Friday, March 4, 1966," and the watch on my wrist shows 10:15.

Moreover, since an omniscient being by any account knows all necessary truths, including the truths of arithmetic, this omniscient being knows how much time elapses between my birth and my writing these words and between these words and my death. But I *am* writing these words just *now*, and on this view of omniscience an omniscient being is incapable of knowing that that is what I am now doing, and for all this omniscient being knows I might just as well be dead or as yet unborn. That is what knowing everything amounts to if knowing "everything" does not include always knowing what time it is. Alternatively, that is what knowing the state of the universe at every instant comes to if that phrase is interpreted in the way required by the claim that it is possible to have that sort of knowledge all at once.

According to this familiar account of omniscience, the knowledge an omniscient being has of the entire scheme of contingent events is in many relevant respects exactly like the knowledge you might have of a movie you had written, directed, produced, starred in, and seen a thousand times. You would know its every scene in flawless detail, and you would have the length of each scene and the sequence of scenes perfectly in mind. You would know, too, that a clock pictured in the first scene shows the time to be 3:45, and that a clock pictured in the fourth scene shows 4:30, and so on. Suppose, however, that your movie is being shown in a distant theater today. You know the movie immeasurably better than do the people in the theater who are now seeing it for the first time, but they know one big thing about it you don't know, namely, what is now going on on the screen.

Thus the familiar account of omniscience regarding contingent events is drastically incomplete. An omniscient being must know not only the entire scheme of contingent events from beginning to end at once, but also *at what stage of realization that scheme now is*. It is in this sense of knowing what time it is that it is essential to claim in premise (3) that a being that knows everything always knows what time it is, and it is in this sense that always knowing what time it is entails incessant change in the knower, as is claimed in premise (4).

In orthodox Christianity the prevalence of the incomplete account of omniscience regarding contingent events effectively obscures the incompatibility of omniscience and immutability. Aquinas, for example, is not content with proving merely that "it is impossible for God to change in any way." He goes on in the *Summa theologica* (Book I, Q. 14, art. 15) to argue that "since God's knowledge is his substance, as is clear from the foregoing, just as his substance is altogether immutable, as was shown above, so *his knowledge likewise must be altogether invariable.*" What Aquinas, Ockham, and others *have* recognized is that God's knowledge cannot be variable if God is to remain immutable. What has *not* been seen is that God's knowledge cannot be altogether invariable if it is to be perfect, if it is to be genuine omniscience.

Objection D: A perfect being transcends space and time. Such a being is therefore not subject to change, whether as a consequence of knowing what time it is or for any other reason.

The importance of this objection lies in its introduction of the pervasive, mysterious doctrine of the trancendence of space and time, a doctrine often cited by orthodox Christians as if it were both consistent with their theology and explanatory of the notion that God sees all time at a glance. It seems to me to be neither.

In *Proslogium* Chapters XIX and XX Anselm apostrophizes the being transcendent of space and time as follows:

> Thou wast not, then, yesterday, nor wilt thou be tomorrow; but yesterday and today and tomorrow thou art; or, rather, neither yesterday nor today nor tomorrow thou art, but simply *thou art, outside all time.* For yesterday and today and tomorrow have no existence except in time, but thou, although nothing exists without thee, nevertheless dost not exist in space or time, but all things exist in thee. For nothing contains thee, but thou containest all.

For present purposes the spatial aspect of this doctrine may be ignored. What is meant by the claim that an entity transcends time? The number 2 might, I suppose, be said to transcend time in the sense that it does not age, that it is no older now than it was a hundred years ago. I see no reason to quarrel with the doctrine that a perfect being transcends time in *that* sense, since under that interpretation the doctrine is no more than a gloss on the principle of immutability. But under that interpretation the doctrine begs the question of premise (4) rather than providing a basis for objecting to it.

Only one other interpretation of the doctrine of the transcendence of time suggests itself, and that is that from a God's-eye point of view there is no time, that the passage of time is a universal human illusion. (Whatever else may be said of this interpretation, it surely cannot be considered compatible with such essential theses of Christian doctrine as the Incarnation and the Resurrection.) Under this interpretation the doctrine of the transcendence of time does have a devasting effect on the argument, since it implies either that there are no true propositions of the form 'it is now t_n' or that there is exactly one (eternally) true proposition of that form. Thus under this interpretation premise (3) either is vacuous or has a single trivializing instance, and premise (4) is false. But this interpretation preserves the immutability of a perfect being by imposing immutability on everything else, and that is surely an inconceivably high price to pay, in the view of Christians and non-Christians alike.

The remaining three objections are directed against premises (1) or (2) and may, therefore, be considered not so much criticisms of the argument as attempts to revise the principle of immutability or the principle of omniscience in the light of the argument. Objections E and F have to do with premise (2), Objection G with premise (1).

Objection E: Since a perfect being transcends time it is logically impossible that a perfect being know what time it is and hence logically impossible that such a being know everything. But it is no limitation on a perfect being that it cannot do what is logically impossible. Therefore, its not knowing absolutely everything (in virtue of not knowing what time it is) does not impair its perfection.

Objections E and F are attempts to hedge on omniscience as philosophers and theologians have long since learned to hedge on omnipotence. In Objection E this attempt depends on directly invoking one of the stanlard limitations on omnipotence, but the attempt does not succeed. Perhaps the easiest way of pointing up its failure is to produce analogous inferences of the same form, such as this: since I am a human being and a human being is a mortal rational animal, it is logically impossible that I should live forever: therefore it is no limitation on me that I must die—or this: since I am a creature of limited power, it is logically impossible that I be capable of doing whatever is logically possible; therefore it is no limitation on me that I cannot do whatever is logically possible. What is wrong with all these inferences is that the crucial limitation is introduced in the initial description of the being in question, after which it does of course make sense to deny that mere consequences of the limiting description are to be introduced as if they constituted additional limitations. It is not an *additional* limitation on a legless man that he cannot walk, or on a mortal being that it must die, or on a creature of limited power that it cannot do whatever it might choose to do. No more is it an *additional* limitation on a being that is *incapable* of knowing what time it is that it *does not* know what time it is. But any claim to perfection that might have been made on behalf of such a being has already been vitiated in the admission that its transcendence of time renders it incapable of omniscience.

Objection F: Just as in explicating the concept of omnipotence we have been forced to abandon the naive formula 'a perfect being can do anything' and replace it with 'a perfect being can do anything the doing of which does not impair its perfection', so the argument suggests that the naive formula 'a perfect being knows everything' must be revised to read 'a perfect being knows everything the knowing of which does not impair its perfection'. Thus, since the argument does show that knowing what time it is impairs the perfection of the knower, it cannot be a part of the newly explicated omniscience to know what time it is.

Even if Objection F could be sustained, this particular grasping of the nettle would surely impress many as just too painful to bear, for in deciding whether or not to try to evade the conclusion of the argument in this way it is important to remember that in the context of the argument 'knowing what time it is' means knowing *what is going on.* Objection F at best thus provides an exceptionally costly defense of absolute perfection, emptying it of much of its content in order to preserve it; for under the newly explicated notion of omniscience Objection F commits one to the view that it is impossible for a *perfect, omniscient* being to know what is going on.

Objection F attempts to draw an analogy between an explication of omnipotence and a proposed explication of omniscience, borrowing strength from the fact that in the case of omnipotence such an explication has long since been recognized as a necessary condition of the coherence of the notion. In evaluating this attempt it is helpful to note that here are at least three types of provisos that may be inserted into formulas of omnipotence for that purpose. The first is relevant to omnipotence generally, the second specifically to eternal omnipotence, and the third specifically to eternal omnipotence as one perfect characteristic of a being possessed of certain other perfect characteristics. (For present purposes it is convenient to say simply that the third is relevant specifically to eternal omnipotence as one aspect of an absolutely perfect being.) These three types of provisos may be exemplified in the following three formulas of omnipotence:

I. A being that is omnipotent (regardless of its other characteristics) can do anything provided that (a) the description of what is to be done does not involve a logical inconsistency.

II. A being that is eternally omnipotent (regardless of its

other characteristics) can do anything provided that (a) . . . and (b) the doing of it does not constitute or produce a limitation on its power.

III. A being that is absolutely perfect (and hence eternally omnipotent) can do anything provided that (a) . . . and (b) . . . and (c) the doing of it does not constitute a violation of somes aspect of its perfection other than its power.

Provisos of type (c) only are at issue in Objection F, no doubt because provisos of types (a) and (b) have no effective role to play in the explication of omniscience. No being knows anything that *is not* the case; *a fortiori* no omniscient being knows anything that *cannot be* the case. So much for type (a). As for type (b), since certain things the description of which involves no logical inconsistency would if done incapacitate the doer—committing suicide, for example, or creating another omnipotent being—there is good reason for such a proviso in the explication of eternal omnipotence. It might likewise be claimed that an omniscient being knows everything except things that would if known limit the being's *capacity for knowledge,* the formal justification for this claim being just the same as that for the corresponding omnipotence-claim. The significant difference between these two claims is that the omniscience-claim is evidently vacuous. There is no reason to suspect that there *are* things that would if known limit the knower's capacity for knowledge. More directly to the point at issue in the argument, there is no reason whatever to think that knowing what is going on is a kind of knowing that limits the knower's capacity for knowledge. Thus although a type (b) proviso is needed in the explication of eternal omnipotence in order to preserve the coherence of the notion of eternal omnipotence, no such proviso need be inserted into the formula of omniscience in order to preserve the coherence of that notion.

The putative analogy in Objection F presupposses that a proviso of type (c) will preserve omniscience as it preserves omnipotence in such a (Cartesian) argument as the following. It is impossible for an absolutely perfect being to lie, for although such a being, as omnipotent, has the power to lie, the exercise of that power would violate the perfect goodness of the being. To say that it is impossible for an absolutely perfect being to lie is not to say that it lacks the power to lie but rather that its absolute perfection in another aspect—perfect goodness —necessitates its refraining from the exercise of that power. Whether or not this line of argument succeeds in doing what it is designed to do, it seems clear that there is no genuine analogue for it in the case of omniscience. Consider the following candidate. It is impossible for an absolutely perfect being to know what is going on, for although such a being, as omniscient, has the power to know what is going on, the exercise of that power would violate the immutability of the being. To say that it is impossible for an absolutely perfect being to know what is going on is not to say that it lacks the power to know what is going on but rather that its absolute perfection in another aspect—immutability—necessitates its refraining from the exercise of that power. A being that has the power to do something that it refrains from doing may not thereby even jeopardize its omnipotence. All the same, a being that has the power to know something that it refrains from knowing does thereby forfeit its omniscience. Omniscience is not the *power to know* everything; it is the *condition of knowing* everything, and that condition cannot be preserved through even a single instance of omitting to exercise the power to know everything.

Therefore, whatever strength Objection F seems to derive from its appeal to the putative analogy betwen omnipotence and omniscience in this respect is illusory, and this attempted evasion of the argument's conclusion reduces to an arbitrary decision to sacrifice omniscience to immutability.

Objection G: The traditional view of philosophers and theologians that absolute perfection entails absolute immutability is mistaken, founded on the misconception that in a perfect being any change would have to be for the worse. In particular the kind of change entailed by always knowing what time it is is a kind of change that surely cannot be construed as deterioration, even when it is ascribed to an absolutely perfect being. No doubt an absolutely perfect being must be immutable in most and perhaps in all other respects, but the argument shows that absolute perfection *entails* mutability in at least this one respect.

Objection G proceeds on the asumption that immutability is ascirbed to a perfect being for only one reason—namely, that all change in such a being must constitute deterioration. There is, however, a second reason, as has been indicated at several points in the discussion so far—namely, that any change in a "perfect" being must indicate that the being was in some respect not in the requisite state of completion, actualization, fixity. The aspect of absolute completion is no less essential an ingredient in the concept of absolute perfection than is the aspect of absolute excellence. Moreover, those such as Aquinas and Ockham who argue against the mutability of a perfect being's *knowledge* would surely agree that the change they are intent on ruling out would not constitute *deterioration*, since they regularly base their arguments on the inadmissibility of *process* in an absolutely perfect being.

An absolutely perfect being may be described as a being possessing all logically compossible perfections. Thus if the argument had shown that omniscience and immutability were logically incompossible, it would have called for no more than an adjustment in the concept of absolute perfection, an adjustment of the sort proposed in Objection G. The proposition 'things change' is, however, not necessarily but only contingently true. If as a matter of fact nothing else ever did change, an omniscient being could of course remain immutable. In Objection G, however, an obsolutely perfect being has been confused with a being possessing all *really* compossible perfections, the best of all *really* possible beings. Perhaps, as the objection implies, the most *nearly* absolutely perfect being in the circumstances that happen to prevail *would* be mutable in the respect necessitated by always knowing what time it is. But that is of consequence to the argument, which may be taken as showing that the prevailing circumstances do not admit of the existence of an absolutely perfect being.

This concluding section of the paper is in the nature of an appendix. It might be subtitled "Omniscience and Theism"; for it may be shown that the doctrine that God knows everything is incompatible also with theism, the doctrine of a personal God distinct from other persons.[8]

Consider these two statements.

S_1. Jones knows that he is in a hospital.
S_2. Jones knows that Jones is in a hospital.

S_1 and S_2 are logically independent. It may be that Jones is an amnesia case. He knows perfectly well that he is in a hospital, and after reading the morning papers he knows that Jones is in a hospital. An omniscient being surely must know all that Jones knows. Anyone can know what S_2 describes Jones as knowing, but no one other than Jones can know what S_1 describes Jones as knowing. (A case in point: Anyone could have proved that Descartes existed, but that is not what Descartes proved in the Cogito, and what he proved in the Cogito could not have been proved by anyone else.) The kind of knowledge S_1 ascribes to Jones is, moreover, the kind of knowledge characteristic of every self-conscious entity, of every person. Every person knows certain propositions that no *other* person *can* know. Therefore, if God is omniscient, theism is false; and if theism is true, God is not omniscient.

It may fairly be said of God, as it once was said of William Whewell, that "omniscience [is] his foible."

[8] The following argument was suggested to me by certain observations made by Professor Hector Castañeda in a paper entitled "He," presented at the Wayne State University philosophy colloquium in the fall of 1964.

2

THE LANGUAGE OF
RELIGIOUS DISCOURSE

THEOLOGY AND FALSIFICATION

ANTONY FLEW

Let us begin with a parable. It is a parable developed from a tale told by John Wisdom in his haunting and revelatory article 'Gods'.[1] Once upon a time two explorers came upon a clearing in the jungle. In the clearing were growing many flowers and many weeds. One explorer says, 'Some gardener must tend this plot.' The other disagrees, 'There is no gardener'. So they pitch their tents and set a watch. No gardener is ever seen. 'But perhaps he is an invisible gardener.' So they set up a barbed-wire fence. They electrify it. They patrol with blood-hounds. (For they remember how H. G. Wells's *The Invisible Man* could be both smelt and touched though he could not be seen.) But no shrieks ever suggest that some intruder has received a shock. No movements of the wire ever betray an invisible climber. The bloodhounds never give cry. Yet still the Believer is not convinced. 'But there is a gardener, invisible, intangible, insensible to electric shocks, a gardener who has no scent and makes no sound, a gardener who comes secretly to look after the garden which he loves.' At last the Sceptic despairs, 'But what remains of your original assertion? Just how does what you call an invisible, intangible, eternally elusive gardener differ from an imaginary gardener or even from no gardener at all?'

In this parable we can see how what starts as an assertion, that something exists or that there is some analogy between certain complexes of phenomena, may be reduced step by step to an altogether different status, to an expression perhaps of a

Reprinted with permission of The Macmillan Company (New York) and the Student Christian Movement Press Limited (London) from *New Essays in Philosophical Theology* by Antony Flew and Alasdair MacIntyre, eds. First published in 1955.

[1] *P.A.S.* 1944–5, reprinted as Ch. X of *Logic and Language*, Vol I (Blackwell, 1951), and in his *Philosophy and Psychoanalysis* (Blackwell, 1953).

'picture preference'.[2] The Sceptic says there is no gardener. The Believer says there is a gardener (but invisible, etc.). One man talks about sexual behaviour. Another man prefers to talk of Aphrodite (but knows that there is not really a super-human person additional to, and somehow responsible for, all sexual phenomena).[3] The process of qualification may be checked at any point before the original assertion is completely withdrawn and something of that first assertion will remain (Tautology). Mr. Wells's invisible man could not, admittedly, be seen, but in all other respects he was a man like the rest of us. But though the process of qualification may be, and of course usually is, checked in time, it is not always judiciously so halted. Someone may dissipate his assertion completely without noticing that he has done so. A fine brash hypothesis may thus be killed by inches, the death by a thousand qualifications.

And in this, it seems to me, lies the peculiar danger, the endemic evil, of theological utterance. Take such utterances as 'God has a plan', 'God created the world', 'God loves us as a father loves his children'. They look at first sight very much like assertions, vast cosmological assertions. Of course, this is no sure sign that they either are, or are intended to be, assertions. But let us confine ourselves to the cases where those who utter such sentences intend them to express assertion. (Merely remarking parenthetically that those who intend or interpret such utterances as crypto-commands, expressions of wishes, disguised ejaculations, concealed ethics, or as anything else but assertions, are unlikely to succeed in making them either properly orthodox or practically effective).

Now to assert that such and such is the case is necessarily equivalent to denying that such and such is not the case.[4] Sup-

---

[2] Cf. J. Wisdom, 'Other Minds,' *Mind*, 1940; reprinted in his *Other Minds* (Blackwell, 1952).

[3] Cf. Lucretius, *De Rerum Natura*, II, 655–60,
    Hic siquis mare Neptunum Cereremque vocare
    Constituet fruges et Bacchi nomine abuti
    Mavolat quam laticis proprium proferre vocamen
    Concedamus ut hic terrarum dictitet orbem
    Esse deum matrem dum vera re tamen ipse
    Religione animum turpi contingere parcat.

[4] For those who prefer symbolism: $p \equiv \sim\sim p$.

pose then that we are in doubt as to what someone who gives
vent to an utterance is asserting, or suppose that, more radically, we are sceptical as to whether he is really asserting anything at all, one way of trying to understand (or perhaps it
will be to expose) his utterance is to attempt to find what he
would regard as counting against, or as being incompatible
with, its truth. For if the utterance is indeed an assertion, it
will necessarily be equivalent to a denial of the negation of that
assertion. And anything which would count against the assertion, or which would induce the speaker to withdraw it and
to admit that it had been mistaken, must be part of (or the
whole of) the meaning of the negation of that assertion. And to
know the meaning of the negation of an assertion, is as near
as makes no matter, to know the meaning of that assertion.[5]
And if there is nothing which a putative assertion denies then
there is nothing which it asserts either; and so it is not really
an assertion. When the Sceptic in the parable asked the
Believer, 'Just how does what you call an invisible, intangible, eternally elusive gardener differ from an imaginary gardener or even from no gardener at all?" he was suggesting
that the Believer's earlier statement had been so eroded by
qualification that it was no longer an assertion at all.

Now it often seems to people who are not religious as if
there was no conceivable event or series of events the occurrence
of which would be admitted by sophisticated religious people to
be a sufficient reason for conceding 'There wasn't a God after
all' or 'God does not really love us then'. Someone tells us that
God loves us as a father loves his children. We are reassured.
But then we see a child dying of inoperable cancer of the throat.
His earthly father is driven frantic in his efforts to help, but
his Heavenly Father reveals no obvious sign of concern. Some
qualification is made—God's love is 'not a merely human love'
or it is 'an inscrutable love', perhaps—and we realize that such
sufferings are quite compatible with the truth of the assertion
that 'God loves us as a father (but, of course, . . .)'. We are
reassured again. But then perhaps we ask: what is his assurance

---

[5] For by simply negating $\sim p$ we get $p : \sim\sim \equiv p$.

of God's (appropriately qualified) love worth, what is this
apparent guarantee really a guarantee against? Just what would
have to happen not merely (morally and wrongly) to tempt but
also (logically and rightly) to entitle us to say 'God does not
love us' or even 'God does not exist'? I therefore put to the
succeeding symposiasts the simple central questions, 'What
would have to occur or to have occurred to constitute for you
a disproof of the love of, or of the existence of, God?'

R. M. HARE

I wish to make it clear that I shall not try to defend
Christianity in particular, but religion in general—not because
I do not believe in Christianity, but because you cannot understand what Christianity is, until you have understood what
religion is.

I must begin by confessing that, on the ground marked
out by Flew, he seems to me to be completely victorious. I
therefore shift my ground by relating another parable. A certain
lunatic is convinced that all dons want to murder him. His
friends introduce him to all the mildest and most respectable
dons that they can find, and after each of them has retired,
they say, 'You see, he doesn't really want to murder you; he
spoke to you in a most cordial manner; surely you are convinced now?' But the lunatic replies 'Yes but that was only his
diabolical cunning; he's really plotting against me the whole
time, like the rest of them; I know it I tell you'. However, many
kindly dons are produced, the reaction is still the same.

Now we say that such a person is deluded. But what is he
deluded about? About the truth or falsity of an assertion? Let
us apply Flew's test to him. There is no behaviour of dons that
can be enacted which he will accept as counting against his
theory; and therefore his theory, on this test, asserts nothing.
But it does not follow that there is no difference between what
he thinks about dons and what most of us think about them—
otherwise we should not call him a lunatic and ourselves

sane, and dons would have no reason to feel uneasy about his presence in Oxford.

Let us call that in which we differ from this lunatic, our respective *bliks*. He has an insane *blik* about dons; we have a sane one. It is important to realize that we have a sane one, not no *blik* at all; for there must be two sides to any argument— if he has a wrong *blik*, then those who are right about dons must have a right one. Flew has shown that a *blik* does not consist in an assertion or system of them; but nevertheless it is very important to have the right *blik*.

Let us try to imagine what it would be like to have different *bliks* about other things than dons. When I am driving my car, it sometimes occurs to me to wonder whether my movements of the steering-wheel will always continue to be followed by corresponding alterations in the direction of the car. I have never had a steering failure, though I have had skids, which must be similar. Morevover, I know enough about how the steering of my car is made, to know the sort of thing that would have to go wrong for the steering to fail—steel joints would have to part, or steel rods break, or something—but how do I know that this won't happen? The truth is, I don't know; I just have a *blik* about steel and its properties, so that normally I trust the steering of my car; but I find it not at all difficult to imagine what it would be like to lose this *blik* and acquire the opposite one. People would say I was silly about steel; but there would be no mistaking the reality of the difference between our respective *bliks*—for example, I should never go in a motor-car. Yet I should hesitate to say that the difference between us was the difference between contradictory assertions. No amount of safe arrivals or bench-tests will remove my *blik* and restore the normal one; for my *blik* is compatible with any finite number of such tests.

It was Hume who taught us that our whole commerce with the world depends upon our *blik* about the world; and that differences between *bliks* about the world cannot be settled by observation of what happens in the world. That was why, having performed the interesting experiment of doubting the ordinary man's *blik* about the world, and showing that no proof could be given to make us adopt one *blik* rather than another, he turned to backgammon to take his mind off the problem. It seems, indeed, to be impossible even to formulate as an assertion the normal *blik* about the world which makes me put my confidence in the future reliability of steel joints, in the continued ability of the road to support my car, and not gape beneath it revealing nothing below; in the general non-homicidal tendencies of dons; in my own continued well-being (in some sense of that word that I may not now fully understand) if I continue to do what is right according to my lights; in the general likelihood of people like Hitler coming to a bad end. But perhaps a formulation less inadequate than most is to be found in the Psalms: 'The earth is weak and all the inhabiters thereof: I bear up the pillars of it'.

The mistake of the position which Flew selects for attack is to regard this kind of talk as some sort of *explanation*, as scientists are accustomed to use the word. As such, it would obviously be ludicrous. We no longer believe in God as an Atlas— *nous n'avons pas besoin de cette hypothèse*. But it is nevertheless true to say that, as Hume saw, without a *blik* there can be no explanation; for it is by our *bliks* that we decide what is and what is not an explanation. Suppose we believed that everything that happened, happened by pure chance. This would not of course be an assertion; for it is compatible with anything happening or not happening, and so, incidentally, is its contradictory. But if we had this belief, we should not be able to explain or predict or plan anything. Thus, although we should not be *asserting* anything different from those of a more normal belief, there would be a great difference between us; and this is the sort of difference that there is between those who really believe in God and those who really disbelieve in him.

The word 'really' is important, and may excite suspicion. I put it in, because when people have had a good Christian upbringing, as have most of those who now profess not to believe in any sort of religion, it is very hard to discover what they really believe. The reason why they find it so easy to think that they are not religious, is that they have never got into the frame of mind of one who suffers from the doubts to which religion is the answer. Not for them the terrors of the primitive jungle. Having abandoned some of the more picturesque fringes of religion, they think that they have abandoned the whole thing—whereas in fact they still have got, and could not live without, a religion of a comfortably substantial, albeit highly sophisticated, kind, which differs from that of many 'religious people' in little more than this, that 'religious people' like to sing Psalms about theirs—a very natural and proper thing to do. But nevertheless there may be a big difference lying behind—the difference between two people who, though side by side, are walking in different directions. I do not know in what direction Flew is walking; perhaps he does not know either. But we have had some examples recently of various ways in which one can walk away from Christianity, and there are any number of possibilities. After all, man has not changed biologicaly since primitive times; it is his religion that has changed, and it can easily change again. And if you do not think that such changes make a difference, get acquainted with some Sikhs and some Mussulmans of the same Punjabi stock; you will find them quite different sorts of people.

There is an important difference between Flew's parable and my own which we have not yet noticed. The explorers do not *mind* about their garden; they discuss it with interest, but not with concern. But my lunatic, poor fellow, minds about dons; and I mind about the steering of my car; it often has people in it that I care for. It is because I mind very much about what goes on in the garden in which I find myself, that I am unable to share the explorers' detachment.

BASIL MITCHELL

Flew's article is searching and perceptive, but there is, I think something odd about his conduct of the theologian's case. The theologian surely would not deny that the fact of pain counts against the assertion that God loves men. This very incompatibility generates the most intractable of theological problems—the problem of evil. So the theologian *does* recognize the fact of pain as counting against Christian doctrine. But it is true that he will not allow it—or anything—to count decisively against it; for he is committed by his faith to trust in God. His attitude is not that of the detached observer, but of the believer.

Perhaps this can be brought out by yet another parable. In time of war in an occupied country, a member of the resistance meets one night a stranger who deeply impresses him. They spend that night together in conversation. The Stranger tells the partisan that he himself is on the side of the resistance—indeed that he is in command of it, and urges the partisan to have faith in him no matter what happens. The partisan is utterly convinced at that meeting of the Stranger's sincerity and constancy and undertakes to trust him.

They never met in conditions of intimacy again. But sometimes the Stranger is seen helping members of the resistance, and the partisan is grateful and says to his friends, 'He is on our side'.

Sometimes he is seen in the uniform of the police handing over patriots to the occupying power. On these occasions his friends murmur against him: but the partisan still says, 'He is on our side'. He still believes that, in spite of appearances, the Stranger did not deceive him. Sometimes he asks the Stranger for help and receives it. He is then thankful. Sometimes he asks and does not receive it. Then he says, 'The Stranger knows best'. Sometimes his friends, in exasperation, say 'Well, what *would* he have to do for you to admit that you were wrong and that he is not on our side?' But the partisan refuses to answer. He will not consent to put the Stranger to the test. And sometimes his friends complain, 'Well, if *that's* what you mean by his being on our side, the sooner he goes over to the other side the better'.

The partison of the parable does not allow anything to count decisively against the proposition 'The Stranger is on our side'. This is because he has committed himself to trust the Stranger. But he of course recognizes that the Stranger's ambiguous behaviour *does* count against what he believes about

him. It is precisely this situation which constitutes the trial
of his faith.

When the partisan asks for help and doesn't get it, what
can he do? He can (*a*) conclude that the stranger is not on
our side or; (*b*) maintain that he is on our side, but that he
has reasons for withholding help.

The first he will refuse to do. How long can he uphold the
second position without its becoming just silly?

I don't think one can say in advance. It will depend on
the nature of the impression created by the Stranger in the first
place. It will depend, too, on the manner in which he takes the
Stranger's behaviour. If he blandly dismisses it as of no consequence, as having no bearing upon his belief, it will be
assumed that he is thoughtless or insane. And it quite obviously
won't do for him to say easily, 'Oh, when used of the Stranger
the phrase "is on our side" *means* ambiguous behaviour of
this sort'. In that case he would be like the religious man who
says blandly of a terrible disaster 'It is God's will'. No, he will
only be regarded as sane and reasonable in his belief, if he
experiences in himself the full force of the conflict.

It is here that my parable differs from Hare's. The partisan
admits that many things may and do count against his belief:
whereas Hare's lunatic who has a *blik* about dons doesn't
admit that anything counts against his *blik*. Nothing *can*
count against *bliks*. Also the partisan has a reason for having
in the first instance committed himself, viz. the character of the
Stranger; whereas the lunatic has no reason for his *blik* about
dons—because, of course, you can't have reasons for *bliks*.

This means that I agree with Flew that theological utterances must be assertions. The partisan is making an assertion
when he says, 'The Stranger is on our side.'

Do I want to say that the partisan's belief about the
Stranger is, in any sense, an explanation? I think I do. It explains and makes sense of the Stranger's behaviour: it helps
to explain also the resistance movement in the context of
which he appears. In each case it differs from the interpretation
which the others put upon the same facts.

'God loves men' resembles 'the Stranger is on our side'

(and many other significant statements, e.g. historical ones) in not being conclusively falsifiable. They can both be treated in at least three different ways: (1) As provisional hypotheses to be discarded if experience tells against them; (2) As significant articles of faith; (3) As vacuous formulae (expressing, perhaps, a desire for reassurance) to which experience makes no difference and which make no difference to life.

The Christian, once he has committed himself, is precluded by his faith from taking up the first attitude: 'Thou shalt not tempt the Lord thy God'. He is in constant danger, as Flew has observed, of slipping into the third. But he need not; and, if he does, it is a failure in faith as well as in logic.

ANTONY FLEW

It has been a good discussion: and I am glad to have helped to provoke it. But now—at least in *University*—it must come to an end: and the Editors of *University* have asked me to make some concluding remarks. Since it is impossible to deal with all the issues raised or to comment separately upon each contribution, I will concentrate on Mitchell and Hare, as representative of two very different kinds of response to the challenge made in 'Theology and Falsification'.

The challenge, it will be remembered, ran like this. Some theological utterances seem to, and are intended to, provide explanations or express assertions. Now an assertion, to be an assertion at all, must claim that things stand thus and thus; *and not otherwise.* Similarly an explanation, to be an explanation at all, must explain why this particular thing occurs; *and not something else.* Those last clauses are crucial. And yet sophisticated religious people—or so it seemed to me—are apt to overlook this, and tend to refuse to allow, not merely that anything actually does occur, but that anything conceivably could occur, which would count against their theological assertions and explanations. But in so far as they do this their supposed explanations are actually bogus, and their seeming assertions are really vacuous.

Mitchell's response to this challenge is admirably direct, straightforward, and understanding. He agrees 'that theological utterances must be assertions'. He agrees that if they are to be assertions, there must be something that would count against their truth. He agrees, too, that believers are in constant danger of transforming their would-be assertions into 'vacuous formulae'. But he takes me to task for an oddity in my 'conduct of the theologian's case. The theologian surely would not deny that the fact of pain counts against the assertion that God loves men. This very incompatibility generates the most intractable of theological problems, the problem of evil'. I think he is right. I should have made a distinction between two very different ways of dealing with what looks like evidence against the love of God: the way I stressed was the expedient of qualifying the original assertion; the way the theologian usually takes, at first, is to admit that it looks bad but to insist that there is—there must be—some explanaion which will show that, in spite of appearances, there really is a God who loves us. His difficulty, it seems to me, is that he has given God attributes which rule out all possible saving explanations. In Mitchell's parable of the Stranger it is easy for the believer to find plausible excuses for ambiguous behaviour: for the Stranger is a man. But suppose the Stranger is God. We cannot say that he would like to help but cannot: God is omnipotent. We cannot say that he would help if he only knew: God is omniscient. We cannot say that he is not responsible for the wickedness of others: God creates those others. Indeed an omnipotent, omniscient God must be an accessory before (and during) the fact to every human misdeed; as well as being responsible for every non-moral defect in the universe. So, though I entirely concede that Mitchell was absolutely right to insist against me that the theologian's first move is to look for an *explanation*, I still think that in the end, if relentlessly pursued, he will have to resort to the avoiding action of *qualification*. And there lies the danger of that death by a thousand qualifications, which would, I agree, constitute 'a failure in faith as well as in logic'.

Hare's approach is fresh and bold. He confesses that 'on the ground marked out by Flew, he seems to me to be completely

victorious'. He therefore introduces the concept of *blik*. But
while I think that there is room for some such concept in
philosophy, and that philosophers should be greatful to Hare
for his invention, I nevertheless want to insist that any attempt
to analyse Christian religious utterances as expressions or affir-
mations of a *blik* rather than as (at least would-be) assertions
about the cosmos is fundamentally misguided. *First,* because
thus interpreted they would be entirely unorthodox. If Hare's
religion really is a *blik,* involving no cosmological assertions
about the nature and activities of a supposed personal creator,
then surely he is not a Christian at all? *Second,* because thus interpreted, they could scarcely do the job they do. If they were
not even intended as assertions then many religious activities
would become fradulent, or merely silly. If 'You ought *because*
it is God's will' asserts no more than 'You ought', then the
person who prefers the former phraseology is not really giving
a reason, but a fraudulent substitute for one, a dialectical dud
cheque. If 'My soul must be immortal *because* God loves his
children, etc.' asserts no more than 'My soul must be immortal',
then the man who reassures himself with theological arguments
for immortality is being as silly as the man who tries to clear
his overdraft by writing his bank a cheque on the same account.
(Of course neither of these utterances would be distinctively
Christian: but this discussion never pretended to be so confined.) Religious utterances may indeed express false or even
bogus assertions: but I simply do not believe that they are not
both intended and interpreted to be or at any rate to presuppose assertions, at least in the context of religious practice;
whatever shifts may be demanded, in another context, by the
exigencies of theological apologetic.

One final suggestion. The philosophers of religion might
well draw upon George Orwell's last appalling nightmare *1984*
for the concept of *doublethink*. '*Doublethink* means the power
of holding two contradictory beliefs simultaneosuly, and accepting both of them. The party intellectual knows that he is
playing tricks with reality, but by the exercise of *doublethink*
he also satisfies himself that reality is not violated' (*1984,*
p. 220). Perhaps religious intellectuals too are sometimes driven

to doublethink in order to retain their faith in a loving God in
face of the reality of a heartless and indifferent world. But of
this more another time, perhaps.

<h2 align="center">I. M. CROMBIE[7]</h2>

There are some who hold that religious statements cannot
be fully meaningful, on the ground that those who use them
allow nothing to count decisively against them, treat them, that
is, as incapable of falsification. This paper is an attempted
answer to this view; and in composing it I have had particularly
in mind an article by Antony Flew [See above] and an unpublished paper read by A. M. Quinton to the Aquinas Society
of Oxford. I shall offer only a very short, and doubtless tenden-
tious, summary of my opponents' views.

Briefly, then, it is contended that there are utterances made
from time to time by Christians and others, which are said by
those who make them to be statements, but which are thought
by our opponents to lack some of the properties which anything
must have before it deserves to be called a statement. 'There is
a God', 'God loves us as a father loves his children', 'He shall
come again with glory . . .' are examples of such utterances.
Prima facie such utterances are neither exhortations, nor questions, nor expressions of wishes; *prima facie* they appear to
assert the actuality of some state of affairs; and yet (and this
is the objection) they are allowed to be compatible with any
and every state of affairs. If they are compatible with any
and every state of affairs, they cannot mark out some one state
of affairs (or group of states of affairs); and if they do not
mark out some one state of affairs, how can they be statements?
In the case of any ordinary statement, such as 'It is raining',
there is at least one situation (the absence of falling water)
which is held to be incompatible with the statement, and it is

---

[7] This paper was composed to be read to a non-philosophical audience. In composing it I have also filched shamelessly (and shamefully no
doubt distorted) some unpublished utterances of Dr. A. M. Farrer's.

the incompatibility of the situation with the statement which gives the statement its meaning. If, then, religious 'statements' are compatible with anything and everything, how can they be statements? How can the honest inquirer find out what they mean, if nobody will tell him what they are incompatible with? Are they not much more like such exhortations as 'Keep smiling', whose confessed purpose is to go on being in point whatever occurs? Furthermore, is it not true that they only appear to be statements to those of us who use them, because we deceive ourselves by a sort of conjuring trick, oscillating backwards and forwards between a literal interpretation of what we say when we say it, and a scornful rejection of such anthropomorphism when anybody challenges us? When we *say*: 'He shall come again with glory . . .', do we not picture real angels sitting on real clouds; when asked whether we really mean the clouds, we hedge; offer perhaps another picture, which again we refuse to take literally; and so on indefinitely. Whatever symbolism we offer, we always insist that only a crude man would take it literally, and yet we never offer him anything but symbolism; deceived by our imagery into supposing that we have something in mind, in fact there is nothing on which we are prepared to take our stand.

This is the position I am to try to criticize. It is, I think, less novel than its clothes; but none the less it is important. I turn to criticism.

Let us begin by dismissing from our inquiry the troublesome statement 'There is a God' or 'God exists'. As every student of logic knows, all statements asserting the existence of something offer difficulties of their own, with which we need not complicate our embarrassment.

That being dismissed, I shall want to say of statements about God that they consist of two parts. Call them, if you like, subject and predicate. Whatever you call them, there is that which is said, and that which it is said about—namely God. It is important to make this distinction, for different problems arise about the different parts. As a first approximation towards isolating the difference, we may notice that the predicate is normally composed of ordinary words, put to un-ordinary uses, whereas the subject-word is 'God', which has no other use. In the expression 'God loves us', the word 'God' is playing, so to speak, on its Home Ground, the phrase 'loves us' is playing Away. Now there is one set of questions which deal with the problem of why we say, and what we mean by saying, that God loves us, rather than hates us, and there is another set of questions concerned with the problem of what it is that this statement is being made about.

To approach the matter from an angle which seems to me to afford a good view of it, I shall make a few observations about the epistemological nature of religious belief. Let me caution the reader that, in doing so, I am not attempting to describe how religious belief in fact arises.

Theoretically, then, not in how it arises, but in its logical structure, religious belief has two parents; and it also has a nurse. Its logical mother is what one might call *undifferentiated theism*, its logical father is particular events or occasions interpreted as theophanic, and the extra-parental nurture is provided by religious activity.

A word, first, about the logical mother. It is in fact the case that there are elements in our experience which lead people to a certain sort of belief, which we call a belief in God. (We could, if we wished, call it rather an attitude than a belief, so long as we were careful not to call it an attitude to life; for it is of the essence of the attitude to hold that nothing whatever in life may be identified with that towards which it is taken up.) Among the elements in experience which provoke this belief or attitude, perhaps the most powerful is what I shall call a sense of contingency. Others are moral experience, and the beauty and order of nature. Others may be actual abnormal experience of the type called religious or mystical. There are those to whom conscience appears in the form of an unconditional demand; to whom the obligation to one's neighbour seems to be something imposed on him and on me by a third party who is set over us both. There are those to whom the beauty and order of nature appears as the intrusion into nature of a realm of beauty and order beyond it. There are those who believe themselves or others to be enriched by moments of direct access to the divine. Now there

are two things that must be said about these various theistic
interpretations of our experience. The first is that those who
so interpret need not be so inexpert in logic as to suppose that
there is anything of the nature of a deductive or inductive
argument which leads from a premiss asserting the existence of
the area of experience in question to a conclusion expressing
belief in God. Nobody who takes seriously the so-called moral
argument need suppose that the *prima facie* authority of conscience cannot be naturalistically explained. He can quite well
acknowledge that the imperativeness wihch so impresses him
could be a mere reflection of his jealousy of his father, or a
vestigial survival of tribal taboo. The mystic can quite well
acknowledge that there is nothing which logically forbids
the interpretation of the experience which he enjoys in terms
of the condition of his liver or the rate of his respirations. If,
being acquainted with the alternative explanations, he persists
in rejecting them, it need not be, though of course it sometimes
is, because he is seized with a fallacious refutation of their
validity. All that is necessary is that he should be honestly convinced that, in interpreting them, as he does, theistically, he
is in some sense facing them more honestly, bringing out more
of what they contain or involve than could be done by interpreting them in any other way. The one interpretation is pre-
ferred to the other, not because the latter is thought to be
refutable on paper, but because it is judged to be uncon-
vincing in the light of familiarity with the facts. There
is a partial parallel to this in historical judgment. Where you
and I differ in our interpretation of a series of events, there
is nothing outside the events in question which can over-
rule either of us, so that each man must accept the interpretation which seems, on fair and critical scrutiny, the most convincing to him. The parallel is only partial, however, for in
historical (and literary) interpretation there is something which
to some extent controls one's interpretation, and that is one's
general knowledge of human nature; and in metaphysical
interpretation there is nothing analogous to this. That, then,
is my first comment on theistic interpretations; for all that these
journeys of the mind are often recorded in quasi-argumentative

form, they are not in any ordinary sense arguments, and their validity cannot be assessed by asking whether they conform to the laws either of logic or of scientific method. My second comment upon them is, that, in stating them, we find ourselves saying things which we cannot literally mean. Thus the man of conscience uses some such concept as the juridical concept of authority, and locates his authority outside nature; the man of beauty and order speaks of an intrusion from another realm; the mystic speaks of experiencing God. In every case such language lays the user open to devastating criticism, to which he can only retort by pleading that such language, while it is not to be taken strictly, seems to him to be the natural language to use.

To bring these points into a somewhat stronger light, let me say something about the sense of contingency, the conviction which people have, it may be in blinding moments, or it may be in a permanent disposition of a man's mind, that we, and the whole world in which we live, derive our being from something outside us. The first thing I want to say about this is that such a conviction is to no extent like the conclusion of an argument; the sense of dependence feels not at all like being persuaded by arguments, but like seeing, seeing, as it were, through a gap in the rolling mists of argument, which alone, one feels, could conceal the obvious truth. One is not *persuaded* to believe that one is contingent; rather one feels that it is only by persuasion that one could ever believe anything else. The second thing I want to say about this conviction of contingency is that in expressing it, as Quinton has admirably shewn, we turn the word 'contingent' to work which is not its normal employment, and which it cannot properly do.

For the distinction between necessity and contingency is not a distinction between different sorts of entities, but between different sorts of statement. A necessary statement is one whose denial involves a breach of the laws of logic, and a contingent statement is one in which this is not the case. (I do not, of course, assert that this is the only way in which these terms have been used in the history of philosophy; but I do assert that this is the only use of them which does not give rise to impossible difficulties. I have no space to demonstrate this here; and indeed I do not think that it is any longer in need of demonstration.) But in this, the only coherent, sense of 'contingent', the existence of the world may be contingent fact, but so unfortunately is that of God. For *all* existential statements are contingent; that is to say, it is never true that we can involve ourselves in a breach of the laws of logic by merely denying of something that it exists. We cannot therefore in this sense contrast the contingent existence of the world with the necessary existence of God.

It follows that if a man persists in speaking of the contingency of the world, he must be using the term in a new or transferred sense. It must be that he is borrowing[8] a word from the logician and putting it to work which it cannot properly do. Why does he do this, and how can he make clear what precisely this new use is? For it is no good saying that when we are talking about God we do not use words in their ordinary senses unless we are prepared to say in what senses it is that we do not use them. And yet how can we explain to the honest inquirer what is the new sense in which the word 'contingent' is being used when we use it of the world? For it is proper to use it, in this sense, of everything with which we are acquainted, and improper to use it only of God, with whom we are not acquainted, how can the new use be learnt? For we normally learn the correct use of a word by noticing the differences between the situations in which it may be applied and those in which it may not; but the word 'contingent' is applicable in all the situations in which we ever find ourselves. If I said that everything but God was flexible, not of course in the ordinary sense, but in some other, how could you discover what the new sense was?

The answer must be that when we speak of the world as contingent, dependent, an effect or product, and so contrast it with a necessary, self-existent being, a first cause or a creator,

---

[8] It might be argued that, historically, the borrowing was the other way round. To decide that we should have to decide where the frontier between logic and metaphysics really comes in the work of those whose doctrine on the relationship between these disciplines is unsatisfactory.

we say something which on analysis will not do at all (for devastating criticisms can be brought against all these formulations), but which seems to us to be the fittest sort of language for our purpose. Why we find such language appropriate, and how, therefore, it is to be interpreted, is not at all an easy question; that it does in some way, it may be in some logically anomalous way, convey the meaning of those who use it, seems however to be an evident fact. How it is that the trick is worked, how it is that this sort of distortion of language enables believers to give expression to their beliefs, this it is the true business of the natural theologian to discuss. Farrer, for example, in *Finite and Infinite,* has done much to elucidate what it is that one is striving to express when one speaks of the contingency of the world, and so to enlighten the honest inquirer who wishes to know how the word 'contingent' is here being used.

What I have said about contingency and necessity applies also to obligation and its transcendent ground (or goodness and its transcendent goal), to design and its transcendent designer, to religious experience and its transcendent object. In all these cases we use language which on analysis will not do, but which seems to us to be appropriate for the expression of our beliefs; and in all these cases the question can be, and is, discussed, why such language is chosen, and how it is to be understood.

That then is the logical mother of religious belief; call her natural theism, or what you will, she is a response, not precisely logical, and yet in no sense emotional or evaluative, to certain elements in our experience, whose characteristic is that they induce us, not to make straightforward statements about the world, but to strain and distort our media of communication in order to express what we make of them. In herself she is an honest woman; and if she is sometimes bedizened in logical trappings, and put out on the streets as an inductive argument, the fault is hardly hers. Her function is, not to prove to us that God exists, but to provide us with a 'meaning' for the word 'God'. Without her we should not know whither statements concerning the word were to be referred; the subject in theological utterances would be unattached. All that we should know of them is that they were not to be referred to anything with which we are or could hope to be acquainted; that, and also that they were to be understood in terms of whatever it is that people suppose themselves to be doing when they build churches and kneel down in them. And that is not entirely satisfactory; for while there is much to be said in practice for advising the honest inquirer into the reference of the word 'God' to pursue his inquiry by familiarizing himself with the concrete activity of religion, it remains true that the range and variety of possible delusions which could induce such behaviour is theoretically boundless, and, as visitors to the Pacific coast of the United States can testify, in practice very large.

The logical father of religious belief, that which might bring us on from the condition of merely possessing the category of the divine, into the condition of active belief in God, this consists, in Christianity (and if there is nothing analogous in other religions, so much the worse for them), in the interpretation of certain objects or events as a manifestation of the divine. It is, in other words, because we find, that, in thinking of certain events in terms of the category of the divine, we can give what seems to us the most convincing account of them, that we can assure ourselves that the notion of God is not just an empty aspiration. Without the notion of God we could interpret nothing as divine, and without concrete events which we felt impelled to interpret as divine we could not know that the notion of divinity had any application to reality. Why it is that as Christians we find ourselves impelled to interpret the history of Israel, the life and death of Christ, and the experience of his Church as relevatory of God, I shall not here attempt to say; it is an oft-told tale, and I shall content myself with saying that we can hardly expect to feel such an impulsion so long as our knowledge of these matters is superficial and altogether from without. Whyever we feel such an impulsion, it is not, of course, a logical impulsion; that is, we may resist it (or fail to feel it) without thereby contravening the laws of logic, or the rules of any pragmatically accredited inductive procedure. On the anthropological level the history of Israel, Old and New, is certainly the history of a religious development from its tribal origins. We may decide, or we may not, that it is something more, something beyond the wit of man to invent, something which seems to us to be a real and coherent communication from a real and coherent, though superhuman, mind. We may decide, or we may not; neither decision breaks the rules, for in such a unique matter there are no rules to conform to or to break. The judgment is our own; and in the language of the New Testament it judges us; that is, it reveals what, up to the moment of our decision, the Spirit of God has done in us— but that, of course, is to argue in a circle.

Belief, thus begotten, is nurtured by the practice of the Christian life by the conviction so aroused (or, of course, not aroused; but then it is starvation and not nurture) that the Christian warfare is a real warfare. Something will have to be said about this later on, but for the moment I propose to dismiss it, and to return to the consideration of the significance of religious utterances in the light of the dual parentage of religious belief.

I have argued that unless certain things seem to us to be signs of divine activity, then we may hope that theer is a God, but we cannot properly believe that there is. It follows from this that religious belief must properly involve treating something as revelatory of God; and that is to say that it must involve an element of authority (for to treat something as divine revelation is to invest it with authority). That what we say about God is said on authority (and, in particular, on the authority of Christ) is of the first importance in considering the significance of these statements. In what way this is so, I shall hope to make clear as we go along.

If we remember that our statements about God rest on the authority of Christ, whom we call his Word, we can see what seems to me the essential clue to the interpretation of the logical nature of such utterances, and that is, in a word, the notion of parable. To elucidate what I mean by 'parable' (for I am using the word in an extended sense) let us consider Christ's action on Palm Sunday, when he rode into Jerusalem on an ass. This action was an act of teaching. For it had been said to Jerusalem that her king would come to her riding upon an ass.

Whoever, therefore, deliberately chose this method of entry, was saying in effect: 'What you are about to witness (namely my Passion, Death and Resurrection) is the coming of the Messianic King to claim his kingdom'. The prohpecy of Messiah's kingdom was to be interpreted, not in the ordinary sense, but in the sense of the royal kingship of the Crucified. To interpret in this way is to teach by violent paradox, indeed, but none the less it is to teach. Part of the lesson is that it is only the kings of the Gentiles that lord it over their subjects; if any man will be a king in Israel (God's chosen people), he must humble himself as a servant; part of it is that the Crucifixion is to be seen as Messianic, that is as God's salvation of his chosen people. Now the logical structure which is involved here is something like this:—You are told a story (Behold, thy king cometh, meek and lowly, and riding upon an ass). You will not know just what the reality to which the story refers will be like until it happens. If you take the story at its face value (an ordinary, though humble, king, bringing an ordinary political salvation), you will get it all wrong. If you bring to bear upon its interpretation all that the Law and the Prophets have taught you about God's purposes for his people, though you will still not know just what it will be like until it happens, none the less you will not go wrong by believing it; for then you will know that Christ ought to have suffered these things, and to enter into his glory, and so you will learn what the story has to tell you of God's purposes for man, and something therefore, indirectly, of God. If you remember what Isaiah says about humility and sacrifice, you will see that what is being forecast is that God's purposes will be accomplished by a man who fulfills the Law and the Prophets in humble obedience.

This story is that [sic] one that can be fairly fully interpreted. There are others that cannot. There is, for example, Hosea's parable in which he likens himself to God, and Israel to his unfaithful wife, and expresses his grief at his wife's unfaithfulness. If, now, you ask for this to be fully interpreted, if you ask Hosea to tell you what he supposes it is like for the Holy One of Israel, of whom no similitude may be made, to be grieved, demanding to know, not what would happen in such

a case to the unfaithful sinner who had provoked the divine
wrath, but what the condition of the divine mind in itself, then
no doubt he would have regarded the very question as blas-
phemous. As an inspired prophet, he felt himself entitled to say
that God was grieved, without presuming to imagine what such
a situation was like, other than in its effects. What he said was
said on authority; it was not his own invention, and therefore
he could rely on its truth, without supposing himself to understand its full meaning. In so far as Hosea's parable is 'interpreted', the interpretation is confined to identifying the *dramatis
personae* (Hosea = God, his wife = Israel). It is noteworthy
that the interpretation which is sometimes given to the parables
of the New Testament is usually of the same sketchy kind (The
reapers are the angels). In Plato's famous parable of prisoners
in a cave, it is quite possible to describe the situation which the
parable seeks to illuminate. One can describe how a man can
begin by being content to establish rough laws concerning what
follows what in nature, how he may proceed from such a condition to desire explanations of the regularities which are forced
on his attention, rising thus to more abstract and mathematical
generalizations, and then, through the study of mathematics, to
completely abstract speculation. One cannot similarly describe
the situation which the parable of the Prodigal Son is intended
to illustrate (or rather one can only describe the human end of
it); and no attempt is ever made to do so.

I make no apology for these paragraphs about the Bible;
after all the Bible is the source of Christian belief, and it cannot but illuminate the logical nature of the latter to consider
the communicational methods of the former. But we must turn
back to more general considerations. It is, then, characteristic
of a parable that the words which are used in it are used in
their ordinary senses. Elsewhere this is not always so. If you
spaek of the virtues of a certain sort of car, the word 'virtue',
being applied to a car, comes to mean something different from
what it means in application to human beings. If you speak of
hot temper, the word 'hot' does not mean what it means in the
ordinary way. Now many people suppose that something of the
latter sort is happening in religious utterances. When God is said

to be jealous, or active in history, it is felt that the word 'jealous' or 'active' must be being used here in a transferred sense. But if it is being used in a transferred sense, some means or other must be supplied whereby the new sense can be taken. The activity of God is presumably not like the activity of men (it does not make him hot or tired); to say then that God is active must involve modifying the meaning of the word. But, if the word is undergoing modification, it is essential that we should know in what direction. In the case of ordinary transfers, how do we know what sort of modification is involved? This is a large question, but roughly, I think, the answer is, in two ways. Firstly there is normally a certain appropriateness, like the appropriateness of 'hot' in 'hot temper'; and secondly we can notice the circumstances in which the word gets used and withheld in its transferred sense. If I hear the phrase 'Baroque music', the meaning of the word 'Baroque' in its normal architectural employment may set me looking in a certain direction; and I can clinch the matter by asking for examples, 'Bach? Buxtehude? Beethoven?' But for either of these ways to be of any use to me, I must know something about *both* ends of the transfer. I must know something about Baroque architecture, *and* I must be able to run through musical styles in my head, to look for the musical analogue of Baroque features. If I cannot stumble on your meaning without assistance, I can still do so by eliciting from you that Bach and Buxtehude are, Handel and Mozart are not, examples of the sort of music you have in mind. This is informative to me if and only if I know something of Buxtehude and Bach, Handel and Mozart.

Now we all know what it is like for a man to be active. We can quote examples, decide correctly, and so forth. But what about divine activity? Surely we cannot have it both ways. Either God can be moderately like a man, so that the word 'active', used of him, can set us looking in the right direction; od he can be quite unlike a man, in which case it cannot. Nor can we be helped by the giving of examples, unless it is legitimate to point to examples of divine activity—to say, 'Now here God is being active, but not there.' This constitutes the force of Flew's demand that we should tell him how statements about

God can be falsified. In essence Flew is saying: 'When you speak about God, the words which occur in the predicate part of your statements are not being used in the ordinary sense; you make so great a difference between God and man, that I cannot even find that the words you use set me looking in anything that might perhaps be the right direction. You speak of God as being outside time; and when I think what I mean by "activity", I find that that word, as used about a timeless being, suggests to me nothing whatsoever. There is only one resort left; give me examples of when one of your statements is, and is not, applicable. If, as no doubt you will say, that is an unfair demand, since they are always applicable (e.g. God is always active, so that there are no cases of his inactivity to be pointed to), I will not insist on actual examples; make them up if you like. But do not point to *everything* and say, "*That* is what I mean"; for *everything* is not *that*, but this and this and this and many other mutual incompatibles; and black and white and red and green and kind and cruel and coal and ink and everything else together cannot possibly elucidate to me the maening of a word.'

As I have said, the answer must be that when we speak about God, the words we use are intended in their ordinary sense (for we cannot make a transfer, failing familiarity with both ends of it), although we do not suppose that in their ordinary interpretation they can be strictly true of him. We do not even know how much of them applies. To some extent it may be possible to take a word like 'activity' and whittle away that in it which most obviously does not apply. It is, however, an exaggeration, at the least, to suppose that this process of whittling away leaves us in the end with a kernel about which we can say that we know that it does apply. A traditional procedure is to compose a scale on which inanimate matter is at the bottom, the characteristically human activities, such as thinking and personal relationship, at the top, and to suppose that the scale is pointing towards God; and so on this assumption the first thing to do is to pare away from the notion of human activity whatever in it is common to what stands below it on the scale—for example actual physical moving about. Taking the human residue, we try to decide what in it is positive, and what is negative, mere limitation. The tenuous ghost of a concept remaining we suppose to be the essential structure of activity (that structure which is common to running and thinking) and so to be realized also in divine activity. Perhaps this is how we imagine our language to be related to the divine realities about which we use it; but such ghostly and evacuated concepts are clearly too tenuous and elusive to be called the meanings of the words we use. To think of God thus is to think of him not in our own image, but in the rarefied ghost of our own image; and so we think of him in our own image, but do not suppose that in so thinking of him we begin to do him justice. What we do, then, is in essence to think of God in parables. The things we say about God are said on the authority of the words and acts of Christ, who spoke in human language, using parable; and so we too speak of God in parable—authoritative parable, authorized parable; knowing that the truth is not literally that which our parables represent, knowing therefore that now we see in a glass darkly, but trusting, because we trust the source of the parables, that in believing them and interpreting them in the light of each other, we shall not be misled, that we shall have such knowledge as we need to possess for the foundation of the religious life.

So far so good. But it is only the predicates of theological utterances which are parabolic; it is only in what is *said about* God that words are put to other than customary employment. When we say 'God is merciful', it is 'merciful' that is in strange company—deprived of its usual escort of human sentiments. But the word 'God' only occurs in statements about God. Our grasp of this word, therefore, cannot be derived from our grasp of its in ordinary human contexts, for it is not used in such contexts. How then is our grasp of it to be accounted for? In other words, if I have given some account of how, and in what sense, we understand the meaning of the things we say about God, I have still to give some account of how, and in what sense, we know what it is that we are saying them about.

In thus turning back from the predicate to the subject of religious utterances, we are turning from revealed theology to natural theology, from the logical father to the logical mother of religious belief. And the answer to the question: 'What grasp have we of the meaning of the word "God"?' must be dealt with along the following lines. Revelation is important to the believer not for what it is in itself (the biography of a Jew, and the history of his forerunners and followers), nor because it is revelation of nothing in particular, but because it is revelation of God. In treating it as something important, something commanding our allegiance, we are bringing to bear upon it the category of the transcendent, of the divine. Of the nature of that category I have already spoken. In other words, there must exist within a man's mind the contrast between the contingent and the necessary, the derivative and the underivative, the finite and the infinite, the perfect and the imperfect, if anything is to be for him a revelation of God. Given that contrast, we are given also that to which the parables or stories are referred. What is thus given is certainly not knowledge of the object to which they apply; it is something much more like a direction. We do not, that is, know to what to refer our parables; we know merely that we are to refer them out of experience, and out of it *in which direction*. The expression 'God' is to refer to that object, whatever it is, and if there be one, which is such that the knowledge of it would be to us knowledge of the unfamiliar term in the contrast between finite and infinite.

Statements about God, then, are in effect parables, which are referred, by means of the proper name 'God', out of our experience in a certain direction. We may, if we like, by the process of whittling away, which I have mentioned, try to tell ourselves what part of the meaning of our statements applies reasonably well, what part outrageously badly; but the fact remains that, in one important sense, when we speak about God, we do not know what we mean (that is, we do not know what that which we are talking about is like), and do not need to know, because we accept the images, which we employ, on authority. Because our concern with God is religious and not speculative (it is contemplative in part, but that is another matter), because our need is, not to know what God is like, but to enter into relation with him, the authorized images serve our purpose. They belong to a type of discourse—parable—with which we are familiar, and therefore they have communication value, although in a sense they lack descriptive value.

If this is so, how do we stand with regard to verification and falsification? Must we, to preserve our claim to be making assertions, be prepared to say what would count aginst them? Let us see how far we can do so. Does anything count against the assertion that God is merciful? Yes, suffering. Does anything count decisively against it? No, we reply, because it is true. Could anything count decisively against it? Yes, suffering which was utterly, eternally and irredeemably pointless. Can we then design a crucial experiment? No, because we can never see all of the picture. Two things at least are hidden from us; what goes on in the recesses of the personality of the sufferer, and what shall happen hereafter.

Well, then, the statement that God is merciful is not testable; it is compatible with any and every tract of experience which we are in fact capable of witnessing. It cannot be verified; does this matter?

To answer this, we must make up our minds why the demand for verification or falsification is legitimate. On this large matter I shall be summary and dogmatic, as follows. (1) The demand that a statement of fact should be verifiable is a conflation of two demands. (2) The *first* point is that all statements of fact must be verifiable in the sense that there must not exist a *rule of language* which precludes testing the statement. That is to say, the way the statement is to be taken must not be such that to try to test it is to show that you do not understand it. If I say that it is wrong to kill, and you challenge my statement and adduce as evidence against it that thugs and headhunters do so out of religious duty, then you have not understood my statement. My statement was not a statement of fact, but a moral judgment, and your statement that it should be tested by anthropological investigations shows that you did not understand it. But so long as there exists no *logical* (or we might say *interpretational*) ban on looking around for verification, the existence of a *factual* ban on verification does not matter. 'Caesar had mutton before he crossed the Rubicon' cannot in fact be tested, but by trying to devise ways of testing it you do not show that you have not understood it; you are merely wasting your time. (3) The *second* point is that, *for me, fully* to understand a statement, *I* must know what a test of it would be like. If I have no idea how to test whether somebody had mutton, then I do not know what 'having mutton' means. This stipulation is concerned, not with the logical nature of the expression, but with its communication value for me. (4) There are then two stipulations, and they are different. The first is a logical stipulation, and it is to the effect that nothing can be a statement of fact if it is untestable in the sense that the notion of testing it is precluded by correctly interpreting it. The second is a communicational stipulation, and it is to the effect that nobody can fully understand a statement, unless he has a fair idea how a situation about which it was true would differ from a situation about which it was false.

Now with regard to these two stipulations, how do religious utterances fare? With regard to the first, there is no language rule implicit in a correct understanding of them which precludes putting them to the test (there may be a rule of faith, but that is another matter). If a man says, 'How can God be loving, and allow pain?' he does *not* show that he has misunderstood the statement that God is loving. There *is* a *prima facie* incompatibility between the love of God, and pain and suffering. The Christian maintains that it is *prima facie* only; others maintain that it is not. They may argue about it, and the issue cannot be decided; but it cannot be decided, not because (as in the case of e.g. moral or mathematical judgments) the appeal to facts is *logically* the wrong way of trying to decide the issue, and shows that you have not understood the judgment; *but* because, since our experience is limited in the way it is, we cannot get into position to decide it, any more than we can get into position to decide what Julius Caesar had for breakfast before he crossed the Rubicon. For the Christian the operation of getting into position to decide it is called dying; and, though we can all do that, we cannot return to report what we find. By this test, then, religious utterances can be called statements of fact; that is their *logical* classification.

With regard to the second stipulation, the case is a little complicated, for here we are concerned with communication value, and there are the two levels, the one on which we remain within the parable, and the other on which we try to step outside it. Now, on the first level we know well enough how to test a statement like 'God loves us'; it is, for example, like testing 'My father loves me'. In fact, of course, since with parents and schoolmasters severity is notoriously a way of displaying affection, the decisive testing of such a statement is not easy; but there is a point beyond which it is foolish to continue to have doubts. Now, within the parable, we are supposing 'God loves us' to be a statement like 'My father loves me', 'God' to be a subject similar to 'My father', 'God loves us' being thus related to 'My father loves me' as the latter is related to 'Aristotle's father loved him'. We do not suppose that we can actually test 'God loves us', for reasons already given (any more than we can test the one about Aristotle); but the communication value of the statement whose subject is 'God' is derived from the communication value of the same statement with a different proper name as subject. If we try to step outside the parable, then we must admit that we do not know what the situation about which our parable is being told is like; we should only know if we could know God, and know even as also we have been known; see, that is, the unfolding of the divine purposes in their entirety. Such ignorance is what we ought to expect. We do not know how what we call the divine wrath differs from the divine mercy (because we do not know how they respectively resemble human wrath and mercy); but we do know how what *we mean* when we talk about the wrath of God differs from what *we mean* when we talk about his mercy, because then we are within the parable, talking within the framework of admitted ignorance, in language which we accept because we trust its source. We know what is meant *in* the parable, when the father of the Prodigal sees him coming a great way off and runs to meet him, and we can therefore think in terms of this image. We know that we are here promised that whenever we come to ourselves and return to God, he will come to meet us. This is enough to encourage us to return, and to make us alert

to catch the signs of the divine response; but it does not lead
us to presume to an understanding of the mind and heart of
God. In talking we remain within the parable, and so our statements communicate, we do not know how the parable applies,
but we believes that it does apply, and that we shall one day
see how. (Some even believe, perhaps rightly, that in our earthly
condition we may by direct illumination of our minds be
enabled to know progressively more about the realities to which
our parables apply, and in consequence about the manner of
their application).

Much of what I have said agrees very closely with what the
atheist says about religious belief, except that I have tried to
make it sound better. The atheist alleges that the religious man
supposes himself to know what he means by his statements only
because, until challenged, he interprets them anthropomor-
phically; when challenged, however, he retreats rapidly back-
words towards complete agnosticism. I agree with this, with two
provisos. The first is that the religious man does not suppose
himself to know what he means by his statements (for what
religious man supposes himself to be the Holy Ghost?); he
knows what his statements mean within the parable, and believes
that they are the right statements to use. (Theology is not a
science; it is a sort of art of enlightened ignorance.) The
second proviso is that the agnosticism is not complete; for the
Christian, under attack, falls back not in any direction, but in
one direction; he falls back upon the person of Christ, and the
concrete realities of the Christian life.

Let us consider this for a moment with regard to the divine
love. I could be attacked in this sort of way:—'You have contended', my opponent might argue, 'that when we say that God
loves us the communication value of the statement is determined
by the communication value of a similar statement about a
human subject; and that we know the statement to be the right
statement, but cannot know *how* it is the right statement, that
is, what the divine love is like. But this will not do. Loving is
an activity with two poles, the lover and the loved. We may not
know the lover, in the case of God, but we *are*, and therefore
must know, the loved. Now, to say that the image or parable

of human love is the right image to use about God must imply
that there is some similarility or analogy between human and
divine love. Father's love may be superficially very unlike
mother's, but, unless there is some similarity of structure between them, we cannot use the same word of both. But we cannot believe that there is any similarity between the love of God
and human love, unless we can detect some similarity between
being loved by God and being loved by man. But if being loved
by God is what we experience all the time, then it is not like
being loved by man; it is like being let down right and left. And
in the face of so great a discrepancy, we cannot believe that
God loves us, if that is supposed to be in any sense a statement
of sober fact.'

I cannot attempt to answer this objection; it involves the
whole problem of religion. But there is something I want to say
about it, which is that the Christian does not attempt to evade
it either by helter-skelter flight, or by impudent bluff. He has his
prepared positions on to which he retreats; and he knows that
if these positions are taken, then he must surrender. He does
not believe that they can be taken, but that is another matter.
There are three main fortresses behind which he goes. For,
first, he looks for the resurrection of the dead, and the life of
the world to come; he believes, that is, that we do not see all of
the picture, and that the parts which we do not see are precisely
the parts which determine the design of the whole. He admits
that if this hope be vain then we are of all men the most
miserable. *Second*, he claims that he sees in Christ the verification, and to some extent also the specification, of the divine
love. That is to say, he finds in Christ not only convincing evidence of God's concern for us, but also what sort of love the
divine love is, what sort of benefits God is concerned to give us.
He sees that, on the New Testament scale of values, it is better
for a man to lose the whole world if he can thereby save his
soul (which means his relationship to God); and that for that
hope it is reasonable to sacrifice all that he has, and to undergo
the death of the body and the mortification of the spirit. *Third*,
he claims that in the religious life, of others, if not as yet in his
own, the divine love may be encountered, that the promise 'I

will not fail thee nor forsake thee' is, if rightly understood, confirmed there. If, of course, this promise is interpreted as involving immunity from bodily suffering, it will be refuted; but no reader of the New Testament has any right so to interpret it. It is less glaringly, but as decisively, wrong to interpret it as involving immunity from spiritual suffering; for in the New Testament only the undergoing of death (which means the abdication of control over one's destiny) can be the beginning of life. What then does it promise? It promises that to the man who begins on the way of the Christian life, on the way that is of seeking life through death, of seeking relationship with God through the abdication of the self-sovereignty claimed by Adam, that to him the fight will be hard but not impossible, progress often indiscernible, but real, progress which is towards the paring way of self-hood, and which is therefore often given through defeat and humiliation, but a defeat and humiliation which are not final, which leave it possible to continue. This is the extra-parental nurture of religious belief of which I spoke earlier, and it is the third of the prepared positions on to which the Christian retreats, claiming that the image and reflection of the love of God may be seen not only hereafter, not only in Christ, but also, if dimly, in the concrete process of living the Christian life.

One final word. Religion has indeed its problems; but it is useless to consider them outside their religious context. Seen as a whole religion makes rough sense, though it does not make limpidity.

AN EMPIRICIST'S VIEW OF THE
NATURE OF RELIGIOUS BELIEF

R. B. BRAITHWAITE

'The meaning of a scientific statement is to be ascertained by reference to the steps which would be taken to verify it.' Eddington wrote this in 1939. Unlike his heterodox views of the *a priori* and epistemological character of the ultimate laws of physics, this principle is in complete accord with contemporary philosophy of science; indeed it was Eddington's use of it in his expositions of relativity theory in the early 1920's that largely contributed to its becoming the orthodoxy. Eddington continued his passage by saying: 'This [principle] will be recognised as a tenet of logical positivism—only it is there extended to all statements.'[1] Just as the tone was set to the empiricist tradition in British philosophy—the tradition running from Locke through Berkeley, Hume, Mill to Russell in our own time —by Locke's close association with the scientific work of Boyle and the early Royal Society, so the contemporary development of empiricism popularly known as logical positivism has been greatly influenced by the revolutionary changes this century in physical theory and by the philosophy of science which physicists concerned with these changes—Einstein and Heisenberg as well as Eddington—have thought most consonant with relativity and quantum physics. It is therefore, I think, proper for me to take the verificational principle of meaning, and a natural adaptation of it, as that aspect of contemporary scientific thought whose bearing upon the philosophy of religion I shall discuss this afternoon. Eddington, in the passage from which I have quoted, applied the verificational principle to the meaning

Reprinted from *An Empiricist's View of the Nture of Religious Belief* (Cambridge: Cambridge University Press, 1955), by permission of the publisher.
[1] A. S. Eddington, *The Philosophy of Physical Science* (1939), p. 189.

of scientific statements only. But we shall see that it will be necessary, and concordant with an empiricist way of thinking, to modify the principle by allowing *use* as well as *verifiability* to be a criterion for meaning; so I believe that all I shall say will be in the spirit of a remark with which Eddington concluded an article published in 1926: 'The scientist and the religious teacher may well be content to agree that the *value* of any hypothesis extends just so far as it is verified by actual experience.'[2]

I will start with the verificational principle in the form in which it was originally propounded by logical positivists—that the meaning of any statement is given by its method of verification.[3]

The implication of this general principle for the problem of religious belief is that the primary question becomes, not whether a religious statement such as that a personal God created the world is true or is false, but how it could be known either to be true or to be false. Unless this latter question can be answered, the religious statement has no ascertainable meaning and there is nothing expressed by it to be either true or false. Moreover a religious statement cannot be believed without being understood, and it can only be understood by an understanding of the circumstances which would verify or falsify it. Meaning is not logically prior to the possibility of verification: we do not first learn the meaning of a statement, and afterwards consider what would make us call it true or false; the two understandings are one and indivisible.

It would not be correct to say that discussions of religious belief before this present century have always ignored the problem of meaning, but until recently the emphasis has been upon the question of the truth or the reasonableness of religious belief rather than upon the logically prior question as to the meaning of the statements expressing the beliefs. The argument usually proceeded as if we all knew what was meant by the

[2] *Science, Religion and Reality*, ed. by J. Needham (1926), p. 218 (my italics).

[3] The principle was first explicitly stated by F. Waismann, in *Erkenntnis*, vol. 1 (1930), p. 229.

statement that a personal God created the world; the point at issue was whether or not this statement was true, or whether there were good reasons for believing it. But if the meaning of a religious statement has to be found by discovering the steps which must be taken to ascertain its truth–value, an examination of the methods for testing the statement for truth–value is an essential preliminary to any discussion as to which of the truth-values—truth or falsity—holds of the statement.

There are three classes of statement whose method of truth-value testing is in general outline clear: statements about particular matters of empirical fact, scientific hypotheses and other general empirical statements, and the logically necessary statements of logic and matehmatics (and their contradictories). Do religious statements fall into any of these three classes? If they do, the problem of their meaningfulness will be solved: their truth-values will be testable by the methods appropriate to empirical statements, particular or general, or to mathematical statements. It seems to me clear that religious statements as they are normally used, have no place in this trichotomy. I shall give my reasons very briefly, since I have little to add here to what other empiricist philosophers have said.

(1) Statements about particular empirical facts are testable by direct observation. The only facts that can be directly known by observation are that the things observed have certain observable properties or stand in certain observable relations to one another. If it is maintained that the *existence* of God is known by observation, for examples, in the 'self-authenticating' experience of 'meeting God', the term 'God' is being used merely as part of the description of that particular experience. Any interesting theological proposition, e.g. that God is personal, will attribute a property to God which is not an observable one and so cannot be known by direct observation. Comparison with our knowledge of other people is an unreal comparison. I can get to know things about an intimate friend at a glance, but this knowledge is not self-authenticating; it is based upon a great deal of previous knowledge about the connexion between facial and bodily expressions and states of mind.

(2) The view that would class religious statements with scientific hypotheses must be taken much more seriously. It would be very unplausible if a Baconian methodology of science had to be employed, and scientific hypotheses taken as simple generalizations from particular instances, for then there could be no understanding of a general theological proposition unless particular instances of it could be directly observed. But an advanced science has progressed far beyond its natural history stage; it makes use in its explanatory hypotheses of concepts of a high degree of abstractness and at a far remove from experience. These theoretical concepts are given a meaning by the place they occupy in a deductive system consisting of hypotheses of different degrees of generality in which the least general hypotheses, deducible from the more general ones, are generalizations of observable facts. So it is no valid criticism of the view that would treat God as an empirical concept entering into an explanatory hypothesis to say that God is not directly observable. No more is an electric field of force or a Schrödinger wave-function. There is no prima facie objection to regarding such a proposition as that there is a God who created and sustains the world as an explanatory scientific hypothesis.

But if a set of theological propositions are to be regarded as scientific explanations of facts in the empirical world, they must be refutable by experience. We must be willing to abandon them if the facts prove different from what we think they are. A hypothesis which is consistent with every possible empirical fact is not an empirical one. And though the theoretical concepts in a hypothesis need not be explicitly definable in terms of direct observation—indeed they must not be if the system is to be applicable to novel situations—yet they must be related to some and not to all of the possible facts in the world in order to have a non-vacuous significance. If there is a personal God, how would the world be different if there were not? Unless this question can be answered God's existence cannot be given an empirical meaning.

At earlier times in the history of religion God's personal existence has been treated as a scientific hypothesis subjectable to empirical test. Elijah's contest with the prophets of Baal was an experiment to test the hypothesis that Jehovah and not Baal controlled the physical world. But most educated believers at the present time do not think of God as being detectable in this sort of way, and hence do not think of theological propositions as explanations of facts in the world of nature in the way in which established scientific hypotheses are.

It may be maintaind, however, that theological propositions explain facts about the world in another way. Not perhaps the physical world, for physical science has been so successful with its own explanations; but the facts of biological and psychological development. Now it is certainly the case that a great deal of traditional Christian language—phrases such as 'original sin', 'the old Adam', 'the new man', 'growth in holiness' —can be given meanings within statements expressing general hypotheses about human personality. Indeed it is hardly too much to say that almost all statements about God as immanent, as an indwelling spirit, can be interpreted as asserting psychological facts in metaphorical language. But would those interpreting religious statements in this way be prepared to abandon them if the empirical facts were found to be different? Or would they rather re-interpret them to fit the new facts? In the latter case the possibility of interpreting them to fit experience is not enough to give an empirical meaning to the statements. Mere consistency with experience without the possibility of inconsistency does not determine meaning. And a metaphorical description is not in itself an explanation. This criticism also holds against attempts to interpret theism as an explanation of the course of history, unless it is admitted (which few theists would be willing to admit) that, had the course of history been different in some specific way, God would not have existed.

Philosophers of religion who wish to make empirical facts relevant to the meaning of religious statements but at the same time desire to hold on to these statements whatever the empirical facts may be are indulging, I believe, in a sort of 'doublethink' attitude: they want to hold that religious statements both are about the actual world (i.e. are empirical statements) and also are not refutable in any possible world, the characteristic of statements which are logically necessary.

(3) The view that statements of natural theology resemble the propositions of logic and mathemaics in being logically necessary would have as a consequence that they make no assertion of existence. Whatever exactly be the status of logically necessary propositions, Hume and Kant have conclusively shown that they are essentially hypothetical. $2 + 3 = 5$ makes no assertion about there being any things in the world; what it says is that, *if* there is a class of five things in the world, *then* this class is the union of two mutually exclusive sub-classes one comprising two and the other comprising three things. The logical-positivist thesis, due to Wittgenstein, that the truth of this hypothetical proposition is verified not by any logical fact about the world but by the way in which we use numerical symbols in our thinking goes further than Kant did in displacing logic and mathematics from the world of reality. But it is not necessary to accept this more radical thesis in order to agree with Kant that no logically necessary proposition can assert existence; and this excludes the possibility of regarding theological propositions as logically necessary in the way in which the hypothetical propositions of mathematics and logic are neecssary.

The traditional arguments for a Necessary God—the ontological and the cosmological—were elaborated by Anselm and the scholastic philosophers before the concurrent and interrelated development of natural science and of mathematics had enabled necessity and contingency to be clearly distinguished. The necessity attributed by these arguments to the being of God may perhaps be different from the logical necessity of mathematical truths; but, if so, no method has been provided for testing the truth-value of the statement that God is necessary being, and consequently no way given for assigning meaning to the terms 'necessary being' and 'God'.

If religious statements cannot be held to fall into any of these three classes, their method of verification cannot be any of the standard methods applicable to statements falling in these classes. Does this imply that religious statements are not verifiable, with the corollary, according to the verificational principle, that they have no meaning and, though they purport to say something, are in fact nonsensical sentences? The earlier logical positivists thought so: they would have echoed the demand of the precursor Hume that a volume ('of divinity or school metaphysics') which contains neither 'any abstract reasoning concerning quantity or number' nor 'any experimental reasoning concerning matter of fact and existence' should be committed to the flames; though their justification for the holocaust would be even more cogent than Hume's. The volume would not contain even 'sophistry and illusion': it would contain nothing but meaningless marks of printer's ink.

Religious statements, however, are not the only statements which are unverifiable by standard methods; moral statements have the same peculiarity. A moral principle, like the utilitarian principle that a man ought to act so as to maximize happiness, does not seem to be either a logically necessary or a logically impossible proposition. But neither does it seem to be an empirical proposition, all the attempts of ethical empiricists to give naturalistic analyses having failed. Though a tough-minded logical positivist might be prepared to say that all religious statements are sound and fury, signifying nothing, he can hardly say that of all moral statements. For moral statements have a use in guiding conduct; and if they have a use they surely have a meaning—in some sense of meaning. So the verificational principle of meaning in the hands of empiricist philosophers in the 1930's became modified either by a glossing of the term 'verification' or by a change of the verification principle into the use principle: the meaning of any statement is given by the way in which it is used.[4]

Since I wish to continue to employ verification in the restricted sense of ascertaining truth-value, I shall take the principle of meaning in this new form in which the word 'verification' has disappeared. But in removing this term from the statement of the principle, there is no desertion from the

---

[4] See L. Wittgenstein, *Philosophical Investigations* (1953), especially §§ 340, 353, 559, 560.

spirit of empiricism. The older verificational principle is subsumed under the new use principle: the use of an empirical statement derives from the fact that the statement is empirically verifiable and the logical-positivist thesis of the 'linguistic' character of logical and mathematical statements can be equally well, if not better, expressed in terms of their use than of their method of verification. Moreover the only way of discovering how a statement is used is by an empirical enquiry; a statement need not itself be empirically verifiable, but that it is used in a particular way is always a straightforwardly empirical proposition.

The meaning of any statement, then, will be taken as being given by the way it is used. The kernel for an empiricist of the problem of the nature of religious belief is to explain, in empirical terms, how a religious statement is used by a man who asserts it in order to express his religious conviction.

Since I shall argue that the primary element in this use is that the religious assertion is used as a moral assertion, I must first consider how moral assertions are used. According to the view developed by various moral philosophers since the impossibility of regarding moral statements as verifiable propositions was recognized, a moral assertion is used to express an *attitude* of the man making the assertion. It is not used to assert the proposition that he has the attitude—a verifiable psychological proposition; it is used to show forth or evince his attitude. The attitude is concerned with the action which he asserts to be right or to be his duty, or the state of affairs which he asserts to be good; it is a highly complex state, and contains elements to which various degres of importance have been attached by moral philosophers who have tried to work out an 'ethics without propositions'. One element in the attitude is a feeling of approval towards the action; this element was taken as the fundamental one in the first attempts, and views of ethics without propositions are frequently lumped together as 'emotive' theories of ethics. But discussion of the subject during the last twenty years has made it clear, I think, that no emotion or feeling of approval is fundamental to the use of moral assertions; it may be the case that the moral asserter has some specific feeling directed on to the course of action said to be right, but this is not the most important element in his "pro-attitude' towards the course of action: what is primary is his intention to perform the action when the occasion for it arises.

The form of ethics without propositions which I shall adopt is therefore a conative rather than an emotive theory: it makes the primary use of a moral assertion that of expressing the intention of the asserter to act in a particular sort of way specified in the assertion. A utilitarian, for example, in asserting that he ought to act so as to maximize happiness, is thereby declaring his intention to act, to the best of his ability, in accordance with the policy of utilitarianism: he is not asserting any proposition, or necessarily evincing any feeling of approval; he is subscribing to a policy of action. There will doubtless be empirical propositions which he may give as reasons for his adherence to the policy (e.g. that happiness is what all, or what most people, desire), and his having the intention will include his understanding what is meant by pursuing the policy, another empirically verifiable proposition. But there will be no specifically moral proposition which he will be asserting when he declares his intention to pursue the policy. This account is fully in accord with the spirit of empiricism, for whether or not a man has the intention of pursuing a particular behaviour policy can be empirically tested, both by observing what he does and by hearing what he replies when he is questioned about his intentions.

Not all expressions of intentions will be moral assertions: for the notion of morality to be applicable it is necessary either that the policy of action intended by the asserter should be a general policy (e.g. the policy of utilitarianism) or that it should be subsumable under a general policy which the asserter intends to follow and which he would give as the reason for his more specific intention. There are difficulties and vaguenesses in the notion of a general policy of action, but these need not concern us here. All that we require is that, when a man asserts that he ought to do so-and-so, he is using the assertion to declare thta he resolves, to the best of his ability, to do so-and-so. And he will not necessarily be insincere in his assertion if he suspects,

at the time of making it, that he will not have the strength of
character to carry out his resolution.

The advantage this account of moral assertions has over
all others, emotive non-propositional ones as well as cognitive
proopsitional ones, is that it alone enables a satisfactory answer to be given to the question: What is the reason for my
doing what I think I ought to do? The answer it gives is that,
since my thinking that I ought to do the action is my intention
to do it if possible, the reason why I do the action is simply
that I intend to do it, if possible. On every other ethical view
there will be a mysterious gap to be filled somehow between
the moral judgment and the intention to act in accordance
with it: there is no such gap if the primary use of a moral
assertion is to declare such an intention.

Let us now consider what light this way of regarding moral
assertions throws upon assertions of religious conviction. The
idealist philosopher McTaggart described religion as 'an emotion resting on a conviction of a harmony between ourselves and
the universe at large',[5] and many educated people at the present
time would agree with him. If religion is essentially concerned
with emotion, it is natural to explain the use of religious assertions on the lines of the original emotive theory of ethics and
to regard them as primarily evincing religious feelings or emotions. The assertion, for example, that God is our Heavenly
Father will be taken to express the asserter's feeling secure in
the same way as he would feel secure in his father's presence.
But explanations of religion in terms of feeling, and of religious
assertions as expressions of such feelings, are usually propounded by people who stand outside any religious system; they
rarely satisfy those who speak from inside. Few religious men
would be prepared to admit that their religion was a matter
merely of feeling: feelings—of joy, of consolation, of being
at one with the universe—may enter into their religion, but to
evince such feelings is certainly not the primary use of their
religious assertions.

This objection, however, does not seem to me to apply to
treating religious assertions in the conative way in which recent

[5] J. M. E. McTaggart, *Some Dogmas of Religion* (1906), p. 3.

moral philosophers have treated moral statements—as being primarily declarations of adherence to a policy of action, declarations of commitment to a way of life. That the way of life led by the believer is highly relevant to the sincerity of his religious conviction has been insisted upon by all the moral religions, above all, perhaps, by Christianity. 'By their fruits ye shall know them.' The view which I put forward for your consideration is that the intention of a Christian to follow a Christian way of life is not only the criterion for the sincerity of his belief in the assertions of Christianity; it is the criterion for the meaningfulness of his assertions. Just as the meaning of a moral assertion is given by its use in expressing the asserter's intention to act, so far as in him lies, in accordance with the moral principle involved, so the meaning of a religious assertion is given by its use in expressing the asserter's intention to follow a specified policy of behaviour. To say that it is belief in the dogmas of religion which is the cause of the believer's intending to behave as he does is to put the cart before the horse: it is the intention to behave which constitutes what is known as religious conviction.

But this assimilation of religious to moral assertions lays itself open to an immediate objection. When a moral assertion is taken as declaring the intention of following a policy, the form of the assertion itself makes it clear what the policy is with which the assertion is concerned. For a man to assert that a certain policy ought to be pursued, which on this view is for him to declare his intention of pursuing the policy, presupposes his understanding what it would be like for him to pursue the policy in question. I cannot resolve not to tell a lie without knowing what a lie is. But if a religious assertion is the declaration of an intention to carry out a certain policy, what policy does it specify? The religious statement itself will not explicitly refer to a policy, as does a moral statement; how then can the asserted of the statement know what is the policy concerned, and how ca.. he intend to carry out a policy if he does not know what the policy is? I cannot intend to do something I know not what.

The reply to this criticism is that, if a religious assertion is regarded as representaive of a large number of assertions of the same religious system, the body of assertions of which the particular one is a representative specimen is taken by the asserter as implicitly specifying a particular way of life. It is no more necessary for an empiricist philosopher to explain the use of a religious statement taken in isolation from other religious statements than it is for him to give a meaning to a scientific hypothesis in isolation from other scientific hypotheses. We understand scientific hypotheses, and the terms that occur in them, by virtue of the relation of the whole system of hypotheses to empirically observable facts; and it is the whole system of hypotheses, not one hypothesis in isolation, that is tested for its truth-value against experience. So there are good precedents, in the empiricist way of thinking, for considering a system of religious assertions as a whole, and for examining the way in which the whole system is used.

If we do this the fact that a system of religious assertions has a moral function can hardly be denied. For to deny it would require any passage from the assertion of a religious system to a policy of action to be mediated by a moral assertion. I cannot pass from asserting a fact, of whatever sort, to intending to perform an action, without having the hypothetical intention to intend to do the action if I assert the fact. This holds however widely fact is understood—whether as an empirical fact or as a non-empirical fact about goodness or reality. Just as the intention-to-act view of moral assertions is the only view that requires no reason for my doing what I assert to be my duty, so the similar view of religious assertions is the only one which connects them to ways of life without requiring an additional premiss. Unless a Christian's assertion that God is love (*agape*)—which I take to epitomize the assertions of the Christian religion—be taken to declare his intention to follow an agapeistic way of life, he could be asked what is the connexion between the assertion and the intention, between Christian belief and Christian practice. And this question can always be asked if religious assertions are separated from conduct. Unless religious principles are moral principles, it makes no sense to speak of putting them into practice.

The way to find out what are the intentions embodied in a set of religious assertions, and hence what is the meaning of the assertions, is by discovering what principles of conduct the asserter takes the assertion to involve. These may be ascertained both by asking him questions and by seeing how he behaves, each test being supplemental to the other. If what is wanted is not the meaning of the religious assertions made by a particular man but what the set of assertion would mean were they to be made by anyone of the same religion (which I will call their *typical* meaning), all that can be done is to specify the form of behaviour which is in accordance with what one takes to be the fundamental moral principles of the religion in question. Since different people will take different views as to what these fundamental moral principles are, the typical meaning of religious assertions will be different for different people. I myself take the typical meaning of the body of Christian assertions as being given by their proclaiming intentions to follow an agapeistic way of life, and for a description of this way of life—a description in general and metaphorical terms, but an empirical description nevertheless—I should quote most of the Thirteenth Chapter of I Corinthians. Others may think that the Christian way of life should be described somewhat differently, and will therefor take the typical meaning of the assertions of Christianity to correspond to their different view of its fundamental moral teaching.

My contention then is that the primary use of religious assertions is to announce allegiance to a set of moral principles: without such allegiance there is no 'true religion'. This is borne out by all the accounts of what happens when an unbeliever becomes converted to a religion. The conversion is not only a change in the propositions believed—indeed there may be no specifically intellectual change at all; it is a change in the state of will. An excellent instance is C. S. Lewis's recently published account of his conversion from an idealist metaphysic—'a religion [as he says] that cost nothing'—to a theism where he faced (and he quotes George MacDonald's phrase) 'something to be neither more nor less other than *done*'. There was no intellectual change, for (as he says) 'there

had long been an ethic (theoretically) attached to my Idealism':
it was the recognition that he had to do something about it, that
'an attmept at complete virtue must be made'.[6] His conversion
was a re-orientation of the will.

In assimilating religious assertions to moral assertions I
do not wish to deny that there are any important differences.
One is the fact already noticed that usually the behaviour policy
intended is not specified by one religious assertion in isolation.
Another difference is that the fundamental moral teaching of
the religion is frequently given, not in abstract terms, but by
means of concrete examples—of how to behave, for instance,
if one meets a man set upon by thieves on the road to Jericho.
A resolution to behave like the good Samaritan does not, in
itself, specify the behaviour to be resolved upon in quite
different circumstances. However, absence of explicitly recognized general principle does not prevent a man from acting in
accordance with such principles; it only makes it more difficult
for a questioner to discover upon what principles he is acting.
And the difficulty is not only one way round. If moral principles
are stated in the most general form, as most moral philosophers
have wished to state them, they tend to become so far removed
from particular courses of conduct that it is difficult, if not
impossible, to give them any precise content. It may be hard
to find out what exactly is involved in the imitation of Christ;
but it is not very easy to discover what exactly is meant by the
pursuit of Aristotle's *eudaemonia* or of Mill's *happiness*. The
tests for what it is to live agapeistically are as empirical
as are those for living in quest of happiness; but in each case
the tests can best be expounded in terms of examples of particular situations.

A more important difference between religious and purely
moral principles is that, in the higher religions at least, the conduct preached by the religion concerns not only external but
also internal behaviour. The conversion involved in accepting
a religion is a conversion, not only of the will, but of the heart.
Christianity requires not only that you should behave towards

[6] C. S. Lewis, *Surprised by Joy* (1955), pp. 198, 212–13.

your neighbour as if you loved him as yourself: it requires that you should love him as yourself. And though I have no doubt that the Christian concept of *agape* refers partly to external behaviour—the agapeistic behaviour for which there are external criteria—yet being filled with *agape* includes more than behaving agapeistically externally: it also includes an agapeistic frame of mind. I have said that I cannot regard the expression of a feeling of any sort as the primary element in religious assertion; but this does not imply that intention to feel in a certain way is not a primary element, nor that it cannot be used to discriminate religious declarations of policy from declarations which are merely moral. Those who say that Confucianism is a code of morals and not, properly speaking, a religion are, I think, making this discrimination.

The resolution proclaimed by a religious assertion may then be taken as referring to inner life as well as to outward conduct. And the superiority of religious conviction over the mere adoption of a moral code in securing conformity to the code arises from a religious conviction changing what the religious man wants. It may be hard enugh to love your enemy, but once you have succeeded in doing so it is easy to behave lovingly towards him. But if you continue to hate him, it requires a heroic perseverance continually to behave as if you loved him. Resolutions to feel, even if they are only partly fulfilled, are powerful reinforcements of resolutions to act.

But though these qualifications may be adequate for distinguishing religious assertions from purely moral ones, they are not sufficient to discriminate between assertions belonging to one religious system and those belonging to another system in the case in which the behaviour policies, both of inner life and of outward conduct, inculcated by the two systems are identical. For instance, I have said that I take the fundamental moral teaching of Christianity to be the preaching of an agapeistic way of life. But a Jew or Buddhist may, with considerable plausibility, maintain that the fundamental moral teaching of his religion is to recommend exactly the same way of life. How then can religious assertions be distinguished into those which are Christian, those which are Jewish, those which are Buddhist, by the policies of life which they respectively recommend if, on examination, these policies turn out to be the same?

Many Christians will, no doubt, behave in a specifically Christian manner in that they will follow ritual practices which are Christian and neither Jewish nor Buddhist. But though following certain practices may well be the proper test for membership of a particular religious society, a church, not even the most ecclesiastically-minded Christian will regard participation in a ritual as the fundamental characteristic of a Christian way of life. There must be some more important difference between an agapeistically policied Christian and an agapeistically policied Jew than that the former attends a church and the latter a synagogue.

The really important difference, I think, is to be found in the fact that the intentions to pursue the behaviour policies, which may be the same for different religions, are associated with thinking of different *stories* (or set of stories). By a story I shall here mean a proposition or set of propositions which are straightforwardly empirical propositions capable of empirical test and which are thought of by the religious man in connexion with his resolution to follow the way of life advocated by his religion. On the assumption that the ways of life advocated by Christianity and by Buddhism are essentially the same, it will be the fact that the intention to follow this way of life is associated in the mind of a Christian with thinking of one set of stories (the Christian stories) while it is associated in the mind of a Buddhist with thinking of another set of stories (the Buddhist stories) which enables a Christian assertion to be distinguished from a Buddhist one.

A religious assertion will, therefore, have a proposiitonal element which is lacking in a purely moral assertion, in that it will refer to a story as well as to an intention. The reference to the story is not an assertion of the story taken as a matter of empirical fact: it is a telling of the story, or an alluding to the story, in the way in which one can tell, or allude to, the story of a novel with which one is acquainted. To assert the whole set of assertions of the Christian religion is both to tell the Christian doctrinal story and to confess allegiance to the Christian way of life.

The story, I have said, is a set of empirical propositions, and the language expressing the story is given a meaning by the standard method of understanding how the story-statements can be verified. The empirical story-statements will vary from Christian to Christian; the doctrines of Christianity are capable of different empirical interpretations, and Christians will differ in the interpretations they put upon the doctrines. But the interpretations will all be in terms of empirical propositions. Take, for example, the doctrine of Justification by means of the Atonement. Matthew Arnold imagined it in terms of

> . . . a sort of infinitely magnified and improved Lord Shaftesbury, with a race of vile offenders to deal with, whom his natural goodness would incline him to let off, only his sense of justice will not allow it; then a younger Lord Shaftesbury, on the scale of his father and very dear to him, who might live in grandeur and splendour if he liked, but who prefers to leave his home, to go and live among the race of offenders, and to be put to an ignominious death, on condition that his merits shall be counted against their demerits, and that his father's goodness shall be restrained no longer from taking effect, but any offender shall be admitted to the benefit of it on simply pleading the satisfaction made by the son;— and then, finally, a third Lord Shaftesbury, still on the same high scale, who keeps very much in the background, and works in a very occult manner, but very efficaciously nevertheless, and who is busy in applying everywhere the benefits of the son's satisfaction and the father's goodness.[7]

Arnold's 'parable of the three Lord Shaftesburys' got him into a lot of trouble: he was 'indignantly censured' (as he says) for wounding 'the feelings of the religious community by turning into ridicule an august doctrine, the object of their solemn faith'.[8] But there is no other account of the Anselmian doctrine

[7] Matthew Arnold, *Literature and Dogma* (1873), pp. 306–7.
[8] Matthew Arnold, *God and the Bible* (1875), pp. 18–19.

of the Atonement that I have read which puts it in so morally favourable a light. Be that as it may, the only way in which the doctrine can be understood verificationally is in terms of human beings—mythological beings, it may be, who never existed, but who nevertheless would have been empirically observable had they existed.

For it is not necessary, on my view, for the asserter of a religious assertion to believe in the truth of the story involved in the assertions: what is necessary is that the story should be entertained in thought, i.e. that the statement of the story should be understood as having a meaning. I have secured this by requiring that the story should consist of empirical propositions. Educated Christians of the present day who attach importance to the doctrine of the Atonement certainly do not believe an empirically testable story in Matthew Arnold's or any other form. But it is the fact that entertainment in thought of this and other Christian stories forms the context in which Christian resolutions are made which serves to distinguish Christian assertions from those made by adherents of another religion, or of no religion.

What I am calling a *story* Matthew Arnold called a *parable* and a *fairy-tale*. Other terms which might be used are *allegory, fable, tale, myth*. I have chosen the word 'story' as being the most neutral term, implying neither that the story is believed nor that it is disbelieved. The Christian stories include straightforward historical statements about the life and death of Jesus of Nazareth; a Christian (unless he accepts the unplausible Christ-myth theory) will naturally believe some or all of these. Stories about the beginning of the world and of the Last Judgment as facts of past or of future history are believed by many unsophisticated Christians. But my contention is that belief in the truth of the Christian stories is not the proper criterion for deciding whether or not an assertion is a Christian one. A man is not, I think, a professing Christian unless he both proposes to live according to Christian moral principles and associates his intention with thinking of Christian stories; but he need not believe that the empirical propositions presented by the stories correspond to empirical fact.

But if the religious stories need not be believed, what function do they fulfil in the complex state of mind and behaviour known as having a religious belief? How is entertaining the story related to resolving to pursue a certain way of life? My answer is that the relation is a psychological and causal one. It is an empirical psychological fact that many people find it easier to resolve upon and to carry through a course of action which is contrary to their natural inclinations if this policy is associated in their minds with certain stories. And in many people the psychological link is not appreciably weakened by the fact that the story associated with the behaviour policy is not believed. Next to the Bible and the Prayer Book the most influential work in English Christian religious life has been a book whose stories are frankly recognized as fictitious—Bunyan's *Pilgrim's Progress;* and some of the most influential works in setting the moral tone of my generation were the novels of Dostoevsky. It is completely untrue, as a matter of psychological fact, to think that the only intellectual considerations which affect action are beliefs: it is *all* the thoughts of a man that determine his behaviour; and these include his phantasies, imaginations, ideas of what he would wish to be and do, as well as the propositions which he believes to be true.

This important psychological fact, a commonplace to all students of the influence of literature upon life, has not been given sufficient weight by theologians and philosophers of religion. It has not been altogether ignored; for instance, the report of the official Commission on Doctrine in the Church of England, published in 1938, in a section entitled 'On the application to the Creeds of the conception of symbolic truth' says: 'Statements affirming particular facts may be found to have value as pictorial expressions of spiritual truths, even though the supposed facts themselves did not actually happen. . . . It is not therefore of necessity illegitimate to accept and affirm particular clauses of the Creeds while understanding them in this symbolic sense.'[9] But the patron saint whom I claim for my way of thinking is that great but neglected Christian

9 *Doctrine in the Church of England* (1938), pp. 37–8.

thinker Matthew Arnold, whose parable of the three Lord Shaftesburys is a perfect example of what I take a religious story to be. Arnold's philosophy of religion has suffered from his striking remarks being lifted from their context: his description of religion as *morality touched by emotion* does not adequately express his view of the part played by imagination in religion. Arnold's main purpose in his religious writings was that of 'cementing the alliance between the imagination and conduct'[10] by regarding the propositional element in Christianity as 'literature' rather than as 'dogma'. Arnold was not prepared to carry through his programme completely; he regarded *the Eternal not ourselves that makes for righteousness* more dogmatically than fictionally. But his keen insight into the imaginative and poetic element in religious belief as well as his insistence that religion is primarily concerned with guiding conduct make him a profound philosopher of religion as well as a Christian teacher full of the 'sweet reasonableness' he attributed to Christ.

> *God's wisdom and God's goodness!*—Ay, but fools
> Mis-define these till God knows them no more.
> *Wisdom and goodness, they are God!*—what schools
> Have yet so much as heard this simpler lore?[11]

To return to our philosophizing. My contention that the propositional element in religious assertions consists of stories interpreted as straightforwardly empirical propositions which are not, generally speaking, believed to be true has the great advantage of imposing no restriction whatever upon the empirical interpretation which can be put upon the stories. The religious man may interpret the stories in the way which assists him best in carrying out the behaviour policies of his religion. He can, for example, think of the three persons of the Trinity in visual terms, as did the great Christian painters, or as talking to one another, as in the poems of St. John of the Cross. And since he need not believe the stories he can interpret them in

[10] Matthew Arnold, *God and the Bible* (1875), p. xiii.
[11] From Matthew Arnold's sonnet 'The Divinity' (1867).

ways which are not consistent with one another. It is disastrous for anyone to try to believe empirical propositions which are mutually inconsistent, for the courses of action appropriate to inconsistent beliefs are not compatible. The needs of practical life require that the body of believed proposition should be purged of inconsistency. But there is no action which is appropriate to thinking of a proposition without believing it; thinking of it may, as I have said, produce a state of mind in which it is easier to carry out a particular course of action, but the connexion is causal: there is no intrinsic connexion between the thought and the action. Indeed a story may provide better support for a long range policy of action if it contains inconsistencies. The Christian set of stories, for example, contains both a pantheistic sub-set of stories in which everything is a part of God and a dualistic Manichaean sub-set of stories well represented by St. Ignatius Loyola's allegory of a conflict between the forces of righteousness under the banner of Christ and the forces of darkness under Lucifer's banner. And the Marxist religion's set of stories contains both stories about an inevitable perfect society and stories about a class war. In the case of both religions the first sub-set of stories provides confidence, the second spurs to action.

There is one story common to all the moral theistic religions which has proved of great psychological value in enabling religious men to persevere in carrying out their religious behaviour policies—the story that in so doing they are doing the will of God. And here it may look as if there is an intrinsic connexion between the story and the policy of conduct. But even when the story is literally believed, when it is believed that there is a magnified Lord Shaftesbury who commands or desires the carrying out of the behaviour policy, that in itself is no reason for carrying out the policy: it is necessary also to have the intention of doing what the magnified Lord Shaftesbury commands or desires. But the intention to do what a person commands or desires, irrespective of what this command or desire may be, is no part of a higher religion; it is when the religious man finds that what the magnified Lord Shaftesbury commands or desires accords with his own moral judgement that he decides to obey or to accede to it. But this is no new decision, for his own moral judgement is a decision to carry out a behaviour policy; all that is happening is that he is describing his old decision in a new way. In religious conviction the resolution to follow a way of life is primary; it is not derived from believing, still less from thinking of, any empirical story. The story may psychologically support the resolution, but it does not logically justify it.

In this lecture I have been sparing in my use of the term 'religious belief' (although it occurs in the title), preferring instead to speak of religious assertions and of religious conviction. This was because for me the fundamental problem is that of the meaning of statements used to make religious assertions, and I have accordingly taken my task to be that of explaining the use of such assertions, in accordance with the principle that meaning is to be found by ascertaining use. In disentangling the elements of this use I have discovered nothing which can be called 'belief' in the senses of this word applicable either to an empirical or to a logically necessary proposition. A religious assertion, for me, is the assertion of an intention to carry out a certain behaviour policy, subsumable under a sufficiently general principle to be a moral one, together with the implicit or explicit statement, but not the assertion, of certain stories. Neither the assertion of the intention nor the reference to the stories includes belief in its ordinary senses. But in avoiding the term 'belief' I have had to widen the term 'assertion', since I do not pretend that either the behaviour policy intended or the stories entertained are adequately specified by the sentences used in making isolated religious assertions. So assertion has been extended to include elements not explicitly expressed in the verbal form of the assertion. If we drop the linguistic expression of the assertion altogether the remainder is what may be called religious belief. Like moral belief, it is not a species of ordinary belief, of belief in a proposition. A moral belief is an intention to behave in a certain way: a religious belief is an intention to behave in a certain way (a moral belief) together with the entertainment of certain stories associated with the intention in the mind of the believer. This solution of the problem of religious belief seems to me to do justice both to the empiricist's demand that meaning must be tied to empirical use and to the religious man's claim for his religious beliefs to be taken seriously.

Seriously, it will be retorted, but not objectively. If a man's religion is all a matter of following the way of life he sets before himself and of strengthening his determination to follow it by imagining exemplary fairy-tales, it is purely subjective: his religion is all in terms of his own private ideals and of his own private imaginations. How can he even try to convert others to his religion if there is nothing objective to convert them to? How can he argue in its defence if there is no religious proposition which he believes, nothing which he takes to be the fundamental truth about the universe? And is it of any public interest what mental techniques he uses to bolster up his will? Discussion about religion must be more than the exchange of autobiographies.

But we are all social animals; we are all members one of another. What is profitable to one man in helping him to persevere in the way of life he has decided upon may well be profitable to another man who is trying to follow a similar way of life; and to pass on information that might prove useful would be approved by almost every morality. The autobiography of one man may well have an influence upon the life of another, if their basic wants are similar.

But suppose that these are dissimilar, and that the two men propose to conduct their lives on quite different fundamental principles. Can there be any reasonable discussion between them? This is the problem that has faced the many moral philosophers recently who have been forced, by their examination of the nature of thinking, into holding non-propositional theories of ethics. All I will here say is that to hold that the adoption of a set of moral principles is a matter of the personal decision to live according to these principles does not imply that beliefs as to what are the practical consequences of following such principles are not relevant to the decision. An intention, it is true, cannot be logically based upon anything except another intention. But in considering what conduct to intend to practise, it is highly relevant whether or not the consequences of practising that conduct are such as one would intend to secure. As R. M. Hare has well said, an ultimate decision to accept a way of life, 'for from being arbitrary, . . . would be the most well-founded of decisions, because it would be based upon a consideration of everything upon which it could possibly be founded'.[12] And in this consideration there is a place for every kind of rational argument.

Whatever may be the case with other religions Christianity has always been a personal religion demanding personal commitment to a personal way of life. In the words of another Oxford philosopher, 'the questions "What shall I do?" and "What moral principles should I adopt?" must be answered by each man for himself'.[13] Nowell-Smith takes this as part of the meaning of morality: whether or not this is so, I am certain that it is of the very essence of the Christian religion.

---

[12] R. M. Hare, *The Language of Morals* (1952), p. 69.
[13] P. H. Nowell-Smith, *Ethics* (1954), p. 320.

THEOLOGY AND VERIFICATION

JOHN HICK

To ask "Is the existence of God verifiable?" is to pose a question which is too imprecise to be capable of bein answered.[1] There are many different concepts of God, and it may be that statements employing some of them are open to verification or falsification while statements employing others of them are not. Again, the notion of verifying is itself by no means perfectly clear and fixed; and it may be that on some views of the nature of verification the existence of God is verifiable, whereas on other views it is not.

Instead of seeking to compile a list of the various different concepts of God and the various possible senses of "verify," I wish to argue with regard to one particular concept of deity, namely the Christian concept, that divine existence is in principle verifiable; and as the first stage of this argument I must indicate what I mean by "verifiable."

I

The central core of the concept of verification, I suggest, is the removal of ignorance or uncertainty concerning the truth

Reprinted from *Theology Today*, 17 (1960), by permission of *Theology Today* and the author.

[1] In this paper I assume that an indicative sentence expresses a factual assertion if and only if the state in which the universe would be if the putative assertion could correctly be said to be true differs in some experienceable way from the state in which the universe would be if the putative assertion could correctly be said to be false, all aspects of the universe other than that referred to in the putative assertion being the same in either case. This criterion acknowledges the important core of truth in the logical positivist verification principle. "Experienceable" in the above formulation means, in the case of alleged subjective or private facts (*e.g.*, pains, dreams, after-images, etc.), "experienceable by the subject in question" and, in the case of alleged objective or public facts, "capable in principle of being experienced by anyone." My contention is going to be that "God exists" asserts a matter of objective fact.

of some proposition. That *p* is verified (whether *p* embodies a theory, hypothesis, prediction, or straigthforward assertion) means that something happens which makes it clear that *p* is true. A question is settled so that there is no longer room for rational doubt concerning it. The way in which grounds for rational doubt are excluded varies, of course, with the subject matter. But the general feature common to all cases of verification is the ascertaining of truth by the removal of grounds for rational doubt. Where such grounds are removed, we rightly speak of verification having taken place.

To characterize verification in this way is to raise the question whether the notion of verification is purely logical or is both logical and psychological. Is the statement that *p* is verified simply the statement that a certain state of affairs exists (or has existed), or is it the statement also that someone is aware that this state of affairs exists (or has existed) and notes that its existence establishes the truth of *p?* A geologist predicts that the earth's surface will be covered with ice in 15 million years time. Suppose that in 15 million years time the earth's surface *is* covered with ice, but that in the meantime the human race has perished, so that no one is left to observe the event or to draw any conclusion concerning the accuracy of the geologist's prediction. Do we now wish to say that his prediction has been verified, or shall we deny that it has been verified, on the ground that there is no one left to do the verifying?

The range of "verify" and its cognates is sufficienty wide to permit us to speak in either way. But the only sort of verification of theological propositions which is likely to interest us is one in which human beings participate. We may therefore, for our present purpose, treat verification as a logico-psychological rather than as a purely logical concept. I suggest, then, that "verify" be construed as a verb which has its primary uses in the active voice: I verify, you verify, we verify, they verify, or have verified. The impersonal passive, it is verified, now becomes logically secondary. To say that *p* has been verified is to say that (at least) someone has verified it, often with the implication that his or their report to this effect is generally accepted. But it is impossible, on this usage, for *p* to have been verified without someone having verified it. "Verification" is thus primarily the name for an event which takes place in human consciousness.[2] It refers to an experience, the experience of ascertaining that a given proposition or set of propositions is true. To this extent verification is a psychological notion. But of course it is also a logical notion. For needless to say, not *any* experience is rightly called an experience of verifying *p*. Both logical and psychological conditions must be fulfilled in order for verification to have taken place. In this respect, "verify" is like "know." Knowing is an experience which someone has or undergoes, or perhaps a dispositional state in which someone is, and it cannot take place without someone having or undergoing it or being in it; but not by any means every experience which people have, or every dispositional state in which they are, is rightly called knowing.

With regard to this logico-psychological concept of verification, such questions as the following arise. When *A*, but nobody else, has ascertained that *p* is true, can *p* be said to have been verified; or is it required that others also have undergone the same ascertainment? How public, in other words, must verification be? Is it necessary that *p* could in principle be verified by anyone, without restriction, even though perhaps only *A* has in fact verified it? If so, what is meant here by "in principle"; does it signify, for example, that *p* must be verifiable by anyone who performs a certain operation; and does it imply that to do this is within everyone's power?

These questions cannot, I believe, be given any general answer applicable to all instances of the exclusion of rational doubt. The answers must be derived in each case from an investigation of the particular subject matter. It will be the object of subsequent sections of this article to undertake such an investigation concerning the Christian concept of God.

Verification is often construed as the verification of a

[2] This suggestion is closely related to Carnap's insistence that, in contrast to "true," "confirmed" is time-dependent. To say that a statement is confirmed, or verified, is to say that it has been confirmed at a particular time—and, I would add, by a particular person. See Rudolf Carnap, "Truth and Confirmation," Feigl and Sellars, *Readings in Philosophical Analysis*, 1949, pp. 119 f.

prediction. However, verification, as the exclusion of grounds for rational doubt, does not necessarily consist in the proving correct of a prediction; a verifying experience does not always need to have been predicted in order to have the effect of excluding rational doubt. But when we are interested in the verifiability of propositions as the critierion for their having factual meaning, the notion of prediction becomes central. If a proposition contains or entails predictions which can be verified or falsified, its charatcer as an assertion (though not of course its character as a true assertion) is thereby guaranteed.

Such prediction may be and ofter are conditional. For example, statements about the features of the dark side of the moon are rendered meaningful by the conditional predictions which they entail to the effect that if an observer comes to be in such a position in space, he will make such-and-such observations. It would in fact be more accurate to say that the prediction is always conditional, but that sometimes the conditions are so obvious and so likely to be fulfilled in any case that they require no special mention, while sometimes they require for their fulfillment some unusual expedition or operation. A prediction, for example, that the sun will rise within twenty-four hours is intended unconditionally, at least as concerns conditions to be fulfilled by the observer; he is not required by the terms of the prediction to perform any special operation. Even in this case, however, there is an implied negative condition that he shall not put himself in a situation (such as immuring himself in the depths of a coal mine) from which a sunrise would not be perceptible. Other predictions, however, are explicitly conditional. In these cases it is true for any particular individual that in order to verify the statement in question he must go through some specified course of action. The prediction is to the effect that if you conduct such an experiment you will obtain such a result; for example, if you go into the next room you will have such-and-such visual experiences, and if you then touch the table which you see you will have such-and-such tactual experiences, and so on. The content of the "if" clause is of course alwaye determined by the particular subject matter. The logic of "table" determines what you must do to verify statements about tables; the logic of "molecule" determines what you must do to verify statements about molecules; and the logic of "God" determines what you must do to verify statements about God.

In those cases in which the individual who is to verify a proopsition must himself first perform some operation, it clearly cannot follow from the circumstances that the proposition is true that everybody has in fact verified it, or that everybody will at some future time verify it. For whether or not any particular person performs the requisite operation is a contingent matter.

I I

What is the relation between verification and falsification? We are all familiar today with the phrase, "theology and falsification." A. G. N. Flew and others,[3] taking their cue from John Wisdom,[4] have raised instead of the question, "What possible experiences would verify 'God exists'?" the matching question, "What possible experiences would falsify 'God exists'? What conceivable state of affairs would be incompatible with the existence of God?" In posing the question in this way it was apparently assumed that verification and falsification are symmetrically related, and that the latter is apt to be the more accessible of the two.

In the most common cases, certainly, verification and falsification are symmetrically related. The logically simplest case of verification is provided by the crucial instance. Here it is integral to a given hypothesis that if, in specified circumstances, A occurs, the hypothesis is thereby shown to be true, whereas if B occurs the hypothesis is thereby shown to be false. Verification and falsification are also smymetrically related in the testing of such a proposition as "There is a table in the next room." The verifying experiences in this case are experiences

---

[3] A. G. N. Flew, editor, *New Essays in Philosophical Theology*, 1955, Chapter VI. [The chapter may be found on p. 107 in this book.]

[4] "Gods," *Proceedings of the Aristotelian Society*, 1944–45. Reprinted in A. G. N. Flew, editor, *Logic and Language*, First Series, 1951, and in John Wisdom, *Philosophy and Psycho-Analysis*, 1953.

of seeing and touching, predictions of which are entailed by the proposition in question, under the proviso that one goes into the next room; and the absence of such experiences in those circumstances serves to falsify the proposition.

But it would be rash to assume, on this basis, that verification and falsification must always be related in this symmetrical fashion. They do not necessarily stand to one another as do the two sides of a coin, so that once the coin is spun it must fall on one side or the other. There are cases in which verification and falsification each correspond to a side on a different coin, so that one can fail to verify without this failure constituting falsification.

Consider, for example, the proposition that "there are three successive sevens in the decimal determination of π." So far as the value of π has been worked out, it does not contain a series of three sevens, but it will always be true that such a series may occur at a point not yet reached in anyone's calculations. Accordingly, the proposition may one day be verified, if it is true, but can never be falsified, if it is false.

The hypothesis of continued conscious existence after bodily death provides an instance of a different kind of such asymmetry, and one which has a direct bearing upon the theistic problem. This hypothesis has built into it a prediction that one will after the date of one's bodily death have conscious experiences, including the experience of remembering that death. This is a prediction which will be verified in one's own experience if it is true, but which cannot be falsified if it is false. That is to say, it can be false, but *that* it is false can never be a fact which anyone has experientially verified. But this circumstance does not undermine the meaningfulness of the hypothesis, since it is also such that if it be true, it will be known to be true.

It is important to remember that we do not speak of verifying logically necessary truths, but only propositions concerning matters of fact. Accordingly verification is not to be identified with the concept of logical certification or proof. The exclusion of rational doubt concerning some matter of fact is not equivalent to the exclusion of the logical possibility of error or illusion. For truths concerning fact are not logically necessary. Their contrary is never self-contradictory. But at the same time the bare logical possibility of error does not constitute ground for rational doubt as to the veracity of our experience. If it did, no empirical proposition could ever be verified, and indeed the notion of empirical verification would be without use and therefore witnout sense. What we rightly seek, when we desire the verification of a factual proposition, is not a demonstration of the logical impossibility of the proposition being false (for this would be a self-contradictory demand), but such weight of evidence as suffices, in the type of case in question, to exclude rational doubt.

III

These features of the concept of verification—that verification consists in the exclusion of grounds for rational doubt concerning the truth of some proposition; that this means its exclusion from particular minds; that the nature of the experience which serves to exclude grounds for rational doubt depends upon the particular subject matter; that verification is often related to predictions and that such predictions and that such predictions are often conditional; that verification and falsification may be asymmetrically related; and finally, that the verification of a factual proposition is not equivalent to logical certification—are all relevant to the verification of the central religious claim, "God exists." I wish now to apply these discriminations to the notion of eschatological verification, which has been briefly employed by Ian Crombie in his contribution to *New Essays in Philosophical Theology*,[5] and by myself in *Faith and Knowledge*.[6] This suggestion has on each occasion been greeted with disapproval by both philosophers and theologians. I am, however, still of the opinion that the notion of eschatological verification is sound; and further, that no viable alternative to it has been offered to establish the factual character of theism.

[5] *Op. cit.*, p. 126.
[6] Cornell University Press, 1957, pp. 150–62.

The strength of the notion of eschatological verification is that it is not an *ad hoc* invention but is based upon an actually operative religious concept of God. In the language of Christian faith, the word "God" stands at the center of a system of terms, such as Spirit, grace, Logos, incarnation, Kingdom of God, and many more; and the distinctly Christian conception of God can only be fully grasped in its connection with these related terms.[7] It belongs to a complex of notions which together constitute a picture of the universe in which we live, of man's place therein, of a comprehensive divine purpose interacting with human purposes, and of the general nature of the eventful fulfillment of that divine purpose. This Christian picture of the universe, entertaining as it does certain distinctive expectations concerning the future, is a very different picture from any that can be accepted by one who does ot believe that the God of the New Testament exists. Further, these differences are such as to show themselves in human experience. The possibility of experiential confirmation is thus built into the Christian concept of God; and the notion of eschatological verification seeks to relate this fact to the logical problem of meaning.

Let me first give a general indication of this suggestion, by repeating a parable which I have related elsewhere,[8] and then try to make it more precise and eligible for discussion. Here, first, is the parable.

Two men are travelling together along a road. One of them believes that it leads to a Celestial City, the other that it leads nowhere; but since this is the only road there is, both must travel it. Neither has been this way before, and therefore neither is able to say what they will find around each next corner. During their journey they meet both with moments of refreshments and delight, and with moments of hardship and danger. All the time one of them thinks of his journey as a

---

[7] Its clear recognition of this fact, with regard not only to Christianity but to any religion, is one of the valuable features of Ninian Smart's *Reasons and Faiths* (1958). He remarks, for example, that "the claim that God exists can only be understood by reference to many, if not all, other propositions in the doctrinal scheme from which it is extrapolated" (p. 12).

[8] *Faith and Knowledge,* pp. 150 f.

pilgrimage to the Celestial City and interprets the pleasant parts as encouragements and the obstacles as trials of his purpose and lessons in endurance, prepared by the king of that city and designed to make of him a worthy citizen of the place when at last he arrives there. The other, however, believes none of this and sees their journey as an unavoidable and aimless ramble. Since he has no choice in the matter, he enjoys the good and endures the bad. But for him there is no Celestial City to be reached, no all-encompassing purpose ordaining their journey; only the road itself and the luck of the road in good weather and in bad.

During the course of the journey the issue between them is not an experimental one. They do not entertain different expectations about the coming details of the road, but only about its ultimate destination. And yet when they do turn the last corner it will be apparent that one of them has been right all the time and the other wrong. Thus although the issue between them has not been experimental, it has nevertheless from the start been a real issue. They have not merely felt differently about the road; for one was feeling appropriately and the other inappropriately in relation to the actual state of affairs. Their opposed interpretations of the road constituted genuinely rival assertions, though assertions whose assertion-status has the peculiar characteristic of being guaranteed retrospectively by a future crux.

This parable has of course (like all parables) strict limitations. It is designed to make only one point: that Christian doctrine postulates an ultimate unambiguous state of existence *in patria* as well as our present ambiguous existence *in via*. There is a state of having arrived as well as a state of journeying, an eternal heavenly life as well as an earthly pilgrimage. The alleged future experience of this state cannot, of course, be appealed to as evidence for theism as a present interpretation of our experience; but it does suffice to render the choice between theism and atheism a real and not a merely empty or verbal choice. And although this does not affect the logic of the situation, it should be added that the alternative interpretations are more than theoretical, for they render different practical plans and policies appropriate now.

The universe as envisaged by the theist, then, differs as a totality from the universe as envisaged by the atheist. This difference does not, however, from our present standpoint within the universe, involve a difference in the objective content of each or even any of its passing moments. The theist and the atheist do not (or need not) expect different events to occur in the successive details of the temporal process. They do not (or need not) entertain divergent expectations of the course of history viewed from within. But the theist does and the atheist does not expect that when history is completed it will be seen to have led to a particular end-state and to have fulfilled a specific purpose, namely that of creating "children of God."

The idea of an eschatological verification of theism can make sense, however, only if the logically prior idea of continued personal existence after death is intelligible. A desultory debate on this topic has been going on for several years in some of the philosophical periodicals. C. I. Lewis has contended that the hypothesis of immortality "is an hypothesis about our own future experience. And our understanding of what would verify it has no lack of clarity."[9] And Morris Schlick agreed, adding, "We must conclude that immortality, in the sense defined [i.e. 'survival after death,' rather than 'never-ending life'], should not be regarded as a 'metaphysical problem' but is an empirical hypothesis, because it possesses logical verifiability. It could be verified by following the prescription: 'Wait until you die!' "[10] However, others have challenged this conclusion, either on the ground that the phrase "surviving death" is self-contradictory in ordinary language or, more substantially, on the ground that the traditional distinction between soul and body cannot be sustained.[11] I should like to address myself

[9] "Experience and Meaning," *Philosophical Review*, 1934, reprinted in Feigl and Sellars, *Readings in Philosophical Analysis*, 1949, p. 142.

[10] "Meaning and Verification," *Philosophical Review*, 1936, reprinted in Feigl and Sellars, *op. cit.*, p. 160.

[11] E.g. A. G. N. Flew, "Death," *New Essays in Philosophical Theology*; "Can a Man Witness his own Funeral?" *Hibbert Journal*, 1956.

to this latter view. The only self of which we know, it is said, is the empirical self, the walking, talking, acting, sleeping individual who lives, it may be, for some sixty to eighty years and then dies. Mental events and mental characteristics are anlayzed into the modes of behavior and behavioral disposition of this empirical self. The human being is described as an organism capable of atcing in the "high-level" ways which we characterize as intelligent, thoughtful, humorous, calculating, and the like. The concept of mind or soul is thus not the concept of a "ghost in the machine" (to use Gilbert Ryle's loaded phrase[12]), but of the more flexible and sophisticated ways in which human beings behave and have it in them to behave. On this view there is no room for the notion of soul in distinction from body and if there is no soul in distinction from body, there can be no question of the soul surviving the death of the body. Against this philosophical background the specifically Christian (and also Jewish) belief in the resurrection of the flesh, or body, in contrast to the Hellenic notion of the survival of a disembodied soul, might be expected to have attracted more attention than it has. For it is consonant with the conception of man as an indissoluble psychophysical unity, and yet it also offers the possibility of an empirical meaning for the idea of "life after death."

Paul is the chief Biblical expositor of the idea of the resurrection of the body.[13] His view, as I understand it, is this. When someone has died he is, apart from any special divine action, extinct. A human being is by nature mortal and subject to annihilation by death. But in fact God, by an act of sovereign power, either sometimes or always resurrects or (better) reconstitutes or recreates him—not, however, as the identical physical organism that he was before death, but as a *soma pneumatikon*, ("spiritual body") embodying the dispositional characteristics and memory traces of the deceased physical organism, and inhabiting an environment with which the *soma pneuma-*

---

[12] *The Concept of Mind,* 1949, which contains an important exposition of the interpretation of "mental" qualities as characteristics of behavior.

[13] I Cor. 15.

tikon is continuous as the *ante-mortem* body was continuous with our present world. In discussing this notion we may well abandon the word "spiritual," as lacking today any precise established usage, and speak of "resurrection bodies" and of "the resurrection world." The principal questions to be asked concern the relation betwen the physical world and the resurrection world, and the criteria of personal identity which are operating when it is alleged that a certain inhabitant of the resurrection world is the same person as an individual who once inhabited this world. The first of these questions turns out on investigation to be the more difficult of the two, and I shall take the easier one first.

Let me sketch a very odd possibility (concerning which, however, I wish to emphasize not so much its oddness as its possibility!), and then see how far it can be stretched in the direction of the notion of the resurrection body. In the process of stretching it will become even more odd than it was before; but my aim will be to show that, however odd, it remains within the bounds of the logically possible. This progression will be presented in three pictures, arranged in a self-explanatory order.

First picture: Suppose that at some learned gathering in this country one of the company were suddenly and inexplicably to disappear, and that at the same moment an exact replica of him were suddenly and inexplicably to appear at some comparable meeting in Australia. The person who appears in Australia is exactly similar, as to both bodily and mental characteristics, with the person who disappears in America. There is continuity of memory, complete similarity of bodily features, including even fingerprints, hair and eye coloration and stomach contents, and also of beliefs, habits, and mental propensities. In fact there is everything that would lead us to identify the one who appeared with the one who disappeared, except continuity of occupancy of space. We may suppose, for example, that a deputation of the colleagues of the man who disappeared fly to Australia to interview the replica of him which is reported there, and find that he is in all respects but one exactly as though he had travelled from say, Princeton to Melbourne, by conventional means. The only difference is that he describes how, as he was

sitting listening to Dr. Z reading a paper, on blinking his eyes
he suddenly found himself sitting in a different room listening
to a different paper by an Australian scholar. He asks his colleagues how the meeting had gone after he ceased to be there,
and what they had made of his disappearance, and so on. He
clearly thinks of himself as the one who was present with them
at their meeting in the United States. I suggest that faced with
all these circumstances his colleagues would soon, if not immediately, find themselves thinking of him and treating him as the
individual who had so inexplicably disappeared from their
midst. We should be extending our normal use of "same person"
in a way which the postulated facts would both demand and
justify if we said that the one who appears in Australia is the
same person as the one who disappears in America. The factors
inclining us to identify them would far outweigh the factors
disinclining us to do this. We should have no reasonable alterna-
itve but to extend our usage of "the same person" to cover the
strange new case.

Second picture: Now let us suppose that the event in
America is not a sudden and inexplicable disappearance, and
indeed not a disappearance at all, but a sudden death. Only, at
the moment when the individual dies, a replica of him as he
was at the moment before his death, complete with memory up
to that instant, appears in Australia. Even with the corpse on
our hands, it would still, I suggest, be an extension of "same
person" required and warranted by the postulated facts, to say
that the same person who died has been miraculously recreated
in Australia. The case would be considerably odder than in the
previous picture, because of the existence of the corpse in
America contemporaneously with the existence of the living
person in Australia. But I submit that, although the oddness of
this circumstance may be stated as strongly as you please, and
can indeed hardly be overstated, yet it does not exceed the
bounds of the logically possible. Once again we must imagine
some of the deceased's colleagues going to Australia to interview the person who has suddenly appeared there. He would
perfectly remember them and their meeting, be interested in

what had happened, and be as amazed and dumbfounded about it as anyone else; and he would perhaps be worried about the possible legal complications if he should return to America to claim his property; and so on. Once again, I believe, they would soon find themselves thinking of him and treating him as the same person as the dead Princetonian. Once again the factors inclining us to say that the one who died and the one who appeared are the same person would outweigh the factors inclining us to say that they are different people. Once again we should have to extend our usage of "the same person" to cover this new case.

Third picture: My third supposal is that the replica, complete with memory, etc. appears, not in Australia, but as a resurrection replica in a different world altogether, a resurrection world inhabited by resurrected persons. This world occupies its own space, distinct from the space with which we are now familiar. That is to say, an object in the resurrection world is not situated at any distance or in any direction from an object in our present world, although each object in either world is spatially related to each other object in the same world.

Mr. X, then, dies. A Mr. X replica, complete with the set of memory traces which Mr. X had at the last moment before his death, comes into existence. It is composed of other material than physical matter, and is located in a resurrection world which does not stand in any spatial relationship with the physical world. Let us leave out of consideration St. Paul's hint that the resurrection body may be as unlike the physical body as is a full grain of wheat from the wheat seed, and consider the simpler picture in which the resurrection body has the same shape as the physical body.[14]

In these circumstances, how does Mr. X know that he has been resurrected or recreated? He remembers dying; or rather he remembers being on what he took to be his death-bed, and becoming progressively weaker until, presumably, he lost consciousness. But how does he know that (to put it Irishly) his

14 As would seem to be assumed, for example, by Irenaeus (*Adversus Haereses*, Bk. II, Ch. 34, Sec. 1).

"dying" proved fatal; and that he did not, after losing consciousness, begin to recover strength, and has now simply waked up?

The picture is readily enough elaborated to answer this question. Mr. X meets and recognizes a number of relatives and friends and historical personages whom he knows to have died; and from the fact of their presence, and also from their testimony that he has only just now appeared in their world, he is convinced that he has died. Evidences of this kind could mount up to the point at which they are quite as strong as the evidence which, in pictures one and two, convince the individual in question that he has been miraculously translated to Australia. Resurrected persons would be individually no more in doubt about their own identity than we are now, and would be able to identify one another in the same kinds of ways, and with a like degree of assurance, as we do now.

If it be granted that resurrected persons might be able to arrive at a rationally founded conviction that their existence is *post-mortem*, how could they know that the world in which they find themselves is in a different space from that in which their physical bodies were? How could such a one know that he is not in a like situation with the person in picture number two, who dies in America and appears as a full-blooded replica in Australia, leaving his corpse in the U. S. A.—except that now the replica is situated, not in Australia, but on a planet of some other star?

It is of course conceivable that the space of the resurrection world should have properties which are manifestly incompatible with its being a region of physical space. But on the other hand, it is not of the essence of the notion of a resurrection world that its space should have properties different from those of physical space. And supposing it not to have different properties, it is not evident that a resurrected individual could learn from any direct observations that he was not on a planet of some sun which is at so great a distance from our own sun that the stellar scenery visible from it is quite unlike that which we can now see. The grounds that a resurrected person would

have for believing that he is in a different space from physical
space (supposing there to be no discernible difference in spatial
properties) would be the same as the grounds that any of us
may have now for believing this concerning resurrected individuals. These grounds are indirect and consist in all those
considerations (*e.g.*, Luke 16: 26) which lead most of those
who consider the question to reject as absurd the possibility
of, for example, radio communication or rocket travel between
earth and heaven.

V

In the present context my only concern is to claim that this
doctrine of the divine creation of bodies, composed of a material
other than that of physical matter, which bodies are endowed
with sufficient correspondence of characteristics with our present
bodies, and sufficient continuity of memory with our present
consciousness, for us to speak of the same person being raised
up again to life in a new environment, is not self-contradictory.
If, then, it cannot be ruled out *ab initio* as meaningless, we may
go on to consider whether and how it is related to the possible
verification of Christian theism.

So far I have argued that a survival prediction such as is
contained in the *corpus* of Christian belief is in principle subject to future verification. But this does not take the argument
by any means as far as it must go if it is to succeed. For
survival, simply as such, would not serve to verify theism. It
would not necessarily be a state of affairs which is manifestly
incompatible with the non-existence of God. It might be taken
just as a surprising natural fact. The atheist, in his resurrection
body, and able to remember his life on earth, might say that
the universe has turned out to be more complex, and perhaps
more to be approved of, than he had realized. But the mere
fact of survival, with a new body in a new environment, would
not demonstrate to him that there is a God. It is fully compatible with the notion of survival that the life to come be, so
far as the theistic problem is concerned, essentially a continua-

tion of the present life, and religiously no less ambiguous. And in this event, survival after bodily death would not in the least constitute a final verification of theistic faith.

I shall not spend time in trying to draw a picture of a resurrection existence which would merely prolong the religious ambiguity of our present life. The important question, for our purpose, is not whether one can conceive of after-life experiences which would *not* verify theism (and in point of fact one can fairly easily conceive them), but whether one can conceive of after-life experiences which *would* serve to verify theism.

I think that we can. In trying to do so I shall not appeal to the traditional doctrine, which figures especially in Catholic and mystical theology, of the Beatific Vision of God. The difficulty presented by this doctrine is not so much that of deciding whether there are grounds for believing it, as of deciding what it means. I shall not, however, elaborate this difficulty, but pass directly to the investigation of a different and, as it seems to me, more intelligible possibility. This is the possibility not of a direct vision of God, whatever that might mean, but of a *situation* which points unambiguously to the existence of a loving God. This would be a situation which, so far as its religious significance is concerned, contrasts in a certain important respect with our present situation. Our present situation is one which in some ways seems to confirm and in other ways to contradict the truth of theism. Some events around us suggest the presence of an unseen benevolent intelligence and others sugest that no such intelligence is at work. Our situation is religiously ambiguous. But in order for us to be aware of this fact we must already have some idea, however vague, of what it would be for our situation to be not ambiguous, but on the contrary wholly evidential of God. I therefore want to try to make clearer this presupposed concept of a religiously unambiguous situation.

There are, I suggest, two possible developments of our experience such that, if they occurred in conjunction with one another (whether in this life or in another life to come), they would assure us beyond rational doubt of the reality of God, as conceived in the Christian faith. These are, *first,* an experience of the fulfillment of God's purpose for ourselves, as this has been disclosed in the Christian revelation; in conjunction, *second,* with an experience of communion with God as he has revealed himself in the person of Christ.

The divine purpose for human life, as this is depicted in the New Testament documents, is the bringing of the human person, in society with his fellows, to enjoy a certain valuable quality of personal life, the content of which is given in the character of Christ—which quality of life (*i.e.* life in relationship with God, described in the Fourth Gospel as eternal life) is said to be the proper destiny of human nature and the source of man's final self-fulfillment and happiness. The verification situation with regard to such a fulfillment is asymmetrical. On the one hand, so long as the divine purpose remains unfulfilled, we cannot know that it never will be fulfilled in the future; hence no final falsification is possible of the claim that this fulfillment will occur—unless, of course, the prediction contains a specific time clause which, in Christian teaching, it does not. But on the other hand, if and when the divine purpose *is* fulfilled in our own experience, we must be able to recognize and rejoice in that fulfillment. For the fulfillment would not be for us the promised fulfillment without our own conscious participation in it.

It is important to note that one can say this much without being cognizant in advance of the concrete form which such fulfillment will take. The before-and-after situation is analogous to that of a small child looking forward to adult life and then, having grown to adulthood, looking back upon childhood. The child possesses and can use correctly in various contexts the concept of "being grown-up," although he does not know, concretely, what it is like to be grown-up. But when he reaches adulthood he is nevertheless able to know that he has reached it; he is able to recognize the experience of living a grown-up life even though he did not know in advance just what to expect. For his understanding of adult maturity grows as he himself matures. Something similar may be supposed to happen in the case of the fulfillment of the divine purpose for human life.

That fulfillment may be as far removed from our present condition as is mature adulthood from the mind of a little child;
nevertheless, we possess already a comparatively vague notion
of this final fulfillment, and as we move towards it our concept
will itself become more adequate; and if and when we finally
reach that fulfillment, the problem of recognizing it will have
disappeared in the process.

The other feature that must, I suggest, be present in a state
of affairs that would verify theism, is that the fulfillment of
God's purpose be apprehended *as* the fulfillment of God's purpose and not simply as a natural state of affairs. To this end it
must be accompanied by an experience of communion with God
as he has made himself known to men in Christ.

The specifically Christian clause, "as he has made himself
known to men in Christ," is essential, for it provides a solution
to the problem of recognition in the awareness of God. Several
writers have pointed out the logical difficulty involved in any
claim to have encountered God.[15] How could one know that it
was *God* whom one had encountered? God is described in Christian theology in terms of various absolute qualities, such as
omnipotence, omnipresence, perfect goodness, infinite love, etc.,
which cannot as such be observed by us, as can their finite
analogues, limited power, local presence, finite goodness, and
human love. One can recognize that a being whom one "encounters" has a given finite degree of power, but how does one
recognize that he has *un*limited power? How does one observe
that an encountered being is *omni*present? How does one per-
ceive that his goodness and love, which one can perhaps see to
exceed any human goodness and love, are actually infinite?
Such qualities cannot be given in human experience. One might
claim, then, to have encountered a Being whom one presumes,
or trusts, or hopes to be God; but one cannot claim to have
encountered a Being whom one resognized to be the infinite,
almighty, eternal Creator.

This difficulty is met in Christianity by the doctrine of the
Incarnation—although this was not among the considerations

15 For Example, H. W. Hepburn, *Christianity and Paradox*, 1958,
pp. 56 f.

which led to the formulation of that doctrine. The idea of incarnation provides answers to the two related questions: "How do we know that God has certain absolute qualities which, by their very nature, transcend human experience?" and "How can there be an eschatological verification of theism which is based upon a recognition of the presence of God in his Kingdom?"

In Christianity God is known as "the God and Father of our Lord Jesus Christ."[16] God is the Being about whom Jesus taught; the Being in relation to whom Jesus lived, and into a relationship with whom he brought his disciples; the Being whose *agape* toward men was seen on earth in the life of Jesus. In short, God is the transcendent Creator who has revealed himself in Christ. Now Jesus' teaching about the Father is part of that self-disclosure, and it is from this teaching (together with that of the prophets who preceded him) that the Christian knowledge of God's transcendent being is derived. Only God himself knows his own infinite nature; and our human belief about that nature is based upon his self-revelation to men in Christ. As Karl Barth expresses it, "Jesus Christ is the knowability of God."[17] Our beliefs about God's infinite being are not capable of observational verification, being beyond the scope of human experience, but they are susceptible of indirect verification by the removal of rational doubt concerning the authority of Christ. An experience of the reign of the Son in the Kingdom of the Father would confirm that authority, and therewith, indirectly, the validity of Jesus' teaching concerning the character of God in his infinite transcendent nature.

The further question as to how an eschatological experience of the Kingdom of God could be known to be such has already been answered by implication. It is God's union with man in Christ that makes possible man's recognition of the fulfillment of God's purpose for man as being indeed the fulfillment of *God's* purpose for him. The presence of Christ in his Kingdom marks this as being beyond doubt the Kingdom of the God and Father of the Lord Jesus Christ.

16 II Cor. 11:31.
17 *Church Dogmatics*, Vol. II, Pt. I, p. 150.

It is true that even the experience of the realization of the promised Kingdom of God, with Christ reigning as Lord of the New Aeon, would not constitute a logical certification of his claims nor, accordingly, of the reality of God. But this will not seem remarkable to any philosopher in the empiricist tradition, who knows that it is only a confusion to demand that a factual proposition be an analytic truth. A set of expectations based upon faith in the historic Jesus as the incarnation of God, and in his teaching as being divinely authoritative, could be so fully confirmed in *post-mortem* experience as to leave no grounds for rational doubt as to the validity of that faith.

V I

There remains of course the problem (which falls to the New Testament scholar rather than to the philosopher) whether Christian tradition, and in particular the New Testament, provides a sufficiently authentic "picture" of the mind and character of Christ to make such recognition possible. I cannot here attempt to enter into the vast field of Biblical criticism, and shall confine myself to the logical point, which only emphasizes the importance of the historical question, that a verification of theism made possible by the Incarnation is dependent upon the Christian's having a genuine contact with the person of Christ, even though this is mediated through the life and tradition of the Church.

One further point remains to be considered. When we ask the question, *"To whom* is theism verified?"* one is initially inclined to assume that the answer must be, "To everyone." We are inclined to assume that, as in my parable of the journey, the believer must be confirmed in his belief, and the unbeliever converted from his unbelief. But this assumption is neither demanded by the nature of verification nor by any means unequivocably supported by our Christian sources.

We have already noted that a verifiable prediction may be conditional. "There is a table in the next room" entails conditional predictions of the form: if someone goes into the next room he will see, etc. But no one is compelled to go into the next room. Now it may be that the predictions concerning human experience which are entailed by the proposition that God exists are conditional predictions and that no one is compelled to fulfill those conditions. Indeed we stress in much of our theology that the manner of the divine self-disclosure to men is such that our human status as free and responsible beings is respected, and an awareness of God never is forced upon us. It may then be a condition of *post-mortem* verification that we be already in some degree conscious of God by an uncompelled response to his modes of revelation in this world. It may be that such a voluntary consciousness of God is an essential element in the fulfillment of the divine purpose for human nature, so that the verification of theism which consists in an experience of the final fulfillmemt of that purpose can only be experienced by those who have already entered upon an awareness of God by the religious mode of apperception which we call faith.

If this be so, it has the consequence that only the theistic believer can find the vindication of his belief. This circumstance would not of course set any restriction upon who can become a believer, but it would involve that while theistic faith can be verified—found by one who holds it to be beyond rational doubt—yet it cannot be proved to the nonbeliever. Such an asymmetry would connect with that strain of New Testament teaching which speaks of a division of mankind even in the world to come.

Having noted this possibility I will only express my personal opinion that the logic of the New Testament as a whole, though admittedly not always its explicit content, leads to a belief in ultimate universal salvation. However, my concern here is not to seek to establish the religious facts, but rather to establish that there are such things as religious facts, and in particular that the existence or non-existence of the God of the New Testament is a matter of fact, and claims as such eventual experiential verification.

ESCHATOLOGICAL VERIFICATION

KAI NIELSEN

Professor John Hick, in carrying on a discussion initiated by Professors Wisdom and Flew, argues that (1) divine existence, as it is understood in the New Testament, is taken to be a matter of objective fact, and (2) statements which assert that existence are empirically verifiable.[1] Hick does not try to show that "God exists" is true and that Christian claims have been established; rather, in "Theology and Verification" he is concerned with the *logically* prior question of whether it is *intelligible* to claim that divine existence is a fact.

I shall argue that Hick has not at all succeeded in establishing what he has set out to establish and that we have no good reasons for believing that such crucial theistic utterances are used to make statements of fact that are either verifiable or confirmable in principle. (Although I cannot accept Hick's central claims, I should like to record that it is a pleasure to read and evaluate critically Hick's writings, for he writes with a clarity and forthrightness of statement that allow his arguments to be appraised readily. The turgid obscurity typical of Tillich, Bultmann, Niebuhr, Buber, and Maritain may give some the illusory sense that they have grasped the esoteric "essence" of religion, but such a manner of writing does not actually contribute to an understanding of religion or to an appraisal of the claims of religion. There is enduring intellectual value in writing so that one's claims can be understood and appraised.)

I

Recognizing that the central intellectual perplexity for enlightened contemporary theists is not the difficulty of proving

From the *Canadian Journal of Theology*, 9 (1963). Reprinted with the permission of the *Canadian Journal of Theology* and the author.
[1] John Hick, "Theology and Verification," *Theology Today*, 17 (1960), 12–31. [The article may be found on p. 164 in this book.]

theistic claims but the difficulty of establishing their intelligibility, Hick's primary concern is to refute claims that religious sentences have uses which are *merely* mythical, quasi-moral, ceremonial, emotive, or ideological, and to establish that they characteristically are used to make factual statements—that is, that such sentences as "God exists" or "The world was created by an act of God" typically function to make assertions of "supernatural fact."

It is Hick's contention that "divine existence is in principle verifiable" (p. 12). For a statement to have *factual meaning* it must, Hick argues, contain or entail "predictions which can be verified or falsified" (p. 14). Hick does not contend that God's existence can be *falsified* but, contending that verification and falsification are in this context asymmetrically related, Hick argues that God's existence can in principle be verified. He does not claim that the verification can come in this life. The verification is eschatological; it will come, if at all, in the next life. It need not necessarily come as a "vision" but may be an experience of the fulfilment of God's purpose for ourselves, as it has been given to us in Christian revelation, in conjunction with "an experience of communion with God as he has revealed himself in the person of Christ" (p. 27).

Hick claims in "Theology and Verification," as he did in *Faith and Knowledge*,[2] that the notion of "eschatological verification is sound; and further, that no viable alternative to it has been offered to establish the factual character of theism" (p. 18). He also claims that it is not "an *ad hoc* invention but is based upon an actually operative religious concept of God" (p. 18).

It is important to note how Hick's insistence that the verification must be eschatological allows him to come to terms with Wisdom's argument that the existence of God is not *now* an experimental issue. Hick contends, in opposition to Wisdom, that the sophisticated Christian does not merely have different feelings or attitudes about the world and man's place in it. He does not view life in just a different way; that is, his difference

[2] Ithaca: Cornell University Press, 1957.

with the atheist is not the same as that which exists where two
people see the same ambiguous figure in two different ways
(e.g. the duck-rabbit, seen as either a duck or a rabbit). The
Christian's and the atheist's "opposed interpretations" of man's
life and the nature of reality are "genuinely rival assertions,
though assertions whose status has the peculiar characteristic
of being guaranteed retrospectively by a future crux" (p. 19).
There is then a real factual issue between the atheist and theist;
it is not just a matter of rival ways of "seeing," "viewing," or
"looking" at man's nature and destiny. But Hick does agree
with Wisdom that in *this life* we are like men looking at an
ambiguous figure. We cannot now settle by any appeal to experience the issue between the theist and atheist. There are no
signs that can unambiguously count as pointing to God; there
is no *present* evidence adequate to make it meaningful to assert
"There is a God" where this sentence is used to make a statement of objective fact; but "Christian doctrine postulates an
ultimate unambiguous state of existence *in patria* as well as our
present ambiguous existence *in via*" (p. 19). But Hick makes it
perfectly clear that this postulated state of an "eternal heavenly
life as well as an earthly pilgrimage" cannot "be appealed to as
evidence for theism as a present interpretation of our experience . . ." (p. 19). If we simply regard our experiences in this
life they are too ambiguous to allow us correctly to claim that
theism is a verifiable position. If we so limit our appeal, a
claim such as Wisdom's is quite compelling. But, Hick argues,
we do not need so to limit it. We can *conceive* what it would be
like to have an after-life and we can *conceive* what it would be
like to verify that there is a God in the "resurrection world" of
the next life. Thus, while we cannot possibly have any present
evidence for or against theism, and must now live by faith if we
are to believe, we can *conceive* what it would be like to have
evidence in the next life; and so the existence of God is, after
all, a factual issue and "the choice between theism and atheism
is a real and not merely empty or verbal choice" (p. 19).

It seems to me that Hick is correct in affirming that any
reasonably orthodox Christian—I do not speak of Tillichians—

would surely wish to regard the question of divine existence as a factual, substantive issue. If an orthodox Christian discovered that he and the atheists were *only* differing in picture preferences, he would then assert that the very foundations of Christianity had been destroyed. Religious talk is certainly embedded in myth and overlaid with ceremonial expressions; and it most certainly guides our behaviour and calls for a basic alteration of our attitudes; but, as Hick recognizes, certain key religious statements are also thought by believers to be factual assertions. If utterances such as "There exists a creator of the heavens and the earth" are not taken by believers to be factual assertions—myth-embedded as they are—theistic religious talk and hence Christianity itself would lose the character it has. If our task is to understand Christianity and not simply to redefine it to fit some antecedently held intellectual or moral ideal, we must come to grips with this assertional element in Christianity. Hick has courageously and honestly attempted to do just that. Like Barth and Crombie, and unlike Tillich and Braithwaite, Hick attempts to elucidate the Christian religion that we actually meet, and in one way or another contend with, in daily life; we sense here that Hick is actually trying to analyse the claims the Christian ordinarily makes. And this, to my way of thinking, is just what we must do if we ever are to get anywhere in an understanding of religion. I am not saying that this is all that either a theologian or a philosopher needs to do, but he at least must do this. Perhaps in that way he will make Christianity or Judaism sound very absurd; but perhaps they are absurd. (We must not forget Kierkegaard here.)

While I am in complete agreement with Hick on this methodological issue, Hick fails, in my judgment, to make the basic claims of Christianity intelligible on the very grounds on which he rightly recognizes that the believer demands they should be intelligible. Hick's arguments are clear and straightforward until he gets to the very crux of his argument and then they become incoherent. Hick recognizes the difficulty of trying to speak of God and he argues that language is never quite adequate to state the facts of which religious people are aware. He speaks as if thought could speed ahead of language and, independently of the forms of language, grasp what is the case. It is natural to want to say this, but can we really "escape language" in this way? Is it really an intelligible claim?[3] Given such complications, it seems to me aparent that we are in real darkness as to whether "there are such things as religious facts" (p. 31). It seems to me that the more plausible conclusion, given such a situation, would be that religious discourse itself is in conceptual confusion (and not just the theological and philosophical accounts of it).[4] This, of course, would be welcome news to the secularist and most unwelcome news to all but the most rabidly Kierkegaardian defenders of the faith. Thus it is understandable that theologians such as Hick, Farrer, and Crombie should try to make an intelligible elucidation of religious concepts. I shall not attempt here to show that religious discourse itself is in a state of conceptual confusion, but merely try to show that Hick's account of such discourse is not successful. But if my analysis is correct, the following problem, relevant to the wider issue mentioned above, is suggested. If Hick utterly fails to establish how "There is a God" is in *any way* verifiable and if Hick is right (as I think he is) in his claim that statements asserting divine existence typically are *intended* to be factual, verifiable claims, then, given the care and the skill with which he has stated the arguments pro and con, would it not be reasonable to assume there is something wrong with our *first-order* God-talk itself? If it can be shown, as I think it can, that the analyses of Crombie, Farrer, and Mascall result in similar failures, does not the assumption of the incoherent quality of the discourse itself grow stronger? It seems

---

[3] I shall not pursue this question here, but a study of the work of Pierce or Wittgenstein raises serious questions about the very possibility of thoughts that have no linguistic expression. For brief and more readily accessible analyses that bring out some of the crucial difficulties, see Alice Ambrose, "The Problem of Linguistic Inadequacy," in Max Black (ed.), *Philosophical Analysis* (Ithaca: Cornell University Press, 1950), pp. 15–37, and William Kennick, "Art and the Ineffable," *Journal of Philosophy*, 58 (1961), 309–20.

[4] I have tried to show how this is in an article, "Speaking of God," *Theoria*, 28 (1962), 110–37.

to me that this issue needs to be faced by theologians in a way in which it has not yet been faced.[5]

The above assumes that Hick's arguments will not do. I have yet to establish this. But it should make apparent the importance for the Christian of making out a case somewhat along the lines that Hick attempts.

I I

In making out his case for eschatological verification, Hick argues that it is intelligible to say that there is a continued existence after death. Hick is perfectly aware that we cannot take such a claim as simply a noble myth, but that it must be regarded as an empirical assertion if his case for eschatological verification is to be made out. As Hick himself recognizes, the truth of such a claim is not sufficient for his case, but without it eschatological verification is unintelligible (pp. 25–6).

Hick does not argue for what he takes to be the "Hellenic notion of the survival of a disembodied soul" (p. 21) but for "the specifically Christian (and also Jewish) belief in the resurrection of the flesh or body." God "by an act of sovereign power . . . resurrects or (better) reconstitutes or recreates" at least some human beings, giving them a "resurrection body" in "the resurrection world." The relation of the "resurrection body" to the "resurrection world" is obscure and puzzling, to put it conservatively. Hick readily acknowledges that such conceptions are very odd, but, however odd, they are (he avers) intelligible empirical claims. (Even *assuming* their *intelligibility,* I should think their very oddness and extreme implausibility would be a very good reason for those who tie their belief in God to such notions to give up their belief and place a belief in God in the same class with a belief in Santa Claus or in the Easter Bunny.) I doubt very much that either conception is intelligible. After all, what is this "resurrection world"? What

[5] This issue is obviously evaded in J. N. Hartt's obscure survey of the state and prospects of contemporary theology, "The Theological Situation after Fifty Years," *Yale Review,* 51 (1961), 84f.

counts as a space that is "a different space" from physical space? Has any meaning or use been given to the words "non-physical space"? What are we supposed to be contrasting with physical space, that either has or fails to have "properties which are manifestly incompatible with its being a region of physical space"? What is it to have a property manifestly incompatible with being a region in physical space? There is the assumption that these words have a use or a sense, but they do not and Hick does not provide us with one. But I wish to by-pass all these questions here. For the sake of the discussion, I shall not only grant Hick that all these notions are meaningful as empirical statements but I shall also grant that they are true.

The survival of a "resurrection boy" in a "resurrection world" is only a necessary but not a sufficient condition for the verifiability of theism. Hick puts it this way: "Survival, simply as such, would not serve to verify theism. It would not necessarily be a state of affairs which is manifestly incompatible with the non-existence of God. It might be taken just as a surprising natural fact" (p. 25). Hick must now show how it can be the case that when our "resurrection body" gets to "the resurrection world" we shall then come to know God.

In trying to complete his case for eschatological verification, Hick attempts to show that one can "conceive of after-life experiences which would serve to verify theism" (p. 26). He is looking for a conceivable *situation* "which points unambiguously to the existence of a loving God" (p. 26). Hick suggests that there are "two possible developments of our experience such that, if they occurred in conjunction with one another, . . . they would assure us beyond rational doubt of the reality of God, as conceived in the Christian faith" (p. 26). As we have seen, they are (1) an experience of God's purpose for ourselves as it has been disclosed in Christian revelation, and (2) "an experience of communion with God as he has revealed himself in the person of Christ" (p. 27).

The initial difficulty we feel about (1) and (2) is that they seem to presuppose some understanding of that very thing we are trying to understand. But let us see what Hick tries to do with these claims. He starts by telling us (*a*) that the content of

(1) is "depicted in the New Testament documents" and (*b*) that these documents indicate (at least to the believer) that to experience the "divine purpose for human life" is "to enjoy a certain valuable quality of personal life, the content of which is given in the character of Christ . . ." (p. 27). This experienced "quality" is "said to be the proper destiny of human nature and the source of man's final self-fulfilment and happiness" (p. 27). That there is such a divine purpose cannot be falsified but it can be verified. (I am troubled about the claim that something can be verified but not falsified, but for the sake of the argument I shall let Hick's claim here pass unexamined.) But how is Hick's claim here even verifiable in principle, without the *assumption* of God—a divine Creator? We are trying to come to understand how "There is a God" or "God created man" could have a factual meaning, but Hick's analysis requires us to presuppose the very thing we are trying to understand, for to speak of "the proper *destiny* of human nature" or of "man's *final* self-fulfilment" *assumes* that man is a creature of God, a divine artefact created by God with a purpose—an "essential human nature" that can be realized. Without such an *assumption*, talk of man's proper destiny or final self-fulfilment is without sense. Hick is asking us to pull ourselves up by our own bootstraps, for unless we understand what it is for there to be a God who created man with a purpose we can make nothing at all of (1).

I add "nothing at all" deliberately, for the believer's understanding of "God exists" or "God loves us" is not—as Hick claims—sufficiently analogous to a child's understanding of what it is to be an adult. Hick's analogy is faulty because the child, as soon as he can recognize anything at all, sees adults around him and is constantly in their presence, but Hick has not shown us how we can have a like idea of what "the divine purpose for us is" or what we mean by "God." We indeed know that these words have great emotional appeal for us, and we know that they would not have that appeal if religious discourse were treated simply as (*a*) a species of ceremonial discourse, (*b*) moral discourse touched with emotion, or (*c*) expressions of human commitment embedded in a mythical framework. Beyond this, we know that there are certain analytic statements we can make

about "God" (e.g. "God is eternal" and the like). But what we
do not know is what it would be like to verify "There is divine
existence." We have no idea at all of what it would be like for
that statement to be either true or false. Here the believer is in a
much worse position than the child. And, as we have seen, to
appeal to the divine purpose for man assumes we already know
what it would be like to verify that our lives have such a purpose. We do not know what must be the case for it to be true
or false that our lives have a purpose, a *telos,* a destiny or final
fulfilment. Our actions may be purposive and we may so live
that there is some purpose in our lives without its even being
intelligible that human life has a purpose or some final end.[6]
We do not understand how to break into this closed circle with
either God or man's destiny or a Christian revelation of our
"essential human nature." It is indeed true that we, who have
been brought up as Christians or in close proximity to Christians, know how to use this discourse. In *that sense* it is sheer
nonsense to say Christian chatter is meaningless, but Hick has
not shown us how we understand this use of language as a
factual or statement-making type of discourse. We do not know
what must happen for us to assert correctly that so and so is
"apprehended as the fulfilment of God's purpose and not simply
as a natural state of affairs" (p. 28).

Can (2) help? I think we are no better off here. (2) is the
"experience of communion with God as he has made himself
known to men in Christ" (p. 28). Hick acknowledges that we
do not know what it would be like to encounter directly an
infinite, almighty, eternal Creator. But Jesus, or Christ, comes
in as the mediator. "Only God himself knows his own infinite
nature; and our human belief about that nature is based upon
his self-revelation to men in Christ" (p. 29). Hick quotes with
approval Barth's contention that "Jesus Christ is the knowability
of God" (p. 29).

----

[6] Kurt Baier, *The Meaning of Life* (Canberra: University College,
1957), pp. 20f., has remarked appropriately that religionists often "mistakenly conclude that there can be no purpose *in* life because there is no
purpose *of* life; that men cannot themselves adopt and achieve purposes
because man, unlike a robot or a watchdog, is not a creature with a
purpose."

There is—as R. W. Hepburn has stressed in his *Christianity and Paradox*[7]—an ambiguity in this sort of claim. "Jesus was born in Bethlehem" or "Jesus died on the cross" are straightforward empirical statements. There is no puzzle at all about their logical status. Where "Jesus" and "Christ" are equivalent we can of course make substitutions and the resulting statements will also be uncontroversial. But "Jesus" and "Christ" are not equivalent, for "Jesus is the Christ" is supposed to be informative. "Christ" or "The Christ" is not intended simply to refer to a man—no matter how extraordinary. "Jesus," by contrast, simply refers to an extraordinary man. We well enough understand the referent of "Jesus," but where "Christ" is not equivalent to "Jesus," what does "Christ" refer to? Unless we already understand what is meant by "God," how can we possibly understand words such as "Christ," "The Christ," "The Son of God," or "Our Lord Jesus Christ"? How can utterances incorporating them be used to make verifiable statements? What would count as verifying them? What *conceivable* experiences, post-mortem or otherwise, would tell us what it would be like to encounter not just Jesus, but the Christ, the Son of God, and the Son of Man, or our Lord, where "Our Lord" does not just mean a wise teacher or a monarch whom we meet either now or hereafter? If we do not know what it would be like to verify "God exists" directly, we have no better idea of what it would be like to verify "The Son of God exists," where "The Son of God" is not identical in meaning with "Jesus." (*If* they are identical in meaning, "The Son of God exists" can provide no logical bridge to "God exists.") The same sort of thing can be said for "The Christ"; and if it is said that "Jesus" and "The Christ" are not identical but we have verified that Jesus is the Christ, then I will reply that Hick has not shown us how we can verify this statement. He has not shown us how we can logically move from "Jesus exists" to "The Christ exists" where they are not identical.

Hick apart, how could we verify "Jesus is the Christ"? What would count as evidence for it? If we say we verify it indirectly by verifying "Jesus lived and acted in a certain way,"

[7] London: Watts, 1958.

then again it can be asked what grounds warrant our saying that the verifiable statement, "Jesus lived and in his thirty-third year died on the cross," or any statement or statements of that logically unambiguous type, counts as evidence for "Jesus is the Christ." I do not see that we have any warrant for saying that it is evidence for such a claim. We might decide that Jesus was a powerful man; we might verify that he did many quite amazing things; our moral insight might lead us to say he was a superlatively good and wise man; but how would this at all point, ambiguously or unambiguously, to Jesus' being the Christ, unless we independently understood what was meant by "The Christ" or "X's being the Christ"?

No empirical sense has been given to Hick's "an experience of the reign of the Son in the Kingdom of the Father"; and we are in no position to say, as Hick does, that this confirms Jesus's authority to reveal God's nature and purpose and thus we can verify that there is a God. No method of verification has been given; we do not know what conceivable experiences would count for or against "God exists" and thus Hick has failed to give us any grounds for saying that "There is a God" or "God exists" "asserts a matter of objective fact" (p. 12).

Hick might reply that I am, in effect, arguing like a rationalist. I want a purely logical argument to prove that such experiences are experiences which point to God; but, as Hick correctly remarks, "the exclusion of rational doubt concerning some matter of fact is not equivalent to the exclusion of the logical possibility of error or illusion" (p. 17). To ask for the latter is to ask for what is self-contradictory; it is (in effect) to ask that a factual proposition be analytic. If we take this rationalist stand, then to have a post-mortem experience of "the Kingdom of God with Christ reigning as Lord of the New Aeon, would not constitute a logical certification of his claims nor, accordingly, of the reality of God" (p. 29). If in our "resurrection bodies" in "the resurrection world" we assert "Jesus is ruling over us all with love and justice" the truth of this statement would not entail the truth of the statement "There is a God" or "There is a divine purpose which is revealed through Jesus," but, Hick argues, such a post-mortem experience of

Jesus's reign would leave no grounds for rational doubt of these theistic claims.

I of course agree with Hick that a statement of evidence for a statement *p* need not be equivalent to the statement *p*. My evidence for "My glasses are on the desk" may be "I looked around a moment ago and I saw them there," but the first statement is not equivalent to, and is not entailed by, the second statement; but if this is granted should we not say the same thing here about Jesus as the mediator for God? Our evidence is a certain post-mortem experience of Jesus. It is true that I know what it would be like to see my glasses, while, apart from claims about a "direct vision of God"—claims which Hick does not espouse—I cannot, even in the next life, directly observe God (p. 26). But, after all, there are certainly very many statements that are only indirectly verifiable. We speak of a magnetic field or a superego and we cannot see either, but there are recognized procedures for verifying statements embodying such conceptions. They are a part of a whole network of conceptions, but within the appropriate scientific context there are recognized procedures of verification for statements using such concepts. Why can we not properly say the same thing about Jesus and Christianity?

One important difference is that in science we are more and more willing to take a conventionalist attitude toward such theoretical conceptions. Such conceptions can be seen as useful devices for systematically predicting and retrodicting certain observable events. But once having learned the lesson that not all substantives have a substance, we no longer feel incumbent to ask if there are any such things as magnetic fields or superegos. Such concepts are pragmatically useful constructs since they enable us to make predictions and assessments of behaviour with greater ease than if we did not have such concepts, but we can be quite agnostic about whether there are such things.[8] But the believer cannot be agnostic in this way about God, and he cannot regard the concept of God, *simply* as an important construct or as a useful heuristic device in his confessional group,

[8] Cf. J. J. C. Smart, "The Reality of Theoretical Entities," *Australasian Journal of Philosophy*, 34 (1956), 1–12.

and still remain a believer. (Note that this last statement is analytic.) As Hick argues, to claim "There is a God" is to make what purports to be an objective factual claim. But where we are willing to say that so-and-so is an objective factual claim we must know what could count as a confirmation of it. Sometimes our evidence is only indirect, but to know what the evidence unambiguously points to we must know what would count as observing or experiencing what the indirect evidence is indirect evidence of. As I sit upstairs I say to my wife, "The children are playing downstairs." I could give as indirect evidence: "They are laughing down there and someone is running around in the living room." But I only do this because I know what it would be like to see the children laughing and running around in the living room. But if we have no idea of what it would be like to experience that which we *supposedly* have indirect evidence for, then we in fact do not actually understand what it would be like to have evidence (direct or indirect) for it. We do not even understand what it could *mean* to say there is a so-and-so such that we have no idea at all of what it would be like to experience it, but something else can be experienced which is evidence for it. The "it" here cannot refer to anything, for in such a case how could we *possibly understand* what it is that our putative "evidence" is supposed to be evidence for? This is just the difficulty we have in using Jesus as the evidence for God. Hick's correct remarks about statements of evidence not being equivalent to statements of what they are evidence for is thus not to the point. We still do not know what is *meant* by saying that a post-mortem encounter with Jesus counts as the indirect (but sole) evidence for the existence of God. Thus we do not have a right to say, as Hick does, that we know what it would be like for our faith to be "so fully confirmed in post-mortem experience as to leave no doubt as to the validity of that faith" (p. 29).

III

Such conclusions as I have arrived at here might, if correct, lead Hick to a conclusion he merely suggests at the end of his essay (pp. 30f.). There he suggests certain considerations that would lead one to the conclusion "that only the theistic believer can find vindication of his belief." If one becomes a believer one's theistic faith can be verified; but the non-believer cannot verify it. Hick's reasoning is as follows. It may be that predictions concerning human experience which give us good grounds for asserting that God exists are conditional predictions, one is compelled to fulfill the relevant conditions.

> It may then [Hick argues] be a condition of post-mortem verification that we be already in some degree conscious of God by an uncompelled response to his modes of revelation in this world. It may be that such a voluntary consciousness of God is an essential element in the fulfilment of the divine purpose for human nature, so that the verification of theism which consists in an experience of the final fulfilment of that purpose can only be experienced by those who have already entered upon an awareness of God by the religious mode of apperception which we call faith (p. 30).[9]

Once more Hick in effect asks us to assume just what is in question. Granted, we can only verify "There is a table in the next room" if we can carry out certain conditional predictions which the statement entails. But these conditional predictions, these operations, are themselves very well understood. No one needs to approach them by faith, for any normal observer (where "normal observer" can itself be objectively and empirically specified) can verify them. But we have seen above how "God exists" does not have any comparable conditional statements which can be so verified or are so verifiable and hence so understood by a normal observer. We must, instead, appeal to that "apperception" we call faith.

This necessity makes "God exists" a very different sort of chowder. There is a further logical difficulty. If we understand what a statement (conditional or otherwise) *means*, then it is

[9] Hick presents a similar argument in his "Meaning and Truth in Theology," in Sidney Hook (ed.), *Religious Experience and Truth* (New York: New York University Press, 1960), pp. 208–10. Cf. Paul Edwards' response, *ibid.*, pp. 245–7.

proper to speak of having faith in its truth, or having faith that the evidence for it outweighs the evidence against it, or that certain experiences will verify it. *Given* these conditions, we could be fideists and approach God simply on trust. But what we cannot do is have faith in a proposition we do not understand, for in such a situation we literally cannot know *what* it is we are supposed to have faith in. If we cannot conceive of there being a state of affairs that would make "God exists' true or false, we cannot understand what conceivable state of affairs we are being asked to accept on faith. We can, by an act of faith, accept as true an antecedently understood proposition. In *that sense*, faith can precede understanding; but it does not make sense to say that we can certify the *meaning* of a proposition by faith; in that sense, understanding must precede faith. We can only have faith in something whose meaning we already understand; otherwise we cannot possibly have any idea what we are being asked to accept on faith. Hick assumes that, as knights of faith, we can somehow be conscious of God even though there is no understanding of what it would be like for there to be a God. But in such a situation we literally cannot have faith in God, for the statement "He has faith in God" cannot be used by him or by anyone else to make a factual claim and thus it cannot, in the requisite sense, have a meaning or a use.

There may indeed be a place for fideism but not on the level at which Hick sets the discussion. Questions of what is *meant* by x cannot possibly be settled by faith or trust. At the most, faith might lead us to try to fulfil certain conditions, but we would still have to understand independently of our faith *what* to fulfil. If my argument is in the main correct, we do not understand what it would be like to fulfil conditions which, once fulfilled, would result in anything that would count as a verification of God's existence. This being so, Hick's forthright argument has not established "that the existence or non-existence of the God of the New Testament is a matter of fact, and claims as such eventual experiential verification."

ABOUT 'GOD'

PAUL ZIFF

My text is a text: the utterance 'God exists.' The question is: does he?

1. The English utterance 'God exists' occurs in religious discourses in English (not in "religious language"—there is no such thing). The expression 'God' in that utterance is evidently a noun; furthermore, it is not a count noun (like 'bean') since it does not require an article. This is not to deny that there is also a count noun 'god' in English. Thus one can say 'If God exists then a god exists' or even 'God is a god.' This indicates that 'God' is not a noun like 'man' in 'Man is a rope stretched over an abyss' for one cannot say 'Man is a man.'

That 'God' is neither a pronoun nor a mass noun in the utterance 'God exists' is indicated by the fact that it is neither a pronoun nor a mass noun in English religious discourses; that it is neither a pronoun nor a mass noun in these discourses is indicated by various facts; e.g., that it does not occur in such environments as 'How much . . . exists?' 'A quantity of . . . exists'; that it takes 'he' as an anaphoric substitute as in, 'That God exists may be doubted but that some men think he exists, that cannot be doubted'; that the "wh—" form employed in connection with 'God' is generally 'who'; and so forth.

Hence it is reasonably clear that 'God' in 'God exists' is a proper noun, i.e., a proper name, or for short, a name.

2. A name may be introduced into a particular discourse either by both extralinguistic and introlinguistic means or simply by intralinguistic means. Since I take it that no one claims to have learned to use the name 'God' by extralinguistic means, i.e., no one (that I am concerned with) claims to have had the referent of the name 'God' indicated to him by osten-

Reprinted from *Religious Experience and Truth*, Sidney Hook, ed. (New York: New York University Press, 1961), by permission of New York University Press and the author.

sion, we may take it that the name 'God' has been introduced into those religious discourses in which it occurs solely by intralinguistic means.

'God' then is a name like 'Caesar' or 'Pegasus' but not like your name.

3. To introduce a name into a discourse by intralinguistic means alone it is necessary to associate certain expressions of the discourse with the name. Since these expressions will have certain conditions associated with them, this means that derivatively the name will have certain conditions associated with it.

(To state the matter more clearly but less precisely, what I am saying is probably that which is intended by those who claim that certain names are introduced into a discourse by means of descriptions.)

4. Consider the name 'Dietrich or Leipzig': I tell you that Dietrich wrote theological tracts entitled "On the Divine Pseudonyms" and "Celestial Conundrums." I tell you that he lived in Leipzig about 1400.

I have now introduced the name 'Dietrich of Leipzig, into the present discourse. I have done so by associating with it certain expressions and, thus, derivatively a certain set of conditions. Thus the referent of the name 'Dietrich of Leipzig,' if it has one, is that which satisfied a certain set of conditions, viz., a set having as its members the conditions of being a man, a resident of Leipzig about 1400, the author of certain theological tracts, and so forth.

5. I shall say that, speaking in what I take to be a familiar and relatively unproblematic way, the set of conditions we take to be associated with a name determines our conception of the referent of the name. Thus, given that the name 'Dietrich of Leipzig' has been introduced into the present discourse, you now have a certain conception of Dietrich.

6. Though a name may at one time have associated with it a certain set of conditions, at another time it may have associated with it a slightly different or even radically different set of conditions. If so, one's conception of the referent of the name will most likely have altered.

Thus your present conception of Dietrich may tarnish and

alter in time. You may discover that he did not write the tract on pseudonyms; if so, you will then have a slightly different conception of Dietrich. Or you may discover that he did not write the tract on celestial conundrums, but rather a tract on infernal paradoxes, and indeed that he did not live in Leipzig about 1400. If so, you will then have a radically different conception of Dietrich.

A name is a fixed point in a turning world. But as the world turns, our conception of that which is named by a name may change.

7. The questions whether the name 'Dietrich of Leipzig' has a referent, whether Dietrich ever existed, whether any such person as Dietrich ever existed, or whether anything answering to our conception of Dietrich ever existed can all be answered in much the same way.

It is necessary to specify the relevant set of conditions associated with the name and then determine whether anything or anyone ever satisfied the conditions of the set.

8. Questions whether the name 'God' has a referent, whether God exists, whether any such being as God exists, or whether anything answering to our conception of God exists can all be anwsered in much the same way and in much the same way as the analogous questions about Dietrich.

It is necessary to specify the relevant set of conditions associated with the name and then determine whether anything or anyone satisfies the conditions of the set.

9. But whether God exists is, in fact, a genuine question depends on (at least) two distinct factors: first, on the intelligibility of the conditions associated with the name, and secondly, on the consistency of that set of conditions.

To determine whether the conditions are intelligible and, if so, both self-commiting and mutually consistent, it is necessary to determine precisely what they are.

10. The first problem then is to specify the conditions associated with the name 'God.' And it is here that the confusion endemic in religious discourse takes its locus. We need not confuse the excubant theologian's febrile concept with that of a plain or even plainer man.

Different theistic groups are likely to have somewhat different and even competing conceptions of God. Presumably the God of the Christians is identical with the God of the Jews: yet Christians apparently suppose that the referent of the name 'God' satisfies the condition of either having been crucified or having had a crucified son; while Jews apparently suppose that the referrent of the name 'God' satisfies the condition of neither having been crucified nor having a crucified son. (It follows that either Jews or Christians are laboring under a misconception.)

Within a particular theistic group, the members of the group are likely to have different conceptions of God. And even a particular member of a theistic group is likely to have different conceptions of God at different periods of his life. To simplify matters I shall suppose that for the moment we are largely concerned with some particular conception of God.

11. All sorts of conditions have been associated with the name 'God'. For the purposes of the preesnt discussion it is useful to sort some of these conditions into two groups, viz., unproblematic conditions and problematic conditions.

12. Some unproblematic conditions are the conditions of being a being, a force, a person, a father, a son, a creator, spatiotemporal, crucified, just, good, merciful, powerful, wise, and so forth.

I class these conditions as unproblematic because its seems clear to me that each condition is, in fact, satisfied or readily satisfiable by something or someone; furthermore, that each condition is satisfied or readily satisfiable is a fairly obvious matter.

13. Some problematic conditions are the conditions of being omnipotent, omniscient, eternal, creator of the world, a non-spatiotemporal being, a spirit, the cause of itself, and so forth.

I class these conditions as problematic simply for this reason: if someone were to maintain that a traditional conception of God is unintelligible, I should think he would base his claim on the prior claim that such conditions as these are fundamentally unintelligible.

So the question is: are such conditions as these somehow unintelligible?

14. To suppose that the conditions in questions are unintelligible is to suppose that one cannot understand them. But understanding admits of degrees—I think there can be no doubt but that some of us at any rate have some understanding of these conditions.

I know that if something satisfies the condition of being an omnipotent being then there is nothing that it cannot do owing to a lack of power, e.g., such a being could transport a stone from the earth to the sun in less than one second. I know that if something is the cause of itself then we cannot succeed in finding another cause. I know that if something is the creator of the world then prior to its act of creation the world did not exist. And so forth. That I can make such inferences indicates that I have some understanding of the conditions involved.

15. The only general sort of reason I can think of to suppose that the conditions in question are somehow unintelligible is that it is evidently difficult to establish whether or not any of them are, in fact, satisfied. But although this is something of a reason to suppose that the conditions in question are somehow unintelligible, I do not think it is a good reason.

Understanding a condition is one thing; knowing how to establish that it is satisfied is another. For example, suppose I agree to do something on the condition that my friend George approves of it. There is no difficulty in understanding this condition though there may be some difficulty in establishing that it is satisfied. Suppose that I agree to do it on the condition that Caesar would have approved of it—there is still no difficulty in understanding the condition though there could be considerable difficulty in establishing that it is satisfied. And now suppose that I agree to do it on the condition that the last man ever to live, were he alive now, would approve of it: There is still no difficulty in understanding the condition and yet I have no idea how to actually establish that such a condition is satisfied.

16. I do not wish to deny that what I have called "problematic" conditions associated with the name 'God' pose all sorts

of conceptual problems, including problems of verification and confirmation. Thus, is there a difference between the condition of being a spirit and that of being spirits? If so, how do we count spirits? What principle of individuation is employed? (This is, of course, an old question, but all these questions are old questions.) Again, what is one to understand by creation *ex nihilo*? Of course, as Collingwood pointed out, one doesn't create something out of anything; thus we speak of creating a disturbance, a design. Even so, creation takes place in a certain environment, under certain environing conditions. The conception of first nothing and then something is a difficult one.

But despite such problems as these I do not think there can be any serious question about the intelligibility of the conditions in question. That they pose problems merely shows, if it shows anything, that the conception of God is a difficult one.

17. Similarly, I am include to suppose that there can be no great problems about the self-consistency and mutual consistency of the conditions in question. Again, there are problems of a sort. I would not deny it; how can something satisfy both the condition of being a being and that of being nonspatiotemporal? I suppose numbers might be said to be nonspatiotemporal, but then numbers are not beings. Such problems, however, are readily dealt with in obvious ways: contradiction can always be avoided by an appropriate and judicious feat of logistic legerdemain; conditions can always be weakened, modified, and so made compatible. This game has been played for over a thousand years.

18. Consequently it seems reasonable to suppose that whether God exists is an intelligible question. To answer it we need do nothing more than determine whether the conditions asssociated with the name 'God' are satisfied. Since that is evidently difficult to do, the interesting question then is: why is it difficult and can it be done, now or ever?

19. The difficulty in establishing whether or not God exists is obviously partially attributable to the character of what I called the "problematic" conditions associated with the name 'God'. All such conditions seem to involve some extreme form of either generalization or abstraction.

Thus the condition of being omniscient is an obvious generalization over the condition of being informed or learned. The condition of being the creator of the world can be thought of as a generalization over the condition of being a creator. On the other hand, the condition of being a non-spatiotemporal being can be viewed as the result of an abstraction from the condition of being a spatiotemporal being. The ease of such abstraction is testified to by the fact that plain people sometimes say they find it difficult to keep body and soul together.

20. The question we are concerned with is whether a certain set of conditions, conditions involving simultaneous generalization and abstraction, are satisfied. Questions of such a character are, I believe, not unreasonably classed as theoretic questions. Simultaneous generalization and abstraction is frequently a striking characteristic of scientific laws and hypotheses; thus a scientist may speak of all rigid bodies, of all bodies free of impressed forces, and so forth.

That a certain question is reasonably classed as a theoretic question is of interest only in that it indicates that one can reasonably expect to answer such a question only within the framework provided by a theory of some sort.

21. It is or should be evident that the question whether God exists can be answered only within the framework provided by some theory if it can be answered at all. For it is or should be obvious that no simple set of observations unsupplemented by powerful theoretic considerations can serve to determine whether or not anything satisfies the conditions in question, e.g., that of being an omnipotent being. That a certain being did not perform a certain task could not in itself establish that the being was not onmipotent, no matter what the task was. Again, that the being performed the task would not establish its omnipotence, and again that no matter what the task was. Projection or extrapolation of some sort is required but that is possible only within a theoretical framework.

22. But the difficulty in providing a final answer to the question whether God exists is only partially owing to problems posed by what I have called "problematic" conditions. It is primarily owing to the fact that, in fact, there is not one but

indefinitely many questions to answer. That each question is asked by the utterance 'Does God exist?' only shows that we put old names to new uses. The sense of the question 'Does God exist?' depends on the conditions associated with the name 'God': these may vary from case to case and they change in time.

23. Consider a plain man's conception of God: the name 'God' has associated with it the conditions of being an omnipotent being, creator of the world, and so forth. Then in answer to the question 'Does God exist?' one can say this: There is no reason to suppose so; there is excellent reason to suppose that no such being exists.

It is a tenet of present physical theory that no physical object can attain a velocity greater than the speed of light. Consequently, according to present physical theory, no being has it in its power to transport a stone from the earth to the sun in one second. But this is to say that no omnipotent being exists. Hence, according to present physical theory, nothing answering to the plain man's conception of God exists.

Present physical theory may be mistaken; that is always possible. But that possibility is irrelevant here. For no matter what form physical theory may take in the future, it seems reasonable to suppose that it will impose certain limits on experience: the existence of limits is incompatible with the existence of an omnipotent being.

24. Present physical theory, however, does not suffice to establish the nonexistence of God; at best, it suffices to establish the nonexistence of God as now conceived of by a plain man.

Man's conception of the world he lives in changes; that his conception of a creator of the world also changes is only to be expected. In consequence the question 'Does God exist?' may be freshly conceived, and so conceived may call for a fresh answer. That the answers to the old questions have always been no proves nothing. The answer to tomorrow's question is something that one can only be blank about.

PROFESSOR TILLICH'S CONFUSIONS

PAUL EDWARDS

1. Anthropomorphic and Metaphysical Conceptions of God

There is a tendency among believers, especially those who are professional philosophers, to make God as unlike human beings as possible. The opposite tendency, of regarding God as very much like a human being, only wiser, kinder, juster, and more powerful, is also, of course, quite common. In Hume's *Dialogues Concerning Natural Religion*, the believers in God, Demea and Cleanthes, are spokesmen for these two positions respectively. "His ways", remarks Demea, "are not our ways. His attributes are perfect, but incomprehensible." "When we mention the supreme Being", it may indeed be "more pious and respectful" to retain various of the terms which we apply to human beings, but in that case we "ought to acknowledge, that their meaning is totally incomprehensible; and that the infirmities of our nature do not permit us to reach any ideas, which in the least correspond to the ineffable sublimity of the divine attributes".[1] Cleanthes denounces Demea and those who share his views as "atheists without knowing it" (*ibid.* p. 159). He maintains that the divine mind must be regarded as a mind in the sense in which we speak of human minds, and when we apply such words as "rational" and "good" and "powerful" to the deity we are using them in one or other of their familiar senses—what we say is by no means incomprehensible.

I shall refer to views like Demea's as "metaphysical" and to those typified by Cleantheseas "anthropomorphic" theology. If this terminology is adopted then Professor Tillich has to be classified as a metaphysical believer. He is quite emphatic in his rejection of the anthropomorphic position to which he dis-

Reprinted from *Mind*, 74 (1965), by permission of *Mind* and the author.
[1] *Dialogues Concerning Natural Religion*, Kemp Smith ed., p. 156.

dainfully applies such labels as "monarchic monotheism". The
God of the anthropomorphic believers, Tillich writes, "is a being beside others and as such a part of the whole of reality. He
certainly is considered its most important part, but as a part and
therefore as subjected to the structure of the whole. He is
supposed to be beyond the ontological elements and categories
which constitute reality. But every statement subjects him to
them. He is seen as a self which has a world, as an ego which
is related to a thou, as a cuase which is separated from its
effect, as having a definite space and an endless time. He is a
being, not being itself."[2] No, God is not "*a being*". "The being
of God is being-itself. . . . If God is *a* being, he is subject to
the categories of finitude, especially to space and substance.
Even if he is called the 'highest being' in the sense of the
'most perfect' and the 'most powerful' being this situation is not
changed. When applied to God, superlatives become diminu-
tives. . . . Whenever infinite or unconditional power and meaning are attributed to the highest being, it has ceased to be *a*
being and has become being-itself".[3] God is that "which transcends the world infinitely". The idea of God is not the idea of
"some*thing* or some*one* who might not exist" (*ST*, p. 205,
Tillich's italics).

Like Demea, Tillich maintains that the words which we
apply to human beings cannot be applied to God in their literal
senses since God is so very far removed from anything finite.
"As the power of being, God transcends every being and also
the totality of beings—the world. . . . Being-itself infinitely
transcends every finite being. There is no proportion or gradua-
tion between the finite and infinite. There is an absolute break,
an infinite 'jump' " (*ST*, p. 237).

There is only one statement that we can make about God in
which we use words "directly and properly", *i.e.* literally, and
that is the statement that "God is being-itself". This statement,
it is true, can be elaborated to mean that "God as being-itself
is the ground of the ontological structure of being without being
subject to this structure himself. He *is* the structure; that is,

2 *The Courage To Be* (from now on referred to as *CB*), p. 184.
3 *Systematic Theology*, Vol. 1 (to be referred to as *ST*), p. 235.

he has the power of determining the structure of everything that has being. . . . If anything beyond this bare assertion is said about God, it no longer is a direct and proper statement" (*ST*, p. 239). Tillich does indeed in various places say such things as that God is Love or that God is living. But these, as well as any other statements ascribing characteristics to God, must be treated as "metaphorical or symbolic"[4] utterances. "Any concrete assertion about God", Tillich makes it clear, "must be symbolic, for a concrete assertion is one which uses a segment of finite experience in order to say something about him" (*ST*, p. 239).

God, as Being-itself, so far transcends any separate, conditioned, finite being that we cannot even properly assert his existence. God is indeed "the creative ground of essence and existence", but it is "wrong . . . to speak of him as existing". "God does not exist." God is "above existence" and "it is as atheistic to affirm the existence of God as it is to deny it" (*ST*, pp. 204-205, 236, 237).

It may at first seem pointless for an unbeliever (like myself) to take issue with a philosopher who concedes that "God does not exist". But Tillich does make other remarks which unbelievers would or should oppose. Thus he speaks of the "actuality of God" (*ST*, p. 239) and he also holds that unlike any contingent, finite entity, Being-itself possesses necessary being (it is not, as we saw, something or someone who might or might not exist) so that, as Sidney Hook has pointed out, "despite Tillich's denial, Being is endowed with a certain kind of existence—that which cannot not be".[5] But in any event, I do not wish to argue that Being-itself does not exist. To do so would presuppose that Tillich's talk about Being-itself is intelligible and this is what I wish to deny.

---

[4] *CB*, p. 179. When making admissions of this kind, Tillich seems to use "symbolic", "metaphorical", and "analogous" interchangeably and I shall also follow this practice. It is fair to add that in discussing the history of religious Tillich uses "symbol" in other ways also. For a critical discussion of Tillich's various uses of this word, see W. Alston's "Tillich's Conception of the Religious Symbol," in S. Hook (ed.), *Religious Experience and Language*, New York University Press, 1961.

[5] 'The Quest for 'Being,' " *Journal of Philosophy*, 1953, p. 719.

When I say, with certain reservations to be explained below, that Tillich's assertions about Being-itself are unintelligible, I am not merely applying the general positivistic condemnation of metaphysics to this particular system. The war-cry of the early logical positivists that "metaphysics is nonsense" does seem to be open to serious objections. For one thing, it is notoriously difficult to formulate a criterion of meaning which does not rule out either too much or too little and which does not have the appearance of being, in cerain respects, arbitrary and question-begging. There can also be no doubt that metaphysical systems are much more complex than some of the enemies of metaphysics believed—frequently they have all kinds of interesting and curious "links" to experience and they are only on the rarest occasions purely "transcendent". Granting this, it seems to me that the logical positivists nevertheless deserve great credit for helping to call attention to certain features of many sentences (and systems) commonly called "metaphysical". The metaphysicians are sometimes obscurely, but never, to my knowledge, clearly aware of these features. On the contrary, they manage by various stratagems to hide these features both from themselves and others. When, in non-philosophical contexts, it is found that a sentence possesses one or more of these characteristics, we do not hesitate to call it meaningless. We do not hesitate to say that it fails to assert anything.

I propose to show now that many of the most important sentences of Tillich's metaphysical system do possess certain of these features. Since they are put forward not merely as expressions of devout feeling or as vehicles of edifying pictures but as truth-claims, it would be interesting to know why, if they really possess the features in question, they should not be rejected as meaningless.

Throughout this article I am using "meaningless", "unintelligible", "devoid of cognitive content", "failing to make an assertion", "saying nothing at all", and "lacking referential meaning" interchangeably. I am aware that, as widely used, not all these expressions have the same meaning or the same force. For example, if I say to a taxi driver, "Go to Amsterdam

Avenue and 82nd Street!" this is "intelligible", it is "meaning-ful", it "says something", but it would not be said to possess "cognitive content" by those who use this expression at all, we would not say that I used the sentence to make an assertion and most of those who used the word "referent" would say that this sentence, like imperatives generally, was without referential meaning. I do not think that this departure from widespread uses is of any consequence for the purposes of this article, but in any event I would be willing to argue that Tillich's theology is all of the things mentioned—meaningless, unintelligible, and all the rest.

2. Tillich's Theology Is Compatible
With Anything Whatsoever

We normally regard as empty, as devoid of (cognitive) meaning or content a sentence which, while pretending to assert something, is on further examination found to be compatible with any state of affairs. If, for example, I say "Bomba is going to wear a red tie tonight" and if I do not withdraw my statement even if he shows up wearing a brown or a black or a grey tie, and if it further becomes clear that I will not consider my statement refuted even if Bomba wears no tie at all and in fact that I will consider it "true", no matter what happens anywhere, then it would be generally agreed that I have really said nothing at all. I have in this context deprived the expression "red tie" of any meaning. I have excluded no conceivable state of affairs and this, in the context in which people are attempting to make factual assertions, is generally considered a sufficient ground for condemning the sentence in question as empty or devoid of content.

Now, unless I have misunderstood Tillich, exactly the same is true of *his* belief in God. However, before showing this, it would be well to bring out as forcibly as possible the enormous difference between Tillich's position and the anthropomorphic theology of Cleanthes and of most ordinary believers. Cleanthes at one stage produces what he call the "illustration" of the "heavenly voice". Suppose, he says, that an articulate voice were heard in the clouds, much louder and more melodious than any which human art could ever reach: Suppose that this voice were extended in the same instant over all nations, and spoke to each nation in its own language and dialect: Suppose, that the words delivered not only contain a just sense and meaning, but convey some instruction altogether worthy of a benevolent Being, superior to mankind." We can make this more definite by supposing that the voice made statements about the cure and prevention of all kinds of illnesses, such as cancer, which are as yet very imperfectly understood, as well as about a large number of other unsolved scientific problems and that upon examination every one of these statements turned out to be true. It is clear that if such a voice were heard, Cleanthes would regard this as confirmation of the existence of God in the sense in which he asserted it. I think it is equally clear that most ordinary believers would be jubilant if such events occurred and that they too would regard their belief confirmed. I do not know how Tillich would in fact react to such events, but I know how he *should* react. The only attitude consistent with his position would be to be (theoretically) wholly indifferent to what happened. The heavenly voice would in no way whatever be a confirmation of *his* theology.

Since heavenly voices do not actually exist, this departure from anthropomorphic theology may not seem to be to Tillich's disadvantage. His position, moreover, may seem to possess a considerable advantage over that of believers in an anthropomorphic God who is declared to be *all*-powerful and *perfectly* good. It has often been shown that the existence of evil falsifies the belief in such a God, and it is generally admitted, even by those who stick to this belief, that the fact of evil presents a ticklish problem. Tillich's theology, however, is immune to any such attack. Since he does not maintain either that God is all-powerful, in the literal sense, or that he is all-good, in the literal sense, Tillich's theology does not imply that there is no evil in the world, in any of the ordinary senses of the word. In fact, even if the world were immensely more full of evil than it is, if it were such a frightful place that Nazi concentration camps and cancer hospitals would be regarded, by comparison, as utopian places of health and happiness and justice—even such a state of affairs would in no way falsify Tillich's view. Being-itself, *i.e.* God, would still be "actual".

The same would hold for any other aspect of the world. Whether human beings discover more and more order in the world or not, whether future scientific developments show space to be finite or infinite or neither, whether new observations confirm the steady-state theory of Hoyle and Bondi or the "bing-bang" cosmology of Gamow and Lemaitre—it all makes no difference: Being-itself would still be actual. Being-itself, as we noted, is not "something or someone who might or might not be". This may be true of the anthropomorphic deity, but not of Being-itself.

I hope that my point is clear now. Tillich's theology is indeed safe from anti-theological arguments based on the existence of evil, but only at the exprense of *being compatible with anything whatever*. All of us normally regard this, as I tried to show, as a reason for calling a sentence meaningless or devoid of cognitive content.

3. Being-itself and Irreducible Metaphors

As we saw, Tillich readily admits that only in the basic statement of his system are all words used in their literal senses. All other statements about Being-itself are "symbolic" or "metaphorical". Tillich not only repeatedly makes general statements to this effect, he also tells us on many, though *not* on all, occasions when he discusses the characteristics of Being-itself that the words he uses in characterizing the Ultimate Reality are not to be understood literally. Thus he writes, "If one is asked how nonbeing is related to being-itself, one can only answer metaphorically: being 'embraces' itself and nonbeing. Being has nonbeing 'within' itself as that which is eternally present and eternally overcome in the process of the divine life" (*CB*, p. 34). Again: "In a metaphorical statement (and every assertion about being-itself is either metaphorical or symbolic) one could say that being includes nonbeing but nonbeing does not prevail against it. 'Including' is a spatial metaphor which indicates that being embraces itself and that which is opposed to it, non-being. Nonbeing belongs to being, it cannot be separated from it" (*CB*, p. 179). Again: "The divine life participates in every life as its ground and aim. God participates in everything that is; he has community with it; he shares in its destiny. Certainly such statements are highly symbolic. . . . God's participation is not a spatial or temporal presence. It is meant not categorically but symbolically. It is the parousia, the 'being with' of that which is neither here nor there. If applied to God, participation and community are not less symbolic than individualization and personality" (*ST*, p. 245). And again: "But in God as God there is no distinction between potentiality and actuality. Therefore, we cannot speak of God as living in the proper or nonsymbolic sense of the word 'life'" (*ST*, p. 242).

Tillich sees nothing at all wrong in his constant employment of metaphors. On the contrary, he stresses the fact that without employing terms taken from "segments of finite experience", theological sentences would have little or no emotional force. "Anthropomorphic symbols", he writes, "are adequate for speaking of God religiously. Only in this way can he be the living God for man" (*ST*, p. 242). Tillich is indeed aware of the objection of certain philosophers that it is illegitimate to use terms which have a reasonably well-defined meaning in everyday contexts to make assertions about a reality that is infinitely removed from the contexts in which these expressions were originally introduced. He dismisses this objection without much ado. Such "accusations are mistaken", Tillich replies, "they miss the meaning of ontological concepts. . . . It is the function of an ontological concept to use some realm of experience to point to characteristics of being-itself which lie above the split between subjectivity and objectivity and which therefore cannot be expressed literally in terms taken from the subjective or the objective side. They must be understood not literally but analogously." This, however, Tillich insists, "does not mean that they have been produced arbitrarily and can easily be replaced by other concepts. Their choice is a matter of experience and thought, and subject to criteria which determine the adequacy or inadequacy of each of them" (*CB*, p. 25).

The rejoinder that "of course" the terms in question are used "analogously", "symbolically" or "merely as metaphors" exercises the same hypnotic spell over Tillich as it has on metaphysicians in the past. He seems to think that it is a solution of the problem. In fact, however, it is nothing of the sort. It is an implicit admission that a problem exists. The concession by an author that he is using a certain word metaphorically is tantamount to admitting that, in a very important sense and a sense relevant to the questions at issue between metaphysicians and their critics, he does not mean what he says. It does not automatically tell us what he does mean or whether in fact he means anything at all. When Bradley, for example, wrote that "the Absolute enters into . . . evolution and progress" it is clear that the word "enter" is used in a metaphorical and not a literal sense. But realizing this does not at once tell us what, if anything, Bradley asserted.

Often indeed when words are used metaphorically, the context or certain special conventions make it clear what is asserted. Thus, when a certain historian wrote that "the Monroe Doctrine has always rested on the broad back of the British navy", it would have been pedantic and foolish to comment "what on earth does he mean—doesn't he know that navies don't have backs?" Or if a man, who has been involved in a scandal and is advised to flee his country, rejects the advice and says, "No, I think I'll stay and face the music", it would be absurd to object to his statement on the ground that it is not exactly music that he is going to hear. In these cases we know perfectly well what the authors mean although they are using certain words metaphorically. But we know this because we can eliminate the metaphorical expression, because we can specify the content of the assertion in non-metaphorical language, because we can supply the literal equivalent.

The examples just cited are what I shall call "reducible

metaphors". I prefer this to the phrase "translatable metaphor" because of certain ambiguities in the use of "translatable". We sometimes say of the English version of a foreign original—*e.g.* of the Kalisch version of the *Rosenkavalier*—that it is a bad or inadequate translation although it does in fact reproduce all the truth-claims contained in the original. Conversely we sometimes, as in the case of the Blitzstein version of the *Dreigroschenoper*, speak of a magnificent translation although we know that *not* all truth-claims of the original have been reproduced. In the present context, however, we are exclusively concerned with reproduction of truth-claims and in calling a metaphor "reducible" all I mean is that the truth-claims made by the sentence in which it occurs can be reproduced by one or more sentences all of whose components are used in literal senses.

Now, Tillich and many other metaphysicians fail to notice the difference between metaphors which are reducible in the sense just explained and those which are not. When a sentence contains an irreducible metaphor, it follows at once that the sentence is devoid of cognitive meaning, that it is unintelligible, that it fails to make a genuine assertion. For what has happened is that the sentence has been deprived of the referent it would have had, assuming that certain other conditions had also been fulfilled, if the expression in question had been used in its literal sense. To say that the metaphor is irreducible is to say in effect that no new referent can be supplied.

It will be instructive to look at an actual case in which a philosopher gave this very reason for his accusation that certain statements by another philosopher were devoid of meaning. I am referring to Berkeley's attack on Locke's claim that the material substratum "supports" the sense-qualities. Berkeley first pointed to the original context in which the word "support" is introduced, as when we say that pillars support a building. He then pointed out that since, according to Locke, the material substratum is a "something, x, I know not what" whose characteristics are unkown and indeed unknowable, and, since, therefore, it is not known to resemble pillars in any way, Locke could not possibly have been using the word "support" in its "usual or literal sense". "In what sense therefore", Berkeley went on, "must it be taken? . . . What that is they (Locke and those who share his view) do not explain." Berkeley then concluded that the sentences in question have "no distinct meaning annexed"[6] to them.

Let us consider some possible answers to Berkeley's criticism without in any way implying that Locke himself would have approved of any of them. Perhaps the most obvious answer would be that Locke should never have spoken of the material substratum as an unknowable entity. It should really be understood as an aggregate of material particles to which certain adjectives like mass- and velocity-predicates can be applied in their literal senses. Locke's statement that the material substratum supports the sense-qualities can then be translated into some such statement as that the particular "gross" sense-qualities perceived at any moment are, in part, causally dependent on the distribution and velocities of the particles in question. On this view there would be no irreducible metaphors in the original sentence.

A second line of defence would begin by admitting that the material substratum *would* be completely unknowable, if sensory observation were the only method of becoming acquainted with objective realities. In fact, however, it would be said, we possess a "super-sensuous" faculty with which we "experience" such realities as material and spiritual substances. We could, if we wanted, introduce a set of terms as the symbols literally referring to the data disclosed by this super-sensuous faculty and we could exchange information about these with all who share in the possession of the faculty. If we call this the "intellectual language", then, so this defence of Locke would run, sentences with metaphors when containing terms from the "sensory level", can be translated into sentences in the intellectual language which will be free from metaphors.

Finally, in view of our later discussion, it is worth looking at a particularly naïve and lame answer to Berkeley. A defender of Locke, when confronted with the question "You do not mean 'support' in its literal sense, what then do you mean?" might say, "I mean that the material substratum holds the sense qualities together". The answer to this is obvious. "Hold together" is no more used in its literal sense than "support" and hence the difficulty has in no way been removed.

Turning now to Tillich metaphysical theology, it seems perfectly clear from numerous of his general observations that Being-itself is, even in principle, inaccessible to anybody's observation. In this respect it is exactly like Locke's material substratum. We do not and cannot have a stock of literally meaningful statements about it at our disposal which would serve as the equivalents of Tillich's "symbolic" statements. The metaphors in Tillich's sentences are, in other words, irreducible and hence, if my general argument has been correct, the sentences are unintelligible. If Tillich's statements are not to become propositions of physics or psychology or history no way out corresponding to the first of the defences of Locke is feasible. And unlike certain contemporary writers, Tillich does not avail himself of an appeal to mystical experience which would correspond to the second defence. For, if I understand Tillich correctly, he denies that even the mystic experiences Being-itself. The (true) "idea of God", Tillich writes, "transcends both mysticism and the person-to-person encounter".[7] As I shall show in a moment, Tillich does avail himself of a line of defence corresponding to the third of the defences of Locke. We already saw, however, that such a defence is altogether futile.

It may be said that I have not been fair to Tillich and other metaphysicians who defend themselves by insisting that they are using certain expressions metaphorically or analogously. It may be said that I have emphasized the negative implications of this admission—that the words in question are not used in their literal senses—without doing justice to its positive implications. For, it may be argued, when it is said that a certain word is used "analogously", it *is* implied that the term has a

---

[7] *CB*, p. 178. I am not sure that I have here correctly understood Tillich. He also seems to be saying the opposite at times—that mystics do have "direct access" to Being-itself. If that is Tillich's position then some of the criticisms which follow would not apply, but it would then be open to a number of other objections.

referent, namely a referent which is in some important respect similar to the referent it has when used literally.

This objection rests on a confusion. We must here distinguish two possible meanings of the assertion that a certain word is used "analogously". This may, firstly, mean no more than that the word in question is *not used literally*. But it may also amount to the much stronger claim that the word *has a referent* and hence that the sentence in which it occurs is, if certain other conditions are fulfilled, cognitively significant. If "analogously" is used in the former sense, then of course I would not for a moment deny that the relevant words are used analogously in Tillich's sentences and in the sentences of other metaphysicians. But this is an innocuous admission. For to say that the words are used analogously in this sense has no tendency whatever to imply that the sentences in which they occur possess cognitive meaning. "If "analogously" is used in the second sense, then, as just observed, it would automatically follow that the sentences are, if other conditions are also fulfilled, cognitively significant; but in that event I would deny that the terms we have discussed are used analogously in Tillich's sentences or in the sentences of other metaphysicians. To put the matter very simply: merely saying that a sentence, or any part of it, has meaning does not by itself give it meaning. Such a claim does not assure us that the sentence is intelligible. Similarly the claim that a sentence has an "analogous" referent is a claim and no more—it may be false. If I say, to use an example given by Sidney Hook,[8] that the sea is angry, the word "angry" really has a referent which is analogous to its referent when used literally. I can in this case specify the features of the sea to which I am referring when I call it angry and I can also specify the similarities between these features and the anger of human beings. If, however, I say that Being-itself is angry, I could not independently identify the features of Being-itself to which I am supposedly referring. Nor of course could I specify the similarities between the anger of human beings and the putative anger of Being-itself. My claim that

8 "The Quest for Being," *op. cit.* p. 715.

"angry" is used analogously in this sentence in a sense in which this implies that it has a referent would be false or at any rate baseless.

The narcotic effect of such phrases as "symbolic language" or "analogous sense" is only a partial explanation of Tillich's failure to be clear about the irreducibility of his metaphors. To tell the whole story one has to take notice of an aspect of Tillich's philosophizing which I have so far ignored. What I have so far brought out may be called Tillich's "modest" side— "modest" because he does not in the passages in question claim any literal knowledge about Being-itself. But there is also what may be called Tillich's "dogmatic" side. He then seems to be jotting down in a matter-of-fact way the characteristics of Being-itself, much as a doctor might jot down descriptions of the symptoms displayed by a patient. He then writes as if he had a completely unobstructed view of the Ultimate Reality. Thus we are told as a plain matter of fact and without the use of any quotaiton marks that "God is infinite because has has the finite (and with it that element of non-being which belongs to finitude) within himself united with his infinity". The expression "divine life", we are told, points to "this *situation*" (*ST*, p. 252, my italics). "The divine life", Tillich admits, "is infinite mystery", but we can nevertheless say that "it is not infinite emptiness. It is the ground of all abundance, and it is abundant itself" (*ST*, p. 251). Again, we are told, without the use of any quotation marks, and I do not think their absence is a mere oversight, that God "is the eternal process in which separation is posited and is overcome by reunion" (*ST*, p. 242). In one place, to give one more illustration of the dogmatic side of his philosophy, Tillich discusses the question of whether will or intellect are dominant "in God". He quotes the rival views of Aquinas and Duns Scotus and he notes that Protestants have tended to favour the latter position which subordinates the intellect. Tillich easily resolves this dispute as if he were reading off the truth by a quick glance at God. "Theology", he writes, "must balance the new with the old (predominantly Catholic) emphasis on the form character of the divine life" (*ST*, p. 248), *i.e.* it must assign equal rank to will and intellect in God. The divine life, we are assured, "inescapably unites possibility with fulfillment. Neither side threatens the other nor is there a threat of disruption" (*ST*, p. 247).

Tillich, the dogmatist, does not hesitate to offer translations or what I have called reductions of his "symbolic" statements about God. We can also express literally, for example, what we mean "symbolically" when we say that God is living. "God lives," the reduction runs, "insofar as he is the ground of life" (*ST*, p. 242). Again, our symbolic statement that God is personal "does not mean that God is *a* person. It means that God is the ground of everything personal and that he carries within himself the ontological power of personality" (*ST*, p. 245). And if we symbolically say God is "his own destiny" we thereby "point to . . . the participation of God in becoming and in history" (*ST*, p. 249).

I wish to make two observations concerning all this. Firstly, although Tillich gives the impression that the metaphors have been eliminated in these and similar cases, this is not so.: He never seems to have noticed that even in his basic statement, when elaborated in terms of "ground" and "structure", these words are used metaphorically and not literally. When Tillich writes that God or Being-itself "is the ground of the ontological structure of being and has the power of determining the structure of everything that has being", the word "ground", for example, is clearly not used in any of its literal senses. Being-itself is surely not claimed to be the ground of the ontological structure in the sense in which the earth is the ground beneath our feet or in the sense in which the premises of a valid argument may be said to be the ground for accepting the conclusion. Similar remarks apply to the use of "structure", "power", and "determine". Hence when we are told that "God lives insofar as he is the ground of life" or that "God is personal" means "God is the ground of everything personal and . . . carries within himself the ontological power of personality", expressions like "ground" and "carry within himself" and even "power" are not used literally. Tillich is here in no better a position than the supporter of Locke who substituted "hold together" for "support". That Tillich does not succeed in breaking

through the circle of expressions *lacking* literal significance, *i.e.*
lacking referential meaning, is particularly clear in the case of
the "translation" of the sentence "God is his own destiny". By
this "symbolic characterization, as we just saw, we "point"
among other things to "the participation of God in becoming
and in history". But a little earlier, in a passage which I also
reproduced, we were informed that "God's participation is not
a spatial or temporal presence" and twice in the same paragraph
we were given to understand that when "applied to God", participation "is meant not categorically but symbolically". In other
words, one metaphorical statement is replaced by another but
literal significance is never achieved.

Tillich constantly engages in "circular" translations of this
sort. Again and again he "explains" the meaning of one "symbolically" used expression in terms of another which is really no
less symbolic. Thus in a passage reproduced at the beginning
of section 3 of this article the sentence "being includes nonbeing" which contains the admittedly symbolic word "include"
is translated into "nonbeing belongs to being, it cannot be
separated from it". "Belong" and "separate" are no longer put
inside quotation marks and one is apt to suppose that some
progress has been made. Countless other illustrations of this
practice could be given.

Secondly, I have the impression that, in spite of his distaste
for "monarchic monotheism", Tillich occasionally relapses into
something not too different from it. When offering translations
such as those just quoted and generally when assessing the
adequacy of certain symbols as "pointers" to the "divine life"
Tillich seems to think that he has at his disposal a stock of
literal truths about God not too different from those asserted by
anthropomorphic believers. There is a remarkable passage in
which this is strikingly evident:

> Religious symbols are double-edged. They are directed
> toward the infinite which they symbolize *and* toward the finite
> through which they symbolize it. They force the infinite down
> to finitude and the finite up to infinity. They open the divine
> for the human and the human for the divine. For instance, if

God is symbolized as 'Father,' he is brought down to the human relationship of father and child. But at the same time this human relationship is consecrated into a pattern of the divine-human relationship. If 'Father' is employed as a symbol for God, fatherhood is seen in its theonomous, sacramental depth. . . . If God is called the 'king,' something is said not only about God but also about the holy character of kinghood. If God's work is called 'making whole' or 'healing,' this not only says something about God but also emphasizes the theonomous character of all healing. . . . The list could be continued (*ST*, pp. 240-241).

Now, if it were known or believed that God is "majestic" in the same sense in which human beings have sometimes been called that, it would make sense to call God a "king" and it would be right to prefer this symbol to symbols like "slave" or "waiter" or "street-cleaner". Similarly, if it were known or believed that God is "concerned with the welfare" of all human beings in the literal sense of this expression, then it would make sense to speak of him as our "father" and it would be right to prefer this symbol to symbols like "daughter" or "soprano" or "carpenter". An anthropomorphic believer has criteria at his disposal in such cases, but Tillich's non-anthropomorphic theology necesarily deprives him of it. Tillich says very correctly that this list of adjectives "could be continued". Since the "comparison" between fathers and kings on the one hand and the infinitely transcending, infinitely mysterious, indescribable Being-itself, on the other, is a bogus comparison, God may no less appropriately be said to be a soprano, a slave, a street-cleaner, a daughter, or even a fascist and a hater than a father or a king.

4. Bombastic Redescriptions of Empirical Facts

Readers who were less critical than Berkeley did not realize the meaninglessness of the sentence "the material substance supports the sense-qualities" or its equivalents chiefly because of the presence of words like "support" which automatically call up certain images. Similarly, I have no doubt that the presence of such words as "embrace" and "resist" and the mental pictures connected with them prevents many a reader from realizing the meaninglessness of Tillich's talk about being and nonbeing and their mutual relations. But there is also another reason why this unintelligibility is not always obvious. The reason is that, *in a certain sense,* some of Tillich's sentences are *not* unintelligible.

In this connection I wish to call attention to a technique which is employed by Tillich as well as by many other metaphysicians and certainly by all other existentialists with whose writings I am familiar. I will call it the technique of "bombastic redescription" and I think that one simple illustration will make quite clear what I am referring to. Some well-known chronological facts about Freud may be stated in the following words:

Freud was born in 1856 and died in 1939   (1)

The very same facts may also be expressed in a much more bombastic fashion:

In 1856 Freud migrated from nonbeing to being and
then in 1939 he returned from being to nonbeing   (2)

Now, let us assume for a moment that the author of (2) is not a metaphysician and does not in fact claim that (2) asserts anything over and above what is asserted by (1). In that events we cannot accuse him of uttering either a meaningless sentence or a falsehood, since what he says is perfectly intelligible and moreover true, or of performing an illegitimate inference; (2) does follow from (1) no less than for example "some mortal beings are men" follows from "some men are mortal". We can, however, point out that our author is employing needlessly high-sounding language to express a truth which can be stated much more simply and that (2) does not embody any grand new "insight" into anything whatever.

Let us next assume that the author of (2) is a metaphysician who assures us that (2) is not a set of simple biographical statements but belongs to "ontology"—the study of "being" and "non-being". He assures us that (2) asserts a great deal more than (1). In that event we would be entitled to reply, first, that it is not at all clear what, if anything, (2) means now, and secondly, that if it does mean more than (1), the step from (1) to (2) is not warranted. Our ontologist is thus either guilty of making a meaningless pronouncement and of performing an invalid inference or at the very least of the latter.

Let us finally assume that we are dealing with an exceedingly nebulous ontologist whose writings hardly ever contain anything that can be dignified as an "argument" or a "definition". Among his many observations about being and nonbeing he on one occasion includes sentence (2) and somewhere, not too remote in space, there also occurs sentence (1). This nebulous ontologist, unlike the other two people we considered, has not committed himself to any view about the relation between (2) and (1) and, because of this omission, he enjoys the best of two worlds. To certain uncritical readers, (2) will appear to be a profound metaphysical utterance—surely not just a redescription of the familiar facts asserted by (1). At the same time, however, (1) does remain in the background and the pictures aroused by it will tend to be vaguely associated also with (2). It will be felt that it is unfair to accuse the author of "wild speculation" since his ontological statement is "firmly rooted" in experience: after all, Freud was born in 1856 and he did die in 1939.

A more critical reader could, however, confront our nebulous ontologist with the following dilemma: either (2) merely asserts what is already asserted by (1)—in that event it is nothing but a bombastic redescription of familiar facts which hardly needed an ontologist or a metaphysician for their discovery, and in that event, furthermore, it is an *empirical* proposition and its truth is in no way incompatible with empiricism or positivism or any of the doctrines despised by ontologists; or else (2) does assert more—in that event it is not at all clear what, if anything, it does assert and secondly, as already pointed out, in that event it does not follow from (1).

In much of what he is doing, Tillich, no less than other existentialists, closely resembles this nebulous ontologist. Like that ontologist he talks grandiloquently about being and nonbeing and he goes even one better in talking about "not-yet-being". Tillich's observations about being and nonbeing and non-yet-being correspond to sentence (2). Like the ontologist, Tillich also either explicitly mentions certain well-known em-

pirical facts in conjunction with his ontological pronounce-
ments or, when he does not actually mention them, the language
chosen nevertheless very strongly tends to call these facts to the
reader's mind and, I am pretty certain, to Tillich's mind also.
This would correspond to sentence (1). Finally, like out nebulous ontologist, Tillich leaves the relation between his ontological remarks and the background empirical facts suitably vague.
In this way what he says simultaneously enjoys the appearance
of being profound, of revealing to us special insights into super-
empirical facts—facts about transcendent realms to which science and ordinary observation have no access but too which
"existential analysis" holds the clue—and of being quite intelligible and indeed "firmly rooted" in human experience, in the
"existential situation". Tillich is of course open to the same
objection as our nebulous ontologist. He cannot, logically, have
it both ways: either his ontological talk is merely a bombastic
redescription of certain empirical facts which are often trivial
and in no instance new; or it is not clear what, if anything, his
sentences assert and in any event they are not then warranted
by any of the empirical facts presented to the reader.

I will now give a few illustrations of this procedure. In
each case, I will first summarize, in bald and untarnished language, the empirical facts of the case whether they are openly
mentioned by Tillich or whether they merely hover discreetly
in the background. We might refer to this as the cash-value of
the doctrine in question. I will then state the corresponding
ontological doctrine and whenever possible I will reproduce
Tillich's own words. The reader can judge for himself whether
one is justified in confronting Tillich with the dilemma mentioned in the last paragraph.

Let us begin with the subject of man's most heroic deeds.

Cash-value: Selfishness and other unadmirable motives
are involved in even the best human actions.

Ontological doctrine: "Even in what he considers his best
deed nonbeing is present and prevents if from being perfect.
. . . Nonbeing is mixed with being in his moral self-affirmation
as it is in his spiritual and ontic self-affirmation (*CB*, p. 52).

Let us turn next to man's "creatureliness".

> Cash-value: Human beings have not always existed; all of them are born and before they were born or rather before they were conceived they did not exist; all of them also eventually die, and after they die they are dead, they are not then alive.

> Ontological doctrine: Nonbeing in man has a dialectical character.

> Full statement of ontological doctrine: "The doctrine of man's creatureliness is another point in the doctrine of man where nonbeing has a dialectical character. Being created out of nothing means having to return to nothing. The stigma of having originated out of nothing is impressed on every creature. . . . Being, limited by nonbeing, is finitude. Nonbeing appears as the 'not yet' of being and as the 'no more' of being . . . everything which participates in the power of being is 'mixed' with nonbeing. It is being in process of coming from and going toward nonbeing. It is finite" (*ST*, pp. 188-189).

Nonbeing, as we just found, appears at times as the "not-yet" of being. Ontologists can therefore hardly neglect the question of man's relation to "not-yet-being" and Tillich promptly addresses himself to this problem.

> Cash-value: Human beings frequently fail to have attributes which they may or will possess at a later time—for example, babies sometimes don't have hair, but later on their heads are covered with hair; a person may at one time know only his native language, but several yersa later he may have mastered other languages as well, etc. etc.

> Ontological doctrine: "Being and not-yet-being are 'mixed' in him (man), as they are in everything finite" (*ST*, p. 236).

5. Being, Nonbeing and "Some Logicians"

Tillich is much irked by "some logicians" who "deny that nonbeing has conceptual character and try to remove it from the philosophical scene except in the form of negative judgments" (*CB*, p. 34). As against the logicians, Tillich insists on "the mystery of non-being" and he recommends that the "fascinating" and "exasperating" question, "What kind of being must we attribute to non-being?" should be taken seriously. His answer to the logicians is worth reproducing in full:

> There are two possible ways of trying to avoid the question of nonbeing, the one logical. . . . One can assert that nonbeing is a negative judgment devoid of ontological significance. To this we must reply that every logical structure which is more than merely a play with possible relations is rooted in an ontological structure. The very fact of logical denial presupposes a type of being which can transcend the immediate given situation by means of expectations which may be disappointed. An anticipated event does not occur. This means that the judgement concerning the situation has been mistaken, the necessary conditions for the occurrence of the expected event have been non-existent. Thus disappointed, expectation creates the distinction between being and nonbeing. But how is such an expectation possible in the first place? What is the structure of this being which is able to transcend the given situation and to fall into error? The answer is that man, who is this being, must be separated from his being in a way which enables him to look at it as something strange and questionable. And such a separation is actual because man participates not only in being but also in nonbeing. Therefore, the very structure which makes negative judgements possible proves the ontological character of nonbeing. Unless man participates in non-being, no negative judgements are possible. The mystery of nonbeing cannot be solved by transforming it into a type of logical judgement (*ST*, p. 187).

Elsewhere, if I understand him correctly, Tillich repeatedly quotes, as support of his view concerning the reality of nonbeing, the existence of such "negativities" as "the transitoriness of everything created and the power of the 'demonic' in the human soul and history" (*CB*, pp. 33–34). I am certain that Tillich would also endorse Heidegger's appeal to such a "negative" phenomena as loathing, refusal, mercilessness, and renunciation[9] and William Barrett's discussion of the effects of blindness[10] as evidence for the same position. There are so many confusions here that it is difficult to know where to begin. Probably the most serious defect of Tillich's discussion is his failure to be clear about the real point at issue between himself and the "logicians". By the "logicians" Tillich presumably means philosophers like Russell, Carnap and Ayer[11] who deny that such words as "nothing" and "nobody" and "not" are names or descriptions. Although they deny *this*, there are two other things which the "logicians" do not deny. Firstly, they do not deny the existence of the various phenomena to which Tillich refers as "negatives". They do not deny that human beings quite often behave destructively, that they feel disgust, hatred, or what have you. Nor do they deny that human beings sometimes become blind or crippled in various ways and that the loss of eyes, limbs, or other parts of their bodies produces vast amounts of grief. Not only do the logicians not deny any of these phenomena, but it is difficult to see how anybody could believe or argue that such denials are logically implied by the view that "nothing" is not a name or a description. Yet,

---

9 *Existence and Being*, p. 373.

10 *Irrational Man*, pp. 256–257.

11 Russell discusses the subject of negation in "The Philosophy of Logical Atomism," which is reprinted in *Logic and Knowledge*, in *An Enquiry Meaning and Truth* and in *Human Knowledge—Its Scope and Limits*; Carnap in "The Elimination of Metaphysics through Logical Analysis of Language," which is reprinted in Ayer's *Logical Positivism*; Ayer discusses the subject in "Jean-Paul Sartre," *Horizon*, 1945, in "Some Aspects of Existentialism," *Rationalist Annual*, 1948 and in "Negation," reprinted in his *Philosophical Essays*. It is perhaps worth adding that the "logicians" are divided among themselves on the question of whether, in Russell's words, "there are facts which can only be asserted in sentences containing the word 'not'". William Barrett, who is the most lucid of the existentialist defenders of Nothingness, seems to think that their case would be helped if it could be shown, to use Russell's words once more, that "the world cannot be completely described without the employment of logical words like 'not'". This, however is a confusion. From the admission that "not" or "nothing" are indispensable it in no way follows that these words are names or descriptions since it is anything but obvious that only names and descriptions are indispensable.

unless such denials are implied by this view, references to phenomena like hatred or blindness are completely beside the point.

The logicians, furthermore, do not deny that "not" and "nothing" are words in the "object-language" and that sentences in which they occur are frequently just as "descriptive of reality" as affirmative sentences. I do not know of any "logician" who has ever denied, for example, that the sentence "there is no butter in the refrigerator" is as descriptive of the world as the sentence "there is butter in the refrigerator" or that the sentence "I know nothing about Chinese grammar" is just as descriptive as the sentence "I know a good deal about German grammar". It is again not easy to see how it could be argued that such denials are logically implied in the view that "nothing" is not a description. I for one also see nothing objectionable in saying that while sentences like "there is butter in the refrigerator" refer to "positive" facts, sentences like "there is no butter in the refrigerator" refer to "negative" facts, that the former sentence refers to the *presence,* while the latter refers to the *absence* of butter in the refrigerator. Whatever misgivings I have about this way of talking concern the use of "fact" and not the use of "positive" and "negative" as qualifying adjectives.[12]

Once the ground is cleared in this way and no appeal is made to such totally irrelevant matters as the existence of hatred and blindness or to the fact that "not" and "nothing" occur in descriptive sentences it is easily seen that the "logicians" are right and that Tillich and other believers in nothingness are wrong. It becomes plain that Tillich and his fellow-existentialists are wrong, not necessarily in believing in some mysterious realm or mode of being which they call "nonbeing" or "nothingness", but in holding that, if there is such a realm, it is named by the word "nothing", *as that word is normally used.* They are wrong, further, in believing that the existence of such "logical structures" as negative judgements implies any

---

[12] For an innocuous use of "unreality" similar to my use of "negative facts," *see* R. L. Cartwright, "Negative Existentials," *Journal of Philosophy,* 1960.

transcendent ontological truths. I need not waste much time over showing that words like "nobody" or "nothing" are not names or descriptions. If somebody asks me, "Who is outside?" and I say "Bomba is outside" and on a second occasion I answer "Mrs. Bomba is outside", "Bomba" and "Mrs. Bomba" function as names—they refer to unmysterious human beings. If on a third occasion I answer "Nobody is outside", the word "nobody" is not the name of a mysterious shadowy human being. It functions as a sign of denial. To say that nobody is outside is to say that it is false to maintain that anybody is outside. Similarly, if I say that Germany is separated from Russia by Poland or that New Jersey and New York are separated by the Hudson River, "Poland" and "the Hudson River" are names of certain things or areas. But to say about two objects or areas, the boroughs of Queens and Brooklyn, for example, that they are separated by nothing, is to say, in Ayer's words, "that they are *not* separated; and that is all that it amounts to".[13] One is not asserting here that the two areas are separated by a mysterious area which is named by the word "nothing". "Nothing", like "nobody", functions as a sign of denial and not as a name —either of something familiar or of something mysterious in a realm to which only specially gifted persons have access.

It is perhaps worth adding that the dispute is not, as Tillich suggests, between himself and existentialists on one side and "some logicians" on the other. It is between the former group and practically the whole of mankind. Ordinary people do *not* believe that "nothing" is a name. I do not suppose that ordinary people hold any explicit view on this subject, but any occasion on which the existentialist theory is presented to them, they regard it as a joke. They simply do not believe that anybody seriously advocates such a position. This surely is the only possible interpretation of the mirth provoked by such exchanges as those between the Messenger and the King of *Alice Through the Looking Glass*.

> "Who did you pass on the road?" the King went on, holding out his hand to the Messenger for some more hay.

[13] "Jean-Paul Sartre," *op. cit.* p. 18.

"Nobody," said the Messenger.

"Quite right," said the King: this young lady saw him too. So of course Nobody walks slower than you."

"I do my best," said the Messenger in a sullen tone. "I'm sure nobody walks much faster than I do."

"He can't do that," said the King, "or else he'd have been here first."

I have often wondered why existential ontologists pay so little attention to caves, hollow tubes and holes in general. These are clear instances of nonbeing which should silence any sceptic. In certain tablecloths, for example, it is the number and the position of the holes which determines the excellence of the tablecloths. This surely shows that holes are real negativities. I was pleased to come across a discussion of this subject in an essay entitled "On the Social Psychology of Holes" by the unjustly forgotten German writer, Kurt Tucholsky. "When a hole is filled", Tucholsky asks, "where does it go? . . . If an object occupies a place, this place cannot also be occupied by another object but what about holes? If there is a hole in a given place can that place be occupied by other holes as well? And why aren't there halves of holes?" In short: what kind of being must we attribute to holes? I hope that Tillich or some other existentialist will before long address himself to this question.

To my knowledge the only people who have believed that "nothing" is a name are certain metaphysicians (including, it is true, some of the most famous like Hegel) and *some* beginning students of philosophy who in their first gropings tend to assume that all words are names.

Tillich is right in regarding disappointed expectations and the erroneous beliefs connected with them, as one of the motives for the introduction of various negative terms. He is wrong, incidentally, if he thinks that it is only the motive—such phenomena as disagreement, refusal to give information, ignorance, rejection, in a sense in which this is not simply disagreement, have also made it necessary to employ these expressions. His statement that "every logical structure is rooted in an ontological structure" is true in the case of negation if it means no more than, firstly, that negative terms would not have been introduced into our various languages if it were not for disappointed expectations, disagreement, ignorance and other phenomena of the kinds just mentioned and, secondly, that they frequently occur in sentences which are descriptive of reality. His statement is not true if it means that the word "nothing" names a special reality which needs existentialists or some rival group of ontologists for its exploration. Tillich's error becomes very evident when we reflect that words like "or" and "and" also have "existential roots". We would not have introduced them if we never hesitated, if our knowledge in a given field were always complete, if we never felt the need to enumerate our possessions, etc. Again, there is no doubt that sentences containing "or" and "and" are frequently descriptive of reality. Yet not even Tillich has had the heart to add and-being or or-being to his ontological inventory.

3

RELIGIOUS EXPERIENCE

THE IRRELEVANCE TO RELIGION OF
PHILOSOPHIC PROOFS FOR THE
EXISTENCE OF GOD

STEVEN M. CAHN

Philosophic proofs for the existence of God have a long and distinguished history. Almost every major Western philosopher has been seriously concerned with defending or refuting such proofs. Furthermore, many contemporary philosophers have exhibited keen interest in such proofs. A survey of the philosophical literature of the past decade reveals quite a concentration of work in this area.[1]

One might expect that religious believers would be vitally interested in discussions of this subject. One might suppose that when a proof of God's existence is presented and eloquently defended, believers would be most enthusiastic, and that when a proof is attacked and persuasively refuted, believers would be seriously disappointed. But this is not at all the case. Religious believers seem remarkably uninterested in philosophic proofs for the existence of God. They seem to consider discussion of such proofs as a sort of intellectual game which has no relevance to religious belief or activity. And this view is shared by proponents of both supernaturalist and naturalist varieties of religion. For example, Søren Kierkegaard, a foremost proponent of supernaturalist religion, remarked: "Whoever therefore attempts to demonstrate the existence of God . . . [is] an excellent subject for a comedy of the higher lunacy!"[2] The same essential

Reprinted from the *American Philosophical Quarterly, 6* (1969), by permission of the *American Philosophical Quarterly.*

[1] For a partial bibliography, see Robert C. Coburn's "Recent Work in Metaphysics," *American Philosophical Quarterly*, vol. 1 (1964), pp. 218–220. Two comprehensive treatments of the subject are Wallace I. Matson's *The Existence of God* (Ithaca, Cornell University Press, 1966) and Antony Flew's *God and Philosophy* (London, Hutchinson & Co., 1966).

[2] *Philosophical Fragments*, tr. by David F. Swenson (Princeton University Press, 1936), ch. III, p. 34.

point is made in a somewhat less flamboyant manner by Mordecai M. Kaplan, a foremost proponent of naturalist religion, who remarks that the "immense amount of mental effort to prove the existence of God . . . was in vain, since unbelievers seldom become believers as a result of logical arguments."[3]

In what follows, I wish to explain just why religious believers have so little interest in philosophic proofs for the existence of God. I wish to show that their lack of interest is entirely reasonable, and that whatever the philosophic relevance of such proofs, they have little or no relevance to religion.

The three classic proofs for the existence of God are the ontological, the cosmological, and the teleological. Each of these proofs is intended to prove something different. The ontological argument is intended to prove the existence (or necessary existence) of the most perfect conceivable Being. The cosmological argument is intended to prove the existence of a necessary Being who is the Prime Mover or First Cause of the universe. The teleological argument is intended to prove the existence of an all-good designer and creator of the universe.

Suppose we assume, contrary to what most philosophers, I among them, believe, that all of these proofs are valid. Let us grant the necessary existence (whatever that might mean) of the most perfect conceivable Being, a Being who is all-good and is the designer and creator of the universe. What implications can be drawn from this fact which would be of relevance to human life? In other words, what difference would it make in men's lives if God existed?[4]

Perhaps some men would feel more secure in the knowledge that the universe had been planned by an all-good Being. Others, perhaps, would feel insecure, realizing the extent to which their very existence depended upon the will of this

[3] *The Future of the American Jew* (New York, The Macmillan Company, 1948), p. 171.

[4] I am not concerned here with the implications of God's omniscience and omnipotence for man's free will. It is possible to interpret these divine attributes in such a way as not to entail the loss of man's free will, and for the purposes of this essay, I shall assume such an interpretation.

Being. In any case, most men, either out of fear or respect, would wish to act in accordance with the moral code advocated by this Being.

Note, however, that the proofs for the existence of God provide us with no hint whatever as to which actions God wishes us to perform, or what we ought to do so as to please or obey Him. We may affirm that God is all-good and yet have no way of knowing what the highest moral standards are. All we may be sure of is that whatever these standards may be, God always acts in accordance with them. One might assume that God would have implanted the correct moral standards in men's minds, but this seems doubtful in view of the wide variance in men's moral standards. Which of these numerous standards, if any, is the correct one is not known, and no appeal to a proof for the existence of God will cast the least light upon the matter.

For example, assuming that it can be proven that God exists, is murder immoral? One might argue that since God created man, it is immoral to murder, since it is immoral to destroy what God in His infinite wisdom and goodness has created. This argument, however, fails on several grounds. First, if God created man, He also created germs, viruses, disease-carrying rats, and man-eating sharks. Does it follow from the fact that God created these things that they ought not to be eliminated? Secondly, if God arranged for men to live, He also arranged for men to die. Does it follow from this that by committing murder we are assisting the work of God? Thirdly, if God created man, He provided him with the mental and physical capacity to commit murder. Does it follow from this that God wishes men to commit murder? Clearly, the attempt to deduce moral precepts from the fact of God's existence is but another case of trying to do what Hume long ago pointed out to be logically impossible, viz., the deduction of normative judgments from factual premises. No such deduction is valid, and, thus, any moral principle is consistent with the existence of God.

The fact that the proofs of God's existence afford no means of distinguishing good from evil has the consequence that no man can be sure of how to obey God and do what is best in His eyes. One may hope that his actions are in accord with God's standards, but no test is available to check on this. Some seemingly good men suffer great ills, and some seemingly evil men achieve great happiness. Perhaps in a future life these things are rectified, but we have no way of ascertaining which men are ultimately rewarded and which are ultimately punished.

One can imagine that if a group of men believed in God's existence, they would be most anxious to learn His will, and consequently, they would tend to rely upon those individuals who claimed to know the will of God. Diviners, seers, and priests would be in a position of great influence. No doubt competition between them would be severe, for no man could be sure which of these oracles to believe. Assuming that God made no effort to reveal His will by granting one of these oracles truly superhuman powers (though, naturally, each oracle would claim that he possessed such powers), no man could distinguish the genuine prophet from the fraud.

It is clear that the situation I have described is paralleled by a stage in the actual development of religion. What men wanted at this stage was some way to find out the will of God. Individual prophets might gain a substantial following, but prophets died and their vital powers died with them. What was needed on practical grounds was a permanent record of God's will as revealed to His special prophet. And this need was eventually met by the writing of holy books, books in which God's will was revealed in a permanent fashion.

But there was more than one such book. Indeed, there were many such books. Which was to be believed? Which moral code was to be followed? Which prayers were to be recited? Which rituals were to be performed? Proofs for the existence of God are silent upon these crucial matters.

There is only one possible avenue to God's will. One must undergo a personal experience in which one senses the presence of God and apprehends which of the putative holy books is the genuine one. But it is most important not to be deceived in this experience. One must be absolutely certain that it is God whose presence one is experiencing and whose will one is apprehending. In other words, one must undergo a self-validating experience, one which carries its own guarantee of infallibility.

If one undergoes what he believes to be such an experience, he then is certain which holy book is the genuine one, and consequently he knows which actions, prayers, and rituals God wishes him to engage in. But notice that if he knows this, he has necessarily validated the existence of God, for unless he is absolutely certain that he has experienced God's presence, he cannot be sure that the message he has received is true. Thus, he has no further need for a proof of God's existence.

For one who does not undergo what he believes to be such a self-validating experience, several possibilities remain open. He may accept the validity of another person's self-validating experience. He thereby accepts the holy book which has been revealed as genuine, and he thereby also accepts the existence of God, since unless he believed that this other person had experienced the presence of God, he would not accept this person's opinion as to which is the genuine book.

It is possible, however, that one does not accept the validity of another person's supposedly self-validating experience. This may be due either to philosophical doubts concerning the logical possibility of such an experience[5] or simply to practical doubts that anyone has, in fact, ever undergone such an experience. In either case, adherence to a particular supernatural religion is unreasonable.

But having no adherence to a supernatural religion does not imply that one does not still face the serious moral dilemmas which are inherent in life. How are these dilemmas to be solved? To believe that God exists is of no avail, for one cannot learn His will. Therefore, one must use one's own judgment. But this need not be solely an individual effort. One may join others in a communal effort to propound and promulgate a moral code. Such a group may have its own distinctive prayers and rituals which emphasize various aspects of the group's beliefs. Such a

---

[5] Such doubts are forcefully expressed in C. B. Martin's *Religious Belief* (Ithaca, Cornell University Press, 1959), ch. V. [The chapter may be found on p. 246 in this book.]

naturalistic religious organization does not depend upon its members' belief in the existence of God, for such a belief is irrelevant to the religious aims and activities of the group.

Is it surprising then that proponents of both supernaturalist and naturalist religion are uninterested in philosophic proofs for the existence of God? Not at all. A supernaturalist believes in God because of a personal self-validating experience which has shown him (or someone he trusts) not only that God exists, but also what His will is. A philosophic proof of the existence of God is thus of no use to the supernaturalist. If the proof is shown to be valid, it merely confirms what he already knows on the much stronger evidence of personal experience. If the proof is shown to be invalid, it casts no doubt on a self-validating experience.

On the other hand, a naturalist believes either that no one has learned or that no one can learn the will of God. If, therefore, a proof for the existence of God is shown to be valid, this has no implications for the naturalist, for such a proof does not provide him with any information which he can utilize in his religious practice. If, on the contrary, a proof for the existence of God is shown to be invalid, this casts no doubt on the naturalist's religious views, since these views have been formulated indepenently of a belief in the existence of God.

Who, then, is concerned with philosophic proofs for the existence of God? First, theer are those who believe that if such proofs are invalid, religion is thereby undermined. This is, as I have shown, a wholly erroneous view. Neither supernaturalist nor naturalist religion depends at all upon philosophic proofs for the existence of God. To attack religion on the grounds that it cannot provide a philosophic proof for the existence of God is an instance of *ignoratio elenchi*.

Secondly, there are those who believe that if the philosophic proofs for the existence of God are invalid, our moral commitments are necessarily undermined. This is also, as I have shown, a wholly erroneous view. It is, however, a common view, and one which underlies the so-called moral argument for the existence of God. According to this argument, it is only if one believes in the existence of God that one can reasonably commit oneself to respect the importance of moral values. This argument is invalid, however, for, as I have shown, belief in the existence of God is compatible with any and all positions on moral issues. It is only if one can learn the will of God that one can derive any moral implications from His existence.

Thirdly, there are philosophers who discuss proofs for the existence of God because of the important philosophical issues which are brought to light and clarified in such discussions. So long as philosophers are aware of the purpose which their discussions serve, all is well and good. It is when philosophers and others use discussions of this sort as arguments for and against religion that they overstep their bounds. Religion may be rationally attacked or defended, but to refute philosophic proofs for the existence of God is not to attack religion, and to support philosophic proofs for the existence of God is not to defend religion.

"SEEING" GOD

C. B. MARTIN

Religious people may feel impatient with the harshness of
argument in the last chapter. They may feel confident that they
have something that nonreligious people lack, namely, a direct
experience or apprehension of God. They may claim that such
religious experience is a way of knowing God's existence. This
claim must now be examined.

We shall first consider accounts of religious experience that
seem to sacrifice an existential claim for the security of the
feeling of the moment. There is an influential and subtle group
of religious thinkers who would not insist upon any existential
claim. My remarks are largely irrelevant to this group. It would
be hasty to describe their religious belief as "subjective" or to
employ any other such general descriptive term. For example,
the "call," in even the most liberal and "subjective" Quaker
sects, could not be reduced to statements about feelings. The
"call," among other things, implies a mission or intricate pattern of behavior. The nonsubjective element of the "call" is
evident, because insofar as one failed to live in accordance with
a mission just so far would the genuineness of the "call" be
questioned. It will be seen that this verification procedure is
necessarily not available in the religious way of knowing to be
examined.

In the second part of the chapter we shall consider accounts
of religious experience that are not so easily reduced to mere
subjectivity.

I

We are rejecting logical argument of any kind as the
first chapter of our theology or as representing the process by

Reprinted from C. B. Martin: *Religious Belief.* © 1959 by Cornell
University. Used by permission of Cornell University Press.

which God comes to be known. We are holding that our knowledge of God rests rather on the revelation of His personal Presence as Father, Son, and Holy Spirit. . . . Of such a Presence it must be true that to those who have never been confronted with it argument is useless, while to those who have it is superfluous.[1]

It is not as the result of an inference of any kind, whether explicit or implicit, whether laboriously excogitated or swiftly intuited, that the knowledge of God's reality comes to us. It comes rather through our direct, personal encounter with Him in the Person of Jesus Christ His Son our Lord.[2]

It will not be possible to describe the compelling touch of God otherwise than as the compelling touch of God. To anyone who has no such awareness of God, leading at it does to the typically religious attitudes of obeisance and worship, it will be quite impossible to indicate what is meant; one can only hope to evoke it, on the assumption that the capacity to become aware of God is part of normal nature like the capacity to see light or to hear sound.[3]

The arguments of the theologians quoted have been taken out of context. The quotations by themselves do not give a faithful or complete impression of their total argument. The following quotations from Professor Farmer indicate two further lines of argument which cannot be discussed here.

For what we have now in mind is no demonstrative proofs *from* the world, but rather confirmatory considerations which present themselves to us when we bring belief in God with us *to* the world. It is a matter of the coherence of the belief with other facts. If we find that the religious intuition which has arisen from other sources provides the mind with a thought in terms of which much else can without forcing be construed,

[1] John Baillie, *Our Knowledge of God* (London: Oxford University Press, 1949), p. 132.

[2] *Ibid.*, p. 143.

[3] H. H. Farmer, *Towards Belief in God* (London: S. C. M. Press, 1942), Pt. II, p. 40.

then that is an intellectual satisfaction, and a legitimate confirmation of belief, which it would be absurd to despise.[4]

We shall first speak in general terms of what may be
called the human situation and need, and thereafter we shall
try to show how belief in God, as particularized in its Christian
form (though still broadly set forth), fits on to this situation
and need.[5]

The alleged theological way of knowing may be described
as follows: I have direct experience (knowledge, acquaintance,
apprehension) of God; therefore I have valid reason to believe
that God exists. By this it may be meant that the statement "I
have had direct experience of God, but God does not exist" is
contradictory. If so, the assertion that "I have had direct experience of God" commits one to the assertion that God exists.
From this it follows that "I have had direct experience of God"
is more than a psychological statement, because it claims more
than the fact that I have certain experiences—it claims that God
exists. On this interpretation the argument is deductively valid.
The assertion "I have direct experience of God" includes the
assertion "God exists." Thus, the conclusion "Therefore, God
exists" follows tautologically.

Unfortunately, this deduction is useless. If the deduction
were to be useful, the addition of the existential claim "God
exists" to the psychological claim of having religious experiences would have to be shown to be warrantable, and this cannot be done.

Consider the following propositions: (1) I feel as if an
unseen person were interested in (willed) my welfare. (2) I
feel an elation quite unlike any I have ever felt before. (3) I
have feelings of guilt and shame at my sinfulness. (4) I feel as
if I were committed to bending all my efforts to living in a
certain way. These propositions state only that I have certain
complex feelings and experiences. Nothing else follows deductively. The only thing that I can establish beyond possible cor-

---

[4] *Ibid.*, p. 113.
[5] *Ibid.*, p. 62.

rection on the basis of having certain feelings and experiences is that I have these feelings and sensations. No matter how unique people may think their experience to be, it cannot do the impossible.

Neither is the addition of the existential claim "God exists" to the psychological claim made good by any inductive argument. There are no tests agreed upon to establish genuine experience of God and distinguish it decisively from the nongenuine.[6] Indeed, many theologians deny the possibility of any such test or set of tests.

The believer may persuade us that something extraordinary has happened by saying, "I am a changed man since 6:37 P.M., May 6, 1939." This is a straightforward empirical statement. We can test it by noticing whether or not he has given up his bad habits. We may allow the truth of the statement even if he has not given up his bad habits, because we may find evidence of bad conscience, self-searching and remorse that had not been present before that date.

However, if the believer says, "I had a direct experience of God at 6:37 P.M., May 6, 1939," this is not an empirical statement in the way that the other statement is. How could we check its truth? No matter how much or how little his subsequent behavior, such as giving up bad habits and so on, is affected, it could never prove or disprove his statement.

An important point to note is that theologians tend to discourage any detailed description of the required experience ("apprehension of God").[7] The more naturalistic and detailed the description of the required experience becomes, the easier would it become to deny the existential claim. One could say, "Yes, I had those very experiences, but they certainly did not convince me of God's existence." The only sure defense here would be for the theologian to make the claim analytic: "You couldn't have those experiences and at the same time sincerely deny God's existence."

The way in which many theologians talk would seem to

[6] This will be qualified in the second part of this chapter.
[7] The detailed descriptions of the Catholic mystics will be discussed later.

show that they think of knowing God as something requiring a kind of sixth sense. The Divine Light is not of a color usually visible only to eagles, and the Voice of God is not of a pitch usually audible only to dogs. No matter how much more keen our senses became, we should be no better off than before. The sixth sense, therefore, must be very different from the other five.

This supposed religious sense has no vocabulary of its own but depends upon metaphors drawn from the other senses. There are no terms which apply to it and it alone. There is a vocabulary for what is sensed but not for the sense. We "see" the Holy, the Numinous, the Divine. In a similar way we often speak of "hearing" the voice of conscience and "seeing" logical connections. By using this metaphor we emphasize the fact that often we come to understand the point of an argument or problem in logic suddenly. We mark this occurrence by such phrases as "the light dawned," "understood it in a flash." Such events are usually described in terms of a complete assurance that one's interpretation is correct and a confidence that one will tend to be able to reproduce or recognize the argument or problem in various contexts in the future. But a vitally important distinction between this "seeing" and the religious "seeing" is that there is a checking procedure for the former but not for the latter. If, while doing a problem in geometry you "see" that one angle is equal to another and then on checking over your proof find that they are not equal after all, you say "I didn't really 'see,' I only thought I did."

The religious way of knowing is described as being unique. No one can deny the existence of feelings and experiences which the believer calls "religious," and one can deny their power. Because of this and because the way of knowing by direct experience is neither inductive nor deductive, theologians have tried to give this way of knowing a special status. One way of doing this is to claim that religious experience is unique and incommunicable.

Professor Baillie, in likening our knowledge of God to our knowledge of other minds, says that it is "like our knowledge of tridimensional space and all other primary modes of knowledge, something that cannot be imagined by one who does not already possess it, since it cannot be described to him in terms of anything else than itself."[8] This kind of comparison is stated in the two sentences following, and we shall now examine the similarities and dissimilarities between them. (1) You don't know what the experience of God is until you have had it. (2) You don't know what the color blue is until you have seen it. Farmer says, "All the basic elements in our experience are incommunicable. Who could describe light and colour to one who has known nothing but darkness?"[9] All that Farmer proves is that a description of one group of sensations A in terms of another set of sensations B is never sufficient for knowing group A. According to this definition of "know," in order to know one must have those sensations. Thus, all that is proved is that, in order to know what religious experience is, one must have a religious experience. This helps in no way at all to prove that such experience is direct apprehension of God and helps in no way to support the existential claim "God exists."

Farmer makes the point that describing the experience of God to an unbeliever is like describing color to a man blind from birth. So it is, in the sense that the believer has usually had experiences which the unbeliever has not. However, it is also very much unlike. The analogy breaks down at some vital points.

The blind man may have genuine, though incomplete knowledge of color. He may have an instrument for detecting wave lengths, and the like. Indeed, he may even increase our knowledge of color. More important still, the blind man may realize the differences in powers of prediction between himself and the man of normal eyesight. He is well aware of the fact that, unlike himself, the man of normal eyesight does not have to wait to hear the rush of the bull in order to be warned.

This point concerning differences in powers of prediction is connected with the problem of how we are to know when someone has the direct experience of God or even when we ourselves have the direct experience of God. It was shown above how the situation is easier in the case of the blind man

[8] Baillie, *Our Knowledge of God*, p. 217.
[9] Farmer, *Towards Belief in God*, p. 41.

knowing about color. It is only when one comes to such a case as knowing God that the society of tests and checkup procedures, which surround other instances of knowing, completely vanishes. What is put in the place of these tests and checking procedures is an immediacy of knowledge that is suposed to carry its own guarantee. This feature will be examined later.

It is true that the man of normal vision has a way of knowing color which the blind man does not have, that is, he can see colored objects. However, as we have seen, it would be wrong to insist that this is the only way of knowing color and that the blind man has *no* way of knowing color. Perhaps Farmer has this in mind when he tries to make an analogy between the incommunicability of the believer's direct knowledge of God to the unbeliever and the incommunicability of the normal man's knowledge of color to the blind man. The analogy is justified if "knowing color" is made synonymous with "having color sensations." On this account, no matter how good his hearing, reliable his color-detecting instruments, and so on, the blind man could not know color, and the man of normal vision could not communicate to him just what this knowledge would be like.

The believer has had certain unusual experiences, which, presumably, the unbeliever has not had. If "having direct experience of God" is made synonymous with "having certain religious experiences," and the believer has had these and the unbeliever has not, then we may say that the believer's knowledge is incommunicable to the unbeliever in that it has already been legislated that in order to know what the direct experience of God is one must have had certain religious experiences. "To anyone who has no such awareness of God, leading as it does to the typically religious attitudes of obeisance and worship, it will be quite impossible to indicate what is meant; one can only hope to evoke it."[10] Reading theological textbooks and watching the behavior of believers is not sufficient.

The theologian has made the analogy above hold at the cost of endangering the existential claim about God which he hoped

[10] *Ibid.,* p. 40.

to establish. If "knowing color" is made synonymous with "having color sensations" and "having direct experience of God" is made synonymous with "having certain religious experiences," then it is certainly true that a blind man cannot "know color" and that a nonreligious man cannot "have direct experience of God." By definition, also, it is true that the blind man and the nonreligious man cannot know the meaning of the phrases "knowing color" and "having direct experience of God," because it has been previously legislated that one cannot know their meaning without having the relevant experiences.

If this analogy is kept, the phrases "knowing color" and "having direct experience of God" seem to make no claim beyond the psychological claims about one's color sensations and religious feelings.

If this analogy is not kept, there is no sense in the comparison of the incommunicability between the man of normal vision and the blind man with the incommunicability between the believer and the unbeliever.

If "knowing color" is to be shaken loose from its purely psychological implications and made to have an existential reference concerning features of the world, then a whole society of tests and checkup procedures, which would be wholly irrelevant to the support of the psychological claim about one's own color sensations, become relevant. For example, what other people see, the existence of light waves, and the description of their characteristics, which needs the testimony of research workers and scientific instruments, all must be taken into account.

Because "having direct experience of God" does not admit the relevance of a society of tests and checking procedures, it tends to place itself in the company of the other ways of knowing which preserve their self-sufficiency, "uniqueness," and "incommunicability" by making a psychological and not an existential claim. For example, "I seem to see a piece of blue paper,"[11] requires no further test or checking procedure in order to be considered true. Indeed, if Jones says, "I seem to see a

---

[11] I shall call such statements "low-claim assertions."

piece of blue paper," he not only needs no further corroboration but cannot be shown to have been mistaken. If Smith says to Jones, "It does not seem to me as if I were seeing a piece of blue paper," this cannot rightly raise any doubts in Jones's mind, though it may express Smith's doubts. That is, Smith may feel that Jones is lying. However, if Jones had said, "I see a piece of blue paper," and Smith, in the same place and at the same time, had replied, "I do not see a piece of blue paper," or, "It does not seem to me as if I were now seeing a piece of blue paper," then Smith's remarks can rightly raise doubts in Jones's mind. Further investigation will then be proper, and if no piece of paper can be felt and other investigators cannot see or feel the paper and photographs reveal nothing, then Jones's statement will be shown to have been false. Jones's only refuge will be to say, "Well, I certainly seem to see a piece of blue paper." This is a perfect refuge, because no one can prove him wrong, but its unassailability has been bought at the price of making no claim about the world beyond the claim about his own experience of the moment.

The closeness of the religious statement to the psychological statement can be brought out in another way, as follows. When one wishes to support the assertion that a certain physical object exists, the tests and checking procedures made by Jones himself are not the only things relevant to the truth of his assertion. Testimony of what others see, hear, and so on is also relevant. That is, if Jones wanted to know whether it was really a star that he saw, he could not only take photographs, look through a telescope, and the like but also ask others if they saw the star. If a large proportion of a large number of people denied seeing the star, Jones's claim about the star's existence would be weakened. Of course, he might still trust his telescope. However, let us now imagine that Jones does not make use of the tests and checking procedures (photographs and telescopes) but is left with the testimony of what he sees and the testimony of others concerning what they see. In this case, it is so much to the point if a large number of people deny seeing the star that Jones will be considered irrational or mad if he goes on asserting its existence. His only irrefutable position is to reduce his physical object claim to an announcement concerning his own sensations. Then the testimony of men and angels cannot disturb his certitude. These sensations of the moment he knows directly and immediately, and the indirect and nonimmediate testimony of men and angels is irrelevant. Absolute confidence and absolute indifference to the majority judgment is bought at the price of reducing the existential to the nonexistential.

The religious claim is similar to, though not identical with, the case above in certain important features. We have seen that there are no tests or checking procedures open to the believer to support his existential claim about God. Thus, he is left with the testimony of his own experience and the similar testimony of the experience of others. And, of course, he is not left wanting for such testimony, for religious communities seem to serve just this sort of function.

Let us imagine a case comparable to the one concerning the existence of a physical object. In this case Brown is a professor of divinity, and he believes that he has come to know of the existence of God through direct experience of God. In order to understand the intricate character of what Professor Brown is asserting we must imagine a highly unusual situation. The other members of the faculty and the members of Professor Brown's religious community suddenly begin sincerely to deny his, and what has been their own, assertion. Perhaps the still attend church services and pray as often as they used to do, and perhaps they claim to have the same sort of experiences as they had when they were believers, but they refuse to accept the conclusion that God exists. Whether they give a Freudian explanation or some other explanation or no explanation of their experiences, they are agreed in refusing to accept the existential claim (about God) made by Professor Brown. How does this affect Professor Brown and his claim? It may affect Professor Brown very deeply—indeed, he may die of broken-hearted disappointment at the loss of his fellow believers. However, the loss of fellow believers may not weaken his confidence in the truth of his assertion or in the testimony of his experience. In this matter his experience may be all that ultimately counts for him in establishing his confidence in the truth of his claim about the existence of God. It has been said that religious experience carries its own guarantee, and perhaps the account above describes what is meant by this.

It is quite obvious from these examples that the religious statement "I have direct experience of God" is of a different status from the physical object statement "I see a star" and shows a distressing similarity to the low-claim assertion "I seem to see a star." The bulk of this chapter has so far been devoted to showing some of the many forms this similarity takes. Does this mean then that the religious statement and its existential claim concerning God amount to no more than a reference to the complex feelings and experiences of the believer?

Perhaps the best way to answer this question is to take a typical low-claim assertion and see if there is anything which must be said of it and all other low-claim assertions which cannot be said of the religious statement. One way of differentiating a physical object statement from a low-claim assertion is by means of prefixing the phrase "I seem."[12] For instance, the statement "I see a star" may be transformed into a statement concerning my sensations by translating it into the form "I seem to see a star." The first statement involves a claim about the existence of an object as well as an announcement concerning my sensations and therefore subjects itself to the risk of being wrong concerning that further claim. Whether one is wrong in this case is determined by a society of tests and checking procedures such as taking photographs and looking through telescopes and by the testimony of others that they see or do not see a star. The second statement involves no claim about the existence of an object and so requires no such tests and no testimony of others; indeed, the final judge of the truth of the state-

---

[12] This, clearly, is a superficial and mechanical move, for the prefixing of this phrase ordinarily would result in a qualified and hedging physical object statement. I shall just have to plead that the possibility that such a prefixing should result in a low-claim assertion is here realized.

ment is the person making it. If no existential claim is lost by the addition of this phrase to a statement then the assertion is low-claim. For instance, the statement "I feel pain" loses nothing by the addition "I seem to feel pain."

In the case of the religious statement "I have direct experience of God" the addition of the phrase is fatal to all that the believer wants to assert. "I seem to be having direct experience of God" is a statement concerning my feelings and sensations of the moment, and as such it makes no claim about the existence of God. Thus, the original statement "I have direct experience of God" is not a low-claim assertion. This should not surprise us. We should have known it all along, for is it not an assertion that one comes to know something, namely God, by means of one's feelings and sensations and this something is not reducible to them? The statement is not a low-claim one just because it is used to assert the existence of something. Whether this assertion is warranted and what exactly it amounts to is quite another question.

We are tempted to think that the religious statement must be of one sort or another. The truth is that *per impossible* it is both at once. The theologian must use it in both ways, and which way he is to emphasize at a particular time depends upon the circumstances of its use and most particularly the direction of our probings.

The statement "I seem to be having direct experience of God" is an eccentric one. It is eccentric not only because introspective announcements are unusual and because statements about God have a peculiar obscurity but for a further and more important reason. This eccentricity may be brought out by comparing this statement with others having the same form. A first formulation of this may be put in the following way. In reference to things other than our sensations of the moment knowledge is prior to seeming as if.

The statement "I seem to be looking directly at a chair" has a meaning only insofar as I already *know* what it is like to look directly at a chair. The statement "I seem to be listening to a choir," has a meaning only insofar as I already *know* what it is like to be listening to a choir. The assumption of knowledge in both these cases is one which all normal people are expected to be able to make and do in fact make.

The statement "I seem to be having direct experience of God" does not lend itself so easily to the criterion for meaning exemplified above, because if this statement has meaning only insofar as one already *knows* what it is like to have direct experience of God, the assumption of such knowledge is certainly not one which all normal people may be expected to be able to make or do in fact make. However, it may be said that the assumption of such knowledge as knowledge of what it is like to see a gorgon may not be made of all normal people and, therefore, the case of religious knowledge is in no peculiar position. This objection can be answered when we ask the question "How do we come to learn what it would be like to look directly at a chair, hear a choir, see a gorgon, have direct experience of God?"

It is not that there are no answers to the question concerning how we come to learn what it would be like to have direct experience of God. We are not left completely in the dark. Instead, the point is that the answers to this question are quite different from the answers to the questions concerning how we come to learn what it would be like to look directly at a chair, hear a choir, and see a gorgon. No one in our society has seen a gorgon, yet there are people who, by means of their specialized knowledge of mythical literature, may claim in a perfectly meaningful way that it now seems to them as if they were seeing a gorgon.

Let us imagine a society in which there are no chairs and no one knows anything at all about chairs. If we were to try to teach one of the members of this society what it would be like to see a chair and if we were not allowed to construct a chair, what might we do? We might look around at the furniture and say, "A chair is a kind of narrow settee. It is used to sit on." This would be a beginning. Then we might compare different settees as to which are more chairlike. We might draw pictures of chairs, make gestures with our hands showing the general shape and size of different sorts of chairs. If, on the following day, the person being instructed said, "I had a most unusual dream last night—I seemed to be looking directly at a chair," we should admit that his statement was closer in meaning to a similar one which we who have seen chairs might make than it would be to a similar one which another member might make who had no information or instruction or experience of chairs. We would insist that we had better knowledge of what it is to see a chair than has the instructed member of society who has still actually to see a chair. However, to know pictures of chairs is to know about chairs in a legitimate sense.

But let us now imagine a utopian society in which none of the members has ever been in the least sad or unhappy. If we were to try to teach one of the members of this society what it would be like to feel sad, how would we go about it? It can be said that giving definitions, no matter how ingenious, would be no help; drawing pictures of unhappy faces, no matter how well drawn, would be no help, so long as these measures failed to evoke a feeling of sadness in this person. Compaing the emotion of sadness with other emotions would be no help, because no matter how like other emotions (weariness and the like) are to sadness they fail just because they are not sadness. No, sadness is unique and incomparable.

To anyone who has no such awareness of sadness, leading, as it does, to the typically unhappy behavior of tears and drawn faces, it will be quite impossible to indicate what is meant. One can only hope to evoke it on the assumption that the capacity to become aware of sadness is part of normal human nature like the capacity to see light or to hear sound.

This last paragraph is a play upon a quotation given at the very beginning of this chapter. The following is the original version.

> To anyone who has no such awareness of God, leading as it does to the typically religious attitudes of obeisance and worship, it will be quite impossible to indicate what is meant; one can only hope to evoke it, on the assumption that the

capacity to become aware of God is part of normal human nature like the capacity to see light or to hear sound.[13]

Consider the following statements:

1. We are rejecting logical argument of any kind as the first chapter of our epistemology of aesthetics, or as representing the process by which beauty comes to be known.

2. It is not as the result of an inference of any kind, whether explicit or implicit, whether laboriously excogitated or swiftly intuited, that the knowledge of beauty comes to us.

3. To those who have never been confronted with the experience of seeing the beauty of something, argument is useless. As these statements stand, they are plainly false. Professors of aesthetics and professional art critics often do help us to come to "knowledge of beauty" by all kinds of inference and arguments. They may, and often do, help us to come to a finer appreciation of beautiful things. Knowledge of the rules of perspective and understanding of an artist's departure from them is relevant to an aesthetic appreciation of his work.

However, it is possible to interpret these statements as true, and this is more important for our purpose. There is sense in saying that an art critic, who has vastly increased our aesthetic sensitivity and whose books of art criticism are the very best, may never have known beauty. If there are no signs of this critic ever having been stirred by any work of art, then no matter how subtle his analyses, there is sense in claiming that he has never been confronted with the experience of seeing the beauty of something. This sense just is that we may be determined not to say that a person has seen the beauty of something or has knowledge of beauty if he does not at some time have certain complex emotions and feelings which are typically associated with looking at paintings, hearing music, and reading poetry. To "know beauty" or to "see the beauty of something" here means, among other things, to have certain sorts of emotions and feelings.

The statements on aesthetics given above are a play on a

[13] Farmer, *Towards Belief in God.* p. 40

quotation given at the beginning of this chapter. The following is the original version with the appropriate omissions and transpositions.

> We are rejecting logical argument of any kind as the first chapter of our theology or as representing the process by which God comes to be known. . . .
>
> It is not as the result of an inference of any kind, whether explicit or implicit, whether laboriously excogitated or swiftly intuited, that the knowledge of God's reality comes to us.
>
> . . . To those who have never been confronted with it [direct, personal encounter with God] argument is useless.[14]

As these statements stand they are plainly false. Professors of divinity and clergymen are expected to do what Baillie claims cannot be done.

However, it is possible to interpret these statements as true, and this is more important for our purpose. There is sense in saying that a theologian (who has vastly increased our religious sensitivity and whose books of theology are the very best) may never have known God. If there are no signs of this theologian's ever having been stirred by a religious ritual or act of worship, then, no matter how subtle his analyses, there is sense in claiming that he has never been confronted with God's personal Presence. This sense just is that we are determined not to say that a person has knowledge of God if he does not at some time have certain complex emotions and feelings which are associated with attending religious services, praying and reading the Bible. To "know God" or to be confronted with God's "personal Presence" means, of necessity, having certain sorts of emotions and feelings.

In this section the analogy between seeing blue and experiencing God has been examined and found to be misleading. I shall not deal in this chapter with the connexion between what the believer expects from immortality and his religious belief. This peculiar kind of test or verification has special difficulties which will be treated in another chapter.

---

[14] Baillie, *Our Knowledge of God*, pp. 132, 143.

So far I have tried to indicate how statements concerning a certain alleged religious way of knowing betray a logic extraordinarily like that of statements concerning introspective and subjective ways of knowing. It is not my wish to go from a corect suggestion that the logic is *very, very* like to an incorrect suggestion that their logic is *just* like that of introspective and subjective statements, for, after all, such statements are logically in order.

I have argued that one cannot read off the existence of God from the existence of religious experience. Now, I must insist, in all charity, that *neither* can one read off the *non*-existence of God from the existence of religious experience.

In criticizing some of the foregoing argument, Mr. W. D. Glasgow claims,

> It is essential here for the defender of the religious way of knowing to assert that there are cases where man *knows* himself to be experiencing an objective Deity, just as there are cases where he knows himself to be experiencing a subjective pain. Unless it is insisted that there is such a thing as *cognitive experience* in religion, Martin's assimilation of all religious existential statements to psychological statements (or what ought to be called psychological statements) becomes highly plausible. Indeed, even the phrase "*may* be objective" has no meaning, probably, for Martin, unless theoretically at least it is possible to find out or test whether religious experience *is* objective. The position is only saved, again, if we say that in some cases the agent himself anyhow *does* know.[15]

Glasgow cannot mean "a man *knows* himself to be experiencing an objective Deity" *in just the same way as* "he knows himself to be experiencing a subjective pain." One's pain is not a thing that exists independently of one's experience. I do not establish the existence of my pain on the basis of experience. There is nothing to establish beyond the experience. Presumably

---

[15] W. D. Glasgow, "Knowledge of God," *Philosophy*, XXXII (1957), 236. This article is a criticism of my article "A Religious Way of Knowing," printed in Flew and MacIntyre, *New Essays in Philosophical Theology* (London: S. C. M. Press, 1955), pp. 76–95.

there is something to establish on the basis of religious experience, namely, the presence of God. When Glasgow says "there is such a thing as *cognitive experience* in religion" and "in some cases the agent himself anyhow *does* know," he must be read as saying that the presence of God is known on the basis of religious experience. That is, the presence of God is something over and above the experience itself. The model that Glasgow implies is that a cognitive experience is rather like a photograph of a friend: one can read off from the photograph that it is of that friend: and though this is a misleading model, there is something in it. If I am sitting at my desk and someone asks me if there is an ash tray on my desk, *all* that I have to do is have a look and say "Yes" or "No." But whether or not I know there is an ash tray on my desk is not to be read off simply from what my eyes at that moment told me. For if my eyes can tell me the truth they can tell me a lie, and the difference here would not be decided by what they tell. For me really to have seen and known there was an ash tray, other people must have been able to have seen it if they had looked. If I have only the testimony of my eyes and discount all else, then that testimony is mute concerning the existence of what is external. My eyes can tell me (in an hallucination) of the presence of an ash tray when there is no ash tray.

When someone uses the sentence "I see an ash tray" in such a way that he counts as relevant to its truth *only* his visual experience at the time, he is talking *only* about that experience, though the sentence has the form of making a statement about an ash tray. It does not help if he calls it a "cognitive experience" or if he says that he "anyhow *does* know" or if he says that his experience is "self-authenticating" or is a "direct encounter." We cannot allow a speaker any final authority in the account of how he is using his sentences. If such special dispensation were allowable, conceptual confusion would be rare indeed.

Similarly, I have argued, when someone uses the sentence "I have or have had direct experience of God" in such a way that he counts as relevant to its truth *only* his experience at the time, he is talking *only* about that experience, though the sentence has the form of making a statement about the presence of God, and neither does it help if he calls it a "cognitive experience."

From the fact that someone uses the sentence "I see an ash tray" so that is talking *only* about his visual experience, nothing at all follows about whether or not he is actually seeing an ash tray in front of him. His *statement* may be only about his visual experience itself, and his actual *situation* may be that of seeing the ash tray. Also, from the fact that someone uses the sentence "I have or have had direct experience of God" in such a way that he is talking *only* about his experience at the time, nothing at all follows about whether or not he is actually experiencing the presence of a supernatural being. His *statement* may be only about his experience itself, and his actual *situation* may be that of experiencing the presence of a supernatural being.

The religious person will want, in what he says, to be able to distinguish between a "delusive" and a "veridical" experience of God. The experience should be due to the actual presence of God and not due only to a drug or to self-deception or to the action of Satan. Therefore he must use his sentence to refer to more than an experience that is, in principle, compatible with these and other similar causes.

What makes a form of experience a way of knowing? It is often suggested that the mystic who "sees" God is like a man (in a society of blind men) who sees colors. It is claimed that each has a form of experience and a way of knowing that others lack. Let us now work out this analogy. A society of blind men is told by one of its members that he has come to have a form of experience and a way of knowing by means of which he has been able to discover the existence of things not discoverable by ordinary experience. He says that these things have a *kind* of size (not just like size as it is felt by the blind) and a *kind* of shape (not just like shape as it is felt by the blind) ; he further says that these things are somehow "everywhere" and that they cannot expect to understand what these things are like and what he means by experiencing them unless they themselves have these experiences. He then tells them of a procedure by which they will be able to discover for themselves the existence of these things. He warns them that these things do not always reveal themselves when the procedure is carried out, but, if a person is sufficiently diligent and believes strongly enough in their existence, he will probably come to know by means of unique and incomparable experiences of the existence of these things.

Some people, with faith and diligence, submit themselves to the required procedure, and some of these are rewarded by a kind of experience they have not known before. Color shapes float before them—things that they cannot touch or feel and that are beyond the reach of their senses, and things that may be present to one of their group and not experienced by the others, things that may as well be everywhere as anywhere, since they are locatable only in the sense of being "before" each observer to whom they appear. These people cannot correlate this new form of experience with the rest of experience, they cannot touch or smell these "things." Indeed, they "see" visions, not things. Or rather these people have no way of *knowing* the existence of the things that may or may not exist over and above the momentary experiences. May these experiences all the same be "cognitive"? Yes and no. Yes, there may be something, they know not what, responsible for their having these experiences. No, their experiences are not a way of *knowing* about this something. For the experience of a colored shape that needs no corroboration by the experience of others similarly placed, and that is not related to one's other senses, is not in itself a way of knowing what in the world is responsible for this experience even if there is something beyond the condition of the "observer" that is so responsible. So far, even the people concerned have no *way of knowing* what more is involved than the fact of their experiencing momentary "visions."

I have not denied that the religious mystic may have experiences that others do not. Neither have I denied that there might be some external agency responsible for these experiences. What I have denied is that the mystic's possession of these experiences is in itself a way of knowing the existence or nature of such an agency.

The argument of this chapter lies in an area in which

confusion is common. I shall consider two cases of such confusion especially relevant to what I have been saying.

> You are acquainted with the distinction between feeling and emotion. Feeling, such as pleasure or pain, is in itself a purely subjective experience; emotion implies an objective situation within which there is something which arouses the emotion, and towards which the emotion is directed. The Divine is, it would seem, first experienced in such a situation; and is initially apprehended solely and exclusively as that which arouses certain types of emotion. If the emotion be awe, then the Divine is so far apprehended as the awesome, what Otto has so helpfully entitled the numinous.[16]

There are two questionable assumptions here: first, that whether or not an experience refers to an objective state of affairs can be read off from the experience itself; second, that emotions *must* do so.

The second claim that an emotion as such implies an objective situation can be refuted very simply. My feeling of pleasure while watching a game of football is related to something in my environment, but my feeling of pleasure at a tune running through my head is not. My emotion of awe in the presence of a particularly magnificent race horse is related to something in my environment, but my emotion of awe during a dream of a coronation service is not. Some people have aesthetic emotions aroused by the contemplation of mathematical proofs and theorems, and others have the emotion of fear toward ghosts and goblins.

In a criticism of the argument of the first part of this chapter (as originally published in "A Religious Way of Knowing," in *Mind*, October, 1952) Professor H. D. Lewis seems to be making the first claim, that a reference to an objective state of affairs can be read off from the experience itself.

> He [Martin] seems to think that the only claim to objectivity which an experience may have is that which is

16 N. Kemp Smith, *Is Divine Existence Credible?*, British Academy Lecture (London: British Academy, 1931), p. 23.

established by tests and checking procedures. A man's statement that he "seems to see a blue piece of paper" is thus said to be unassailable only because it is a "claim about his own state of mind." This I would doubt, for the colour expanse which we only seem to see is neither a mere appearance nor a state of mind. It is "out there before me" and real enough while I seem to see it, however many problems may be involved in distinguishing between it and the physical entities. . . . "Having been stirred" by a religious ritual or act of worship, or having "certain sorts of emotions and feelings," is not the essential thing in religious experience; it is what we apprehend that comes first.[17]

However, "what we apprehend," if anything, is the whole problem and cannot "come first." Certainly, people have had special sorts of experience which incline them to claim with the greatest confidence that their experiences are of God. But whether the experiences are or are not of God is not to be decided by describing or having those experiences. For whether anything or nothing is apprehended by experiences is not to be read off from the experiences themselves. The presence of a piece of blue paper is not to be read off from my experience as of a piece of blue paper. Other things are relevant: What would a photograph reveal? Can I touch it? What do others see? It is only when I admit the relevance of such checking procedures that I can lay claim to apprehending the paper, and, indeed, the admission of the relevance of such procedures is what gives meaning to the assertion that I am apprehending the paper. *What I apprehend is the sort of thing that can be photographed, touched, and seen by others.*

It does not help when Lewis says,

> The colour expanse which we only seem to see is neither a mere appearance nor a state of mind. It is "out there before me" and real enough while I seem to see it, however many problems may be involved in distinguishing between it and physical entities.

[17] H. D. Lewis, "Philosophical Surveys X, The Philosophy of Religion, 1945–1952," *Philosophical Quarterly*, IV (July, 1954), p. 263.

Think now of a man who claims to see a blue piece of paper, and when we complain that we cannot, he replies, "Oh, it isn't the sort of thing that can be photographed, touched, or seen by others, but all the same, it is out there before me." Are we to think that he has come upon a special sort of object that is nevertheless "out there" as are desks and tables and the rest of the furniture of the world? No, ontological reference is something to be earned. We earn the designation "out there" of a thing by allowing its presence to be determined by the procedures we all know. We cannot just *say* "out there" of it, and we cannot just *say* "apprehended" of God.

It can be objected, "But God is different, and we never meant that our experiences of God should be checked by procedures relevant to physical objects." Of course not, but what *sort* of checks are there then, so that we are left with more than the mere experiences whose existence even the atheist need not deny?

II

Yet checking procedures are not on all accounts in all ways irrelevant. As in all theological discourse concerning the status of religious experience there are many, many voices, and so far we have listened to too few.

A religious experience is not just an ineffable, indescribable something that comes and goes unbidden and amenable to no criteria of identity. At least, the mystics seldom describe it in this way. There are certain steps one can take to bring about such experiences, and the experiences are describable within limits, and they leave certain kinds of identifiable aftereffects.

Alvarez de Paz and other mystics have emphasized the importance of practicing austerities, conquering the flesh, and mortifying the body.

Of course, this training of the body is not sufficient. The mind must be trained as well. To have a vision of the Holy Virgin one must be acquainted with the basic facts of "Christ's birth and life and death." To have the highest mystical apprehension of the Trinity, as did St. Teresa, one must have some elementary theological training.

Nor is bodily and intellectual training enough, for there must be moral and emotional training as well. The commandment to love one another was given not only to lead us to peace and brotherhood on earth but also to change our hearts so that we might see God.

Yet all of these may not be enough, for it is possible one should train oneself most assiduously in all of these ways and still not have truly religious experience. This possibility is characterized by saying that finally the favor and grace of God are required.

The paradoxical and negative ways in which mystics most often describe their experiences may seem, at first, unsatisfactory. But it helps to consider how similar sorts of descriptions are employed outside the religious context. One might say of one's emotion at a particular time that one felt both love and hate toward someone. This would be understood as a description of a complex emotion that most of us have experienced. And the paradoxical expression is not reducible to "in some ways love, in other ways hate," because it refers not only to different patterns of behaving and feeling but also to a particular feeling at a particular moment.

Alvarez de Paz gives a particularly sharp description that must strike even the most sceptical reader as in no way obscure or evasive.

> One perceives no representation of the face or the body, yet one knows with greater certainty than if one saw it with one's eyes that the person (Jesus Christ or the Blessed Virgin) is present on one's hand or in one's heart. . . . It is as if, in darkness, one should feel at once that someone is at one's side, knowing that he has goodwill and not enmity towards you; while one remains absolutely ignorant whether it is a man or a woman, young or old, handsome or ugly, standing or seated.[18]

It would be wrong for us to legislate against the mystic's claim that his experience is not sensory. For in a nonreligious

[18] Quoted in Joseph Marechal, *Studies in the Psychology of the Mystics* (London: Burns Oates & Washbourne, 1927), p. 110.

context there may be a parallel. Many of us have felt or experienced the presence of some loved one dead or living but distant. (Of course, we do not tend to think that the person is in any way *actually* present unless the person is dead.) Certainly in such cases we do not see or hear the person. It is not even *as if* we heard or saw the person. Making the parallel even closer to the mystical, we do not even have to have any kind of mental image of the loved one. Neither is the presence felt as being in any specific place. The very subtle feelings and emotions typically directed to this one person and no other are now aroused as once they were by this person alone. The unique love and regard this person showed us, we, as it were, receive again. And we can feel ashamed at having done things of which the loved one would disapprove. And so we can feel guided where there is no guide and loved where the lover is dead. The emotion is in shadow felt but is no less real for that.

A child may read of a fairy-story giant who eats the children who do not think he is real and even some who do. He is described in detail (perhaps there is even a picture), and his hatred of children is made too clear. The child may have a bad dream about the giant. Or he may, as in the case above, just feel the giant's presence in no very localized place yet somewhere near. That is, the child reads the story, comes to feel a kind of fear toward the giant, and hates him in a way that others do not. Then the child, hearing and seeing nothing, may, in the dark, feel that fear and sense that hate so strongly that he will claim, even when the light is turned on and in spite of the most tender parental reassurance, that the giant had been in the room. That is, the experience of the child is such that he is left with a certitude which he considers the giant alone could give.

In order to have such an experience, then, with all of the sense of reality and conviction that it carries, it is not necessary that the being whose presence is so felt should ever have existed.

As children we are taught to love Christ in a very special way, and we are taught of Christ's very special love for us. Christ, as a person, is made extremely real to us. That we cannot see or hear him takes very little from his reality. He was once seen and heard, and we are told so much of his life and actions and visible love that we are apt to feel that we know him more clearly than we do any other historical person. As children (or, indeed, as adults) we are encouraged in this feeling by being told that he is somehow, if not actually somewhere, alive. We are told that God loves us as Christ loves us, and we learn that Christ and God are somehow One. So we know roughly how we *should* feel in God's presence. We have as reference countless stories of how others have felt. These experiences are very different, but they form a kind of family. At one extreme there is a visible vision, and at the other extreme there is almost a kind of unconscious trance.

> Let us now speak of the sign which proves the prayer of union to have been genuine. As you have seen, God then deprives the soul of all its senses that he may the better imprint in it true wisdom; it neither sees, hears, nor understands anything while this state lasts. . . . God visits the soul in a manner which prevents its doubting, on returning to itself, that it dwelt in him and that he was within it. . . . But, you may ask, how can a person who is incapable of sight and hearing see or know these things? I do not say that she saw it at the time, but that she perceives it clearly afterwards, not by any vision but by a certitude which remains in the heart which God alone could give. . . . If we did not see it, how can we feel so sure of it? That I do not know: it is the work of the Almighty and I am certain that what I say is the fact. I maintain that a soul which does not feel this assurance has not been united to God entirely, but only by one of its powers, or has received one of the many other favours God is accustomed to bestow on men.[19]

Yet, with all of this, it could be argued that all that has been accomplished is a description of a class of experiences and of methods of obtaining and recognizing them. Their ontological reference has still to be established. It could be dogmatically asserted that these experiences by definition come only through the grace of God, but this would be no more than a way of

[19] St. Teresa, *Interior Castle* (London: Thomas Baker, 1930), pp. 91–93.

stamping one's foot and insisting on, rather than arguing for, that reference. St. Teresa once again is of help. She was plagued during her lifetime not by doubts about the character of her experiences but about their source. Was she perhaps being subtly deceived by Satan? She was not at a loss to provide a kind of settlement procedure.

> I could not believe that Satan, if he wished to deceive me, could have recourse to means so adverse to his purpose as this, of rooting out my faults and implanting virtues and spiritual strength: for I saw clearly that I had become another person by means of these vision. . . . Neither the imagination nor the evil one could represent what leaves such peace, calm, and good fruits in the soul, and particularly the following three graces of a very high order. The first of these is a perception of the greatness of God, which becomes clearer to us as we witness more of it. Secondly, we gain self-knowledge and humility as we see how creatures so base as ourselves in comparison with the Creator of such wonders, have dared to offend Him in the past or venture to gaze on Him now. The third grace is a contempt of all earthly things unless they are consecrated to the service of so great a God.[20]

But now, what more has really been accomplished by this? To say that the source of these experiences is God and not Satan in the absence of further criteria reduces to saying that these experiences have certain sorts of profound effects upon one's character, attitudes, and behavior. And why should an atheist deny any of this? If there is more that cannot be so reduced and if it is inconsistent with the claims of an atheist, it still remains to be said.

Unlike the first section of this chapter, this section has been concerned with views (those of the great Catholic mystics) in which statements about religious experience are not employed as in any way arguments for, or evidence of, the existence of God. The mystics are convinced on other grounds of the existence of God. Religious experience, then, is conceived by them

[20] *Ibid.*, p. 171.

as a way of coming to know better the object of their worship, whose existence is proved or assumed independent of that experience.

This conservative estimate of the status of religious experience in theology is not, however, necessarily safe from censure. The conceptual weight is shifted from the experience to the previously established or assumed notion of the object of the experience. In the previous chapter difficulties were found in typical notions of the qualities of God. No Catholic theologian and few Protestant theologians would claim that religious experience could resolve problems of this conceptual sort.

MYSTICISM AND SEMANTICS

PAUL HENLE

It has been a persistent complaint of mystics that language is inadequate to express their insights, and this complaint is directed not against any given language, as Lucretius objected to the clumsiness of Latin, but against language as such. Thus Boehme says "That which you have seen in my writings is but a glimpse of the mysteries, for a person cannot write them"— and this is only one of innumerable similar statements.

Now this situation poses a curious problem for students of semantics. By his own admission a mystic seer is to be judged not by what he says but rather by what he is trying to say. And he cannot say what he is trying to say. Persistent attempts to formulate his meaning fail. So thoroughly do they fail, moreover, that serious doubts have arisen as to whether mystics even intend anything sensible. Perhaps their failure of expression is a failure of thought, not of language. Perhaps language is adequate to say everything sensible and mystics are merely muddle-headed.

This possibility gives rise to the problem of this paper: Granted that what mystics say often is not cogent, is there any cogency to what they mean? Let us admit at the outset that the only conclusive answer to the problem would consist in exhibiting what mystics intend to say and exhibiting it in a language of some sort. This has been tried for centuries without success, and it is not my purpose here to try to improve on the writings of the mystics themselves. A more modest undertaking is to give up the attempt at a conclusive answer and to content ourselves with a merely probable solution. If we can find other situations in which something sensible cannot be stated, it will give some measure of support to the contention of mystical writers. If the situation can be shown to be closely parallel to

Reprinted from *Philosophy and Phenomenological Research,* 9 (1949), by permission of *Philosophy and Phenomenological Resarch.*

that of the mystics, the contention will be more strongly supported. The sense in which there is something one cannot say is important here. If, by some peculiarity, a language lacks a term for a given concept, this would seem to be an accidental and trivial sort of semantic failure. Ordinarily at least, the missing term could be added and the deficiency of the language remedied. It would be more serious and more in point if symbolisms could be constructed which constitutionally and by their very nature were incapable of expressing certain ideas. It is to such a case that we turn.

Let us, for the sake of illustration, assume the existence of some primitive people who had developed a form of ideographic writing, had some idea of the number system and had worked out some notion of addition, though not of multiplication. Let us assume that they did their actual finding of sums by the aid of counters, so that a census-taker might drop one twig in a jar for each inhabitant of the tribe and keep the jar of twigs as a permanent record. Although more cumbersome, this method would not differ in principle from the system of Roman numerals.

We may go farther, we may assume that our primitive tribe had some rudimentary conception of algebra, had a notation for a variable so that they might speak of any number whatsoever, as we do when we say $(a + b)^2 = a^2 + 2ab + b^2$. Let us assume, however, that instead of using letters of the alphabet to represent variables, they used geometric figures—say, regular plane figures. Thus where we should write

$$a + b = b + a$$

one might expect them to write

$$\triangle + \square = \square + \triangle$$

Naturally, just as we make a distinction in meaning between letters of different size between, 'a' and 'A', so they would distinguish between '$\triangle$' and '$\bigtriangleup$'. In a given sense they use only one size triangle, square, etc. Thus far there seems to be no difference between their algebra and ours, but there is one element of their notation which I have neglected. In the addition of fixed integers, we have seen, they simply heaped together the symbols for the component numbers and, wishing to keep the same sort of notation in their abstract algebra, they represented a + b not as I have shown, by '$\triangle + \square$', but by a superposition of the symbols for the two variables, thus: $\overset{+}{\boxed{\triangle}}$ with a little plus sign over the whole to show the nature of the operation.

A curious result ensues, from the use of this symbolism. Whereas we can easily state the very simple rule of arithmetic that a + b = b + a, this is impossible in their symbolism. If one tries to write it, one comes out with

$$\overset{+}{\boxed{\triangle}} = \overset{+}{\boxed{\triangle}}$$

and this of course is indistinguishable from the formulation of a + b = a + b. Hence they are bound to regard it as an immediate consequence of the law of identity:

$$\triangle = \triangle$$

obtained by substituting '$\overset{+}{\boxed{\triangle}}$' for '$\triangle$'. This result is inevitable and inescapable. With the symbolism at hand there is no way of distinguishing between "a + b" and "b + a". At first one might be tempted to write one '$\overset{+}{\boxed{\triangle}}$' and the other '$\overset{+}{\boxed{\triangle}}$'; but this will not succeed. By the conventions established, '$\triangle$' and '$\triangle$' are different symbols so that if one complex is equivalent to a + b, the other is equivalent to b + c. You may object that this is a very poor symbolism: I shall not dispute the point. All I claim is that it is a symbolism which might be used.

At first sight it might appear that this symbolism made the lives of mathematicians simpler by reducing the number of laws which can be expressed. I regret to inform you that this is not the case, and in fact it has led to a mathematical schism. The orthodox, and generally accepted opinion is that the only general law of addition is that a + b > a, which they write

$$\overset{+}{\boxed{\triangle}} > \boxed{\triangle}$$

The orthodox defy their opponents to formulate any other law.

There has always been a minority, however, never very large and often composed of rather dreamy, solitary individuals, who have persistently maintained that there are other laws of addition as well. When asked to produce another, they often come up with our formula:

$$\boxed{\overset{+}{\triangle}} = \boxed{\overset{+}{\triangle}}$$

When it is pointed out that this is a simple corollary of the law of identity they rather sadly admit that this is true in the usual sense of symbols but that there is a special sense in which the formula is not a tautology. When asked to make explicit the sense they intend, they shake their heads and are unable to do so, but still insist that they mean something. Most people think they are talking nonsense.

An even worse heresy has appeared recently. Substraction has long been known with regard to particular numbers. Symbolically it was performed by taking from the pile of twigs representing one number a pile representing another. By borrowing from a third separate pile, even negative differences could be achieved. Not long ago, a young genius tried to treat subtraction generally, to work out laws of subtraction for all numbers. Using the notation '$\boxed{\overline{\triangle}}$' for 'b — a', he wished to enunciate the rule that in general b — a $\neq$ a — b. He wrote that, in general,

$$\boxed{\overline{\triangle}} \neq \boxed{\overline{\triangle}}$$

He was accused, of course, of violating the law of identity, the most sacred law of logic, and was promptly condemned to death. He met his end rather pensively, confusedly shaking his head. He admitted that what he wrote seemed to contradict itself, but somehow, he was sure, it didn't.

But enough of mythical anthropology. The point is clear. We have before us a symbolism in which it is impossible to formulate certain statements. Attempts to formulate them result in tautologies or self-contradictions. It is fair to say that a statement which cannot be expressed in a given symbolism is in-

effable with regard to that symbolism. The ineffable is thus
established as a perfectly sound semantic concept. Generalizing
from our previous illustration, it is apparent that the principle
of commutativity is ineffable in a commutative symbolism. Other
laws of ineffability can be worked out, though, as yet, this has
not been done. Of course, to show that a statement is ineffable,
one must have a broader symbolism in which it can be expressed, but this does not prevent a statement being ineffable
with regard to some particular symbolism.

Religious mystics may be taken as asserting that their
insights are ineffable with regard to all known symbolisms.
There is no direct way of assessing this claim. But there is indirect evidence. If the claim were correct we might expect, by
analogy to our illustration above, that their writings would
contain tautologies and contradictions. Examination proves this
to be correct. Thus Jacob Bottomley complains: "Oh God. . . .
What shall I speak of thee, when speaking of thee I speak
nothing but contradiction?" And, as for tautologies, you will
recall that, according to Exodus, when God himself revealed
his nature to Moses he could say no more than "I am that I am."
Illustrations of this sort could easily be multiplied.

Thus far we have established a parallel between the case
of our hypothetical primitive mathematicians and religious
mystics. We knew that our mathematicians had something to
say and found their symbolism inadequate to express it. We
find religious mystics behaving in the same way, and conjecture
that they, too, have something to express. But how close is the
parallel really? Is there not a vast difference between the
limited resources of the ideographic symbolism for addition and
the full resources of discursive language? That the difference
exists must of course be admitted, but I think it is a difference
of degree and not of kind. Unfortunately, time is short and I
can only indicate the outline of the reasons.

Let us consider for the moment a case in which one is confronted with a novel situation and attempts to describe it, either
to one's self or to some one else. If the novel experience is that of
a new quality, then it must be simply apprehended and named;
past experience is of no use. If, however, one is confronted with

some structure of related parts, then a previously known relation may be used, by analogy, to describe the present situation. To take a simple case, automobiles are a relatively recent invention, whose prevalence has required considerable extension of our vocabularies. For one thing, it was desirable to have a name for the cover of the motor. The term 'hood' has been adopted, meaning, of course, that part of the auto which bears a similar relation to it had a hood, in the literal sense bears to its wearer. This analogy makes reasonably clear the part of the car intended and so provides a means of assimilating the novel situation to our language.

What we have in this instance is a use of analogy not generally treated in logic texts—an analogy used not as an argument to prove something but as a symbol to bring something within the realm of discourse. It is a semantic use of analogy, a situation in which our established concepts act as a symbolism in terms of which to represent the novel. In just the sense in which, in our mathematical symbolism before, superposition represented addition, so, in this more complex case, the known concept represents the novel situation.

We saw before that certain symbolisms limited what could be expressed in them. Is the same true in the more complex case where concepts serve as symbols. It is easy, I think to show that this is the case. To recur to our illustration, we may of course symbolize a variety of situations by our concept 'hood'. We may describe a part of a cobra or a device on a fireplace to catch smoke, but we cannot describe everything. If, for example, I have a group of small objects laid out on a flat surface—say, a group of pennies on a table—one cannot describe the total situation in terms of the symbol 'hood'. Thus, here also, one's symbolism limits what can be expressed. With regard to the symbolic concept 'hood', statements about the premises on the table are ineffable.

Let us return now to our chief problem, that of mysticism. We have seen that there are some situations not describable by analogy to a given concept. It may be that all our concepts have something in common and so there might be situations which cannot be symbolized in terms of any of them. Bergson has argued for this point of view and certain esthetic theories would support it. If this were true, it might further be the case that a vision of God, or of existence as a whole, possessed features which could not be symbolized by any of our concepts. The result would be the kind of contradictoriness and linguistic chaos one finds in the literature of mysticism. These conjectures are not of course proved and they may be wrong. It may be that our concepts are adequate symbols, for the expression of anything—we shall never know so long as we stay within the realm of our concepts. It may be that all visions—whether of God, or of existence as a whole, or of anything else—could be symbolized consistently by our present conceptual symbolism; this is a possibility. But at least there is also the possibility that our conjectures are correct and that in mysticism there is something which cannot be imparted, using our present concepts as symbols.

Let us sum up briefly what has and has not been shown. (1) We have seen that there are symbolisms in which certain things cannot be said and so are ineffable. This much is established. (2) We have seen reasons for regarding our concepts as a system of symbols in which certain statements may be ineffable. This is not established, and I have only indicated reasons. (3) Such ineffable statements may well be what mystics are trying to express. This has not been established and cannot be, short of finding a new symbolism for expressing what is now inexpressible. (4) Nothing has been claimed regarding the truth of what mystics are trying to express. This lies totally outside the domain of semantics.

Several points come up in the discussion of this paper on which I should like to comment briefly. Professor V. C. Aldrich objected to this account of mysticism on the grounds that, if our present symbolism is inadequate to express a mystic insight, the mystics would have devised a better symbolism in the course of time. I do not think that this follows. There is nothing within a symbolism which would lead one to go beyond it—that depends not merely on a need for a new symbolism, but also on the flash of inspiration which provides it. When and where such inspiration might occur, or even that it should ever occur, are quite unpredictable.

There is another factor in the situation. Symbolisms, I have argued, are limited in their range of application. It well may be—although I do not know how this could be conclusively proved—that all our conceptual symbols derived from ordinary life are such as to exclude some truths about mystical experiences from the range of their application. This would mean that no generally intelligible symbolism for the representation of mystical experiences would be possible. It would leave open, however, the possibility of some unusual experiences, if common to a group, providing the basis for a symbolism. Thus one mystical experience might be symbolized by another and so be accurately described.

It was suggested by Professor R. Frondizi, and others, the insight of a mystic is ineffable not merely relative to our language and our symbolic devices, but absolutely or with regard to any language whatsoever. That mystics have claimed this is undeniable, but how to assess the claim is another matter. If one were to take it seriously one would credit the mystic not merely with insight on religious matters—which one might readily grant—but also with insight into the nature of all symbolic devices, invented and uninvented. If the discovery of a more adequate symbolism must always be fortuitous, as I have suggested, I do not see how this claim can be allowed. A mystic may well find that he can express his meaning in no available symbolism and may be able to devise none which would do better. He might plausibly argue that no concept thus far derived from common experience might serve to symbolize what he intends, but beyond this he cannot go unless mystical experiences be taken as a revelation of semantics as well as of deity.

Professor Arthur E. Murphy argued that one is not entitled to apply the term proposition to what is not formulable in some known symbolism. He would, therefore, not speak to ineffable propositions (unless the proposition were expressible in some other symbolism) but rather of "candidates for propositions." After some consideration, I am convinced that Prof. Murphy's distinction is correct. The "candidate for a proposition" properly speaking is simply the aspect for an experience which one would express if proper symbolism were available. It becomes a proposition when expressed, though it still may remain ineffable relative to some symbolisms.

INEFFABILITY

WILLIAM ALSTON

It [the Godhead] is free of all names and void of all forms. It is one and simple, as God is one and simple, and no man can in any wise behold it.—MEISTER ECKHART

Brahman has neither name or form, transcends merit and demerit, is beyond time, space, and the objects of sense-experience. . . . Supreme, beyond the power of speech to express . . .—SHANKARA

In them [mystical states] the mysterium is experienced in its essential, positive, and specific character, as something that bestows upon man a beautitude beyond compare, but one whose real nature he can neither proclaim in speech nor conceive in thought.—RUDOLPH OTTO

That Soul is not this, it is not that. It is unseizable, for it cannot be seized.—BRIHAD ARANYAKA UPANISHAD

No form belongs to Him, not even one for the Intellect. . . . What meaning can there be any longer in saying: "This and this property belongs to Him"—PLOTINUS

Philologos: How can anyone seriously make statements like this? They seem to be self-defeating. For in making such a statement as "Brahman has neither name nor form . . . [and is] beyond the power of speech to express," isn't one doing (or purporting to do) the very thing which the statement declares to be impossible, namely, attach a name or ascribe a form to Brahman or "express" it in speech? Of course we cannot press this charge until we know the authors' exact intentions. Perhaps they are indulging in rhetorical exaggeration, as I would in

Reprinted from *The Philosophical Review*, 65 (1956), by permission of *The Philosophical Review* and the author.

saying, "Oh, Jane is impossible." If I said this, you wouldn't charge me with self-contradiction on the ground that I was on the one hand implying that "Jane" names an actually existing person and on the other hand asserting that it is impossible (logically or causally) that this person exists. You would take me to be saying. hyperbolically, that Jane is very difficult to get along with, and/or expressing my irritation at her. (Cf. "That outcome is unthinkable," "I *always* say the line 'Scarf up the tender eye of pitiful day' wrong.") Similarly, Shankara may be hyperbolically saying that it is difficult to find the right words to talk about Brahman, and/or expressing the frustration he meets in such attempts. Or perhaps the authors are using terms like "name," "form," "express," and "property" with unstated restrictions and qualifications such that their statements do not involve naming, expressing, attributing forms or properties, and so on, in their use of these terms. On neither of these interpretations would their statements be logically objectionable. But the oracular style of these writings makes it very difficult to know what interpretation to give them.

Mysticus: It is true that most religious writers are rather obscure, on this point as on others. But there is at least one exception—Professor W. T. Stace. In his recent book, *Time and Eternity*,[1] Stace puts forward the proposition that God is ineffable and takes considerable pains to explain exactly what he means, thereby, so it seems to me, giving a precise expression to what the people such as you cited were getting at. He makes it quite clear that he is not speaking hyperbolically, and he makes it quite explicit that the assertions are to be taken unqualifiedly, without any sort of restriction. And yet I cannot see that they are self-defeating in the way you suggest. Here are some of his statements of the thesis:

> To say that God is ineffable is to say that no concepts apply to Him, and that He is without qualities. . . . And this implies that any statement of the form "God is x" is false.[2]

---

[1] Princeton, N. J., 1952.
[2] *Op. cit.,* p. 33.

> Thus to the intellect He is blank, void, nothing. You can-cannot attach any predicate to Him . . . because every predi-cate stands for a concept, so that to affirm a predicate of Him is to pretend that He is apprehensible by the conceptual intellect.[3]

> It is not merely *our* minds which cannot understand God, nor is it merely *our* concepts which cannot reach Him. No mind could understand His Mystery—so long as we mean by a mind a conceptual intellect—and no concepts could appre-hend Him. And this is the same as saying that He is, in His very nature, unconceptualizable, that His Mystery and incom-prehensibility are absolute attributes of Him.[4]

Philologos: These utterances sound uncompromising enough. But there is something very queer about some of them, for example, "He is, in His very nature, unconceptualizable." Is this as if I should say, in speaking of a very bright but in-tractable student, "He is, by his very intelligence, incapable of learning"? Note that I *couldn't* be denying, in a literal sense, that he can learn. For my statement presupposes that he has intelligence, and we wouldn't say of anything that it has intel-ligence unless we suppose that it could learn something. Any evidence that it was in a strict sense incapable of learning would equally be evidence that it had no intelligence. In actually using this sentence I would be employing hyperbole to express vividly the fact that the very intelligence which makes him capable of learning is so quick-triggered that it is *difficult* for him to sub-mit to the prolonged discipline which is essential for thoroughly learning anything. So in the same spirit I might say of an acquaintance, "He is, in his very nature, unconceptualizable" (cf. "His nature is an absolute enigma to me"), thereby exag-geratedly saying that he is hard to understand and expressing my puzzlement at his dark and devious ways. But again I could not mean "unconceptualizable" in a strict sense here;[5] for in

---

[3] *Op. cit.*, p. 42.

[4] *Op. cit.*, pp. 48–49.

[5] A terminological note for the whole paper: I take Stace, and those who talk about this matter in the same way, to be using "concept"

ascribing to him a nature, I have already admitted that he is
conceptualizable, that is, that concepts can be applied to him.
We speak of the nature of x only where we suppose ourselves
able to say various things about x. We wouldn't talk about
human nature unless we supposed we could apply certain concepts to men. Hence I can suppose only that Stace in saying,
"He is, in His very nature, unconceptualizable" is hyperbolically
expressing the *difficulty* of forming concepts which apply strictly
to God. And so we are back to something like "Jane is impossible."[6]

Mysticus: No, I can't agree that Stace is just exaggerating.
But I must admit that the statements you cite are not happy
ones. However, I don't believe they are essential for the statement of his thesis. He doesn't have to speak of God's *nature,* or
of something being an absolute attribute of God. He used those
locutions in order to emphasize that God is unconceptualizable
not just by the human mind but by any mind whatsoever. But
he could have made the point by saying just that (as he also
does) and thereby have avoided tripping himself up in this way.

P.: Let's see what is left after the purge. "To say that God
is ineffable is to say that no concepts apply to Him, . . . that any
statement of the form 'God is x' is false." "Thus you cannot
attach any predicate to Him." But if in saying, "God is in-

---

within the philosophical tradition in which we can be said to apply a
concept to x whenever we predicate anything of x (or attach a predicate
to x); and in which to say that we can apply concepts to x is equivalent
to saying that x is conceptualizable, capable of being apprehended by concepts or by the conceptual intellect, etc. These equivalences are implicit
in the second of the three above quotations from Stace and in the quotation below, p. 510. Therefore, although I hold no brief for this double-
barreled lingo, I shall in the following use "apply a concept to x" as
synonymous with "attach a predicate to x" (or "predicate something of
x"). And, for stylistic purposes, I shall sometimes add as a further
synonym "characterize x." I am under no illusion that the boundaries of
these three terms are precisely drawn in the tradition. In fact a good part
of this paper hinges, in part, on exhibiting their vagueness. But I think
that within the tradition they oscillate together for the most part.

   [6] The same sort of considerations apply to "His Mystery and incom-
prehensibility are absolute attributes of Him."

effable" we are making a true statement, haven't we applied a
concept to Him, viz., the concept of ineffability? Haven't we
attached a predicate to Him, viz., "ineffable"? Haven't we made
a true statement of the form "God is x"? Aren't we in the
position of being able to make a true statement only by doing
the very things which the statement declares impossible, thereby
falsifying it? Is this like a man saying, "I can't spaek English"?
(Cf. the case of a town crier who cries that crying has been
outlawed.)

    M.: Surely you aren't serious. When I say, "God is in-
effable," I am not attempting to apply a concept to Him or
attach a predicate to Him, and so if the statement is true it
would not be correct to say I have succeeded in doing these
things. I am denying that any concepts or predicates can be applied to Him. Of course, the grammatical form of "God is
ineffable" is misleading. It looks like a positive statement, such
as "Jones is ill" or Susie is pretty," but actually it doesn't involve attaching any predicate to anything. Its logical form
would be more clearly exhibited if it were formulated: "It is
not the case that any predicate can be attached to God." This
shows that "God is ineffable" is not really of the *logical* form
"God is x," although it looks as if it were. Similarly, saying
"King Arthur is fictitious" does not constitute attaching a predicate to King Arthur, although it looks as if it did. Hence to say
truly "God is ineffable" we are not required to do what we are
declaring to be impossible.

    P.: So the man who said, "I can't speak English," if
charged with falsifying his own statement, might retort (in
French) that he didn't mean that he couldn't say what he was
saying. (And if the town crier were arrested, he might complain,
"But surely the law doesn't forbid my crying *it*. It's the only
way of publicizing it.") In both these cases the speaker trusts
us to make the sort of qualification that would make his statement intelligible and proper. If we are tempted to interpret
them in a paradoxical way, we draw back and say, "They
couldn't have meant that" and look for some qualification that
will remove the paradox. So Stace perhaps trusted to the circum-

stances to make it plain that he wouldn't count "ineffable" as a predicate because it is negative. But wouldn't it be better to make this explicit and restate the principle as: "No *positive* predicates can be applied to God"?

M.: This qualification is unnecessary. "Ineffability" is not a predicate, in the strict sense of the term. For to "predicate" ineffability of *x* is really to deny something of *x*.

P.: If a pupil who had been directed to give an example of a subject-predicate sentence were to present "Freedom is intangible" or even "God is ineffable," wouldn't he get credit for his answer? And isn't "the concept of impossibility" a proper phrase? So whatever the "strict" sense might be, the point is that Stace is deviating common usage and, in the interests of intelligibility, had best make his deviation explicit.

But now I want to bring out another feature of "God is ineffable" which puzzles me. Let me approach this by asking: "What is is of which ineffability is being predicated, or, if you prefer, of which 'ineffability' is being denied?"

M.: God, of course.

P.: Ah. But what do you mean by "God"?

M.: Stace identifies God with mystical experience. But that seems to me unduly restrictive. I would rather say that God is that toward which we direct religious activities of any sort: worship, prayer, and so forth.

P.: But when you and Stace explain in this way the meaning you attach to "God," aren't you thereby attaching predicates to Him, or at least putting yourself in a position to do so? In other words, in using "God," aren't you presupposing that you can predicate of God whatever phrase you would give to explain your meaning?

M.: There does seem to be something odd here. Perhaps we are overlooking some peculiarity in the way a proper name like "God" is used. Now that I recall, Stace says:

> As every logician knows, any name, any word in any language, except a proper name, stands for a concept or a universal. . . . Neither God nor Nirvana stand for concepts. Both are proper names. It is not a contradiction that Eckhart should use the name God and yet declare Him nameless. For though

He has a proper name, there is for Him no name in the sense of a word standing for a concept.[7]

P.: This theory does not tally with the way you, and Stace, were just now explaining the meaning of "God." But never mind that. Let's look at this conception of proper names for a bit. And first I want to ask: "How do we determine whether a given person understands a given proper name?"[8] Let's start with something a little simpler than "God." Suppose I say to you, "Jane is a spiteful wench." You nod, but for some reason I suspect you are bluffing. So I say, "I don't believe you know who I am talking about." What could you do to vindicate yourself?

M.: I might point out a girl in the room and say, "That is Jane." Or I might just go over and address her by name.

P.: Yes. But this obviously doesn't apply to our problem, since one can't in a literal sense, point out God, or go over and address Him. And so for our purpose we had better stipulate that I make my statement when Jane is not present and that for some reason we can't go to where she is. Or take the case of a historical figure, for example, "Richard II of England," where jointing out is *logically* impossible. How would you prove your understanding in these cases?

M.: In the case of Jane, I might reply to your charge by saying something like "She's Fred's sister-in-law" or "She's the girl with the auburn hair Bob introduced me to last night." In the case of Richard II, I might say, "He was the king deposed by Bolingbroke," or "He was ruler of England from 1377 to 1399."

---

7 *Op. cit.,* p. 24.

8 We do not ordinarily speak of "understanding a proper name." But we do speak of understanding sentences and using them meaningfully; and one of the conditions of understanding or using meaningfully a sentence in which a proper name occurs is knowing who the proper name is a name of (whith certain qualifications which are noted below, p. 514). Hence, in the absence of any other compendious expression, I shall speak of "understanding a proper name, '*N*,'" as synonymous with "knowing who (or what) '*N*' is the name of" or "knowing who (or what) *N* is." This extension of the use of "understanding" will not cause confusion unless it is allowed to obscure the important differences involved.

P.: Good. But doesn't this show that a condition of your understanding me, when I use the proper name of something you cannot point out, is your capacity to provide some such identifying phrase? If you were unable to provide any such phrase, would we say you understand the name?

M.: I suppose not.

P.: And isn't the same true of "God"? Suppose I say to you, "God is a very present help in time of trouble." You nod piously, but for some reason I suspect a failure of communication; perhaps I have reason to think you use the word differently. And so I ask, "What do you mean by 'God'?" You might reply, "The first cause," or "The necessary being," or "The supreme mind holding moral relations with mankind," or "He Who revealed Himself to the prophets," or "The father of Jesus Christ," or "The judge of our sins." If you were unable to give *any* such answer, wouldn't I be justified in concluding that you didn't understand the word "God" in any way? This means that a condition of your understanding any statement containing "God" is your capacity to supply some such identifying phrase, and any such phrase would constitute a predicate which could be attached to God. Hence "God is ineffable" asserts that an essential condition of its meaningfulness does not hold.

M.: Hold on. I might agree with your premise that I couldn't be said to understand a sentence containing "God" unless I could supply an identifying phrase. But your conclusion doesn't follow. Suppose in order to identify Jane I use the phrase "the girl whose picture was on the back page of last night's paper," or in order to identify Richard II, I use the phrase "the protagonist of Shakespeare's play of that name." Would these responses be sufficient to convince you that I had understood your statements containing those proper names?

P.: I suppose so.

M.: But to say that a picture of Jane was on the back page of last night's paper is not to predicate anything of Jane or characterize her in any way. You might well complain that I had not told you that what she is like and that you still can't form a concept of her. And still less have I predicated anything of

Richard II when I have said that Shakespeare wrote a play about him.

P.: Maybe not. But you have said something about them.

M.: True. But to say that x is ineffable is obviously not to say that we can't say anything about x in any sense of "say something about." It is to say that we can't say anything which would involve attaching a predicate to x or characterizing it.

P.: You have overlooked one point, I fear. Even if you can't use those identifying phrases to characterize x, the information contained in these phrases gives you clues as to how to go about characterizing x. You can look at the back page of last night's paper, and on the basis of what you see, you can tell me all sorts of things about Jane. You can read Shakespeare's play and/or study his sources and thereby discover many characteristics of Richard II. Hence it isn't true that you could provide identifying phrases of this sort and yet *not be able* to characterize that which the phrase identifies.

M.: Perhaps. But what about "God"? That's the case we're really interested in. Couldn't I demonstrate my understanding of "God" by saying something like "the object of religious experience," or "the object of worship"? And surely saying that doesn't lead to any characterization lurking in the very *mode* of identification. For in identifying x as the protagonist of a drama, I am presupposing that x is a human being; and to identify x as that a picture of which . . . is to presuppose that x is a visible thing. But to identify x as the object of religious experience or worship is not to imply anything about what sort of entity it is. It does not involve any limitation on what can and cannot be said about it. It is like saying of something that it is an object of thought. That tells us nothing. *Anything* can be thought about.

P.: But doesn't your identifying phrase tell us where to look for more information, just as in the other cases? If you actually use "object of religious experience" as a criterion for identifying God (and aren't just mechanically repeating the phrase), you can find other things to say of God by reflecting on your own religious experience and/or reading what other people have said on the basis of theirs. Thus, depending on what

you are willing to call "religious experience," you could discover that God is infinite bliss, a consuming fire, the ground
of all being, the spirit of love, and so on. Or if your criterion
is "object of worship," you could examine what you take to
be cases of worship and discover what is said of God there,
for example, that He is our father, King of Kings, creator of
heaven and earth, judge of all men, and so forth.

M.: Ah, but the language we use to describe what we meet
in religious experience or to address the object of our worship
is metaphorical language. We don't mean that God is literally a
fire, a father, a King, and so forth. Hence in saying these things
we aren't really predicating anything of God.

P.: The standards for *real* predication seem to be steadily
stiffening. Do you really wish to say that when the poet says:

> There is a garden in her face
> Where roses and white lilies grow,

he is not predicating anything of his lady fair?

M.: Not in the strict sense.

P.: What would you take to be a case of predication in the
strict sense?

M.: "This cup is blue."

P.: "God is a consuming fire" is certainly different from
that. But until you have said just how it is different, that is,
until you have given some criteria for recognizing *real* predication, your general thesis that no predicate can be applied to God
doesn't come to much.

M.: Surely such criteria could be given. But there is something else we have overlooked. There are cases where we would
say that someone understands a sentence even though he doesn't
know who is named by a proper name occurring in the sentence.
Suppose you are rambling on about your acquaintences and
you say, "John Krasnick is a queer duck." Perhaps we are
interrupted then, and I don't have a chance to ask you who
John Krasnick is. Or perhaps I am just not interested in following up this facet of the conversation. It would be strange,

wouldn't it, to say that I didn't understand what you had said?

P.: Yes, it would. But note why. If I were called away just after uttering this sentence, and someone asked you, "Who is John Krasnick?" you would reply, "Oh, I don't know, one of P.'s acquaintances," or perhaps, "Someone P. was just talking about; that's all I know about him." You would have to supply at least this much of an identification if you are to be said to understand my remark.

M.: But if the ability to supply an identifying phrase like "the *x* named '*N*'," or "the *x A* calls '*N*'" is sufficient for understanding a sentence containing a proper name, then I can certainly understand such a sentence without being able to characterize the nominatum. Surely not even you would hold that saying, "*X* is *named by* '*N*'" constitutes a characterization of *x*.

P.: No, I wouldn't. But note what is going on here. Insofar as the only identifying phrase you gave for *N* is "the *x* called '*N*," we are hesitant about saying that you understand, or fully understand, what is being said. If, when I said, "John Krasnick is a queer duck," you had nodded, assented, let it pass, or given other indications that you had understood me, and then it turned out later that the only identifying criterion you could give is "the man P. called 'John Krasnick'," I could accuse you of practicing deception. I might say, "Why didn't you tell me you didn't know who I was talking about?" In other words, when we give the usual indications of having understood a sentence containing a proper name, we are purporting to be able to say more about the nominatum than this.

This is also brought out by the fact that if, after the interruption, someone were to ask you, "Who was P. talking about?" it would be misleading for you to reply, "John Krasnick." For in *using* the proper name, you would be representing yourself as knowing more about him than that I called him "John Krasnick." If that is all you know, the natural thing for you to say would be, "Oh, somebody named 'John Krasnick'." Thus we put this case into a special category.

And this means that the philosopher who *says*, "God is ineffable" could not be interpreted as understanding "God" in this very weak sense. If I were to *say*, "John Krasnick is queer," and couldn't tell you anything about him (except for queerness), apart from the fact that his name is "John Krasnick," you could justifiably accuse me of shamming. You might retort, "You weren't really saying anything." And there is a good reason for this usage. There would be no point in my saying anything about John Krasnick or God or anyone else unless I had some way of identifying them in addition to their being so named. Why should I bother to say of God that He is ineffable rather than effable, why should I care whether He is omnipotent or limited, loving or cruel, conscious or unconscious, if I know Him only as what people call "God"? It is not only that in this case I would have no *basis* for saying one thing rather than the other. More fundamentally, I could have no interest in doing so. People are interested in saying things, and raising questions, about God because they identify Him as the source of their being, the promulgator of their moral laws, the judge of their sins, the architect of their salvation, the object of their worship, or (with Stace) mystical experience. It is because they identify God in such ways that they consider it important to ask and answer questions about Him.

M.: Perhaps you are right. But there is something else which has been worrying me. People differ enormously in verbal ability. Is it not possible for a man to understand a proper name and yet not be able to put this understanding, at least with any adequacy, in a formula?

P.: Perhaps. *Formulation* of an identifying phrase is not the only device for explaining one's understanding of a proper name, though it is the simplest. If the speaker lacks verbal facility, we might try to smoke out his criterion in some other way. We might, for example, present him with various passages from religious literature and note which ones he recognizes as describing God. Or we might describe (or present) various forms of worship and note which he considers appropriate. With sufficient pains we could, in this way, piece out a criterion which he would on reflection recognize as the one he actually uses. And if the most thorough attempts of this sort were persistently frustrated, wouldn't we again be justified in concluding that he wasn't using the word meaningfully?

Another thing. This point doesn't depend on any special features of *intersubjective* communication. I might be doubtful as to whether I really understood a certain name. If so, I would have to use the same devices to assure myself that I did (or didn't).

But let's forget all these difficulties for the moment and suppose that one can say, "God is ineffable" without thereby defeating one's purpose. We are still faced with the question why anyone should accept the statement. Isn't it amply refuted by the facts? Religious literature is crammed full of sentences attaching predicates to God, and there are many men who devote their lives to making such predications.

M.: Oh, no doubt there are many sentences which have a declarative grammatical form and contain "God" as subject. But if you examine them they will all turn out to be either negative or metaphorical. None of them express *conceptions* of God, and so none constitute predication in the strict sense of the term.

P.: Perhaps. But what positive reasons can be adduced for the position?

M.: Mystics, who are in the best position to know, have repeatedly declared God to be ineffable. Just consider, for example, the statements you cited at the beginning of our discussion.

P.: It is true that many mystics have said things which could be interpreted in this way. But if it is a question of authority, many deeply religious men who are not mystics have expressed themselves to the contrary. Of course you could rule out their testimony by defining "God" as what one encounters in mystical experience, or even (with Stace) simply as mystical experience.

M.: I would hesitate to do that. But if we approach God through mystical experience, without ruling out the possibility of other approaches, we can use a diffeernt line of argument.

We can see that mystical experience has certain features which prevent it, or anything discovered in it, from being conceptualized. For example:

> It is of the very nature of the intellect to involve the subject-object opposition. But in the mystic experience this opposition is transcended. Therefore the intellect is incapable of understanding it. Therefore it is incomprehensible, ineffable.[9]

> But the oneness of God is indivisible and relationless. Now this relationless indivisible unity is precisely the character of the mystic intuition as described by all mystics. . . . To say this is only to say that the mystic experience is beyond the capacity of the intellect to handle, since it is the very nature of the intellect to operate by means of separation, discrimination, and analysis.[10]

P.: Leaving aside questions as to the adequacy of the analysis of "intellect" employed here, there is something very strange about these arguments. The conclusion is "Mystical experience is unconceptualizable," and in order to prove it we adduce various characteristics of mystical experience. That is, we have made our success in conceptualizing mystical experience in a certain way a condition for proving that it can't be conceptualized. But how could a successful completion of a task ever enable us to prove that the task is impossible? Wouldn't it rather prove the opposite? Isn't this like giving an inductive argument for the invalidity of induction? Or presenting a documentary film to show that photography is impossible?

M.: You keep making the same mistakes. To say that God is an indivisible unity is not to apply any concept to Him. It is simply to *deny* that there is any distinction of parts in Him.

P.: I begin now to see the situation more clearly. Several times I have pointed out that in saying or defending "God is ineffable," you were saying, or implying your ability to say, something about God. And each time you deny that what is

9 *Op. cit.,* p. 40.
10 *Op. cit.,* pp. 40–41.

being said involves attaching any predicate to God, applying any concepts to Him, or characterizing Him, either because it is negative, or because it is metaphorical, or because it is an extrinsic denomination, and so forth. It begins to appear that you are prepared to deny of anything you are committed to saying of God that it is a predicate and so on. But if this is your tack, then in uttering "God is ineffable," you are just exhibiting a certain feature of your use of "ineffable" (and "predicate," "concept," and so on), rather than saying anything about God. You are expressing your determination not to count as a predicate and so on anything which is said of God. You are like a man who says, "Only empirically testable sentences are meaningful" (cf. "Only scientific method gives us knowledge") and then, whenever presented with a sentence which can't be empiricaly tested, denies that it is meaningful, without giving any reason for all these denials except the lack of empirical testability. After a while we will begin to suspect that he is just showing us how he uses "meaningful," rather than ascribing some property to all the members of a class which has been defined in some independent way.

M.: But I am just using "predicate," "concept," and so on, in their ordinary senses. The only statements which you showed I was committed to making would not ordinarily be thought to involve applying concepts or predicates to God. Similarly *if* the positivist just accepts or rejects examples of meaningful statements according to our ordinary discriminations, he is saying something about the class of statements which would ordinarily be called meaningful.

P.: I'm not at all sure that you are using "predicate" and so on in just the way we ordinarily do, if, indeed, there is any one such way. At least you haven't made that out. Of course, it is only if you are taking "having 'God' as subject" as your sole and sufficient criterion for saying that a sentence doesn't involve predication and so on that you can be accused of uttering a tautology in the strict sense. Insofar as you have other criteria, you are not uttering a tautology. But if you don't state your criteria, and if, whenever you are forced to admit that certain statements containing "God" as subject can be made, you rule these out as examples of "predication" and so on, either without any justification or on the basis of a principle which looks tailor-made for the occasion, we can be excused for suspecting that your utterance approximates to a tautology. Of course alternatively I might suppose that you have no criterion. But then your utterance becomes so indefinite as to assert almost nothing.

If you want to prevent your thesis from oscillating in this limbo betwen tautology and maximum indefiniteness, you had better include a specification of the senses in which you wish to deny that concepts and predicates can be applied to God. With such a specification the thesis might well be significant and worthy of serious consideration. For example, you might restate the position: "God cannot be positively characterized in literal terms." This assertion need not lead to such frustrations as we have been considering. For the speaker could use a nonliteral phrase to identify God; and although the statement itself is presumably literal, it is not positive. And, given a sufficiently precise explication of "literal," this is a thesis well worth consideration. Or you might wish to say, "We can speak only of extrinsic features of God, not of His intrinsic nature," or "God can never be characterized with the precision we can attain in science," or "We can speak of God only in a highly abstract way." None of these utterances need be self-defeating; for (1) in each case the sentence itself does not fall within the class of those declared impossible, and (2) a speaker or hearer can use a criterion for identifying God which does not involve attributing to Him a predicate of the sort which is ruled out. If you are interested in unambiguously communicating a definite thesis and avoiding tripping yourself up in the process, you would be well advised to make such specifications.

M.: Yes, I see that would be better. But how does it happen that so many philosophers make ineffability statements without qualification?

P.: Perhaps something like this is involved. There are many "un . . . able" words which can be applied with all sorts of qualifications, diminishing to an unqualified application. Thus

I can say that our baseball team is unbeatable in our league; or unbeatable by any other college; or unbeatable by any other amateur team; or well-nigh unbeatable (by any team); practically unbeatable; or, simply, unbeatable; or even, to make it still stronger, absolutely unbeatable. The final term in this series, "unbeatable" (or "absolutely unbeatable") is logically just as respectable as any of the others. Though it may be wildly improbable that our baseball team is unbeatable (without qualification), there is no logical self-stultification involved in saying so. (Cf. "unattainable," "unbreakable," "uncontrollable.") With such cases in mind it is easy to feel logically comfortable about saying of God without qualification that He is unconceptualizable or ineffable. But we still might feel more squeamish about this latter case were it not for the fact that there are contexts where we can employ even these terms (or terms very close to them) without qualification. For example: (a) "A fall in the stock market is inconceivable"; (b) "John is unspeakable." Of course as (a) is actually used, it doesn't imply that we can't apply a concept to the falling of the stock market. It simply means that we have every reason to suppose it won't happen. But the verbal similarity between this and "God is unconceptualizable" (where this is intended to imply that we cannot form a concept of God) helps us to suppose that the latter is as legitimate as the former. Similarly (b) is simply a way of saying that John is despicable. But the fact that it has a use helps us to suppose that the verbally similar utterance "God is ineffable" (taken to imply that God cannot be spoken of) also can be given a use. But fully to untangle the muddle in "God is ineffable," we should have to make explicit all the similarities and differences in the ways sentences of this sort function.

If we want to avoid such muddles, we must make explicit the sort of conception, predication, characterization, and so forth we are asserting to be impossible with respect to God in contrast to the sorts we are admitting as possible. To label something ineffable in an unqualified way is to shirk the job of making explicit the ways in which it *can* be talked about;

just as to unqualifiedly label an expression (which is actually used) meaningless is to shirk the job of making explicit the sort of meaning it *does* have in these uses. There may be something in the world which can't be talked about in any way, but if so we can only signalize the fact by leaving it unrecorded.

MYSTICISM AND PHILOSOPHY

RICHARD GALE

This paper will be an attempt to deal with the key problems which mysticism poses for philosophy, these being the alleged ineffability of mystical experiences, the relation between the so-called eternal and temporal orders of being and the objectivity of mystical experiences. We will use Professor Walter Stace's *Time and Eternity* as a springboard for our own critical analysis of these problems.

I. Alleged Ineffability of Mystical Experiences

Basic to Professor Stace's thesis is his claim that mystical experiences, unlike all other types of experience, are completely ineffable, or non-conceptualizable. From this it follows that nothing revealed through mystical experience could possibly be either proved or disproved by anything known through the intellect, which is the process of understanding objects by means of concepts. His discussion, however, is marred by a failure to state clearly in exactly what sense mystical experiences are ineffable. I believe that a careful reading of the book will reveal that four different criteria or senses of ineffability are appealed to. It will be neecssary to discuss each one of these four senses separately to determine, first, whether mystical experiences are ineffable in any of these senses, and, second, if they are ineffable in any sense, whether this sense is trivial, i.e., one which would apply equally well to certain non-mystical experiences.

(1) *Within the mystical experience there is an undifferentiated unity, affording no foothold for any concept.* During the mystical experience, as viewed phenomenologically from the standpoint of the experient, there is a dissolution of the dualism between subject and object as well as a unification of what was

Reprinted from *The Journal of Philosophy*, 57 (1960), by permission of *The Journal of Philosophy* and the author.

originally a multipilicty of objects. For this reason mystical experiences are ineffable.

In opposition to this it can be maintained that mystics as a matter of fact *do* manage to conceptualize their mystical experiences when they are outside them. By applying concepts such as "the undifferentiated unity," "the dissolution of the personal ego," "non-temporal and non-spatial," "the sense of peace and sacredness," etc. to their experiences they succeed in distinguishing mystical from non-mystical experiences.

Professor Stace's counter to this would be that *within* the mystical experience the mystic cannot conceptualize his experience because the use of any concept presupposes a multiplicity of objects as well as the subject-object dualism, and this is just what is wiped out during the experience. In claiming that mystical experiences are ineffable because they cannot be conceptualized by the mystic *while he is within* the experience, Professor Stace seems to be appealing to the following criterion of ineffability: *An experience is ineffable if a proposition describing this experience cannot be either formulated, consciously considered, or verified by the experient during the time that he is actually having the experience.* I will attempt to show that this sense of ineffability is trivial because many non-mystical experiences would equally well qualify as candidates for the title of ineffable.

We would all agree that the experience of wrestling with an alligator is conceptualizable. However, the proposition. "Tarzan is wrestling with an alligator," could not possibly by either formulated, consciously considered, or verified by Tarzan while he is actually having the experience described by the proposition. Similarly, and for slightly different practical reasons, Schnabel is not capable of formulating or verifying the proposition, "Schnabel is concentrating *solely* on interpreting Beethoven's 14th Sonata," while he is actually engaged in performing the sonata; for if he were to attempt to verify this proposition while he was performing the Sonata he would automatically render it false, because that would mean that he could not possibly be concentrating *solely* on interpreting the Sonata.

Because an experience, whether of the mystical or the

Tarzan-Schnabel type, is not conceptualizable by the experiment while he is having the experience, it does not follow that a third person cannot describe the experience at the very moment the experiment is having his experience, or that the experient himself cannot conceptualize his experience after the experience is over.

Professor Stace's answer to this argument would be that there still is a significant difference between mystical experiences and the Schnabel-Tarzan type of experiences, for only in the former is there a complete dissolution of the personal ego. Whether the mystic actually experiences the dissolution of his own ego is open to some doubts, for if this were so how would it be possible for the mystic to remember that *he* had had such an experience? In what sense could it be said to be *his* experience? How can someone experience the dissolution of his ego? But if we waive these difficulties and grant Professor Stace his point that there actually is such a dissolution of the personal ego, this would have no logical relevance to the claim that mystical experiences are ineffable in some unique sense. It would show only that there are different practical reasons why the mystic cannot conceptualize his experience when inside the experience than why Tarzan and Schnabel cannot.

(2) *Mystical experiences are unique, being totally different from all other types of experience.* Mystics themselves claim that they cannot find adequate words to describe their experiences. They have not been able to invent a new language in which their experiences would no longer be ineffable.

However, against this, it can be said that many mystics have been autobiographical mystics. Such mystics manage to communicate the nature of their experience not only to fellow mystics but to many non-mystics as well. When we read the descriptions of mystical experience given by an Eckhart or a Suzuki we seem to know what they are talking about. If we should be soaking in a hot bath one night and suddenly have an experience in which our personal ego was dissolved by melting into an infinite ocean which was an undifferentiated unity and which furthermore gave us a sense of peace and sacredness far transcending anything previously experienced, we would leap to our feet saying with great excitement, "Why that Eckhart wasn't just pulling our leg! There really are such experiences and I just had one!"

There is something woefully inconsistent in Professor Stace's saying, in one breath, that mystical experiences are ineffable—that no concepts can be used to describe them,—and, in the next breath, that there is unanimity among the mystics— that all mystics describe their experiences in pretty much the same way. If one of these claims is true then the other must be false.[1] Also, if mystical experiences were as ineffable as mystics claim they are, then what sense could we make of their claim that their experiences are in principle verifiable if the proper steps are taken? What kind of an experience would serve as a confirming instance?

To say that mystical experiences are ineffable in the sense of not being adequately described by language is to make a trivial claim. No concepts can completely describe any direct experience; they can never serve as substitutes for such experiences. My concept of a loud, deafening noise is not itself a loud, deafening noise. Our experience of yellow is just as unique and ineffable as a mystical experience; we cannot define the color yellow in terms of anything more simple or basic. But this does not mean that we cannot conceptualize our direct experience of yellow and communicate with others about it. If the experience of the color yellor were unique, and accessible to only one person in the universe, then it would be impossibe for this person to communicate with other about this experience. What is presupposed in communicating propositions about simple color experiences as well as as mystical experiences is an experimental awareness on the part of the addressee of the experience referred to by the proposition.

I believe that he real reason for the mystic's claiming some

---

[1] I believe that Professor Stace, in accordance with his latest formulation of the empirical theory of meaning, put forth in "Some Misinterpretations of Empiricism" (*Mind*, 1958), would be forced to attribute empirical meaning to mystical propositions. There he states that a word or sentence has empirical meaning if it refers to some specific but unanalyzable experiential datum or if it is amenable to a process of analysis, the end-terms of which will be such experiential data.

sort of unique ineffability for his experience is to be found in the inestimable significance and value which the experience has for him. It seems that the more highly we prize some experience the more we shun applying concepts to it. Like the composer who shuns writing program notes for his symphony because he fears, and rightly so, that eventually the reading of the program notes will take the place of the direct listening experience of the music, the mystic is afraid that the concepts by which he describes his experience will become surrogates for the experience itself. Both men are telling us by their refusal to conceptualize their experience that it is the direct experience itself which counts and that language is a very poor substitute.

(3) *Propositions describing mystical experiences contain self-contradictions.*[2] Professor Stace finds the basic paradox of the Divine in the contradiction between the positive and negative conceptions of the Divine. "The latter denies all predicates of Him, even that of existence; whereas, the former says that He is the fullness of Being, the ultimate reality" (p. 34).

It seem to me that this alleged contradition between the positive and negative conceptions of the Divine rests on the equivocation of the term "exist." When in the negative conception of the Divine the mystic denies that God *exists,* he means, by "exist," "to be a fact in a spatio-temporal order"; whereas, when from the positive conception of the Divine he claims that God *exists* or *Is,* he means now, by "exist," "to be an eternal or timeless Being," which is supposedly apprehended through mystical experiences. If we distinguish between these two different meanings of "exist" the alleged contradiction between the positive and negative conception of the Divine disappears.

This still does not explain away many seemingly self-contradictory statements made by mystics. They refer to their experi-

[2] Paul Henle, in his excellent article, "Mysticism and Semantics" (*Philosophy and Phenomenological Research,* 1948), claims that the mystic is not entitled to claim that his mystical utterances are ineffable in regard to all symbolism, possible as well as actual. In principle we cannot know that any utterance is ineffable in any possible symbol system; for, in order to know that a certain utterance is ineffable, we should have to find a new symbolism for expressing what is now ineffable. [Paul Henle's article may be found on p. 274 in this book.]

ence as being at once passive and active, personal and impersonal, full and empty, containing a multiplicity of objects and
still being a Oneness without parts, etc. What I will try to show
is that such statements are not literal self-contradictions because
the law of contradiction does not apply to them. The function
of mystical statements is not the cognitive one of literally describing facts in space and time, but rather that of evoking
in the addressee certain feelings and emotions in the same way
that esthetic language does. In the following discussion we will
consider *only* propositions having some sort of empirical
meaning, i.e., propositions referring to something which is a
content of a direct experience. Mystical propositions, while
not having existential import in the strictest sense since they
do not refer to facts in space and time, still come under the
heading of propositions having empirical meaning, since, as we
tried to prove, they do have experiential import.

Now in regard to propositions having empirical meaning
we can say that one proposition contradicts another proposition
only if we first know the time factor of the two propositions.[3]
The law of contradiction has application only to those empirical
propositions in which the time factor can be specified. For this
reason *we can never say that two mystical propositions are
contradictories because the time factor of the two propositions
can never be specified.* The reason why the time factor of a
mystical proposition can never be specified is that such a proposition refers to an experience which is, as the mystic himself
claims, phenomenologically atemporal, containing within itself
no change and therefore no relations of before and after. Therefore when we read in the *Isa Upanishad,* "It (the Self) stirs and
it stirs not," we cannot say that such a proposition is a self-
contradiction because the mystic can never tell us whether it
stirs and also stirs not *at one and the same moment of time.* He
cannot supply us with this information because his experience
is atemporal.

The conclusion to be drawn from this analysis is that mysti-

---

[3] In formulating the law of contradiction Aristotle wrote, "The
same attribute cannot *at the same time* belong and not belong to the
same subject in the same respect" (*Metaphysics,* 1005b, 17).

cal propositions cannot be said to be literally self-contradictory.[4] The law of contradiction is a rule of discourse applying *only* to propositions having a cognitive function, i.e., propositions referring to events locatable in some definite region of space and time. The propositions of the mystics are alogical. They do not violate the law of contradiction—it simply does not apply to them. Professor Stace would agree with the end result of this analysis if not with the means by which it is achieved; for he has said that the function of mystical propositions is not cognitive, but rather that of *evoking* within us a certain type of experience (p. 120). But the evocative function of language is not unique to mystical symbolism; it is equally true of the esthetic use of language, so that we would not have shown that mystical experiences were ineffable in some unique sense. In describing my listening experience of the second movement of Beethoven's 7th Symphony I might say that it is the most tragic and yet the most joyous music I ever heard. If someone should then ask, "Do you mean at the same moment of time?," I would not know how to answer, for, as in the case of mystical propositions, I would not be able to specify the time factor. By describing the movement as being both tragic and joyous I am referring to an emotional quality which permeates the *entire* movement, and the function of my language is to evoke in the addressee an emotional experience of a similar type to the one I had when I listened to the movement.

(4) *Propositions describing mystical experiences contradict propositions describing non-mystical experiences.* This is unquestionably the case, for mystical propositions claim that space, time, and multiplicity are unreal; whereas propositions describing non-mystical experiences deny this. But it does not follow that mystical propositions are empirically meaningless, and consequently that mystical experiences are ineffable. We

[4] Professor Stace writes: "The Ultimate can be neither self-consistent nor self-contradictory, for both of these are logical categories. It is neither logical nor illogical, but alogical" (p. 153). This is in complete concordance with the conclusion reached in this paper. However, Professor Stace's claim that the Ultimate is alogical is obviously inconsistent with his assertion thaat there is a logical contradiction between the negative and positive conceptions of the Ultimate or Divine.

can understand the empirical meaning of each one of a pair of contradictory propositions; it is only the conjunction of these two contradictory propositions into a single proposition which becomes empirically meaningless. If our analysis has been correct, we understand what sort of experiences are being referred to by mystical propositions, and the fact that such proposions contradict propositions refererring to non-mystical experiences does not render mystical experiences ineffable any more than it renders non-mystical experiences ineffable. Because mystical experiences are so different from the ordinary run-of-the mill experiences, the mystic feels that these experiences are mysterious and paradoxical.

II. Relation of the Eternal to the Temporal Order of Being

During the mystical experience the mystic experiences only one order of being, the so-called eternal order. Within his experience there is no opposition between the eternal and temporal since the temporal world then simply does not exist for him; therefore, there is no contradiction for him to be puzzled over or to try and explain away. But most of the mystic's life is lived outside of the mystical moment, and it is then that he feels the contradiction between his mystical and non-mystical experiences. He may then even attempt to reconcile intellectually these two seemingly diametrically opposed realms of being, and so become involved in contradictions.

Professor Stace's answer to the seeming contradiction between the eternal and temporal order of being takes the form of an *exclusive* disjunction: *Either* we take our stand *outside* the mystical experience, as the naturalist does, in which case mystical experiences are purely subjective feelings and emotions; *or* we take our stand *inside* the mystical experience, in which case the natural world of space, time, and multiplicity is unreal or illusory. These two possible standpoints or perspectives are disjuncts in an exclusive disjunction, which means that *we cannot take both of these standpoinds at the same time.* We must affirm one of these disjuncts and so deny the other.

However, in his theory of intersection Professor Stace

makes this disjunction *inclusive*. The eternal and natural order intersect at each point of space and time. We know of such an intersection through the experience of the mystic. The mystic lives in both orders and at the moment of his mystical experience the two orders intersect. The point at which his experience takes place can be considered as a moment of time if viewed from the naturalistic standpoint, or it can be seen from within as the eternal Now-moment. "It is one and the same human consciousness which experiences both the temporal or natural and the eternal and infinite order which is disclosed in mystical illumination. Thus this identity of eternity with a temporal moment is an actual experienced fact, and this fact is what is metaphorically represented by the image of intersection" (p. 82).

Professor Stace's claim that the "identity of eternity with a temporal moment is an actual experienced fact" is ambiguous. It could mean: (1) that one and the same person has mystical experiences and *at other times* has experiences of a non-mystical variety; and (2) that the mystic experiences in the mystical experience the intersection of the two orders. In the case of (1) there is no direct experience of the intersection of the two orders; herein we are still left with an exclusive disjunction betwen the naturalistic and mystic standpoints. In the case of (2) the intersection is the content of a single direct intuitive experience.

I believe that the first interpretation is the only defensible one. It is certainly the case that one and the same person can have both mystical and non-mystical experiences, but it is not true that a person can have an experience which is *at once both* mystical and non-mystical. As the mystic himself has proclaimed, a person cannot at the same time experience both the eternal and the temporal; by definition it follows that if a person is having a mystical experience he cannot at the same time be having a non-mystical experience. Therefore it is not possible for a person to have a single direct experience in which the temporal and timeless realms of being intersect because for this to happen he would have to have an experience which was at once both mystical and non-mystical, and by defintion this is impossible. The intersection of the eternal and the temporal is arrived at through an intellectual interpretation, and can never be the content of any direct experience.

In his theory of intersection, Professor Stace uses at the same time the language of both mystic and naturalist, and in this way attempts to escape the confines of his own exclusive disjunction. By saying that *at a moment in time* a mystic experiences the *eternal* he is employing at the same time the language of both mystic and naturalist, and thereby makes his disjunction inclusive by *adopting both standpoints at the same time.* But insofar as we use the language of the naturalist we must describe the mystical experience as a subjective psychological event taking place at some moment of time, and insofar as we adopt the mystical standpoint we must describe the experience as union with the eternal or infinite and so deny that there is a temporal order. From the latter standpoint there is no *moment in time* at which the experience takes place.

III. Objectivity of Mystical Experience

It may appear that we have been begging the question up to now by referring to mystical experiences as subjective psychological experiences when viewed from the naturalistic standpoint. Some mystics would argue that the same criterion by which we judge a sense experience to be veridical or objective can be used to prove the objectivity of a mystical experience. This is the argument: The criterion for objectivity in sense experience is unanimity or agreement among observers; since there is unanimity among mystics it follows by analogy with the criterion for objectivity in sense experience that mystical experiences are objective. The fact that very few persons have had mystical experiences is not evidence against the objectivity of such experiences; for a mystical proposition, like any non-mystical one, is really a hypothetical statement saying what experiences a person will have *if* certain verifying procedures are followed. However, in the case of propositions about sense experience we can specify exactly what operations must be performed by the verifier; whereas, in the case of mystical propositions, it is far more difficult to do this. The proper steps to be taken by one who wishes to verify a mystical proposition may include living an ascetic life for twenty years—staying out of bars, not watching television, doing breathing exercises, etc. If after following the "mystic way" for twenty years this poor chap still does not have a mystical experience there is the tendency for the mystic to beg the question by definition by saying that this only proves that this person has not taken the proper steps. In this case part of the very definition of what constitutes the proper steps is the stipulation that the verifier must have a mystical experience.

Waiving this difficulty and also granting the claim for unanimity among the mystics, we can still point to a basic flaw in this argument which is due to the fact that the criterion for objectivity which is appealed to is inadequate even in the realm of sense experience. Mere unanimity or agreement among observers is not a sufficient condition for objectivity. *Everybody* who presses his finger on his eyeball will see double, *everybody* who stands at a certain spot in the desert will see the mirage, etc. The true criterion for objectivity is the Kantian one: An experience is objective if its contents can be placed in a spatio-temporal order with other experiences in accordance with scientific laws. The objectivity of a sense experience means the verifiability of further possible sense experiences which are inferred from this experience in accordance with known scientific laws. In accordance with this criterion we would say that our sense experience of seeing things double when we press our finger on our eyeball is subjective—a mere illusion—because the inferences we make from this sense experience to other possible sense experiences do not hold. When we reach out to touch the two objects which we saw we find only one. There is, then, a rupture in the temporal continuity of our experience.

In accordance with this new criterion for objectivity we must classify mystical experiences as subjective because they represent a break in the temporal continuity of our experience. What we have in the case of mystical experience is a moment of eternity, i.e., phenomenological atemporality, suddenly appearing in the midst of a temporal sequence of events. When the mystic reports that during his experience all change and multiplicity were obliterated, we must, from the naturalistic standpoint, tell him that he was "seeing things." Because we cannot fit the content of mystical experiences into a temporal order with other experiences in accordance with scientific laws, we must call these experiences subjective.

Since Professor Stace defines God or the Eternal ostensively in terms of the content of the mystical experience itself, he is not claiming that a mystical experience is evidence for the existence of some Being or Reality which transcends the experience. By God we mean the mystical experience and *nothing more*. If we accept Professor Stace's ostensive definition of God in terms of the mystical experience itself, and if we grant the fact that there are mystical experiences, then it follows that God, *in his sense*, must exist. All of this is perfectly compatible with our classification of mystical experiences as subjective pyschological experiences from the naturalistic standpoint. We cannot add to such psychological facts any existence claim; an existence claim cannot follow either deductively or inductively from a psychological claim. Since mystical experiences do not point beyond themselves to other facts they are irrefutable. We cannot dispute the claim of the mystic because, from the naturalistic standpoint, he is not making an existence claim—he is making only a psychological claim.

Professor Stace argues that each mystic experiences the same reality or Oneness. He states that since the mystic is identical with the One or God during his experience, his experience is identical with all other mystical experiences, whether of himself or of others, and this moment of time is identical with all other moments of time. "And hence there is, from within, no relation at all between one mystical experience and another and therefore no likeness or unlikeness" (p. 84). Professor Stace is writing here from the eternal standpoint; from this standpoint there is no problem of the identity of one mystical experience with another or of one moment of time with another simply because there are no other mystical experiences or moments of time. There is only the undifferentiated unity. But from the naturalistic standpoint it is not true tha the moment of one mystical experience is identical with the moment of every other mystical experience. Two or more mystical experiences can be alike as two peas in a pod as far as the phenomenological content of the experiences are concerned, but they can still be distinguished from each other by the experient's position in space and time. The fact that two mystical experiences are phenomenologically identical is no more evidence for the objective existence of the content of these experiences than is the fact that two dreams are phenomenologically identical evidence for the objective existence of the content of the dreams.

What we are left with, then, is an exclusive disjunction between the mystical and naturalistic standpoint. There is no way of getting rid of the contradiction between the claim of the mystic and the naturalist. Such a dispute is not resolvable by any empirical means; for the very criterion for objectivity in terms of temporal continuity is made from the naturalistic standpoint, and so the mystic would accuse us of begging the question from the outset. The question, "Which is the *true* reality, the one revealed to us in mystical experiences or the one revealed to us in our non-mystical experiences?," is really a value question and cannot be settled by any logical means. What a man takes to be the *really* real is a value judgment expressive of what experiences have the greatest significance for him.

4

FAITH AND REASON

FAITH, LANGUAGE, AND
RELIGIOUS EXPERIENCE: A DIALOGUE

ARTHUR C. DANTO

> *Enwrap in misty cloud, with lips*
> *that stammer, hymn chanters wan-*
> *der and are discontented.*
> Rig Veda, X, 82.

A: The conflict between science and religious faith! Fancy raising *that* old ghost. I thought by now we were all agreed that religious language, like scientific language, has its own validity in the contexts in which it is appropriate to use it. And since the contexts are different, a conflict could hardly arise. Except trivially, one doesn't celebrate Mass in the laboratory. Nor measure mass in the cathedral.

B: That notion of validity may be valid at Oxford. But not here. I'm glad the issue was raised. I believe there is a conflict, and your pun only clouds it over. As if religion were merely a matter of performing rituals! Surely some religious utterances mean to state a truth, and so undertake to do the job which scientific sentences, by common consent, are meant to do. So, in principle, a conflict can arise—even if the conflicting sentences are uttered in laboratory and cathedral respectively.

A: You surely wouldn't want to say that every so-called scientific sentence asserts, or means to assert, a truth: scientific sentences do all sorts of jobs. But considering only those sentences which do mean to do this job—they can conflict with religious sentences only if they are about the same things. But I would deny that this is ever the case.

B: There is nothing which scientific sentences cannot be about. There are no limits set for science in point of subject

Reprinted from *Religious Experience and Truth*, Sidney Hook, ed. (New York: New York University Press, 1961), by permission of New York University Press and the author.

matter. And simply as a matter of fact, scientists and religionists have talked about the same things.

A: Oh, there may well have been such disputes. But these arose only because each party misrepresented the scope of his own discipline. You, apparently, are victim to the same delusion. What do you mean by "faith," for instance?

B: One might do worse than use the old notion of which Professor Hook reminded us: to have faith is to hold for true a belief for which there is insufficient evidence. I may have great confidence in some hypothesis, and believe very strongly that experiment will bear me out. But, quoting Nietzsche, "Strong faith proves only its strength, and not the truth of what is believed in."[1] I have no right to assert my hypothesis until I have other than subjective grounds for doing so. But religious people act as though they had such a right. I'll bet you would drop your language-game immunities fast enough if you had sufficient evidence for any of *your* beliefs!

A: In fact we have evidence, *strong* evidence, but you are doubtless too narrow to regard it as such. But what in general can you mean by "sufficient evidence?" If we set our standard of "sufficient evidence" sufficiently high—none of our beliefs after all admit of perfect certainty—everything becomes faith, for everything we believe is now based upon insufficient evidence. And it would be wholly arbitrary on your part to specify a degree of confirmation such that any sentence confirmed to a lesser degree becomes faith. For I, with equal justification, could specify an upward revision. But anyway, the difference between scientific and religious beliefs cannot simply be a matter of differing degrees of confirmedness. The hypothesis to which you referred a moment back did not pass from religion to science in virtue of successfully passing tests. And should there have been a conflicting hypothesis which was disconfirmed when your hypothesis was confirmed, it would not thereby be relegated to religion.

B: No, but it would become a matter of faith if someone

---

[1] Friedrich Nietzsche, *Human, All too Human,* I.

were to now hold it for true. By faith I shall mean holding a sentence true when there exists evidence which a reasonable man would regard as sufficient for holding its contradictory. We scientists relinquish our beliefs in such circumstances. But not religious people. There, if you like, is the difference between us.

A: I am not prepared to grant this as a characterization of *religious* faith, for which, as I said, evidence is available to those not hardened to reality. You are thinking of such cases as these, perhaps. A man has faith in his success when the world has written him off as a failure. Or in his wife's chastity when half the village knows her for a trull.

B: Exactly. And only consider, if I may play your game, the contexts in which we would say "I believe in . . ." or "I have faith that. . . ." We use such propositional attitudes only when a belief has been challenged, for purpose of expressing our resolve to go on believing. If there were something wrong with the evidence brought against us, or if we were privy to a fact unavailable to our challengers, we would simply say he was wrong and show why. Instead, we take a stand. Of course I can understand this. The man has his back to the wall, and to give up his belief will mean the collapse of his universe. But that doesn't make faith a rational thing. Rationally, we ought to face the facts and not persist in illusion.

A: It is a part of the concept of faith that a man's faith be *tried*, even that he should be alone in his faith. But there are martyrs in the history of science and religion alike. And let me point out that you and I try one another's faiths. Is it not true that you are committed in advance to stand by certain of your beliefs no matter what contravening evidence religion might bring forth?

B: You *want* to try my faith. But you are hardly likely to produce evidence in support of religious beliefs.

A: Why do you say that with such force? Is it not because, as a scientist, there are certain beliefs which you hold, and must go on holding, if you are to do science at all? Beliefs you would not *allow* to be abrogated? The conflict between science and religion is then a conflict between faiths. I have this in mind: you are antecedently committed to the view that there are no ultimate dark spots in the fabric of things, and that everything, in the fullness of time, must yield to scientific understanding and explanation. Einstein wrote: "The regulations valid for the world existence are rational, that is, comprehensible to reason."[2] And surely, to say that there must always be a natural explanation is to announce a creed? If I then insist that there are ultimate mysteries, even claim to be able to point them out, you would remain unshaken in your faith. Unless, indeed, you were to convert. For a conversion it would be—from one faith to another.[3]

B: I am a scientist, interested in finding solutions to problems I regard as genuine. I believe these problems admit of solution, though I may not be clever or lucky enough to find them. If I fail, the fault at least does not lie with the world, and I should hope sooner or later that my colleagues or our successors will do what I could not. If you refer to this, then, indeed, I have faith of a kind. And so perhaps has every scientist. It may even be true that had they not had this faith, science could never have arisen or advanced. But this would then be a psychological fact concerning scientists, or a sociological fact concerning science considered externally. For the "faith" is not part of science itself. You will not find "The universe is comprehensible to reason" listed amongst the sentences which together make up a theory in physics, or chemistry, or what science you will.[4] And even were you to insert it, say as an independent postulate, it would be inert, and play no logical role there: "A wheel that can be turned though nothing else moves with it, is not part of the mechanism."[5] As for the sentences which *are* part of the

---

[2] Albert Einstein, "Science, Philosophy, and Religion," reprinted in Phillip P. Wiener (ed.), *Readings in Philosophy of Science* (New York: Charles Scribner's Sons, 1953), p. 605.

[3] John Wilson, *Language and Christian Belief* (London: The Macmillan Company, 1958), p. 64.

[4] This point was made at the conference by Professor Sidney Morgenbesser.

[5] Ludwig Wittgenstein, *Philosophical Investigations* (New York: The Macmillan Company), 271.

machine, no scientist is prepared to defend them come what
may. Of course, a man might try very hard to make a favorite
hypothesis stick. Like Priestley. But this, while possibly *his*
faith is not science's. I add, by way of an *ad hominem* remark,
that you religionists don't, as a matter of fact, treat science as
a faith amongst faiths. Have you not time and again given up
beliefs of yours which conflicted with science (in *my* sense)?
Do any of you seriously defend Genesis against geology today?
Yet I have not seen any comparable readiness to retreat when
conflicts arise between competing religions.

A: It is not quite true to say that they have been given up—
they have been seen in a new light, and interpreted so as to
remove the alleged conflict.

B: But isn't that just the same thing as to have given them
up? I mean, you obviously are not saying that Genesis is *true*.
Where then does "interpretation" get you? Suppose P and Q
are respectively scientific and religious sentences, that P and Q
are incompatible, and that you accept P. Then let R be an interpretation of Q. If R is equivalent to Q, the conflict remains, for
now R is incompatible with P, and hense false if P is true. If not
equivalent, then R now turns out to be incompatible with Q. So
either you remain in conflict with science, or you enter into
conflict with the faith of your fathers.[6]

A: You miss the point. Genesis was literally false all along.
People failed to see it for what it was, an ambitious metaphor.
And a metaphor may be true though the sentence which ex-
presses it, taken literally, is false.

B: All you tell me is that you have shifted ground since last
century's controversies. And this just makes my point for me.
There was no attempt, until science arose and threatened it, for
religionists to decide that their canon was a tissue of metaphor.
But up to that time there were plenty of opportunities to concede

---

[6] The argument here is particularly directed at the position of
Averroes. See especially "A Decisive Discourse on the Delineation of the
Relation between Religion and Philosophy," in *The Philosophy and
Theology of Averroes,* trans. Mohammad Jamil-ur-Rehman (Baroda:
Gaiekwad's Oriental Series, 1929).

this, since there were plenty of conflicts between religions. In those days you condemned your opponents as heretics or worshippers of false gods. I won't push you on the fact that there are inconsistencies even within your own canon.

A: I want to grant your point and then go on to show how little comes of granting it. Consider this analogy. The camera showed (as Socrates' mirror should have done) that representation was not a sufficient condition for art. Kandinsky showed that it was not even a necessary condition. The essence of art lies elsewhere, and works qualify as artistic independently of whether or not they are representational. The old masters thought differently, but they produced art in spite of not quite understanding what they were doing. So with my forebears. They mislocated the essence of religion and felt themselves obliged to defend every sentence of the canon. The Bible contains religious truth independently of whether it contains literal truth or not. The Genesis controversies had the valuable consequence of making us see this fact.

B: Non-objective religion! You then give up making cognitive claims? The issue goes by default. I win.

A: Not quite. My fundamentalist forebears, well meaning as they were, erred in feeling they must pitch their faith where they did. They might, as I, have given Genesis up and retained their faith intact. Genesis tells a lovely story, and makes a point, but it is bad cosmology and worse geology. But lest this, like illusions in epistemology, threaten every claim to empirical knowledge, I will go further. I will concede that every sentence in the Bible which can possibly conflict with science is to be given up. The Bible, of course, contains a number of true statements, and I understand that it has become a valuable tool for the archeologist. But even such literal truths as there may be are dismissed by me from the body of faith: consider it expunged of whatever sentence science may confirm or disconfirm.

B: That's it, is it not? What do you plan to do, now that religion is finished?

A: It's not finished, only purified. And there still remains a conflict between you and me, though not between science and religion. We believe in, and our faith rests upon, the occurrence of a miracle. Thus: "The Eternal has entered the time-series and become Temporal."[7] I don't suppose science denies this? The denial of it is not included amongst the sentences which make up theories in physics, chemistry, or whatever you regard as science. Nor would it do to list it as an independent postulate, so to speak. For it would not be part of the machinery. To be sure, it is a terribly dark thing I refer to, and utterly incomprehensible to reason, and so conflicts with the belief (dare I say "faith"?) that "the universe is comprehensible to reason." But this you have conceded not to be part of science. We have each effected a purgation. I have cleansed religion of everything which might fall within the province of science. And you have purged science of whatever might clash with religion—including the very principle I would have thought to have animated your entire enterprise. Or do you want to reconsider, and relocate "the universe is comprehensible to reason" within the body of science? In that case, as a scientist, you must stand ready to relinquish it upon discovering dark spots in the universe. Which you now must allow as possible, if only to save your belief from vacuity.

B: You would not really want me to take it back into science. For then, by *your* criterion, you would have to give up your belief in dark spots. For this would not rest upon a claim which would, by my fiat, fall within the province of science. But I need not make this move. For your belief happens to conflict with logic, which I consider part of science. Indeed, you make it very easy for me. To say that something is eternal is to say that temporal predicates are inapplicable to it. It is self-contradictory then to say that something is both temporal and nontemporal. And please spare me any pious reference to life as being bigger than logic and God as being bigger than both. You can't turn your back on logic. You may be irrational enough to believe in what is impossible, just as Tertullian was insane enough to believe in what is absurd. But impossibility (and absurdity) are

[7] Emil Brunner, *Revelation and Reason,* tran. by Olive Wyon (Philadelphia: The Westminster Press, 1946), 294 ff.

given content, after all, by logic. Had you no commitment to logic, you would not have what to believe. The question is why you want to be so perverse.

A: It only *sounds* impossible. But that is because our understanding here is limited. Our faith is that this is what *happened*. But we don't know how or why. We see as through a glass darkly.

B: The fact is that you don't understand *what* you believe in. We scientists at least know what we mean when we assert something, and then we try and find out whether it is true. You seem to work reversely: first you take something for true, and then you hope to find out what it means. Suppose a friend and I are trapped by the proprieties into sitting through a lecture in Turkish. My friend afterwards tells me that every word of it was true. I commend him on his knowledge of an exotic language, but he disclaims such knowledge: he *hopes*, he says, someday to understand Turkish. I call him either weird or silly. But now I think I know what faith is, or at least religious faith. It is not, as I thought, to hold onto a belief in the teeth of contrary evidence. For apparently nothing can count for or against a proposition, the meaning of which we do not know. How then *could* there be a conflict between science and religion? Faith is a matter of defending an incomprehensible proposition.

A: You show your shallowness. The language is, and must be, paradoxical. It makes plain by not making plain. Its purpose is to show how exceptional and how awesome a thing it is which we worship. The paradox is *there*, at the heart of things. Christ was human, and fully so. And he was fully divine as well. Temporal *and* eternal. Ordinarily, of course, "is human" and "is divine" are contrary predicates, and contrast with one another. But contrary predicates are both true of Jesus. Or Krishna, if you are a Hindu. Or Buddha if you accept the *Lotus Sutra*. Christ is a paradoxical entity. I accept logic everywhere but here, and my acceptance of it helps to throw the entire world into contrast with the dark spot at its core.

B: I don't understand a word you say. And neither do you.

A: "It is the duty of the human understanding to understand that there are things which it does not understand, and what these things are. . . . The paradox is not a consession but a category, an ontological relation between an existing cognitive spirit and an eternal truth."[8] So wrote Kierkegaard—who incidentally helped do for religion what Kandinsky did for art.

B: We should have to change our assessment of Kandinsky were we to discover that his paintings showed the world as he *saw* it. For then it would not be a case of nonrepresenting, which was to have been his contribution to the concept of art, but rather a case of representing the world abnormally. Enlarging rather than eliminating the subject matter. But that's inconsistent with what you said.

A: Nonetheless I like your point. Why not represent reaches of reality abstractly which cannot be captured via conventional imagery? Why not describe reaches of reality paradoxically when consistent language fails?

B: But your statement of the paradox begs an important question. The paradox arises only because both contrary predicates are allegedly true of Christ. One of these predicates is "is divine." But divine is a word I fail to understand. Nor can you simply say that to be divine is to be a paradoxical entity. For the paradox arises only because Christ is supposedly *already* divine: his being divine is *one pole* of the paradox. Notice that "is human" contrasts with many predicates. Grant me that it contrasts with "is vegetable." Then to say that something is a human vegetable is to posit a paradoxical entity, as you like to say. But surely you don't believe in every possible impossibility. Hence the object of worship here is doubly obscure. Once because paradoxical. But more basically, once because divine. The predicate which must antecedently be cleared up then is "is divine." What does it mean?

A: It is learnt by ostension. Except God revealed Himself the term would not be in the language. Christ was a divine being, Jesus an individual in history. Those who saw Jesus saw a divine being, given that Christ and Jesus were identical. $Fa \cdot a = b \cdot] \cdot Fb. \ Fa \cdot a = b \cdot] \cdot Fb.$

[8] Sören Kierkegaard, *Journals*, p. 633. Cited by S. R. Hopper in his essay, "Paradox" in *Handbook of Christian Theology* (New York: Meridian Books, Inc., 1958), p. 262.

B: But not everyone apparently saw him as such. What did they fail to *sense?* You call him the Son of God. But you can't teach the meaning of the term by referring back to God, for the problem gets raised all over again. Think of a kind of Prince and Pauper situation: suppose someone were a replica of Jesus, only of merely human provenance. The visual experience of seeing Jesus matches the visual experience of seeing his counterpart, admittedly nondivine. Then divineness cannot be seen, for by hypothesis the visual experiences are identical. But then suppose this were the case for each sense modality. How then is divinity to be sensed and "is divine" learnt?

A: Divinity is sensed by the eye of faith. "The numinous cannot be 'taught.' It has to be awakened from the spirit."[9]

B: Ah, I thought we were going to get a behavioral criterion. I thought you were going to tell me Christ performed miracles but His replica could not.

A: The miracles were signs and portents of His divinity, toward which they pointed. But how should we really understand what we being pointed to only by means of signposts? No, they may have helped cause men to be awakened to divineness. But they were not the object of the awareness. "Is divine" is primitive. It cannot be explicitly defined, and hence cannot be eliminated in favor of the garden variety of observational terms.

B: Could it not perhaps be *reduced?* Let N be a numinous predicate. And F and G observational predicates. Then we could say that if a is F, then a is N if and only if a is G.

A: You know as well as I that this doesn't eliminate N. You might just as well regard it as primitive.

B: Still, we would have a decisive test for numinosity if we could decide upon F and G.

A: We would not. If you put something claimed to be soluble in water which fails to dissolve, then this decisively tells against its being soluble in water. But here it very much would

[9] Rudolph Otto, *The Idea of the Holy,* trans. J. W. Harvey (London: Cumberlege, 1950), p. 67. Cited in Ninian Smart, *Reasons and Faiths* (London: Routledge and Kegan Paul, 1958), p. 27. Smart's book ought to be quite widely read, not least of all because of his use of Oriental materials.

depend upon who was performing the test. You, lacking grace, might get a negative result. But the argument is silly. Numinosity is a manifest property.

B: I *could* get a decisive test providing N were allegedly manifest to somebody. I simply present him with *a*, and then *a* is N if he *says* it is. My only problem is to find a numinosity detector.

A: We call that trusting to authority. And for the bulk of mankind that is the best that can be done. We rely for our knowledge of the mysteries upon saints and prophets. Isn't that the gist of faith?

B: The gist of faith lies in believing that somebody knows what he is talking about. If that's what your faith is, I wish you joy. I prefer clarity. And I know that I haven't a clue as to what divinity means. For *me* there is a disposition on the part of certain entities to elicit "N" from those specially disposed to respond religiously to those entities. But "N" as yet means nothing more to me than that. How, for instance, am I to know whether or not they speak the truth when they say "N"?

A: Aren't you being rash in supposing them to be making an assertion, true or false, to begin with? It may simply be a kind of ejaculation, a wince upon being struck by holiness. Or better—it may be a contingent fact that they respond verbally at all. Instead they could fall prostrate. Or jump. Or clap their hands. And you, in their place, would perhaps not respond at all. Merely peer in puzzlement at their odd behavior or notice nothing out of the ordinary were they not present and reacting. That is, you would be lost and anaesthetic.

B: But could these inspired men not tell me afterward what they saw ("saw") when the reaction occurred?

A: That's just it. They *try*. But it is hard for them, and the words come out sounding paradoxical. For this reason I neglected to take up your point about canonical inconsistencies. Consider: "Grasping without hands, hasting without feet, he sees without eyes, he hears without ears."[10] It is the Self which

---

[10] *Svetāśvatara Upanishad*, III, 19. trans. Max Müller, in Nicol Macnicol (ed.), *Hindu Scriptures* (Everyman's Library).

is here referred to: "smaller than small, greater than great." The writer is not trying to be obscure. But this is the only way he can capture in words a concept which strains the rules of usage.

B: But what really does he *tell* me? Suppose I am told of a new theological discovery, namely that Brahma wears a hat. And then I am told that it is a divine hat and worn infinitely, since Brahma has neither head nor shape. In what sense then is a hat being worn? Why use *these* words? I am told that God exists but in a "different sense" of *exists*. Then if he doesn't exist (in the plain sense) why use *that* word? Or that God loves us—but in a wholly special sense of *love*. Or God is a circle whose center is everywhere and circumference nowhere. But this is then to have neither a center nor a circumference, and hence not to be a circle. One half of the description cancels out the other half. And what is left over but just noise?

A: But we after all speak in such wise even in normal circumstances. A man's wife dies after a long and painful illness. He says he is happy and unhappy at once. Does he contradict himself? I should think not. Or someone says he loves someone and he doesn't. Or that he can and he can't do something. Or that something is and isn't *F*. The conjuncts go together and don't cancel each other out. In a way, Cusanus's "definition" is a sophisticated stammer before the ineffable. The religious man's imagination is exercised in saying, by means of such expressions, what cannot otherwise be said. For the object of his discourse cuts across what in ordinary experience are mutually exclusive categories. And hence is paradoxical.

B: I call that misplaced concreteness. Language may be paradoxical, but not the world.

A: On the contrary. The language is clear—providing we understand the mode of utterance appropriate here. It clearly depicts a mystery. And tries to draw our attention to the mysteriousness. That is the main use of religious language.

B: The issue between us looks clear now. But I cannot accept your analysis.

A: Only because of your faith that there are no dark spots.

B: But this is surely not a *religious* faith if you are right.

For a religious faith is based upon believing in dark spots. That rules me out.

A: I should think it a dark spot indeed if the universe were such that it contained no dark spots. What a miracle it would be if the universe were comprehensible to reason! We are of one mind after all, you and I.

B: We are *not*.

FAITH

RICHARD TAYLOR

"Our most holy religion," David Hume said, "is founded on *faith,* not on reason." (All quotations are from the last two paragraphs of Hume's essay "Of Miracles.") He did not then conclude that it ought, therefore, to be rejected by reasonable men. On the contrary, he suggests that rational evaluation has no proper place in this realm to begin with, that a religious man need not feel in the least compelled to put his religion "to such a trial as it is, by no means, fitted to endure," and he brands as "dangerous friends or disguised enemies" of religion those "who have undertaken to defend it by the principles of human reason."

I want to defend Hume's suggestion, and go a bit farther by eliciting some things that seem uniquely characteristic of *Christian* faith, in order to show what it has, and what it has not, in common with other things to which it is often compared. I limited myself to Christian faith, because I know rather little of any other, and faith is, with love and hope, supposed to be a uniquely Christian virtue.

Faith and Reason

Faith is not reason, else religion would be, along with logic and metaphysics, a part of philosophy, which is assuredly is not. Nor is faith belief resting on scientific or historical inquiry, else religion would be part of the corpus of human knowledge, which it clearly is not. More than that, it seems evident that by the normal, common-sense criteria of what is reasonable, the content of Christian faith is *un*reasonable. This, I believe, should be the starting point, the *datum,* of any discussion of faith and reason.

Reprinted from *Religious Experience and Truth,* Sidney Hook, ed. (New York: New York University Press, 1961), by permission of New York University Press and the author.

It is, for instance, an essential content of the Christian faith that, at a certain quite recent time, God became man, dwelt among us in the person of a humble servant, and then, for a sacred purpose, died, to live again. Now, apologetics usually addresses itself to the *details* of this story, to show that they are not inherently incredible, but this is to miss the point. It is indeed *possible* to believe it, and in the strict sense the story is credible. Millions of people do most deeply and firmly believe it. But even the barest statement of the content of that belief makes it manifest that it does not and, I think, could not, ever result from rational inquiry. "Mere reason," Hume said, "is insufficient to convince us of its veracity." The Christian begins the recital of his faith with the words, "I believe," and it would be an utter distortion to construe this as anything like "I have inquired, and found it reasonable to conclude." If there were a man who could say that in honesty, as I think there is not, then he would, in a clear and ordinary sense, believe, but he would have no religious faith whatsoever, and his beliefs themselves would be robbed of what would make them religious.

Now if this essential and (it seems to me) obvious unreasonableness of Christian belief could be recognized at the outset of any discussion of religion, involving rationalists on the one hand and believers on the other, we would be spared the tiresome attack and apologetics upon which nothing ultimately turns, the believer would be spared what is, in fact, an uncalled-for task of reducing his faith to reason or science, which can, as Hume noted, result only in "exposing" it as neither, and the rationalist would be granted his main point, not as a conclusion triumphantly extracted, but as a datum too obvious to labor.

Faith and Certainty

Why, then, does a devout Christian embrace these beliefs? Now this very question, on the lips of a philosopher, is wrongly expressed, for he invariably intends it as a request for reasons, as a means of putting the beliefs to that unfair "trial" of which Hume spoke. Yet there is a clear and definite answer to this

question, which has the merit of being true and evident to anyone who has known intimately those who dwell in the at-
mosphere of faith. The reason the Christian believes that story
around which his whole life turns is, simply, that he cannot
help it. If he is trapped into eliciting grounds for it, they are
grounds given after the fact of conviction. Within "the circle
of faith," as one symposiast observed, the question whether on
the evidence one *ought* to believe "does not arise." One neither
seeks nor needs grounds for the acceptance of what he cannot
help believing. "Whoever is moved by *faith* to assent," Hume
wrote, "is conscious of a continued miracle in his own person,
which subverts all the principles of his understanding, and
gives him a determination to believe. . . ." It is this fact of faith
which drives philosophers to such exasperation, in the face of
which the believer is nonetheless so utterly unmoved.

The believer sees his life as a gift of God, the world as the
creation of God, his own purposes, insofar as they are noble,
as the purposes of God, and history as exhibiting a divine plan,
made known to him through the Christian story. He sees things
this way, just because they do seem so, and he cannot help it.
This is why, for him, faith is so "easy," and secular arguments
to the contrary so beside the point. No one seeks evidence for
that of which he is entirely convinced, or regards as relevant
what seems to others to cast doubt. The believer is like a child
who recoils from danger, as exhibited, for instance, in what he
for the first time sees as a fierce animal; the child has no difficulty *believing* he is in peril, just because he cannot help believing it, yet his belief results not at all from induction based
on past experience with fierce animals, and no reassurances,
garnered from *our* past experience, relieve his terror at all.

Some Confusions

If this is what religious faith essentially is—if, as a believer
might poetically but, I think, correctly describe it, faith is an
involuntary conviction, often regarded as a "gift," on the part
of one who has voluntarily opened his mind and heart to receive
it—then certain common misunderstandings can be removed.

In the first place, faith should never be likened to an *assumption*, such as the scientist's assumption of the uniformity of nature, or what not. An assumption is an intellectual device for furthering inquiry. It need not be a conviction nor, indeed, even a belief. But a half-hearted faith is no religious faith. Faith thus has that much, at least, in common with knowledge, that it is a *conviction*, and its subjective state is *certainty*. One thus wholly distorts faith if he represents the believer as just "taking" certain things "on faith," and then reasons, like a philosopher, from these beginnings, as though what were thus "taken" could, like an assumption, be rejected at will.

Again, it is a misunderstanding to represent faith as "mere tenacity." Tenacity consists in stubbornly clinging to what one hopes, but of which one is not fully convinced. The child who is instantly convinced of danger in the presence of an animal is not being tenacious or stubborn, even in the face of verbal reassurances, and no more is the Christian whose acts are moved by faith. The believer does not so much *shun* evidence as something that might *shake* his faith, but rather regards it as not to the point. In this he may appear to philosophers to be mistaken, but only if one supposes, as he need not, that one should hold only such beliefs as are rational.

Again, it is misleading to refer to any set of propositions, such as those embodied in a creed, as being this or that person's "faith." Concerning that content of belief in which one is convinced by faith, it is logically (though I think not otherwise) possible that one might be convinced by evidence, in which case it would have no more to do with faith or religion than do the statements in a newspaper. This observation has this practical importance, that it is quite possible—in fact, common—for the faith of different believers to be one and the same, despite creedal differences.

And finally, both "faith" (or "fideism") and "reason" (or "rationalism") can be, and often are, used as pejorative terms, and as terms of commendation. Which side one takes here is arbitrary, for there is no non-question-begging way of deciding. A rationalist can perhaps find reasons for being a rationalist, though this is doubtful; but in any case it would betray a basic misunderstanding to expect a fideist to do likewise. This is brought out quite clearly by the direction that discussions of religion usually take. A philosophical teacher will often, for instance, labor long to persuade his audience that the content of Christian faith is unreasonable, which is a shamefully easy task for him, unworthy of his learning. Then suddenly, the underlying assumption comes to light that Christian beliefs ought, therefore, to be abandoned by rational people! A religious hearer of this discourse might well reply that, religion being unreasonable but nonetheless manifestly worthy of belief, we should conclude with Hume that reason, in this realm at least, ought to be rejected. Now, one can decide *that* issue by any light that is granted him, but it is worth stressing that the believer's position on it is just exactly as good, and just as bad, as the rational sceptic's.

NATURALISM AND FIRST PRINCIPLES

SIDNEY HOOK

In this paper I propose to raise and discuss what I regard as the most fundamental problem in the intellectual enterprise which goes by the name of philosophy, *viz.*, what it means for human behavior to be reasonable or rational. Some philosophers have referred to it as the nature of intelligibility. I have been led to this question primarily because of some recent criticisms of naturalism which charge that this philosophy arbitrarily imposes its own canons of rationality or intelligibility on existence and therefore denies certain important truths about the world and human experience on a priori grounds.

A similar question has also been raised by some fashionable sociological views of knowledge according to which there are irreducibly different modes of knowing illustrated in different cultures so that there is no such thing as a universally, objective valid method of determining rationality or intelligibility, independent of time or society or class, or even of party. On this latter view it is sometimes argued that moral, social and political conflicts are the results of conflicting logics of inquiry. Sometimes the converse is argued, *i.e.*, irreducible social conflicts give rise to irreducibly different criteria of truth. In either case no one method can claim universal and exclusive validity. Indeed, to claim that any one method of establishing truths is better than another is to be guilty of philosophical imperialism almost in the same way that the claim of superiority for the institutions of modern western, democratic society evinces cultural imperialism.

My argument will make—I do not say establish—the following points: (1) that despite all the basic conflicts over first principles of thinking or evidence, there are working truths on the level of practical living which are everywhere recognized and which everywhere determine the pattern of reasonable conduct in secular affairs, *viz.*, the effective use of means to achieve ends. Rationality on this level is not merely as Charles Peirce suggests "being governed by final causes" but so using the means and materials of the situation in which final causes are pursued as to achieve a maximum of functional adaptation between means and ends. (2) Second, this conception of rationality is not limited to our culture and to our time but is supported by the available anthropological evidence. The mind of primitive man, medieval man, communist man, for all the claims that have been made about their differences, is no different from our own. This is not incompatible with believing that in respect to discovering new truth one or another group of men, in virtue of *historical*, perhaps genetic reasons, at a given time may be in possession of superior powers. (3) Third, scientific method is the refinement of the canons of rationality and intelligibility exhibited by the techniques of behavior and habits of inference involved in the arts and crafts of men; its pattern is everywhere discernable even when overlaid with myth and ritual. (4) Fourth, the systematization of what is involved in the scientific method of inquiry is what we mean by naturalism, and the characteristic doctrines of naturalism like the denial of disembodied spirits generalize the cumulative evidence won by the use of this method. (5) Fifth, that the criticisms of naturalism from which the paper takes its point of departure can be met by showing that although the assumptions of naturalism are not necessarily true they are more reasonable than their alternatives. (6) Sixth, "Every reasoning itself holds out some expectation" (Peirce). Ultimately the rules of logic are instruments of discourse which enable us to avoid the shocks and surprises, the disasters and disappointments in attempting to understand the nature of the world and our own intentions and purposes. One method of reasoning is more valid than another because its use enables us to make the knowledge we have today more coherent, and more easily facilitates adding new knowledge to it.

This is the ground plan of the essay. Space permits the development here of only the first five points.

1

That first principles must be justified before we can achieve assured knowledge is a view seemingly held by some philosophers but rarely by anyone else. Scientists, for example, have satisfactorily solved problem after problem without feeling called upon to solve the problem of justifying their first principles. Not only scientists but people of ordinary affairs generally know when something is truer than something else without knowing, or even claiming to know, what is *absolutely* true. To say that we do not have to know what is ultimately or absolutely true or good in order to know what is truer or better, sounds dialectically impossible. But I submit that this is actually the way common sense and science operate. Even the most rationalist of philosophers in their nonprofessional capacity make effective use of everyday knowledge long before they reach their uncertain conclusions about the validity of first principles. It isn't necessary to assert that we know what is absolutely true about the cause of tuberculosis to know that a certain germ has more to do with it than climate. Similarly, few people know what their ultimate values are, and yet almost everyone will claim to know that it is better for human beings to do productive labor for a living than to be recipients of charity. Deny propositions of this sort and insist that declarations of the truer or better must wait upon knowledge of *the* true or *the* good, and the whole of human inquiry anywhere would come to halt.

This is not to assert that there is no problem concerning the jusitfication of first principles or of those rules of procedure which we follow when we reach the knowledge about which there is a maximum of agreement among human beings. What I am asserting is that the justification of rules of procedures is not of a different logical order, possessing so to speak another or higher type of necessity than the actions of which they are the rule. More specifically what I am asserting is that there is no such thing as strictly logical justification of first principles in science or common sense since proof by definition involves the reduction of all statements to indefinable terms and undemonstrable propositions or to propositions themselves so reducible. And secondly, what I am further asserting is that in the sense in which justification of first principles is an intelligible question—as when someone asks me why I regard naturalism as a truer or more adequate doctrine than its rivals —the answer will take the same *general* form of the answers given by those who do the world's work—the cobblers, the carpenters and gardeners—when they are asked to justify one set of procedures rather than alternative ones.

In other words I am saying somewhat differently what William James observed in *The Problems of Philosophy* although it is alleged he sometimes sinned against the meaning of his own words. "Philosophy," he there says, "taken as something distinct from science or human affairs, follows no method peculiar to itself. All our thinking today has evolved gradually out of primitive human thought, and the only really important changes that have come over its manner (as distinguished from the matters in which it believes) are a *greater* hesitancy in asserting its convictions, and the *habit* of seeking verification for them when it can." [my italics]

Such an approach, as I understand it, is the only one that can consistently be advanced by naturalists in justifying their first principles. This has provoked the retort that it is stupendously question-begging, that since the methods and categories of common day activity and science—upon which naturalism relies—are designed to take note only of the existence of certain things, the existence of other things like immaterial entities, cosmic purposes, Gods, and disembodied souls are ruled out *a priori*. The assertion of their existence on the naturalist's view must therefore be assumed to be not merely false but meaningless or contradictory. Since we are concerned here with questions of existential fact, the naturalist who naïvely believes himself to be imbued with a spirit of natural piety for a world he has not created, is taxed with the ironic charge of legislating for all existence.

Before evaluating the charge of circularity it is important to realize that if valid, it holds for *every* philosophical position. We cannot break out of this circularity by invoking only the law of contradiction, unless we are prepared to hold that all knowledge is analytic and that the differences between nature and history, with all their contingency, and mathematics and logic disappear. Certainly, whatever falls outside the scope of the basic explanatory categories of any philosophical position cannot be recognized. This is a tautology. That these categories are restrictive follows from their claim to be meaningful since a necessary condition of a meaningful statement is that it should be incompatible with its opposite. The only legitimate question here is whether they are narrowly restrictive, whether there are matters of knowledge in common experience which they exclude or whose existence they make unintelligible.

Since every philosophic position must start somewhere and make some preliminary or initial assumptions that can be challenged at least verbally by other philosophers, it is always possible to level the charge of circularity. But what shall we therefore conclude? That these assumptions are mere stipulations or arbitrary postulations which express nothing but the *resolutions* of philosophers. This would be voluntarism gone mad. Philosophers might just as well close up shop insofar as they claim for their position some objective validity in reporting or interpreting the facts of experience. For even voluntarism could not sustain itself against the charge of circularity.

The naturalist does not despair because he cannot demonstrate what is by definition indemonstrable. Nor can he rely upon intuitions or revealed dogmas because of their irreducible plurality. He believes he can show that although not demonstrable, his assumptions can be made reasonable to "reasonable" men. And the mark of a "reasonable" man is his willingness to take responsibility for his actions, to explain why he proceeds to do one thing rather than another, and to recognize that it is his conduct, insofar as it is voluntary, which commits him to a principle of belief rather than any form of words where the two seem at odds with each other. The naturalist does not speak, as one of its critics does, in large terms of "justifying philosophical categories as rationally and comprehensively as possible," and then fail to tell us in what specific ways philosophical rationality and comprehensiveness differ from scientific rationality and comprehensiveness. Are the laws of logic and the canons of evidence and relevance any different in philosophy from what they are in science and common sense?

To every critic of naturalism who has charged it with circularity I propose the following. Consider someone who comes to you and proclaims on the basis of some special personal experience that an all-pervasive R substance exists. It is neither physical nor psychical nor social, neither natural nor divine, nor can it be identified by, defined in, or reduced, in any sense of reduction, to any physical, psychical, or social terms. It is subject, so you are told, to no material conditions of determination whatsoever. The very request that these conditions be indicated is brushed aside as revealing a constitutional incapacity or blindness to grasp this unique entity to which all sorts of edifying qualities are attributed in an analogical sense, including a triune gender. It is granted by the believer in R that its existence cannot be logically inferred from whatever *else* is experienced, but he is quick to add that its existence cannot be logically *disproved* without assuming a question-begging philosophical position which rules out the possibility of this unique cosmic process. The next day he reports personal contact with another presence which he calls the analogical father, and the day after, the analogical grandfather, and so on, until even the most fervent supernaturalist finds himself confronted with an embarrassment of supernatural riches.

Embroider the fancy as you will. It is obvious that he can repeat almost word for word the points in the indictment of those who charge naturalists with circular reasoning.

Even if all philosophical positions are *au fond* question begging, there would still remain the task, pursued by all philosophers of determining which of all questions-begging positions is more adequate to the facts of experience. Every philosopher who serious attempts an answer does assume *in fact* that there is some common method of determining when a position is adequate to the facts of experience and when not. The contention of the naturalist is that this common method is in principle continuous with the method which we ordinarily use to hold individuals to responsible utterance about the existence of things in the world—a method which is pre-eminently illustrated in the ways in which men everywhere solve the problem of adaptation of material means to ends.

2

The procedures which are the matrix of reasonable conduct everywhere seem to me to be clearly involved in what broadly speaking we may call the technological aspect of human culture. It is not necessary to maintain that tool using is the only characteristic which differentiates human society from animal societies to recognize that whereas only some nonhuman animals occasionally use natural objects as tools, all human animals, wherever they are found, *make* their own tools. What distinguishes modern society from primitive society is not the presence of inventions but the organization of inventiveness.

Anthropological evidence leaves no doubt that primitive man wherever found solved tremendous problems of adjustments and survival. With a little imagination we can appreciate that starting from scratch such things as the invention of fire and the wheel, the cultivation of plants, domestication of cattle, and the smelting of metal represent inventive feats of a high order. There is an obvious continuity between our own technology and that of our primitive ancestors. "The sapling," says A. A. Goldenweiser, "bent out of its natural position to provide the dynamic factor in a primitive trap, is the remote forerunner of a spring which runs untold millions of watches and performs numerous other tasks in modern technology. The achievement of Alexander the Great in cutting the Gordian knot, though dramatic, did not equal that other achievement—the tying of the first knot. And this knot, in the midst of an ever-growing family of knots, is still with us."[1]

One can multiply illustrations indefinitely of the ingenious ways in which primitive man everywhere chooses between

[1] A. A. Goldenweiser, *Anthropology*, N. Y., 1937, p. 134.

alternate means to achieve the particular end, improves upon these means and tests them by their relative efficacy in achieving determinate results. What stands out in my mind particularly is the impressive functional economy of the Eskimo's composite harpoon, that marvelous contrivance by which he spears seal, walrus, and whale, and especially the way in which the precious point is recovered. Hundreds of decisions must have been made and tested by their consequences before the instrument finally took shape.

The patterns of rationality does not extend of course to all aspects of primitive life any more than it does to our own life, but it points to a universal pattern of intelligibility understood by everyone who grasps the problem which the tool or technical process is designed to solve. Where religion or myth does not influence technology, the indefinite perfectability, so to speak, of the particular instrument is recognized or another one is substituted which gives more reliable results. Thus, for example, the Eskimo will abandon his ingenious harpoon for a gun when he can procure one.

The contention of Levy-Bruhl that primitive man thinks prelogically, that he denies the law of contradiction, that he is unable to isolate and distinguish logically unrelated things or ideas, that he understands by a kind of "participation" is not borne out by a study of primitive technology. Levy-Bruhl's observations are valid enough for the religious beliefs and social customs of the primitives, for their "collective representations" but not for the individual behavior of the primitive in war or hunt or in the field. One might add that Levy-Bruhl's observations can be extended to much of the religious beliefs and social customs of modern society, too. Even if all of Levy-Bruhl's claims are granted they do not invalidate Franz Boas' plausibly argued conclusion that the mental processes of primitive man in respect to inhibition of impulses, power of attention, logical thinking, and inventiveness seem essentially like our ow ..[2]

Despite their differences on other questions there is funda-

[2] F. Boas, *Mind of Primitive Man*, N. Y., 2nd edition, p. 131.

mental agreement among Levy-Bruhl, Boas, Goldenweiser and Malinowski concerning the universality of the experimental, commonsensical, practical approach to the environmental challenge. Malinowski points out that the realms of the profane or secular, and the realms of the religious or supernatural are not confused even when their respective activities are conjoined. The native plants his sweet potato with the most exacting care for the conditions of soil, moisture, and other elements which affect its growth: but in addition, he goes through some religious ritual, supported by a myth, before he believes he has a right to expect a successful crop.

"Can we regard primitive knowledge," asks Malinowski, "which, as we found is both empirical and rational, as a rudimentary stage of science, or is it not at all related to it? If by science be understood a body of rules and conceptions, based on experience and derived from it by logical inference, embodied in material achievements and in a fixed form of tradition and carried on by some sort of social organization—then there is no doubt that even the lowest savage communities have the beginnings of science, however rudimentary."[3]

Similarly, Goldenweiser:

Technique on the one hand, and religion and magic, on the other, present from one angle the opposite poles of the primitive attitude. Industry stands for common sense, knowledge, skill, objective matter of fact achievement. Religion stands for mysticism, a subjective translation of experience, a substitution of mental states for external realities and a reification of such states into presumed existences in a realm which in part is 'another' world but in part also belongs to 'this' world insofar as the two worlds interpenetrate.[4]

What all modern anthropoligists seem to agree on, as I interpret them, is that the religious or mystical elements in primitive experience, with their myths and religious rites, arise

[3] B. Malinowski, *Science, Religion and Reality*, N. Y., 1929, p. 35.
[4] Goldenweiser, *op. cit., pp.* 420–21.

not in competition with the secular knowledge of technology or as a substitute for such knowledge but as a "complement" in situations in which all the available technical means and know-how are not adequate to a desired end, or where events do not clearly or always prosper when the proper instrumentalities are employed. In a world full of dangers and surprises, in a world of time, pain and contingencies, it is not hard to understand the psychological place of religion. It is a safe generalization to say taht the depth of the religious sense is inversely proportionate to the degree of reliable control man exercises over his environment and culture. In this sense religion is a form of faith, emotion, not knowledge: when it is something more than this and competes with science or technology it becomes superstition.

We may restate this a little differently. Science or technology and religion represent two different attitudes toward the mysterious: one tries to solve mysteries, the other worships them. The first believes that mysteries may be made less mysterious even when they are not cleared up, and admits that there will always be mysteries. The second believes that some specific mysteries are final.

The relation between technology and religion is not restricted to primitive societies. Somewhere in the Talmud it is written that if a man's son is ill, the correct thing for him to do is not merely to call a doctor or merely to pray to God but to call a doctor *and* pray to God. And in our own culture this seems to be the function of nonsuperstitious religion. The theology comes as an afterthought. Even those who do not believe in God often look around for Him to thank or to blame somewhat like the atheist in the well-known story who when asked why he nailed a horseshoe over his door replied, "I really don't believe in it but I've heard it brings luck even if you don't."

In modern societies our attitudes are more complex. There is religion and religion. If you pray to God expecting rain or a baby boy, that is one thing. It is bad science, although if Rhine establishes the existence of psychokinesis (the PK effect), a power which some subjects allegedly have to influence the way dice will fall by wishing or willing, this kind of praying may not be bad science. If you pray in order to relieve your mind that is another thing. It is good psychology although there may be better psychology. If you pray without any purpose at all but out of a sense of relief, gratitude, awe or fear—that is not science at all but pure religion or art. "If scientific statements are to be called truths, religious statements should be called something else—comforts, perhaps."[5]

3

I turn now to a brief consideration of the nature of technology and technological behavior. All technological behavior is purposive behavior; the purpose provides a test of relevance, and the achievement of purpose, a ttst of the adequacy of alternative means suggested. Its every features takes note of the compulsions of the environment as well as the much more limited powers of man over the environment. Its knowledge is a form of acknowledgment—an acknowledgment of the nature of materials, the effect of motor action on the redistribution of materials, the importance of sequential order and spatial configuration. It is obviously reconstructive in intent, and makes of a natural order one that is also reasonable. It discounts the immediate qualities of use and enjoyment for the sake of anticipated consequences. Wherever we have a tool or technique, it refers not to a unique situation but a class of situations so that it has a kind of implicit universal import not separable from ultimate indiivdual applications. The better instrument recommends itself to us to the extent that it enables us to make a more reliable prediction of *observable* effects that bear on the purpose in hand—the resolution of the problem. Learning from these simple inductions of experience is usually the first manifestation of intelligence. The violation, or rather the attempted violation of established inductions, like walking off a roof or out of a window, is sometimes the first evidence of insanity.

[5] W. Crawshaw-Williams, "True Truth: or the Higher the Deeper," *Rationalist Annual* (London), 1948, p. 28.

Technological behavior may be overlaid with all sorts of propitiatory rites but it is usually possible to distinguish between the functional and ritualistic aspects of the use of instruments. In its purely functional aspect every feature of the technique can be justified by its normal fruits or consequences. In time the process of adaptation tends to give us structures that are as simple and beautiful in their economy as the ax-handle and oar, turbine and jet plane.

An analysis of the implicit logic of technology and the commonsense operations it involves, reveals that no hard and fast line of separation can be drawn between the general pattern of scientific method and reasonable procedures in the primary knowledge-getting activities of men struggling to control their environment. With the development of new instruments of discovery and measurement, and the use of mathematical notation, science becomes more abstract, more systematic, more precise, more complex. But wherever a man has had an idea sufficiently clear to enable him to draw a valid inference from it, the truth of which he sought to test by some controlled observation or experiment, he was proceeding—no matter how primitively—in a scientific way. The continuity between reasonable procedures in reaching conclusions about matters of fact everyday concern and the procedures by which we make the most esoteric discoveries in the advanced sciences cannot be breached without making the whole enterprise of science a mystery, for every science starts from, and returns to, some of these reasonable procedures. If the common-sense world is radically unreliable or illusory, every theoretical construction which is based upon it or which it tests, is no more credible.

What we might call the first order facts of science are drawn directly from the world of common-sense experience— *e.g.* that a sponge holds more water than a cloth, that a polished surface is a better reflector than an opaque one, that white clothing is cooler than black—all of which were once discoveries. In the development of science no matter what the succession of theories, these first order facts are the last to be challenged. Whether the wave theory or corpuscular theory or any other theory of light is defended, the law which states the inequality of the angles of incidence and refraction when a ray of light passes from one medium to another is not questioned. For the class of phenomena it characterizes must be accounted for irrespective of what other predictions are made. From this point of view the laws of nature may be plausibly interpreted as instrumental devices to bring within the largest explanatory scheme our empirical knowledge of first order facts and successfully to predict future experiences which then become first order facts for all other theories.

Science differs from technology in two important respects. First in generality, and second in purpose. Technology is restricted in its practical reference to useful results; whereas the practical purpose of science, if we choose to use this language, is "the advancement of knowing apart from concern with other practical affairs," *i.e.*, the building up of a systematic body of knowledge.[6]

4

If there is no break in the continuity between life sustaining technological and vocational activities anywhere, and developed scientific activities, there is still less to be said for the view that science is so intimately tied up with culture that we must in Spenglerian fashion speak of Appollonian science, Magian science, and Faustian science with irreducibly different criteria of scientific validity. This is carried to extreme lengths by the current dialectical materialistic interpretation of science which denies its classless, international character and asserts that all sciences, social as well as physical, are class sciences and party sciences. More is meant here than the obvious view that social and political circumstances, interests and ideas have influenced the kind of scientific problems considered, and the direction of their application. The actual content of science is allegedly dependent upon a class or party approach, and the philosophy of dialectical materialism is recommended because by following its lead, problems within science can be presumably solved

[6] J. Dewey, in *Journal of Philosophy*, 1945, p. 206.

which defy solution on the basis of other philosophies. It would follow from this, to paraphrase Mannheim, that different classes think differently about everything, or at least everything important, which is manifestly false. There are no "national truths" in science, and Pierre Duhem is obviously right in his claim that it is only by its deficiencies that a science can become the science of one nation rather than another. The belief that there are "class truths" or "party truths" in science rests upon the elementary confusion between the objective evidence for a theory, which if warranted, is universally valid, with the uses, good, bad, or indifferent that are made of it.

Much more worthy of notice is the claim made that what constitutes "objective evidence for a theory" is an historical conception. The history of science reveals that the conditions which a scientific theory must fulfill to be accepted have been more rigorous at some times than at others. It becomes pointless to speak, then, of scientific method *überhaupt;* there are only scientific methods.

This is a very difficult and interesting questions which I can treat only briefly and with the appearance of a dogmatism I do not feel. As a possible solution of this problem I venture the following: At any given time scientists accept as working truths hypothesis of varying degrees of generality and strength. They are more firmly convinced of the genetic theory of heredity than of the theory of organic evolution. They would be less surprised if the general theory of relativity were abandoned than the special theory. The degree of confirmation which a theory must pass muster at any time seems to be a function of the fruitfulness of previous theories in the field with similar degrees of confirmatory strength in extending our knowledge of the unknown. In addition the strength of an hypothesis is a function of the number of alternative hypotheses that are available as explanations. As a rule the more numerous the confirming instances the stronger the hypothesis. But if there are no alternative hypotheses present, we may be satisfied with far fewer confirming instances than where alternative hypotheses are present.[7] Further, the bearing of an hypothesis upon the direction of inquiry, the leads it opens up to new ways of experiment, must be taken into account.

To use a distinction of Peirce, in science a *valid* reason for believing a theory may not be a conclusive reason or even a strong reason. My contention is that what makes any reason in science a *valid* reason for believing an hypothesis is not historical, but invariant for all historical periods in the growth of science. But whether a reason is a strong reason for believing an hypothesis varies with the presence or absence of other leads and the evidence for them. This is an historical matter since no one can predict how many creative, competing insights will be current when an hypothesis presents its credentials for confirmation. I therefore do not believe that the variations in the degree of confirmatory completeness which scientific hypothesis have had to meet at different times relativizes in any way the logic of scientific method.

In passing it should be noticed that even in the history of mathematics standards of rigor seem to have varied, and for centuries mathematicians believed propositions which were only conclusively proved in the nineteenth and twentieth centuries. No one would infer from this that the notion of mathematical validity is historically conditioned, for despite the variations in rigor they progressively illustrate one underlying logical pattern of proof to which no alternative has ever been formulated.

If the foregoing is sound then I think it constitutes some reason for believing that there is only one reliable method of reaching the truth about the nature of things anywhere and at any time, that this reliable method comes to full fruition in the methods of science, and that a man's normal behavior in adapting means to ends belies his words whenever he denies it. Naturalism as a philosophy not only accepts this method but also the broad generalizations which are established by the use of it; *viz*, that the occurrence of all qualities or events

[7] C. Pierce, *Collected Works*, Vol. II, Par. 2, p. 780.

depends upon the organization of a material system in space-time, and that their emergence, development and disappearance are determined by changes in such organization.

Common sense takes the word "material" as loosely equivalent to the *materials* which men deal as they go from problem to problem; naturalism as a philosophy takes it to refer to the subject matter of the physical sciences. Neither the one nor the other asserts that only what can be observed exists, for many things may be legitimately inferred to exist (electrons, the expanding universe, the past, the other side of the moon) from what is observed; but both hold that there is no evidence for the assertion of the existence of anything which does not rest upon some observed effects.

The objections that have recently been urged against naturalism sometimes proceed from the notion that a philosophical position must justify its general assumption in some absolutely unique way. This is, as we have seen, a blind alley. Naturalism makes no assumptions over and above those that have been made every time the borders of our knowledge have been pushed back. It therefore has the cumulative weight of the historic achievements of common sense and science behind it. *If* we want to acquire new knowledge, the naturalist asserts, we should follow the basic pattern of inquiry—recognize the problem, state the hypotheses, draw the inferences, perform the experiment, and make the observation. There is no logical necessity or guarantee that we will achieve new knowledge this way but it is reasonable to act on the assumption. If one chooses to call this faith, it is certainly of a different order from the faith that new knowledge will suddenly be won in some other way—as different as the faith that "if I sow, reap, mill and bake the wheat, I shall get bread" is from the faith that "manna will fall from heaven." This difference would remain even if men decided not to reach for new knowledge, and depressed by Hiroshima, were to cry "Sufficient unto the day is the knowledge thereof." The connection between the method that one *could* follow and the conclusions that depend upon its being followed, remains unaffected by what one wants or does not want.

It is all the more surprising therefore to hear from one critic that "the most fundamental objection to the naturalist's procedure is that in Peirce's words it 'blocks the path of inquiry' in that it seeks to settle by stipulation the very issue that we need to be reasonable about if we can." Why? Because, he answers, "having committed themselves in advance to a position which identifies reasonable procedure with that which does not differ 'sharply' from that of the more developed sciences, they (the naturalists) will limit the scope of reasonable inquiry to what can be settled by the methods these sciences employ."[8]

This charge rests upon a double confusion—one of interpretation and one of observation. It is not reasonable procedure—what Dewey calls the basic pattern of inquiry—of which the naturalist says that it does not differ sharply from the more developed sciences. It is the techniques and body of knowledge which enable us to control everyday affairs of which he says that they do not differ sharply from the techniques and body of knowledge that the sciences have developed. For some of the techniques and parts of the body of knowledge of the former are always incorporated in the latter. The reasonable procedure—which according to naturalists is emphatically *not* a special technique of any special science—is *identical* in every formal aspect in every field in which we can lay claim to tested and universally agreed on knowledge about the world. How, then, can it serve as an obstacle to further inquiry, unless it is held that some disciplines have a basic pattern of inquiry quite different from that employed by critical common sense and science. What are these disciplines? What is this pattern? And what tested and universally agreed upon knowledge about this world or any other has been won by it? We are not told.

The error of observation derives from the failure to note that the driving motivation of modern naturalism has been not to block but to open up the paths of injury into whole fields which unil now have not been investigated scientifically—

---

[8] Arthur Murphy, in *Journal of Philosophy*, Vol. XLII, p. 413.

especially the social disciplines. If this criticism of the danger threatened by naturalism were just, we should expect to find naturalists opposing attempts to employ scientific method in anthropology, history and economics on the ground that the methods and techniques of mathematical physics—"the more fully developed sciences"—were not applicable to them. But it is precisely the naturalists who by distinguishing between the basic pattern of inquiry and the special techniques applicable to different matters have been trying to banish methodological purism.

It is true that there have been occasions in the past when those concerned with the logic of scientific method have seemed to show excessive caution in evaluating the first efforts of scientific theories struggling to be born. Before the theory of evolution was buttressed by the findings of experimental genetics some biologists regarded its claims as too speculative. Today many scientific psychologists are very dubious about the validity of psychoanalytic theories which are somewhat in the same state as theories of magnetism at the time of Oersted and Oken. But all of these doubts, including those that follow from a too rigorously formulated canon of verifiability, far from obstructing inquiry are a challenge to it, and melt away as fruitful results are achieved and systematized. Such hypercritical doubts about evidence usually lead to suspension of *judgment* not of inquiry; they do not establish or enforce nontrespass signs. The dogmatism of a Comte who ruled out the possibility of our ever learning anything about the internal constitution of the stars, derided the undulatory theory of light, and professed skepticism about the results of microscopic investigation is as rare as it is inconsistent, and was repudiated by his scientific colleagues as soon as his views were made known.

If we take a long view of the history of scientific inquiry, the evidence is overwhelming that it has not been the naturalists who have obstructed investigation into new fields by insisting that the methods of the more advanced sciences be taken as paradigmatic for all inquiry, so much as those who have contested the validity of the naturalist position, particularly in the study of the human body and mind. The deliverances a few years ago by high church dignitaries against psychoanalysis follow a precedent estabilshed by a long line of more distinguished predecessors. An interesting chapter remains to be written on the distortion produced in other fields of science by those who took mathematics as the *model* of all knowledge. But the mathematical ideal for all human knowledge was held by comparatively few naturalists. Those thinkers who took it seriously tended to regard scientific knowledge as mere opinion lost in the welter of appearances and unable to grasp reality.

The most powerful opposition to naturalism comes not from those who feel that it obstructs the path of inquiry and closes the gates to new knowledge but from those who fear that it arbitrarily excludes from the realm of existence and knowledge something which we actually have good reason to believe in, *viz.*, God and man's immortal soul. Naturalism *arbitrarily* excludes the existence of God and man's immortal soul, it is alleged, because its first principles and categories of explanation are such as to make the very assertion of their existence meaningless. If true, this charge would be serious indeed, for the naturalist professes to be open-minded about the possibilities of existence in a world in which his greatest efforts seem so modest in the cosmic scale.

There are many conceptions of God and the soul which are unintelligible because they involve the attribution of contradictory qualities to Him; and there are other conceptions which are so vague and indeterminate in meaning, that nothing significant can be affirmed or denied of them. But it is not difficult to find conceptions that are sufficienctly meaningful to make the contention of the *impossibility* of their existence arrant dogmatism. Are naturalists guilty of this kind of dogmatism?

I do not believe this to be the case. For one thing this would remove the sting from naturalism. Its criticisms of the belief in Deity have not been based on semantic considerations but on what it presumed to be the weight of scientific discovery. Some theologians and even some Catholic scientists like

Duhem have sought to bolster the beliefs in God precisely on the ground that in relation to the categories of naturalistic science, the affirmation as well as the denial of God's existence would be meaningless. Such a view of naturalism is more devastating to atheism than to theism because the atheist does not profess to have any other categories at the disposal of his undersanding while the theist emphatically does.

Secondly, wherever declared naturalists assert that the existence of God is impossible, it will usually be found they are using the term impossible not in the logical or mathematical sense but in the physical or medical sense in which we say that it is impossible for anything to burn or for a man to breathe without oxygen. Neither Professor Ducasse in his recent discussions of immortality nor Professor Ewing in his discussions of the body and its mental attributes have established anything more than what a sophisticated naturalist is prepared to grant them *to begin* with, *viz.*, that God's existence and personal survival are synthetic propositions and that therefore their denial cannot be contradictory or a matter for logic alone to settle. G. E. Moore once observed that the fact that one needs one's eyes for seeing is an empirical discovery, and this is obviously true for more recondite matters like the role of the brain in thinking and of the nerves in feeling. To see without eyes is physiologically impossible but every believer in immortality known to me is convinced that in his disembodied state he will see at least as well as he sees now. The two assertions are not *logically* incompatible for obviously the believer in immortality expects the laws of physiology to be suspended in the hereafter. This is not logically impossible but the absence of a logical impossibility does not constitute a scintilla of evidence against the usual validity of physiological law as we know it. Every reasonable person in his behavior denies the assumption "that we have no right to disbelieve in anything which cannot be logically disproved."[9]

The history of naturalism, it seems to me, has been marked by two main tendencies. The first has interpreted God in the

[9] Crawshaw-Williams, *loc. cit.*

same way as the great historical religions; *viz*, as an omnipotent personal power who guides the destinies of the world He has created—and concluded that the evidence does not warrant belief in the existence of anything corresponding to this conception. The second has reinterpreted the conception of God and used the term "God" to signify a principle of order in the universe, the totality of all things, the possibility of good in the world, or the object of human allegiance. Karl Marx once observed that even the profession of belief in deism on the part of scientists was motivated by a desire to win freedom to continue scientfic inquiry and to escape molestation from those whom we would today call religious fundamentalists. But in most cases the attribution of such motives seems to be entirely gratuitous even though a greater freedom from interference by revealed religion may have been among the effects of the profession of deism.

Whatever the historical facts, the charge of dogmatism against naturalism on the ground that it rules out by definition the possibile existence of God and the soul has often been made. Recently it has been renewed and fortified by quoting from an essay by Mr. Dennes some ambiguous passages which are interpreted to mean that all things in the world *must* ultimately be described and explained in terms of the categories of quality, relation, and event. One critic then asks, "How do we know that the world consists of events, qualities and relations, and nothing more? We know that we must so describe it if we are committed to basic categories of a naturalistic philosophy. . . . But would the nature of a spiritual substance be so determinable?"[10] Another critic referring to the same point writes, "If everything has to be an event, the idea of a timeless God is excluded from the outset and without argument. The writer asserts that his list of categories makes no demand upon the metaphysical commitment of the reader, as though giving up one's belief in God were nothing."[11]

These questions seem to me to misconceive both the mean-

[10] A. E. Murphy, in *Journal of Philosophy*, Vol. XLII, pp. 411, 412.
[11] R. Demos, in *Philosophy and Phenominological Research*, Vol. VII, p. 271.

ing of the text criticized as well as the position of naturalism.
I shall, however, discuss only the latter.

(1) Naturalism is not committed to any theory concerning which categorial *terms* are irreducible or basic in explanation. Naturalists differ among themselves about this in the
same way that scientists may differ among themselves as to
what terms in the language of science should be taken as
primary. What all naturalists agree on is "the irreducibility"
of a certain method by which new knowledge is achieved and
tested. The analysis of this method may be made in terms of
categories like thing, structure, function, power, act, cause,
relation, quantity and event. The choice of which categories
to take as basic in describing a method depends upon the
degree to which they render coherent and fruitful what we
learn by the use of the method. Historically, and up to very
recently, the most widely used category among naturalistic
philosophers has been matter or substance. It is a complete
nonsequitur to assume that because one asserts that the fundamental categories of description are X and Y and Z, and that
they hold universally, he is therefore asserting that the world
cannot be significantly described *except* in terms of X, Y,
and Z, or as so many critics assume that the world consists of
"nothing but" X and Y and Z. One may use categorial terms
A and B and C that are not fundamental and maintain either—
what most naturalists do *not*—that they are logically definable
in terms of X, Y, and Z or—what most naturalists do—that the
conditions under which any existing thing is significantly describable in terms of A, B, and C are such that they are always
describable in terms of X, Y, and Z.

This gives us two possibilities in respect to a term like
substance. It might be defined as a constellation of events
instead of a substratum in which predicates inhere, and all
statements about substances translated without loss of meaning
into statements about organized sets of events or processes.
Or second, an attempt might be made to show that whatever
else a substance is, its manifestations or appearances can always
be described in terms of activities or operating powers, themselves definable as events or powers. This does not require

that substances whether material or spiritual have to be directly observed, but it does require that their presumed manifestations or effects must be observable in our experience, else we can populate the world at will with the creatures of our fancy.

Whether the existence of the identifiable "effects" of an allegedly spiritual substance justifies our belief in the existence of a separable and immortal soul rather than our belief that they are "effects" of a highly organized body in a given culture is something which the naturalist proposes to solve, either (i) by proceeding in the same way and with the same logic that he makes inferences from the presence of certain observable ocurrences to the presence of other unobserved occurrences, or (ii) by examining the experimental evidence for the survival of the soul or personality after the death of the body, which brings us into the field of parapsychology and psychical research.

That the choice of which categorial terms to use in description is a problem independent of determining what actually exists in heaven or earth may be clear if we bear in mind that even if we were to conclude that man has an immortal soul, that would not by itself answer the question whether it was to be described as a spiritual substance or an organized set of spiritual functions. Conversely, Whitehead denies the explanatory primacy of the category of substance, and using the categories of event, quality and relation reaches altogether different conclusions from naturalism.

(2) Nor does naturalism exclude the very idea of a "timeless" God at the outset and without argument, as Mr. Demos alleges. Otherwise, as I have already indicated, it could not deny his existence or be denounced for its atheism. Naturalists use the term "timeless" to designate traits and qualities in existence which either do not change or to which the predication of temporal quality is irrelevant. Circular things exist in time but their circularity is timeless. Before we can assert that there are timeless "entities" in existence which do not change, we should need some experience of them in time in order to distinguish them from what lacks changeless character. The point is not whether timeless nonexistential entities

can be conceived without contradiction. Assume that they can. But Mr. Demos is talking not of a purely conceptual or logic construction from whose meaning we can deduce existence. He is talking about a timeless entity whose existence must be inferred, as in orthodox theology (*e.g.* the Aquinate proofs of the existence of God) from a series of temporal and contingent events. And he must meet the naturalist contention that there is neither empirical nor logical warrant for the leap from what we can observe in our experience in time to a creature outside of time. That there must be some disclosure in time of what is presumed to be outside of time as a starting point of the argument, Mr. Demos must admit, else the whole concept of God is useless for the purposes for which Mr. Demos and orthodox theology invoke him.

(3) If God and man's immortal soul are so conceived that they have no empirical effects, then there is nothing to prevent anyone from imputing any set of logically consistent attributes to them. They would then take their place with other imaginary creatures in the realm of mythology. I can very well understand the refusal of historical religions to take such conceptions of God and the soul seriously, since it makes them completely otiose in understanding the world, superfluous entities that can be shaved away with a flick of Occam's razor.

It is of course true that in modern philosophy the term "God" has stood for many different ideas—natural structure, the order of cause and consequence, the principle of concreation or logical limitation, the experience of value and righteousness. Avowed atheists, like Morris R. Cohen, have described their dedication to truth, and not only out of piety to the memory of Spinoza, as "the intellectual love of God." Naturalists are under no more compulsion to observe terminological taboos than other philosophers although one would expect them to be more careful of the context of familiar terms used to convey new meanings. If anyone gets particular satisfaction out of the use of the term God, then fortunately or unfortunately, he can find it in the writings of most naturalist philosophers. Naturalism, as a philosophy, however, has nothing to do with such linguistic matters important as they may be in other respects. Naturalism as a philosophy is concerned only with those assertions about existence from which something empirically observable in the world follows that would not be the case if existence were denied. And it proposes to treat assertions about God's existence in the same generic way that it treats assertions about the existence of invisible stars or hidden motives or after-images or extrasensory perception. Critics of naturalism who regard this as dogmatic might put their charge to the test by furnishing the reasons or evidence which *they* hold warrant belief in the existence of God or gods, cosmic purpose or personal survival after death.

Some beliefs are reasonable even if we cannot finally confirm or disconfirm them. But if we take technological and practical behavior as the matrix of the reasonable, then beliefs in the existence of supernatural entities are not reasonable. They are not warranted even if they turn out to be true, just as a guess is not warranted knowledge even when it turns out to be true. Santayana somewhere suggests that the reason most people believe in immortality is that they cannot imagine themselves dead. This raises an interesting methodological point since only if we are immortal can we prove it, while the naturalists who deny the immortality of the soul will never have the satisfaction of saying, "We were right." "Wouldn't naturalists be surprised," a critic of the position once observed, "if after they died they woke up in the presence of God." They certainly would be surprised. The degree of their surprise would be the measure of the unreasonableness of the belief. Unreasonable behavior or conduct may sometimes turn our right—*e.g.*, if I gave six to one odds on the toss of a well made coin—but it is no less unreasonable for all that. And what is true for conduct is true for belief. Consequently, in respect to the available evidence in our possession, the naturalist is reasonable in his belief even if it turns out he is wrong about God and survival, while the supernaturalist in respect to the same data is unreasonable even if it turns out he is right. "Faith in the supernatural," says Santayana, "is a desperate wager made by man at the lowest ebb of his fortune." The scientist who predicts that life will disappear because of the second law of thermodynamics will never be around when the last flicker of life dims. The logic of the argument is no different in the case of immortality.

In conclusion, the naturalist believes that his assumptions are reasonable because they express, in a more general way, no more than what is expressed by any nonphilosopher as well as by all philosophers, whatever their school, in their successful working practice on solving problems concerning the nature of things. And by successful is meant here something independent of the categorial terms of naturalism or any other philosophy, something as simple, naïve, and indefeasible as discovering a substance that on friction will burst into flame, building a house that will withstand an earthquake, producing a seed that will yield a better harvest. Naturalism, as a philosophy, is a systematic reflection upon, and elaboration of, the procedures man employs in the successful resolution of the problems and difficulties of human experience. To use a phrase of Peirce, without giving it necessarily his special interpretation, it is "critical commonsensism." But it is more than this. It is a proposal. It is a proposal to continue to follow this general pattern of procedure in all fields of inquiry where it has enabled us to build up a body of knowledge, and to extend it to fields where we have not satisfactorily settled questions *of fact* of any kind. As a proposal it seems hardly less reasonable to the naturalist to follow than, when thirsty, under normal circumstances, to look for some liquid to quench one's thirst. Could any other procedure be more reasonable or as reasonable? Or must we solve *the* problem of induction first? But to raise the problem of induction no less than to solve it assumes that we are already in possession of undisputed knowledge. And to facilitate the transition from the problematic to the undisputed in human affairs has been one of the underlying purposes of all historical forms of naturalism.

IS UNDERSTANDING RELIGION
COMPATIBLE WITH BELIEVING?

ALASDAIR MACINTYRE

Begin with an elementary puzzlement. In any discussion between sceptics and believers it is presupposed that, even for us to disagree, it is necessary to understand each other. Yet here at the outset the central problem arises. For usually (and the impulse to write 'always' is strong) two people could not be said to share a concept or to possess the same concept unless they agreed in at least some central applications of it. Two men may share a concept and yet disagree in some of the judgements they make in which they assert that objects fall under it. But two men who disagreed in *every* judgement which employed the concept—of them what could one say that they shared? For to possess a concept is to be able to use it correctly—although it does not preclude mishandling it sometimes. It follows that unless I can be said to share your judgements at least to some degree I cannot be said to share your concepts.

Yet sceptic and believer disagree *in toto* in their judgements on some religious matters; or so it seems. So how can they be in possession of the same concepts? If I am prepared to say *nothing* of what you will say about God or sin or salvation, how can my concepts of God, sin and salvation be the same as yours? And if they are not, how can we understand each other? There are parties to the discussion who would cut it short precisely at this point, both Protestants who believe that only saving grace can help us to understand the concepts of the Scriptures or the creeds, and sceptics

I owe a great deal in this paper to conversations with Professor Ernest Gellner and Mr. Peter Winch, neither of whom will agree with the use I have made of what I have learned from them.—A. M.

Reprinted from *Faith and the Philosophers*, John Hick, ed. (New York: St. Martin's Press, Inc., 1964), by permission of Princeton Theological Seminary and the editor.

who believe that religious utterances are flatly senseless. But each of these is presently convicted of paradox. For the Protestant will elsewhere deny what is entailed by his position, namely that nobody ever rejects Christianity (since anyone who thinks he has rejected it must have lacked saving grace and so did not understand Christianity and so in fact rejected something else); and the sceptic of this kind has to explain the meaning of religious utterances in order to reject them (that is, he never says—as he would have to if they were flatly senseless—'I can't understand a word of it'). So it seems that we do want to say that a common understanding of religious concepts by sceptics and by believers is both necessary and impossible. This dilemma constitutes my problem.

Someone might argue that this dilemma is an entirely artificial construction on the grounds that the concepts used in religion are concepts also used outside religion and that sceptics and believers agree in the non-religious judgements which make use of such concepts. Since I have said that it is far from neecssary for two men who share a concept to agree in every judgement which they make in which they make use of the concept, there can be no objection to saying that sceptics and believers share the same concept and, *a fortiori*, no difficulty in mutal understanding. But this objection rests upon two mistakes. First of all it ignores those specifically religious concepts which have no counterpart in non-religious contexts; and the concepts I have already cited such as those of God, sin and salvation belong to this class. Secondly, when secular predicates such as 'powerful' and 'wise' are transferred to a religious application, they undergo a change. Certainly they are used analogically; but just this is the point. A new element is introduced with the analogical adaptation of the concept. The transition from 'powerful' to 'omnipotent' is not merely quantitative. For the notion of 'supreme in this or that class' cannot easily be transferred to a being who does not belong to a class (as God does not).[1] And thus a new concept has been manufactured. But if the understanding of this new con-

---

[1] *Summa Theologica*, Part I, Q. 3, Art. 5.

cept can lead theologians to make one set of judgements and
the understanding of what is apparently the same concept can
lead sceptics to make quite another set of judgements, then
how can it be the same concept which is in question? The
dilemma stands. If by any chance examples were to be produced from religions which turned out to use no specifically
religious concepts, and only to use secular predicates, without
change of meaning, then certainly we should have no problems of meaning with them. And with them for that very
reason I am not concerned.

An indirect way of approaching this dilemma as it arises
for the philosophy of religion would be to enquire whether
the same dilemma arises in any other field; and at once it is
clear that there is at least one field in which it *ought* to arise,
namely the study of so-called primitive societies. For anthropologists and sociologists (I intend to use these terms interchangeably) claim to understand concepts which they do not
share. They identify such concepts as *mana*, or *tabu*, without
themselves using them—or so it seems. If we could discover
what anthropological understanding consisted in therefore,
we might be in a stronger position to restate the problem.
And if, as I shall claim, we could also show that the variety
of positions taken up by anthropologists reproduce a variety of
positions already taken up in the philosophy of religion, the
sense of relevance would be even stronger. I want to distinguish
four different positions, each of which has defects.

(A) There is the now unfashionable view of Levy-Bruhl
that primitive thought is pre-logical. When Australian aborigines asserted that the sun is a white cockatoo[2] Levy-Bruhl concluded that he was faced with a total indifference to inconsistency and contradiction. From the standpoint of rational
discourse we can study primitive thought much as we study
natural phenomena. It obeys laws as particles obey laws; but in
speaking, primitives do not follow rules as we do. Therefore
we cannot elucidate the rules that they use. In an important
sense therefore, although we can describe what primitives say,

[2] *Les Fonctions mentales dans les sociétés inférieures*, pp. 76 *et seq.*

we cannot grasp their concepts. For they do not possess concepts in the sense of recognizing that some uses of expression conform to and others break with rules for the use of such expressions. It is of course consistent with this view that we might by a kind of empathy imagine ourselves to be primitives and in this sense 'understand'; but we might equally understand by imaginative sympathy what it is to be a bear or a squirrel.

The counterpart in philosophy of religion to Levy-Bruhl is the kind of position which wants to interpret religious language (or metaphysical language—see R. Carnap, *Philosophy and Logical Syntax*) as expressive of attitudes rather than as affirming or denying that anything is the case. On this view religious language simply does not function as *language*; for it is used either causally to evoke or aesthetically to express feelings or attitudes, and Carnap thinks that language can do these things in precisely the same way in which 'movements' can. We can thus study religious language, as in Levy-Bruhl's writings, only as a natural phenomenon; we cannot grasp its concepts for they cannot, on this view, be conceptual. The problem for writers like Levy-Bruhl and Carnap is that they have to treat their own conclusions as palpably false in order to arrive at them. For unless Levy-Bruhl had grasped that 'white cockatoo' and 'sun' were being used with apparently normal referential intentions, he could not have diagnosed the oddity of asserting that the sun is a white cockatoo; and unless Carnap had grasped the assertive form of religious or metaphysical statement, he would not have had to argue that this language is not assertive but expressive. That is, in Levy-Bruhl and Carnap we find a tacit acknowledgement that primitive *language* and religious *language* are *language*. And that therefore something is there to be construed and not merely described or explained.

(B) At the opposite extreme from Levy-Bruhl is the practice of Professor E. E. Evans-Pritchard in his book *Nuer Religion*, which is of course offered as an explicit refutation of Levy-Bruhl. Like the Australian aborigines, the Sudanese Nuer appear to fly in the face of ordinary rules of consistency and contradiction. 'It seems odd, if not absurd, to a European when he is told that a twin is a bird as though it were an obvious fact, for Neur are not saying that a twin is like a bird but that he is a bird.'[3] Evans-Pritchard begins from the Nuer concept of the divine, *kwoth*. The difficulties in the notion of *kwoth* spring from the fact that *kwoth* is asserted both to be sharply contrasted with the material creation and to be widely present in it. It is both one and many: and the many, as aspects of *kwoth*, are one with each other. In order to tease out the notion Evans-Pritchard has to allow full weight to the social context of practice in which the assertions about *kwoth* are used. By doing this he is able to show that the utterances of the Nuer are rule-governed, and on this rests his claim to have refuted Levy-Bruhl. But Evans-Pritchard takes this to be the same as having made the utterances of the Nuer intelligible. Certainly he has shown us what the Nuer idea of intelligibility is. He has shown why the Nuer think their religion makes sense. But this is not to have shown that the Nuer are right. 'When a cucumber is used as a sacrificial victim Nuer speak of it as an ox. In doing so they are asserting something rather more than that it takes the place of an ox.'[4] When we have grasped the whole of Nuer practice have we grasped what more this could be? Or is there anything left over that we have not understood? Evans-Pritchard would have to answer this last question by 'No'. In doing so he brings out the parallels between his position and the kind of Wittgensteinianism in philosophy of religion exemplified by Mr. Peter Winch.[5]

Winch argues that 'intelligibility takes many and varied forms'; that there is no 'norm for intelligibility in general'.[6] He argues that 'criteria of logic are not a direct gift of God, but arise out of, and are only intelligible in the context of, ways of living or modes of social life as such. For instance, science is one such mode and religion is another; and each

[3] E. E. Evans-Pritchard, *New Religion* (Oxford: Clarendon Press, 1956), p. 131.
[4] Evans-Pritchard, *op. cit.* p. 128.
[5] *The Idea of a Social Science and its Relation to Philosophy* (London: Routledge and Kegan Paul, 1958).
[6] *Op. cit.* p. 102.

has criteria of intelligibility peculiar to itself. So within science or religion actions can be logical or illogical; in science, for example, it would be illogical to refuse to be bound by the results of a properly carried out experiment; in religion it would be illogical to suppose that one could pit one's own strength against God's; and so on. But we cannot sensibly say that either the practice of science itself or that of religion is either illogical or logical; both are non-logical.'[7] It follows from this that anything that counts as a 'way of living' or a 'mode of social life' can only be understood and criticized in its own terms. Winch indeed argues that so far as religion is concerned, a sociologist can only identify religious actions under their religious descriptions and if he answers any questions about them of the form 'Do these two acts belong to the same kind of activity?' the answer will have to be 'given according to criteria which are not taken from sociology, but from religion itself. But if the judgements of identity—and hence the generalizations—of the sociologist of religion rest on criteria taken from religion, then his relation to the performers of religious activity cannot be just that of observer to observed. It must rather be analogous to the participation of the natural scientist with fellow-workers in the activities of scientific investigation.'[8] That is, you can only understand it from the inside.

Winch therefore points to a theoretical justification for Evans-Pritchard's practice, and in so doing exposes its weakness. For there are not two alternatives: *either* embracing the metaphysical fiction of one over-all 'norm for intelligibility in general' *or* flying to total relativism. We can elicit the weakness of this position by considering the conceptual self-sufficiency claimed for 'ways of living' and 'modes of social life'. The examples given are 'religion' and 'science'. But at any given date in any given society the criteria in current use by religious believers or by scientists will differ from what they

[7] *Op. cit.* pp. 100–101.
[8] *Op. cit.* pp. 87–88.

are at other times and places.[9] Criteria have a history. This emerges strikingly if we ask how we are to think of magic on Winch's view. Is magic a 'mode of social life'? Or is it primitive religion? Or perhaps primitive science? For we do want to reject magic, and we want to reject it—in the terms which Winch has taken over for polemical purposes from Pareto—as illogical because it fails to come up to our criteria of rationality. An excellent case here is that of the witchcraft practised by the Azande.[10] The Azande believe that the performance of certain rites in due form affects their common welfare; this belief cannot in fact be refuted. For they also believe that if the rites are ineffective it is because someone present at them had evil thoughts. Since this is always possible, there is never a year when it is unavoidable for them to admit that the rites were duly performed, but that they did not thrive. Now the belief of the Azande is not unfalsifiable in principle (we know perfectly well what would falsify it—the conjunction of the rite, no evil thoughts and disasters). But in fact it cannot be falsified. Does this belief stand in need of rational criticism? And if so by what standards? It seems to me that one could only hold the belief of the Azande rationally *in the absence of* any practice of science and technology in which criteria of effectiveness, ineffectiveness and kindred nations had been built up. But to say this is to recognize the appropriateness of scientific criteria of judgement from our standpoint. The Azande do not intend their belief either as a piece of science or as a piece of non-science. They do not possess these categories. It is only *post eventum*, in the light of later and more sophisticated understanding that their belief and concepts can be classified and evaluated at all.

This suggests strongly that beliefs and concepts are not merely to be evaluated by the criteria implicit in the practice

[9] Consider Kepler using as a criterion in selecting from possible hypotheses what could be expected from a perfect God whose perfection included a preference for some types of geometrical fiugure as against others.

[10] E. Evans-Pritchard, *Witchcraft, Oracles and Magic Among the Azande.*

of those who hold and use them. This conviction is reinforced by other considerations. The criteria implicit in the practice of a society or of a mode of social life are not necessarily coherent; their application to problems set within that social mode does not always yield *one* clear and unambiguous answer. When this is the case people start questioning their own criteria. They try to criticise the standards of intelligibility and rationality which they have held hitherto. On Winch's view it is difficult to see what this could mean. This is to return to the point that criteria and concepts have a history; it is not just activities which have a history while the criteria which govern action are timeless.

What I am quarrelling with ultimately is the suggestion that agreement in following a rule is sufficient to guarantee making sense. We can discriminate different types of example here. There are the cases where the anthropologist, in order to interpret what people say, has to reconstruct imaginatively a possible past situation where expressions had a sense which they no longer bear. Consider theories about what taboo is. To call something taboo is to prohibit it, but it is not to say that it is prohibited. To say that somehing is taboo is to distinguish it from actions which are prohibited but are not ttaboo. We could say that it is to give a reason for a prohibition, except that it is unintelligible what reason can be intended. So some theorists have construed[11] from the uses of taboo. We could say that it is to give a reason for a prohistory of how this sense was lost. One cannot take the sense from the use, for the use affords no sense, although the temptation to tell anthropologists that taboo is the name of a non-natural quality would be very strong for any Polynesian who had read G. E. Moore.

In the case of 'taboo' we can imagine a lost sense for the expression. What about cases, however, where the sense is not lost, but is simply incoherent? According to Spencer and Gillen some aborigines carry about a stick or a stone which is treated as *if* it is or embodies the soul of the individual who

---

[11] See F. Steiner, *Taboo.*

carries it. If the stick or stone is lost, the individual anoints himself as the dead are anointed. Does the concept of 'carrying one's soul about with one' make sense? Of course we can re-describe what the aborigines are doing and transform it into sense, and perhaps Spencer and Gillen (and Durkheim who follows them) mis-describe what occurs. But if their reports are not erroneous, we confront a blank wall here, so far as meaning is concerned, although it is easy to give the rules for the use of the concept.

What follows from this is quite simply that there are cases where we cannot rest content with describing the user's criteria for an expression, but we can criticise what he does. Indeed, unless we could do this we could not separate the case where there are no problems of meaning, the case where now there is no clear sense to an expression, but where once there may well have been one (as with 'taboo') and the case where there appears never to have been a clear and coherent sense available. What matters for our present purposes is that these examples suggest that sometimes to understand a concept involves not sharing it. In the case of 'taboo' we can only grasp what it is for something to be taboo if we extend our insight beyond the rules which govern the use of the expression to the point and purpose which these rules once had, but no longer have, and can no longer have in a different social context. We can only understand what it is to use a thoroughly incoherent concept, such as that of a soul in a stick, if we understand what has to be absent from the criteria of practice and of speech for this incoherence not to appear to the user of the concept. In other words we are beginning to notice requirements for the elucidation of concepts which are necessarily absent from the kind of account given by Evans-Pritchard or by Winch.

We have not only to give the rules for the use of the relevant expressions, but to show what the point could be of following such rules, and in bringing out this feature of the case one shows also whether the use of this concept is or is not a possible one for people who have the standards of intelligibility in speech and action which we have. But do we have to be thus self-centered in our application of criteria? Can we, as it might appear from this, only understand what makes sense to us already? Can we learn nothing from societies or modes of social life which we cannot understand within our present framework? Why dismiss what does not fit easily into that framework? Why not revise the framework? To find a clue to the answering of these questions let us examine yet a third doctrine of intelligibility in anthropology.

(C) Dr. E. R. Leach[12] commits himself to a version of the philosophical theory that the meaning of an expression is nothing other than the way in which the expression is used. Myth is to be understood in terms of ritual, saying in terms of doing. To interpret any statement made by primitive people which appears unintellibible, ask what the people in question do. So Leach writes that 'myth regarded as a statement in words "says" the same thing as ritual regarded as a statement in action. To ask questions about the content of belief which are not contained in the content of ritual is nonsense.'[13] Leach, that is, adopts an opposite standpoint to Evans-Pritchard. Evans-Pritchard insists that the anthropologist has to allow the Nuer to make sense in the Nuer's own terms; Leach insists that his Burmese society must be made sense of in Leach's own terms. What is impressive here is that both Evans-Pritchard and Leach have written anthropological classics and this may be thought to be inconsistent with what I have just said. But the reason why we get insight both into Evans-Pritchard's *Nuer* and Leach's *Kachin* is that both are so explicit in presenting us both with their philosophical assumptions and with the field-material to which they apply those assumptions. Each furnishes us not merely with a finished interpretation but with a view of the task of interpretation while it is being carried out.

In Leach's case, although his attitude is the opposite of that of Evans-Pritchard, the results are oddly similar. In the case of the Nuer everything made sense, for the Nuer were judged on their own terms. In the case of the Kachin everything makes sense, for the rules of interpretation provide

12 *The Political Systems of Highland Burma*, Ball, London, 1954.
13 *Op. cit.*

that every statement which appears not to make sense is to
be translated into one that does. So Leach insists that metaphysical questions about the spirits in whom the Kachin
believe (*nats*) are out of place. We cannot ask if *nats* eat or
where they live for we are not to treat statements about *nats*
as statements at all, but as ritual performances which can be
performed properly or improperly, but which are scarcely true
or false.

The counterpart to Leach in the philosophy of religion
is perhaps Professor R. B. Braithwaite's reinterpretation of the
meaning of religious utterances. Braithwaite sets out a classification of utterances derived from his philosophical empiricism
and asks where religion can be fitted in.[14] The answer is that
the room left for religion is in providing a specification and
a backing for ways of life. I do not want to discuss Braithwaite's position in this paper. I only want to point out that
Braithwaite's way of giving a sense to religious utterances dis-
tracts us from the question. What sense do these utterances have
for those who make them? And because Braithwaite deprives
us of this question, he makes it unintelligible that anyone
should cease to believe, on the grounds that he can no longer
find a sense in such utterances. So also it seems difficult to
see what view Leach could take of a Kachin who was persuaded, for example by a Christian missionary, that his belief
in *nats* was false and idolatrous.

It is therefore true that if the criteria of intelligibility with
which we approach alien concepts are too narrow we may be
liable not only to erroneously dismiss them as senseless but
even more misleasdingly we may try to force them to a sense
which they do not possess. It must seem at this point that my
attempt to illuminate the original dilemma has merely led
to the formulation of the second one. For it seems that we
cannot approach alien concepts except in terms of our own
criteria, and that yet to do this is to be in danger of distortion.
But in fact if we are careful we shall be able to set out some

---

[14] *An Empiricist's View of the Nature of Religious Belief.* [The
essay may be found on p. 140 in this book.]

of the necessary prerequisites for an adequate understanding of beliefs and concepts without this inconsistency.

Against Winch and Evans-Pritchard I have argued that to make a belief and the concepts which it embodies intelligible I cannot avoid invoking my own criteria, or rather the established criteria of my own society. Against Braithwaite and Leach I have argued that I cannot do this until I have already grasped the criteria governing belief and behaviour in the society which is the object of enquiry. And I only complete my task when I have filled in the social context so as to make the transition from one set of criteria to the other intelligible. These requirements can be set out more fully as follows:

(1) All interpretation has to begin with detecting the standards of intelligibility established in a society. As a matter of fact no one can avoid using clues drawn from their own society; and as a matter of exposition analogies from the anthropologist's society will often be helpful. But we have to begin with the society's implicit forms of self-description. Malinowski is contemptuous of the account which, so he says, a Trobriander would give of his own society; but Malinowski's own account of the Trobrianders is curiously like that which he puts in the mouth of his imagined Trobriand informant. And, had it not been, there would have been something radically wrong with it, since how a man describes himself is partially constitutive of what he is. It does not follow from this, as I have already suggested, that the descriptions used or the standards of intelligibility detected will always be internally coherent. And, if they are not, a key task will be to show how this incoherence does not appear as such to the members of the society or else does appear and is somewhat made tolerable.

(2) But in detecting in coherence of this kind we have already invoked *our* standards. Since we cannot avoid doing this it is better to do it self-consciously. Otherwise we shall project to our studies, as Frazer notoriously did, an image of our own social life. Moreover, if we are sufficiently sensitive we make it possible for us to partially escape from our own cultural limitations. For we shall have to ask not just how we

see the Trobrianders or the Nuer, but how they do or would see us. And perhaps what hitherto looked intelligible and obviously so will then appear opaque and question-begging.

(3) We can now pass on to the stage at which the difficult and important question can be put. How is it that what appears in one social context can appear not at make sense in another? What has to be underlined is that answers to this question are not necessarily all going to be of the same form.

There is the type of case where a concept works very well, so long as certain questions are not asked about it, and it may be that for a long time in a given society there is no occasion for raising such questions. The concept of the divine right of kings will undergo a strain which reveals internal incoherences only when rival claimants to sovereignty appear, for it contains no answer to the question Which king has divine right? Then there is the type of case where incoherence and intelligibility are to some extent manifest to the users of the concept. But the use of the concept is so intimately bound up with forms of description which cannot be dispensed with if social and intellectual life is to continue that any device for putting up with the incoherence is more tolerable than dispensing with the concept. A third type of case is that in which the point of a concept or group of concepts lies in their bearing upon behaviour. But changed patterns of social behaviour deprive the concept of point. So that although there is no internal incoherence in the concept, the concept can no longer be embodied in life as it once was, and it is either put to new uses or it becomes redundant. An example of this would be the concept of honour detached from the institutions of chivalry. 'It is difficult', a British historian once wrote, 'to be chivalrous without a horse'. And the change in the importance of the horse in war can turn *Don Quixote* from a romance into a satire.

(D) I must seem to have come a very long way round. And it is therefore perhaps worth trying to meet the charge of irrelevance by saying what I hope the argument has achieved. I first posed the question: in what sense, if any, can sceptic and believer be said to share the same concepts, and so to understand one another? I then tried to show how the anthropologist might be said to grasp concepts which he does not share, in the sense that he does not make the same judgements employing them as do the peole whom he studies. I now want to use my answer on this point to pose a new question which will begin the journey back to the original enquiry. This is still an anthropological question. Up to the seventeenth century we should in our society all have been believers and indeed there would be no question of our being anything else. We should not merely have believed that God existed and was revealed in Christ but we should have found it obvious and unquestionable that this was so. Since the seventeenth century, even for those who believe, the truth and intelligibility of their beliefs is not obvious in the same sense. What accounts for the fact that what was once obvious is now not so? What accounts for the fact that nobody now believes in God in the way mediaeval men did, simply because men are aware of alternatives? And more importantly still, what makes some of the alternatives appear as obvious to modern sceptics as belief in God did for pre-seventeenth-century Christians?

I pose this question as a background to another. If we can understand why one group of men in the past found Christian beliefs obviously true and intelligible and another group now find them opaque, and we can locate the difference between these two groups, perhaps we shall also be able to locate the difference between contemporary believers and contemporary sceptics. And if we do this we shall have solved our original problem. This brief excursus may make clear the relevance of my apparently rambling procedure. So it becomes urgent to attempt an answer, at least an outline, to the anthropological question. And the form of his answer will be to ask which of the different types of answer to the question How is it that what appears intelligible in one social context can appear not to make sense in another? is applicable in the case of the transition from mediaeval belief to modern scepticism.

It is obvious that the internal incoherences in Christian concepts did not go unnoticed in the Middle Ages. The antinomies of benevolent omnipotence and evil, or of divine predestination and human freedom, were never more clearly and acutely discussed. But it is not the case in general that mediaeval thinkers who were dissatisfied with the solutions offered to these antinomies differed in their attitude to belief in God or belief in Christ from thinkers who believed that they or others had offered satisfactory solutions. So the problem becomes: why do the same intellectual difficulties at one time appear as difficulties but no more, an incentive to enquiry but not a ground for disbelief, while at another time they appear as a final and sufficient ground for scepticism and for the abandonment of Christianity? The answers to this question are surley of the second and third types which I outlined in the last section. That is, the apparent incoherence of Christian concepts was taken to be tolerable (and treated as apparent and not real) because the concepts were part of a set of concepts which were indispensable to the forms of description used in social and intellectual life. It is the secularization of our forms of description, constituting part of the secularization of our life, that has left the contradictions high and dry. To take an obvious example, Chrisianity does not and never has depended upon the truth of an Aristotelian physics in which the physical system requires a Prime Mover, and consequently many sceptics as well as many believers have treated the destruction of the Aristotelian argument in its Thomist form as something very little germane to the question of whether or not Christianity is true. But in fact the replacement of a physics which requires a Prime Mover by a physics which does not secularizes a whole area of enquiry. It weakens the hold of the concept of God on our intellectual life by showing that in this area we can dispense with descriptions which have any connection with the concept.

Some Christian theologians such as Paul Tillich have welcomed this process of secularization, describing it in Tillich's terms as a transition from heteronomous to autonomous reason. But the counterpart to secularization is that the specific character of religion becomes clearer at the cost of diminishing its content. Primitive religon is part of the whole form of human life. Durkheim in *The Elementary Forms of the Re-*

ligious Life tried to show, and had at least some success in showing, that the most primitive modes of our categorical grasp of the world are inextricably embedded in religion. Thus it is even difficult to talk of 'religion' in this context, as though one could identify a separate and distinct element. But it is just this distinctiveness which can be identified in our culture. Religious apologists, not sceptics, stress the uniqueness of religious utterance. The slogan 'Every kind of utterance has its own kind of logic' finds a ready response from theologians.

The counterpart to this is an easy toleration for contradiction and incoherence, through the use of such concepts as 'the absurd' (Kierkegaard), 'paradox' (Barth) or 'mystery' (Marcel). We can in fact reach a point at which religion is made logically invulnerable. The attempt in the controversy over the falsification of religious assertions to show that if religion were irrefutable religious utterances would be deprived of sense failed for the same reason that attacks on Azande witchcraft would fail. Religious believers do know what would have to occur for their beliefs to be falsified—they can specify some occurrences with which the existence of omnipotent benevolence is incompatible ('utterly pointless evil' is one commonly used example). But just as the Azande can state what would falsify their assertions about witchcraft—but we could never know that such an occurrence had taken place—so the Christian will leave us in the same difficulty. For the after-life, that which we do not see, may always lend point to otherwise pointless evil, or absurd happenings. This line of argument is certainly open to attack; but the invocation of concepts such as 'mystery' or 'paradox' is always there in the background. Thus the logical invulnerability of Christianity seems to me a position that can be maintained.[15] But only at a cost. The cost is emptiness.

I have already produced reasons to explain why incoherences which only presented problems to an Occam could

---

[15] As I myself did maintain it in 'The Logical Status of Religious Beliefs' in *Metaphysical Beliefs*.

present insuperable obstacles to a T. H. Huxley or a Russell. But now I want to argue that the form of Christian apologetic on moral questions itself exhibits Christian concepts as irrelevant in the modern world in which the way in which the concepts of chivalry became irrelevant in the seventeenth century. For what Christian apologists try to show is that unless we live in a certain way certain ill consequences will follow (broken homes and delinquency, perhaps). But this turns Christianity into a testable nostrum. For we can always ask empirically: do particular religious practices in fact produce higher standards of behavior? Again we return to the very simple point—are Christians in fact different from other people in our society, apart from their ritual practices? And if they are not what is the point of Christian belief, in so far as it issues an injunction? Now, whether Christians are different or not is an empirical question. Certainly empirical enquiry cannot tell us whether Christianity is true or not. But if Christian beliefs belong now to a social context in which their connection with behaviour has ceased to be clear (as it was clear in the Roman empire, say) the question of the truth of Christianity is put into a different perspective.

Christians here will perhaps want to point to the distinctively Christian forms of behaviour of the Confessional Church under Hitler, and this is certainly relevant. For the regressive primitivism of National Socialism with its idols provided a context sufficiently alike to that of early Christianity to make Christianity once more relevant. The Nazis desecularized society with a vengeance. But while to be asked to choose for Christ has a clear meaning when the pracical choices are those of the Nazi society, does this injunction have a clear meaning also in our society? And if it had would we not in fact find Christians united on ways of behaving in a way that they are not?

From an historical point of view, of course, it is most unfair to present Christianity as only the victim of secularization. Christianity, especially Protestant Christianity, was itself a powerful secularizing agent, destroying in the name of God any attempt to deify nature, and so helping to rid the world of magic and making nature available for scientific enquiry. The kind of negative theology which refuses to identify any object with the divine (God is not this, not that) has its final fruit in the kind of atheism which Simone Weil and Tillich both see as a recognition of the fact that God cannot be identified with any particular existing object. But what is left to Simone Weil or Tillich is in fact a religious vocabulary without any remaining secular content. Hegel's irreligion consists in his insight into the possibility of extracting truth from its religious husks. Kierkegaard's answer to Hegel is the assertion of a religion defined entirely in its own religious terms, uncriticizable *ab externo*. Together Hegel and Kierkegaard reflect accurately the status of religion in a secularized environment.

(E) For a sceptic to grasp the point of religious belief, therefore, he has to supply a social context which is now lacking and abstract a social context which is now present, and he has to do this for the mediaeval Christian, just as the anthropologist has to do it for the Azande or the aborigines. But in dialogue with contemporary Christians the sceptic is forced to recognize that they see a point in what they say and do although they lack that context. And therefore either he or they are making a mistake, and not a mistake over God, but a mistake over criteria of intelligibility. What is at issue between sceptic and Christian is the character of the difference between belief and unbelief as well as the issue of belief itself. Thus the sceptic is committed to saying that he understands the Christian's use of concepts in a way that the Christian himself does not, and presumably *vice versa*. The discussion is therefore transferred to another level, and a Christian refutation of this paper would have to provide an alternative account of intelligibility. If I am right, understanding Christianity is incompatible with believing in it, not because Christianity is vulnerable to sceptical objections, but because its peculiar invulnerability belongs to it as a form of belief which has lost the social context which once made it comprehensible. It is now too late to be mediaeval and it is too empty and too easy to be Kierkergaardian. Thus sceptic and believer do not share a common grasp of the relevant concepts any more than anthropologist and Azande do. And if the believer wishes to he can always claim that we can only disagree with him because we do not understand him. But the implications of this defence of belief are more fatal to it than any attack could be.

THE CASE FOR RELIGIOUS NATURALISM

JACK J. COHEN

. . .

"Naturalism" and "supernaturalism" are key words in any discussion of religion. They are also among the most difficult concepts to free of semantic confusion. They are overloaded with prejudices. To illustrate, when the Catholic speaks of "natural law," he posits along with it a conception of nature in which the suspension of that law by a supernatural deity is possible. For him, since naturalism cannot possibly mean a renunciation of miracle, there is no clear demarcation between it and supernaturalism. Yet a distinction between naturalism and supernaturalism is essential if rational communication is to be a possibility. Naturalism cannot be made to mean supernaturalism and vice versa. Let us examine some of the ramifications of these terms.

1

By naturalism I mean the disposition to believe that any phenomenon can be explained by appeal to general laws confirmable either by observation or by inference from observation. The term disposition is used advisedly, since it is perfectly clear that even the most ardent supporter of the scientific method cannot in any "ultimate" sense disprove "miracles." But it is inherent in the naturalist disposition to accept any discontinuities in the affairs of the physical universe or of man as part of the "natural" scheme of things. This is not to say that everything that happens in the universe if necessarily explainable. Only extreme arrogance would lead men to believe

Reprinted from *The Case for Religious Naturalism* (New York: The Reconstructionist Press, 1958), by permission of the Jewish Reconstructionist Foundation, Inc. Footnote and section numbers have been slightly altered for the sake of convenience.

they possessed the potentiality of omniscience. All the naturalist insists upon is that man has only one instrument of knowledge, his reason, and that any knowledge or "vision" purportedly received by man from sources beyond "nature" are products of that same rational faculty operating either in inspired fashion or mistakenly, as the case may be.

The main problem in any definition or description of naturalism is the fog surrounding "nature" itself. This is a concept which appears, in all likelihood, as frequently as any other in the literature of philosophy, science, and religion. It is, therefore, important to realize the great variety of meanings and shades of meanings conferred upon it by the leading thinkers of all ages. Nature is sometimes a designation for the physical universe exclusively of man. It is sometimes held to include man as well. Frequently nature is set off in contrast to man's spiritual qualities, much as the body is contrasted to the spirit. Nature is conceived of as created existence, in contrast to the absolute existence of God. It is the totality of all existence, and it is the orderly process which characterizes that part of reality which man can experience. It is the totality of physical reality, and it is the principle of its operation. Nature is substance, and it is function. And so it goes. Some of these usages contradict one another: some are complementary.

In these pages, nature will be conceived of as the totality of reality—its substance, functioning, and principles of operation—including man and his spiritual qualities. The naturalist thus tends to explore as deeply as possible the pattern of things as they lend themselves to human understanding and to deny the existence of any realm of human knowledge beyond that apprehensible through men's faculties of mind. He would deny that there is a realm of meaning "beyond" the process of life manifest to human investigation.

But to many thinkers human understanding is itself a problem. Are there not methods of arriving at truth, such as intuition and revelation, which are as valid as the scientific method of hypothetical reasoning and experimental verification? Assuming that such methods are different in character from that of science, what are their implications for the mean-

ing of nature? Do they imply a spatial beyondness, such as that
pictured in traditional accounts of heaven and hell? In this case
would not some form of revelation be essential if man were ever
to receive any inkling of that realm? Or is the beyondness an
ontological dimension, a principle of explanation, without which
nature itself is hardly understandable? If so, revelation might
still be considered essential for man's grasp of nature to be
more than a tenuous one.

It is a common assumption that there is a sharp cleavage
between the methods of science and religion, that there are
different roads to truth, and that there are, indeed, different
kinds of truth, each apprehended by its own distinctive method.
I take the view that all hypothetical thinking is a projection
beyond the actually experienced, that all so-called revelations
and intuitions are extensions of such imaginative construction,
and that the ultimate test of their validity must lie in experience. The key to the solution of the foregoing questions I find
in the concepts of transcendence. For this concept opens the
door to harmonizing the so-termed scientific and nonscientific
methods of arriving at truth.

The problem of thinking deserves the kind of extensive
consideration which cannot be given to it here. I shall limit
my discussion of thinking primarily to its connection with the
idea of transcendence which is basic in religious terminology.

Transcendence is a necessary category of all human thinking; but it in no way requires going beyond nature. Consider,
for a moment, scientific method. The scientist, faced with the
problem of relating facts of observation in some pattern of
cause and effect, or of analyzing the factors entering into a
given phenomenon, must necessarily transcend a given situation in order to arrive at a new and more inclusive framework
of explanation. Transcendence in this sense actually adds nothing to nature which is not inherently and essentially involved
in a particular concatenation of events. In the realm of values,
however, it is frequently asserted that transcendence involves
an entirely new category of existence, one which is "beyond"
nature and which can only be grasped by the human mind
through intuition or revelation.

There is really only one method of arriving at knowledge about the universe. What intuitionists and revelationists do is to omit the final step in the process of thought, which is validation. For example, what happens when we try to understand the status of freedom? To say that man is free, in the sense that he *ought* to be free, is to transcend the present state of man and to project for him a new mode of existence. This kind of transcendence seems, on the surface, to add a new dimension to nature, a dimension that has been supplied only by man and that if absent would in no way affect man's understanding of nature. But to conclude that human values are not part of nature is superficial, for it ignores completely man's proneness to transcend his immediate experience. This human characteristic is as much an aspect of nature as an observed fact or the scientific context into which that fact is placed. Furthermore, the fact that man feels he ought to be free is not the final step in the process of value judgment, no matter how dogmatically certain religious theorists insist that we must accept this ideal as moral truth. There are a number of other serious questions that require investigation. What, really, do we mean by human freedom? How does this ideal relate to the other values we hold out for human life? What are the conditions of human intercourse essential to the achievement of freedom? Are not the answers to these questions prerequisites for the acceptance of freedom as an "ought"? And when we have undergone such a process of investigation, have we not at the same time validated our assumption that this "freedom" is part of the very existential framework within which the nature of man becomes more clearly apprehended?

All thinking, in other words, requires acts of imaginative vision about an infinite present and of equally imaginative projection into an always expanding future. The realm of the transcendent is thus the ever-present unknown, the source at one and the same time of intellectual and spiritual challenge and of our future knowledge. But it is all part of nature, for nature, too, has a future, as well as a past and a present.

Some naturalists, on the basis of scientific experience, include in the naturalist disposition a tendency to assume that the universe is an orderly process. But whether or not they make this admittedly unverifiable assumption, all naturalists believe that there is no conscious force outside the universe acting upon it. On the other hand, the assumption that the universe is orderly permits many generalizations about reality that take us far beyond the realm of mere observation. Naturalism is not a commitment to holding as real only those phenomena which are capable of mechanistic determination. Indeed, mechanism is no longer considered to be an adequate explanation of the behavior of even the physical universe. There is too much mystery, creativity, and uncertainty in life for us to countenance mechanism as a satisfactory explanation of reality. But disbelief in mechanism does not warrant belief in arbitrariness. It warrants only reserving judgments about the significance of a particular experience. Man has unraveled the answer to many mysteries, and there is no reason to assume that he will not unravel others. The naturalist believes that solutions can be found to the unsolved mysteries of life, because the still mysterious phenomena are subject to the same natural processes as those already understood.

It should be realized that naturalists do not deny their inability to answer questions like "Was the world created?" and "How was life initiated?" But although they find such questions, at least for the present, unanswerable, they do not posit a cause outside nature; to do this, they assert, would simply add to the mystery.

2

The difficulty with language is that we have to define words with words. I have been using "supernaturalism" in my discussion in connection with naturalism, and I suppose the reader has been wondering if I ever intended to define it. The time has come to do so.

By supernaturalism I mean the belief that there is a power (or powers) operating in the universe not subject to the same restraints as are imposed on natural phenomena. Whatever order does exist is present by virtue of an arbitrary, omnipotent will above nature and is subject to interference at any time. The world, according to this view, exists by the grace of a living God.*

Both the assumption of a self-ordered universe, which is the view taken here, and of a God transcending (in the sense of "beyond") nature and capable of overturning it are acts of faith by which man tries to read meaning into his life. From the perspective of human values, there is perhaps as much evidence that the world is chaotic as that it is orderly. Earthquakes, tornadoes, floods are as real as night and day, summer and winter. Why, then, does not the naturalist posit either chaos or arbitrary rule from above? The answer, which is necessarily psychological rather than ontological, lies in the fact that the assumption of order is at least capable of validation. Every successful experiment points in this direction, and many of the admitted disorders in nature have gradually been explained in terms of natural causes. No such canons of validation have ever been worked out for the existence of an omnipotent God transcending nature.

In the spiritual realm, the struggle between naturalism and supernaturalism is centered in the problem of the source of values. Whence do we derive our ideals of justice, truth, equality? And once derived, how is their fulfillment to be guaranteed? The naturalist would assert, as we have seen, that it is the very nature of man, by virtue of his powers of thinking and willing, to establish values for himself. He would contend further that some values are more worthy than others, in

* Making allowances for the mood of their thinking, we can classify both Reinhold Niebuhr and Paul Tillich in the naturalist camp as described in this volume. However, it seems to me that Niebuhr, in his profound work *The Nature and Destiny of Man*, introduces considerable confusion by setting up an arbitrary and restrictive definition of nature. By denying to nature elements of freedom and spirituality, he is able to refer to the self-transcending aspects of nature, such as freedom and creativity, as "supernatural." Tillich similarly denies to nature the quality of self-transcendence. Supernaturalism for him then becomes the ontological tool by means of which alone man can gain true perspective on himself and on the process of nature. For both these thinkers supernature is the transcendent aspects of reality, not a realm of space and time beyond nature.

the sense that the attainment of specific objectives is dependent
on the integration of certain values rather than others into the
life of the individual and society. For example, given the objective of peace, equality of opportunity is more likely than
class stratification to lead a society toward this goal. The
naturalist would concede also that there are certain values of
spiritual objectives which are absolute in a given context. That
is to say, while peace may not always be desirable—for instance, where freedom is at stake—this does not gainsay the
fact that peace as an objective of mankind is a goal toward
which all men should strive. Naturalism would stop at this point
in the argument, claiming that the further question "Why is
peace more desirable (or more 'good') as a value than war?"
can be answered only by locating peace in the scheme of all
values, the keystone of which is the affirmation of life itself.

Supernaturalism cannot be satisfied with this self-contained
system of values. It seeks to break through the circle and locate
the source of values and the guarantee of their fulfillment in a
cause beyond man. Therefore God beyond nature is invoked
once again, as in the case of the physical world. Otherwise by
virtue of what standard, asks the supernaturalist, do democrats
struggle for their system against that of the totalitarians? Unless democratic ethics are grounded in the will of God—and
God is here interpreted as being a Power who communicates
his values to man, who could never be certain of their truth
without such revelation—they can make no legitimate claim on
the conscience of man. For without such cosmic authority, it is
held, one man's claim would be as valid as another's.

Naturalism and supernaturalism agree on the existence of
moral order, but they differ in their understanding of that
order. Naturalism holds this order, in the form that it is available to human awareness, to be a construct of the human mind,
subject to all its weaknesses. The moral law, in other words, is
for the naturalist a term applied to *man's* understanding of
what is ethically valid. Supernaturalism, equally cognizant of
human frailty, asserts the need for an absolute system of morality whose validity is dependent on its being equated with the
will of God. Naturalism is satisfied to struggle for human

betterment without any guarantee concerning the ultimate triumph of goodness (except the guarantee of potentiality); supernaturalism insists on the existence of God as man's assurance that evil will be banished from the earth (or in the afterlife). In the search for such certainty, supernaturalism has often involved itself in two basic paradoxes: the first, that if God's absolute goodness and omnipotence will necessarily produce an ethical world, then man's conduct is actually of little moment in its achievement; the second, that if God is absolutely good and omnipotent, then evil should be impossible.

Naturalism is not a new approach to reality. But its early formulations lacked the backing of scientific knowledge, which has now been marshaled to support it. Thus, although the Greeks developed a conception of nature and took the first real steps toward the scientific method, their science, being embryonic, scarcely touched the popular religion of the time. Rather was it the dialectician who challenged the traditional beliefs, in much the same way that thinkers and religious geniuses (or virtuosos, to use a term of Max Weber's) had effected changes in other religions in both Eastern and Western Asia. It was not until the cumulative effect of centuries of scientific discovery had swept away the last hope of convincingly explaining the universe by positing a conscious deity that the era of naturalism really arrived.

When religion arose in society, its intellectual foundation was neither supernatural nor natural. Primitive man had only a vague conception of nature as a "self-operative" phenomenon; therefore, he could have no idea of the supernatural, in the refined sense in which we use the term today. Cassirer, in summarizing Renan's views, declares:

> What we today call a miracle, what appears as such to the modern man, can be expressed only through a definite contrast and difference. A miracle is something that falls outside the field of "natural" occurrences which is governed by fixed and universal laws, but for a consciousness that has not yet achieved such a view of nature and its complete subjection to causal order, this contrast has no meaning; the idea of a miracle escapes it. Hence our historical perspective is false

when we transfer to primeval times an antithesis that is valid and decisive for us.[1]

For the ancients, literally everything that happened was caused by the activity of a god or gods. Whether for good or for evil, the final authority was not man's. Man could have a hand in his fate by keeping on good terms with his deity, but it was the deity who managed the world.

Ancient Jewish thinkers made the concept of God's rule more subtle by attributing to man freedom of the will. If everything was in the hands of God, then human behavior could have no independent status. Hence God created man with a peculiar nature of his own, a nature which included freedom. Man's freedom could have meaning only if the world in which he functioned was so orderly as to make sense of his power to choose. Miracles, in turn, were a deliberate and occasional intervention of God in the orderly affairs of His universe in pursuit of some divine purpose. This refinement of the more primitive concept, however, did not eliminate the idea that nature itself was a miracle. This view, as exemplified in the prayer "We will give thanks to Thee—for Thy miracles [the ordinary acts of nature] which are daily with us . . ." permeated the tradition.

The following passage from the writings of Joseph Albo, fifteenth-century Jewish philosopher, should counteract any tendency to credit premodern Judaism with a consistent view of an independent natural law: "Now the existence of rain cannot be ascribed to nature, because it is not a thing which occurs every year at the same time in the same way, like the other natural phenomena. Rain comes at different times, in different ways, in a wonderful manner, not uniformly and naturally."[2] The tradition, like many modern religionists who delight in the limitations of science, ascribed the slightest discontinuity in nature to the operation of a supernatural force. And since there

[1] Ernst Cassier, *The Problem of Knowledge*, Yak University Press, New Haven, 1950, p. 305.

[2] Joseph Albo, *Sefer Ha—'Ikharim*, Jewish Publication Society, Phila., 1946, Vol. 4, p. 65.

are always areas of discontinuity, the belief in the supernatural continues to flourish.

During the many centuries of their progressive discovery of the laws of nature, scientists were unaware of the revolution they were helping to foster. Many of them were as devout as their religious leaders, and some of them were churchmen. Today, however, we realize fully what they wrought. They destroyed the entire intellectual foundation of the then existing Western civilization. That civilization rested on the assumption that since all of life depended on the actions of an omnipotent power, it was necessary for men to abide by the code of behavior which the deity had supposedly revealed to them. It was not only reevaled religion that was undermined; every institution which rested on the assumption that the status quo was God-inspired was weakened. Monarchical governments, for example, even after the Reformation and the break-up of the temporal power of the Roman Church, found justification in the assumption that class distinctions were divinely approved.

The foregoing analysis should make it clear why authoritarian religionists insist on the supernaturalist view; it should also help to explain the usefulness of supernaturalism to a diametrically opposed group, the authoritarian antireligionists. The dogmatic religionist knows that to admit the legitimacy in religion of replacing the supernaturalist position by a naturalist one would be to weaken the authority of orthodoxy. The dogmatic antireligionist, of the Marxist type in particular, stands to gain equally from the pinning of the supernaturalist label on all religion. It helps support his own critique of religion as intellectually reactionary and unworthy of serious consideration as an option for intelligent men. For these two types of minds religion, by definition, includes the assumption that there is a conscious Power beyond nature which brought the universe into being and which ultimately determines its fate. No naturalistic belief can be religion in the eyes of the Marxist, any more than it can in the eyes of the fundamentalist.

The fact is that the identity of religion and supernaturalism that some thinkers try to establish is a historical judgment arising from the fact that religion, during a considerable portion of human history, could hardly have been grounded in any other view. Supernaturalism was for centuries convincing to mankind as a whole; the naturalism of the Greeks had its influence and its small following among the intellectuals, but it never came anywhere near achieving the popularity of supernaturalism. Today, however, given the context of scientific knowledge, it can be urgently argued that supernaturalism is a millstone around the neck of religion: with the spread of education supernaturalism becomes less and less appealing even to nonintellectuals.

Moreover, the identity of religion and supernaturalism can stand only when religion is treated without concern for its bearing on human needs. Taken as an institution which has an independent existence, religion could, of course, be defined as the embodiment of supernaturalism. This would be a structural definition. When viewed functionally, however, as an institution capable of fulfilling certain needs of man, religion cannot so easily be limited; it cannot be restricted in definition to one particular method of saitsfying those needs. We see, then, that a structural definition of religion associates religion with some specific *Weltanschauung;* it follows that when the *Weltanschauung* changes, the religion is undermined. Indeed traditional religionists, who hold to the structural definition, to this day insist that the future of religion depends entirely on its ability to continue to inspire belief in revelation. Those who define religion functionally, on the other hand, take account of the fact that there are often many answers to a single problem and realize that there are thus many pathways in man's eternal quest for fulfillment.

The distinction between these two concepts of religion, the structural and the functional, also involves a presumption about the nature of religious development. Those who hold to the structural definition conceive of religion statically. The church is an end in itself; all other institutions must adapt themselves to its spiritual hegemony. The church never changes; it is eternal. Those who abandon it are sinners, deliberate or unwitting. The church never errs, since it operates on a mandate from God. Proponents of the structural definition of religion also posit certain basic doctrines that are unchangeable and eternal. Adaptation to new conditions is never necessary because the doctrines are assumed to have anticipated their own evolution and to have embodied a method of interpretation at the time of their revelation.

Those who interpret religion functionally, quite otherwise, discern unending change in the conditions of life, change that necessitates constant revision of the doctrines and institutions of religion. They must, then, find some identifying factor common to religion in all its varying forms. If no common factor could be found, then the term religion could justifiably be used only in the narrowest sense. Indeed, we should have to rewrite almost every book containing the word. For it is apparent that the particular sense in which "religion" is understood varies from author to author. This conclusion should show the absurdity of trying to pin "religion" down to a single theology or a single institutional form. An adequate definition, which would enable normal discourse about religion to continue without the necessity of the invention of a new term for each subtle nuance, must therefore provide a suitable generalization. It will perhaps shed light on the problem to use the concept of government as an analogy.

If we examine governments throughout the ages, we find a wide variety of forms, from the patriarchy of the early Hebrews to the republicanism of the United States. The functions of government as well have varied, beginning, among the primitives, with the rudimentary purposes of protection and the securing of food. These minimal needs obviously cannot account for the pyramiding of structure characteristic of subsequent governments. Initially established to care for the basic physical wants, governments were later called upon to answer additional needs, physical, intellectual, and spiritual, resulting from the growth of civilization—the need for internal law and order, for the development of agriculture and industry, for the maintenance (or eradication) of class distinctions, for education and culture, etc. To identify government with the satisfaction of just one of these needs would be an unwarranted circumscription of its function. If we were to apply to government the logic of those who define religion structurally and identify it with a particular response to a particular human need, we should have to eliminate the term government from our vocabulary as the designation for many of our present-day ruling authorities. In the United States the government was once conceived of as an instrument for ensuring the untrammeled exercise of free private enterprise. For some time now the government has been imposing limits on such freedom, yet no one in his right mind would declare that the term government, as applied to the ruling power of our country, has outlived its function and ought to be superseded by a new designation.

If I seem to labor this point, it is because so many liberal intellectuals try to read "religion" out of existence by denying that it can be legitimately employed as a designation for any other attitude than the supernaturalism of a bygone age.

Doubtless there are religions which originated, at least partially, as responses to fear, and doubtless there are a few religions in which fear still plays a significant role. But some religions today exhibit only normal concern with that emotion. Some orthodox churches seek power in order to force their conceptions of truth and salvation on the world, but there are others, for instance the Quakers, which have traditions of serving mankind. Some religions abound in ritual; others, like Unitarianism and Quakerism, are relatively devoid of it. I need not multiply examples. From the standpoint of specific function, there is as much (or as little) reason to provide a new term for every kind of religion as there is for every kind of government.

3

I have tried by semantic analysis to rescue religion from the vested interests, both intellectual and institutional, which would like to appropriate it for their own purposes. Semantics alone, however, cannot solve the problem. Whatever power religion retains as an institution, as an intellectual or emotional factor in modern society, is a mere vestige of past glory. Like the monarch of England, it reigns but does not rule. It is respectable but not respected. Its restoration to its former position of importance in the thinking and behavior of intelligent men and women depends on whether religious spokesmen will have the courage to abandon outmoded positions and strike out in new directions.

SELECTED BIBLIOGRAPHY

Extensive bibliographies of recent work in philosophy of religion can be found in *A Modern Introduction to Philosophy*, Paul Edwards and Arthur Pap, eds. (New York: The Free Press, 1965), and *Philosophical Problems and Arguments: An Introduction*, James W. Cornman and Keith Lehrer (New York: The Macmillan Company, 1968). There have been so many books and articles published in the past twenty years which relate to the topics discussed in this volume that the listing below necessarily omits numerous excellent writings.

BLACKSTONE, WILLIAM, *The Problem of Religious Knowledge*. Englewood Cliffs, N. J.: Prentice-Hall, 1963.

BOCHENSKI, JOSEPH, *The Logic of Religion*. New York: New York University Press, 1965.

CAHN, STEVEN, *Fate, Logic, and Time*. New Haven, Conn.: Yale University Press, 1967, ch. 5.

CAHN, STEVEN, "The Book of Job: The Great Dissent," *Reconstructionist, 31* (1965).

CAMPBELL, C. A., *On Selfhood and Godhood*. New York: Macmillan, 1957.

CHRISTIAN, WILLIAM, *Meaning and Truth in Religion*. Princeton, N. J.: Princeton University Press, 1964.

COHEN, JACK, *The Case for Religious Naturalism*. New York: Reconstructionist Press, 1958.

DUCASSE, C. J., *A Philosophical Scrutiny of Religion*. New York: Ronald Press, 1953.

FERRE, FREDERICK, *Language, Logic, and God*. London: Eyre & Spottiswoode Ltd., 1962.

FLEW, ANTONY, *God and Philosophy*. London: Hutcheson & Co. Ltd., 1966.

FLEW, ANTONY, and ALASDAIR MACINTYRE, eds., *New Essays in Philosophical Theology.* New York: Macmillan, 1955.

HEPBURN,, RONALD, *Christianity and Paradox.* New York: Humanities Press, 1958.

HICK, JOHN, *Philosophy of Religion.* Englewood Cliffs, N. J.: Prentice-Hall, 1963.

HICK, JOHN, *Evil and the God of Love.* New York: Harper & Row, 1966.

HICK, JOHN, *Faith and Knowledge,* 2nd ed. Ithaca, N. Y.: Cornell University Press, 1966.

HICK, JOHN, ed., *Faith and the Philosophers.* New York: St. Martin's Press, 1964.

HOOK, SIDNEY, *The Quest for Being.* New York: St. Martin's Press, 1961, pt. 2.

HOOK, SIDNEY, ed., *Religious Experience and Truth.* New York: New York University Press, 1961.

HUXLEY, JULIAN, *Religion Without Revelation,* rev. ed. New York: New American Library, 1958.

KAPLAN, MORDECAI, *Judaism Without Supernaturalism.* New York: Reconstructionist Press, 1958.

KAUFMANN, WALTER, *Critique of Religion and Philosophy.* New York: Harper & Row, 1958.

KAUFMANN, WALTER, *The Faith of a Heretic.* Garden City, N. Y.: Doubleday, 1961.

LEWIS, H. D., *Our Experience of God.* New York: Macmillan, 1959.

MCCLOSKEY, H. J., "The Problem of Evil," *The Journal of Bible and Religion, 30* (1962).

MACINTYRE, ALASDAIR, *Difficulties in Christian Belief.* London: Student Christian Movement Press, 1959.

MACINTYRE, ALASDAIR, ed., *Metaphysical Beliefs.* London: Student Christian Movement Press, 1957.

MARTIN, C. B., *Religious Belief.* Ithaca, N. Y.: Cornell University Press, 1959.

MASCALL, E. L., *The Secularization of Christianity.* New York: Holt, Rinehart and Winston, 1966.

MATSON, WALLACE, *The Existence of God.* Ithaca, N. Y.: Cornell University Press, 1965.

MATTHEWS, GARETH, "Theology and Natural Theology," *The Journal of Philosophy, 61* (1964).

MITCHELL, BASIL, ed., *Faith and Logic.* London: George Allen & Uniwn Ltd., 1957.

NIELSEN, KAI, "Can Faith Validate God-Talk?" *Theology Today, 20* (1963).

NIELSEN, KAI, "Wittgensteinian Fideism," *Philosophy, 42* (1967).

PIKE, NELSON, "Hume on Evil," *The Philosophical Review, 72* (1963).

PIKE, NELSON, "Omnipotence and God's Ability to Sin," *American Philosophical Quarterly, 6* (1969).

PLANTINGA, ALVIN, *God and Other Minds.* Ithaca, N.Y.: Cornell University Press, 1967.

PRICE, H. H., "Belief 'In' and Belief 'That,'" *Religious Studies, 1* (1965).

PRIOR, A. N., "The Formalities of Omniscience," *Philosophy, 37* (1962).

RAMSEY, IAN, *Religious Languague.* London: Student Christian Movement Press, 1957.

RAMSEY, IAN, *Freedom and Immortality.* London: Student Christian Movement Press, 1960.

ROSS, JAMES, *Philosophical Theology.* Indianopolis, Ind.: Bobbs-Merrill, 1969.

ROYAL INSTITUTE OF PHILOSOPHY LECTURES, *Talk of God,* New York: St. Martin's Press, 1969.

SAVAGE, C. W., "The Paradox of the Stone," *The Philosophical Review, 76* (1967).

SMART, NINIAN, *Reasons and Faiths.* London: Routledge & Kegan Paul, 1958.

STACE, W. T., *Time and Eternity.* Princeton, N.J.: Princeton University Press, 1952.

STACE, W. T., *Mysticism and Philosophy.* Philadelphia: Lippincott, 1960.

STACE, W. T., ed., *Teachings of the Mystics.* New York: New American Library, 1960.

TILLICH, PAUL, *Dynamics of Faith.* New York: Harper & Row, 1957.

WISDOM, JOHN, *Paradox and Discovery.* Oxford: Basil Blackwells, 1965, chs. 1, 5.

ZUURDEEG, WILLIAM, *An Analytical Philosophy of Religion.* Nashville, Tenn.: Abingdon Press, 1958.

70 71 72 73 7 6 5 4 3 2 1